THIRD EDITION

Lendal H. Kotschevar, Ph.D.

Marcel R. Esc

National Restaurant Association
EDUCATIONAL FOUNDATION

Director of Product Development: Marianne Gajewski
Project Manager: Lisa Parker Gates
Production Manager: Virginia Christopher
Assistant Editor: Kate E. Sislin
Cover Design: Julie Streicher
Art Director: Ed Wantuch

National Restaurant Association
EDUCATIONAL FOUNDATION

❧ Contents ❧

A Message from The Educational Foundation

Welcome to *Management by Menu, Third Edition! Management by Menu* was initially written with the idea that the menu is *the* controlling document that affects every area of operation in the facility. This book was revised by Dr. Kotschevar and Mr. Escoffier to reflect the changes that have occurred in the foodservice industry since publication of the second edition. An increase in regulations affecting nutritional claims, advances in computer technology, concern over the responsible service of alcohol, and other changes that have affected foodservice management in general—and menu development in particular—are covered in this edition.

Most operations start with a menu or an idea of what the menu should be. The menu is essential to the concept of a commercial facility, and is a controlling factor in both commercial and noncommercial operations. Using the menu as a management tool in every area of operation, from planning the facility to purchasing food items to promoting items to customers to providing exceptional service, can help ensure success. With over a dozen examples of actual menus, *Management by Menu* serves as a guide both to developing a menu and to using it as a control document.

Management by Menu is part of The Foundation's Management Development Diploma Program. As such, it is combined with a Student Manual and final examination and is offered in schools or as a homestudy course. Students who successfully complete the final examination are awarded a certificate of completion from The Educational Foundation. Students who fulfill the requirements of the program are awarded a Management Diploma from the National Restaurant Association.

The Foundation wishes to thank the reviewers of the *Management by Menu* manuscript who contributed their time and expertise and greatly contributed to the development of the book: Henry Anderson, Professor at Macomb Community College in Mount Clemens, Michigan; Gregory Krzyminski, Instructor at Mid-State Technical College in Wisconsin Rapids, Wisconsin; and Margaret Steiskal, Professor at Columbus Community College in Columbus, Ohio.

Special recognition is also due The Foundation staff who assisted Dr. Kotschevar and Mr. Escoffier in the development of this book. Project Manager Lisa Parker Gates and Assistant Editor Kate E. Sislin coordinated the reviews of each chapter, conducted research, and skillfully edited the text.

Production Manager Virginia Christopher coordinated the design of the cover and text as well as the actual production of the book.

The National Restaurant Association Educational Foundation is dedicated to the advancement of professionalism in the restaurant and foodservice industry, fostering and nurturing it through education. The Foundation provides vital services to the industry through the development of innovative educational programs and materials, the administration of scholarships and work-study grants, and the promotion of industry careers.

It is our belief that this third edition of *Management by Menu* will contribute to the professionalism of the restaurant and foodservice industry and to those individuals about to enter it.

Preface

Management by Menu has had a successful career since its first publication, being used widely in schools, self-study courses, and on-the-job training. It is also used as a resource book for foodservice managers. This third edition has gone through an extensive revision that was aimed at both bringing it up to date and explaining even further how the menu serves as an invaluable tool in managing food services. *Management by Menu* continues to be unique in its presentation of the menu as a central theme that controls and influences all foodservice functions. Other books explain how to set up a menu; none tie the menu in with overall management principles. *Management by Menu* begins with an introduction to the industry and then develops the theme of shaping the menu to best perform its function of controlling and directing a foodservice operation.

Management by Menu, Third Edition is written both for those who are just being introduced to foodservice management and for those who have experience in food service. The book has been found to be suitable for use as a text for introduction to the foodservice industry as well as a text on menu construction and formulation. Others have used it successfully in teaching foodservice management, since the menu is the central core around which management revolves.

Several new developments have been added to the discussions in this revision. Growth in the foodservice industry has been enormous in recent years. Desktop publishing has made designing and printing menus much faster and less expensive for operators. Concern over responsible alcohol service has given a new focus to liquor menu promotions. Consumer interest in nutrition, and legislation governing health claims, have put added responsibility on menu planners to offer nutritious items. Finally, the presence of computers in so many foodservice management functions has put immeasurable information literally at managers' fingertips.

Each chapter of the third edition attempts to aid learning by first presenting objectives and then discussing in depth a distinct part of menu development. Questions are included at the end of each chapter to help emphasize main points and reinforce learning. Five appendixes present support material. Additional aids have been liberally spread throughout the text in the form of exhibits to help emphasize information given in the discussions.

Although terms that are not apt to be immediately understood or that are used in a special way in this text are explained as they are presented, a glossary is included to assist in defining many terms.

Lendal H. Kotschevar, Ph.D., FMP
Distinguished Visiting Professor
Florida International University
Educational Foundation 1992 Ambassador of Hospitality

1

A Look Back at the Foodservice Industry

Objectives

After reading this chapter, you should be able to:

1. Trace the beginnings and growth of the foodservice industry.
2. Identify the major contributions to this growth made by people and events.

INTRODUCTION

The story of humans and food is the story of life itself, and it would ultimately lead us back to the metabolizing of nutrients by a one-celled organism in some warm, shallow sea millions of years ago. Our account is a little less ambitious, seeking only to deal with how the foodservice industry developed to provide food for those who eat away from home; more specifically, how this vast industry is influenced by one particular document to the point that it dominates the industry's management. This document is the *menu*, a list of foods offered along with their prices. This book will explain how to manage a food service using the menu as the controlling factor.

It is said that a science is an organized body of knowledge, and art is the application of the science. We shall try to point out the principles and theories of the science of menu planning and its implementation, as well as the art required. However, first we will trace the beginnings of the foodservice industry, show what it is today, and explain how it consists of a large number of different segments that require different menus to suit various market needs. A single foodservice operation is a member of the larger foodservice industry; the more one knows about this field, what it is and how it grew, the more one can adjust to the overall conditions that affect the foodservice industry as a whole and, in turn, the individual operation.

ANCIENT FOOD SERVICE

The foodservice industry is both old and new. It is old in that humans have prepared and eaten food in groups since the earliest times. It is new in that it has changed considerably in the past 150 years. There is evidence that before 10,000 B.C., tribes in Denmark and the Orkney Islands off the coast of Scotland cooked food in large kitchens and ate together in large groups. Swiss lake dwellers left records that show that they dined in groups around 5000 B.C. Pictorial evidence in the tombs and temples of the ancient Egyptians also show that people knew how to prepare and serve food for large groups. There is also evidence in these pictures that prepared food was sold in marketplaces, just as it is today. Vendors also sold foods in the streets, the same as a mobile unit might today.

We get much knowledge also from ancient tombs. For instance, the tomb of the Egyptian Pharoah Tutankhamen contained many of the foods this king would need in the afterworld, many of which were surprisingly like the foods we have today. (Some wheat kernels left there to make flour were later planted and they grew.) The Ancients also had recipes. The oldest recipe for beer was left on an Assyrian tablet found near Mount Ararat. The Assyrians put their wine and beer in animal-skin containers. The poor drank beer while the wealthy drank wine.

Ancient Chinese records indicate that travelers ate and stayed in roadside inns. In large urban cities, restaurants existed in which rice, wine, and other items were sold. In India the operation of roadside inns, taverns, and food services was so prevalent that ancient laws were passed to control them.

In ancient Mohenjo-Daro, recently excavated in Pakistan, we find evidence that people ate in restaurant-type facilities that were equipped with stone ovens and stoves for quantity food preparation.

The Bible gives many accounts of a mass feeding industry. For instance, accounts tell of Xerxes, the Persian king, giving a banquet that lasted 180 days and of Solomon butchering 22,000 oxen for a public feast. Sardanapalus, the Assyrian king, was a patron of the art of eating and loved huge feasts. He organized a cooking contest at which the top professional cooks vied for honors, much as they do today at the Culinary Olympics held in Frankfurt, Germany, every four years.

The ancient Greeks had a high level of public dining, and much of their social lives took place around banquets at home or at public feasts. Inns and foodservice operations existed. Greece was the land of Epicurus, who spread the philosophy of good eating and good living. The Grecians went all out for their feasts. The Bacchanal feast in honor of the god of wine, Bacchus, was a lavish outlay of food, drink, and revelry. Professional cooks in Greece were honored people and had important parts in plays, where they declaimed their most famous recipes. It was even possible in ancient Greece to copyright a recipe.

The ancient Greeks loved to gather to discuss matters of interest and drink and eat snack foods. These foods were appetizers of different kinds. They learned about these foods from the peoples of Asia, and even today, the custom of having an array of snack foods with beverages when people gather is followed in the Near East and Greece.

The Romans also loved feasting. In fact, several of the emperors were so fond of banquets they bankrupted the nation. Emperor Lucullus, a Roman general, loved lavish banquets, and today whenever the word "Lucullan" is used, it means lavish and luxurious dining. A special rich sauce used to grace meat is called Lucullus Sauce. It is perhaps one of the richest sauces used and has a garnish of cocks' combs. Marc Antony was so pleased with the efforts of Cleopatra's cook that he presented him with a whole city. *Tabernas*, from which we get the word "tavern," were small restaurants in ancient Rome where one could get wine and food. We can see one such restaurant almost intact in the ruins of ancient Pompeii. It had a large service counter where huge urns of wine were kept. In the back area, a huge brick oven and other cooking equipment still stand. These small tabernas were the forerunners of the *trattorias* or small community restaurants of modern Italy. The Romans had a number of laws regulating the sale of foods and the operation of food services.

The first cookbook, titled *Cookery and Dining in Imperial Rome,* was written by a Roman epicure named Apicius, and some of its recipes are still used today. From it we learn that the Roman feast consisted of three courses, each of which had a number of foods served during it: 1) the *gustatio*, a group of appetizers that turned into the Italian antipasto of today; 2) meats and vegetables of different kinds, many of which were rare items imported from foreign lands; and 3) fruits and sweets. Plenty of wine was served throughout. The Romans did not sit at their meals but rather reclined on couches. A lot of the Roman culinary art was preserved during the Dark Ages and emerged as the basis of Italian and French cuisine that later influenced all of European cooking. The Romans had no stoves, but cooked over open fires or in fireplaces, although they did bake in brick ovens. Apicius' life ended tragically; he committed suicide in remorse when he found himself bankrupt after giving a lavish banquet.

FOOD SERVICE IN THE MIDDLE AGES

Following the disintegration of the Roman Empire, group eating became somewhat less lavish. Public eating virtually went underground in the Dark Ages. Some inns functioned along the most protected and traveled highways. We can read about these in the tales of the Crusaders. Chaucer's *Canterbury Tales* revolves around stories told by a group of travelers as they stayed in inns. Quantity food service in its highest form was practiced in the monasteries and abbeys by monks or friars. They considerably advanced the knowledge of baking, wine- and beer-making, and cooking. Many of the master craftsmen who later formed the various foodservice guilds gained much of their knowledge in these religious communities. Some recipes originated by these friars are still used today, such as pound cake and many meat dishes. It was during that time that Benedictine, Cointreau, Grand Marnier, Chartreuse, and other famous liqueurs were developed. These are still made by formulas held secret by the makers.

Eating was quite crude by our standards. The trencher, a large, shallow, oval-shaped wooden bowl, was the main food container from which people ate. It was often filled with a soup, stew, or ragout consisting of meat and vegetables. Bread was used to sop up the liquid and one's own dagger was used to cut up and spear meats and vegetables.

Toward the end of the Middle Ages, eating became somewhat refined and a distinct pattern of courses began to emerge. The French are credited for this change. Their menus had more appetizers, and soups and salads began to appear as first courses. Lighter foods were served at the beginning of the meal, while the heavier ones were served later, followed by desserts.

The English also improved their dining. We know from records left by the court of Henry VIII that they served many elaborate foods and, while the course structure of the meals was not as advanced as the French, they had a pattern somewhat similar to it. The menus emphasized game and most meat, fish, or poultry was spit-roasted. They ate a variety of soups, pastries, and puddings, and often had a sweet meat dish or two at every meal.

During the Middle Ages, various *guilds* arose to organize foodservice professionals. The *Chaine de Rotissieres* (Guild of Roasters) was chartered in Paris in the 12th century. This charter is owned today by the gourmet society of that name. A guild had a monopoly on the production of its specialties and could keep others from manufacturing them.

The guilds developed into the classic kitchen organization of chef and entourage, and codified many of the professional standards and traditions that are still in existence. It was at that time that the chef's tall hat, the *toque*, became a symbol of the apprentice. Later the black hat became the mark of a master chef nominated by his peers as having the right to wear it. The hat was a small, round one made of black silk and could be worn only by chefs elected to wear it. (Black in medieval times was the color indicating nobility.) The modern *Society of the Golden Toque*, an organization of master chefs elected by their peers (as in the French group), was designed to duplicate this honor for great chefs in the United States.

EARLY RENAISSANCE—THE DEVELOPMENT OF HAUTE CUISINE

The Renaissance saw a rise in elegant dining as well as the arts. While the renaissance in dining really began in Italy, its move to France brought fine dining to its highest form. As usual, royalty led the way.

French Cuisine

France has not always been known for its fine food. In medieval times, its food was coarse and plain. However, with the marriage in 1533 of Henry II of France to Catherine de Medici of Florence, Italy, France started toward its ascendancy as the country of *haute cuisine*, or high food preparation. In Italy, the Medicis not only were great patrons of such artists as Michaelangelo, but served the finest food and drink in their households. When Catherine came to France, she brought the master Medici cooks with her, and established herself as dictator of Henry's table and court. Foods never before known in France were soon being served, much to the delight of Henry and his court. Catherine introduced ice cream and many other great dishes that became part of French culinary accomplishments.[1]

All this started the French on their way toward a great improvement in the quality of foods appearing on the tables of the court and elsewhere. Besides fine food, Catherine taught the French to eat with knives, forks, and spoons instead of using their fingers and daggers. She brought these utensils from Florence and introduced them to the nobility. Soon it became a custom for guests to carry their own eating utensils when they went to dine outside their homes.

Henry's nephew, Henry of Navarre, who became Henry IV after his uncle's death, visited the court frequently and became quite fond of a good table. During his reign from 1589 to 1610, he continued to encourage the service of fine foods, and encouraged the more influential households in France to do the same. Henry IV became known in history as a great gourmet, and today we have a famous soup named after him, *Potage Henri IV*, which is dished into a large tureen and has big pieces of chicken and beef in it.

After Henry IV, the court and kings of France continued their interest in food and dining. It was considered the mark of gentility to set a good table and to encourage the development of top chefs and culinary personnel as well as the development of fine recipes. In the 1600s, the courts of the Bourbons, Louis XIII to Louis XV, continued to develop a knowledge of cuisine and to encourage the training of top chefs. Louis XIV, who reigned from 1643 to 1715, was known for his ostentatious and luxurious manner of living, and was very active in the development of good schools where chefs and cooks could be trained. A number of the nobles of the court also became famous for their tables and had fine dishes and sauces named after them. The fine white sauce, *Béchamel,* was named for the count of that name, and Sauce Mornay was named after Count Mornay. A fine sauce highly seasoned with onions was named after Count Soubisse.

Louis XV, who reigned from 1715 to 1774, continued his predecessor's advancement of the science and art of cooking. Maria Leszczynska, his wife, and daughter of the famous Polish king, Stanislaus I, who reigned from 1704 to 1735 and was himself a gourmet and cook, duplicated Catherine de Medici's supervision of the kitchen and set standards for great quality and elaborateness in food service. In addition, Louis XV's mistresses, Madame Pompadour and Madame du Barry, were not only lovers of fine food but proficient cooks, and today we have many fine dishes named after them. Madame du Barry was considered by the king such an excellent cook that he had her awarded the *Cordon Bleu,* an award given only to the best chefs.

The menus of this time were very elaborate. The French had three courses but as many as 20 or more dishes would be served in one. The methods of preparation were also often very elaborate. However, toward the end of this period the menus became more simplified with fewer dishes in each course.

While the French Revolution ended the reign of the Bourbons in 1792, it did not stop the French love of food and drink and French dominance in the art of fine dining. Some of the servants of the nobility and wealthy began to use their cooking skills in restaurants. Some of the nobility that had not lost their heads nor their servants, but had lost their fortunes, opened up their homes and made their living by serving meals. These operations continued the high standards that had previously existed in the homes of the famous. A group of prominent gourmets now came to the fore to support these operations. Some were writers who began to build literature in the art of cooking and eating. Such writers as Brillat-Savarian, who wrote *The Physiology of Taste*; Grimrod de la Reyniere, editor of the world's first gourmet magazine; Alexandre Dumas père, compiler of *The Grand Dictionaire de Cuisine*; and Vicomte de Chateaubriand, after whom the famous steak dish was named, left writings about the foods of the time that mark their period as one of the great ones in fine dining. With the return of Napolean and his crowning, the tables in the homes of the wealthy, nobility, and others assumed their former high level. It was almost as if the time of the Louis kings had returned.

The Coming of the Restaurant

During the development of haute cuisine in Europe, the eating habits of common people away from home continued to be spotty and casual. Crude inns and taverns existed along the main roads where coaches traveled. When people of wealth or high rank traveled and stayed in these inns, they often had their own servants prepare the food. Religious orders continued to care for travelers, but places for common people to go out and dine did not exist. People ate largely in private homes. The common people had neither the resources, equipment, facilities, nor know-how to provide more than simple food. Those in prisons or hospitals were served fare barely above minimal needs.

About 1600 an important development occurred that would influence the growth of the modern foodservice industry. The first coffeehouses (cafés) appeared in France and their spread was rapid in the great cities of Europe. Not much food was served; the fare consisted mostly of coffee and cocoa or mild alcoholic beverages, such as wine. These coffeehouses were largely places where the local gentry and others could go to get the latest news and gossip, discuss matters of interest, and have a good beverage. The coffeehouse was a forerunner of the modern restaurant.

Another important event occurred later in France. In 1760, during the reign of Louis XV, a man named Boulanger opened an eating place that served soups that were believed to be health restorers. These soups were claimed to be highly nutritious and filled with foods that brought about the cure of many ailments. One soup was distinguished by a calf's foot floating in it. Boulanger called his health restorers *restaurers*, and he called his enterprise a *restorante*. We can readily recognize that this became the word restaurant.

The powerful guilds, *Chaine de Rotissieres* and *Chaine de Traiteurs* ("caterers," from the French verb *traiter*, "to treat"), opposed this infringement of Boulanger on their rights as cooks and developers of new dishes. (The guild of bakers also disapproved because it was a threat to their sovereignty.) The guild cooks claimed they had sole right to serve food of this kind, and Boulanger was not a member of their guild. The case gained wide notoriety. Boulanger, however, was adept at public relations and got leading gourmets, the French legislature, King Louis XV, and other influential individuals on his side. Boulanger won his right to operate as a restaurateur, and this decision lessened the powers of the guilds. Boulanger enlarged his menu and included a much wider list of foods that met with great success. Many other coffeehouses followed Boulanger's example, becoming restaurants. Within a 30-year period, Paris had over 500 of these, and the beginnings of the modern foodservice industry.

Other National Cuisines

While France was the leader in the development of serving fine foods, it was not alone. Other nations also developed high levels of food preparation and service.

England was one of these; although its cuisine never approached that of the French in reputation, its tables were worthy of note. Much of the food was of local origin, but because England was a great seapower, some fine additions came from foreign lands. The English blended their food standards with those of Spain and Portugal when Prince Philip, heir to the Spanish throne, married Mary, daughter of Henry VIII and Catherine of Aragon. Mary later became Queen of England, known in history as Bloody Mary. Philip brought a large retinue of servants with him when he moved to England, many of whom were fine cooks. They introduced items into the English cuisine such as sponge cake, famous Spanish hams and bacons, and sherry and port. Even today the British consume these foods to a point that some of them are thought of as original English foods. Philip stayed in England long enough to leave a Spanish flavor to English food. Troubles in the Netherlands, which Spain ruled, took him there and he never returned.

Russia also developed an original and fine cuisine. Catherine the Great thought highly of the French; in fact, French became a language spoken by many in the Russian court. French chefs were imported—later Czar Alexander hired the great French chef, Antoine Carême, to rule over the royal kitchens. This Russian cuisine featured many game animals, fish, and vegetables of Russian origin. The Russians were more robust eaters and drinkers than the French, and their style of eating and drinking reflected this, but often done in an original way. For instance, instead of having a seated appetizer at the table, they liked a large gathering where plenty of vodka was served (it was a much more potent product in those times) along with what they called flying dishes (appetizers), so named because servants carried them around to serve to the guests on platters held high over their heads to allow them to pass through the number of people gathered. The Russians left a rich heritage of foods, some of which were dishes like *stroganoff* (borrowed from Poland), caviar, borscht, and vodka.

The Italians had their own distinctive cuisine. The fine food tradition of the Medicis continued in northern Italy, but because Italy was a land divided into many small, independent *duchies* (headed by dukes) and other political units, a true national cuisine did not develop until later. When it did arrive, it was dominated by pasta, and today Italian pastas are world-renowned. At one time Henry Sell, renowned editor of *Town and Country*, at a dinner in Le Pavilion in New York City, was asked where the greatest food was served in our day. He answered, "In Florence; their great traditions still hold."

Every cuisine is distinguished by individual characteristics from the region where it first took root, and Italy's cuisine is no different. Regional foods greatly influence its cooking. Italy is a long, narrow peninsula jutting out into the Mediterranean, and with its extensive seacoast, has plenty of fish and other seafood. Thus, Italian menus will often offer more fish than meat dishes. Olive oil is the main cooking fat and wine is often served at meals in place of water.

Southern Italian cooking is distinguished by its heavy emphasis on tomato sauces and tomatoes in dishes, especially in those using pasta. More fruits are used, especially citrus. The north places less emphasis on the tomato and has more subtle and delicate seasoning. Garlic is a common ingredient in all Italian cooking, but the North uses it a bit more gently. Veal is more popular in the North, while goat's meat is often seen in the South. Thus, we can see that cuisines are largely defined by resources of the region, and

Italy's cuisine is a good example of this regional influence and of a unique cooking heritage.

Largely through the royal courts of all these countries, the production of great food, the art of eating, and an interest in gastronomy grew. It was an important development, and preceded the modern foodservice industry.

THE INDUSTRIAL REVOLUTION

During the final years of the development of *haute cuisine* in France and in other countries, and the emergence of the *restorante*, another very important event was occurring. The Industrial Revolution, which started at the end of the 18th century, brought about great societal and economic changes. Vast industrial complexes emerged with the consequent loss of the guild system. Commercial trade became an important factor.

For a long time, the gentry, with their wealth in agricultural lands, dominated the political and economic scene in Europe. As the Industrial Revolution grew, this changed. The political upheaval caused by the fall of the Bourbons in France and the coming of Napolean also sped up changes in European society. A new social class emerged as a result of the Industrial Revolution, a middle-class composed of entrepreneurs, shopkeepers, industrialists, and financiers. (For instance, Baron Rothschild, a British financier, became the wealthiest man in the world, with much more money and more influence on society than any nobility had.) This new class began to dominate and affect the social and economic spheres in European society. The newly wealthy demanded a food standard as high as that in the homes of the nobility. Great chefs and retainers were hired. Food was served in exclusive clubs for the wealthy entrepreneurs. Even the lower-income middle class began to ask for food prepared by competent people. Dining out became more popular because these middle-class people could afford it. A true foodservice industry was emerging.

THE ADVANCEMENT OF SCIENCE

Another factor in the development of the foodservice industry, and probably one of the stimulants of the Industrial Revolution, was the development of modern science. Until the 17th century, science was influenced by the Greek philosophers, who based scientific theories on philosophical ones. Modern scientists began to use the *inductive method*, in which scientific theories are based on observable phenomena. It was the development of this scientific method that led to the great enlargement of knowledge and to the advancement of society in general.

Such great men as Galileo, Bacon, Descartes, Pasteur, and others appeared on the scientific scene and developed the kind of knowledge that advanced technology and people's standard of living. This technology affected food processing. Nicolas Appert discovered canning and earned a 2,000-franc reward from Napolean I because it helped him feed his vast armies on his march to conquer Europe. Appert and other scientists made technological discoveries that advanced our ability to produce, preserve, and manufacture food. Soon, more food resources were available. Never before had humans had such a surplus of food. Mass starvation, common in the Middle Ages, appeared to end. The resources needed for the development of a foodservice industry and feeding people away from home were now available.

THE GOLDEN AGE OF CUISINE

Several developments that occurred in France ushered in a new era that perfected dining standards and helped make dining out a central social activity. This era was called the *Golden Age of Cuisine*.

Carême

The Golden Age of Cuisine began around 1800 with the rise of Marie Antoine Carême, who was one of the world's most famous chefs. The century ended with Georges August Escoffier, another chef of equal eminence, who died in 1935. (One of the authors of this text is the grand-nephew of this famous man.) Carême worked as a chef for the French statesman Talleyrand, Czar Alexander I of Russia, and the banking giant, Baron Rothschild.[2] Carême wanted to become an architect, but was never able to do so. Instead, his father apprenticed him as a small boy to Carême's uncle, who operated a small restaurant. Here, Carême learned the basic rudiments of cooking. Originally, Carême was trained to be a pastry chef, and he developed a number of famous dishes in this area; but he branched out and became highly proficient in the other areas of cuisine. He trained many famous chefs, some of whom became chefs at the famous Reform Club of London, considered the apex of jobs for chefs—Carême himself and the famous Escoffier were also rulers of its kitchens.

In his teens, Carême traveled to Paris, where he quickly progressed through the various food production sections to become a chef. He soon attained a position of prominence and was sought by the leading gourmets of the time to prepare foods for them. With them Carême developed many of the basic concepts for the progression of courses in a dinner and the sequence of the proper wines to accompany them. Carême perfected the very delicate soup, *consommé*, which took its name from the word consummate, which means "to bring to completion, perfection, or fulfillment." After he introduced it at a dinner as the first course, Grimod de la Reyniere exclaimed in his approval, "A soup served as the first course of a meal is like the overture to the opera or the porch to the house; it should be a proper introduction to that which is to follow." Carême developed many fine French sauces and dishes. He also originated *pièces montées* such as ice carvings, tallow pieces, and highly decorated foods, that were used as displays, evidently working out his love for architecture. However, Carême's greatest claim to fame, and perhaps his greatest contribution to food preparation, was that he trained a large number of famous chefs who became his disciples and followed him in holding some of the most prominent cooking positions in clubs, restaurants, and hotels. Carême also gave a considerable period of his time to writing, and we still have a rich legacy of his ideas on foods. Undoubtedly, Brillat-Savarin and other great gourmets of the time were considerably influenced by him.

Escoffier and Ritz

Escoffier, like Carême, was an innovator of fine foods. He was sought by royalty and other society leaders, and at one time was the executive chef of the Reform Club. Later in his life, to spread his talents, he became the supervising chef at a number of leading hotels and clubs in London and continental Europe.

It was Escoffier who perfected the classical, or continental, organization of workers in the kitchen and precisely defined the responsibility of each one. Escoffier was the first to use a food checker and to establish the close coordination that an executive chef must have with the chief steward. Escoffier insisted that his men (kitchen workers at the time were exclusively male) dress neatly, never use profanity, and work quietly, with decorum and gentlemanliness. To reduce the amount of noise and talking in his kitchen, he introduced the *aboyeur* (announcer), who took orders from service personnel, and in a clear, loud voice called out the foods ordered to the various production centers. Escoffier wrote many articles and several books, one of which is a cookbook still used all over the world both in homes and foodservices. He is also credited with the invention of Peach Melba and Melba Toast, named for the famous singer, Nellie Melba.

Escoffier was a true scientist, giving careful observations to the reactions of foods to preparation procedures. From these he developed sound rules for the preparation of foods in quantity. He teamed up with the famous hotelier, Cesar Ritz, to operate many of Europe's finest hotels; Escoffier ran the back of the house while Ritz tended to the front. Perhaps at no other time has the level of dining and staying away from home been raised so high as under these two men. Even today the word ritzy means "elegant, ostentatious, fancy, or fashionable."

It was the highly social Edward VII (1841–1910), Prince of Wales and the playboy of Victorian England, who remarked, "Where Mr. Ritz goes, there I go." The informal leaders of culture, society, politics, the arts, and sciences became patrons of these two men. When Ritz and Escoffier died, an era died with them. However, another era was about to be built on their accomplishments. The new era belonged to working people in general, who were beginning to emerge as important figures in society since their wages could help a new foodservice industry develop and survive. A substantial middle class was also coming into its own, and the new market would be shaped largely for them.

Another important contribution of Escoffier was simplifying the menu. He felt that too many foods were served at each course, so he often reduced this to just one food item with an accompaniment. It was he, following Carême and others, who developed the progression of courses in a formal meal to: a light soup, fish, poultry, entree, salad, cheese, and dessert. Each course might have its accompaniment and garnish; the entree would be the heaviest course, with a roast beef meat accompanied by a vegetable and starch food, often a potato. After this course, the meal was to drop in intensity. The salad gave a refreshing respite, with the cheese following to keep up the flagging appetite so the dessert could be appreciated. A formal progression of wines accompanied the courses. We will see this progression of courses later in our discussions; its purpose here is to point out that it was Escoffier who stamped it indelibly into our eating culture. However, Escoffier also did not hesitate to serve very simple luncheons and dinners. He felt that foods above all had to be supremely prepared and not just be exciting to the eye, and food that good should be served in an adequate quantity, and satisfy the appetite.

Exhibit 1.1 shows a fine dinner menu used at the White House when the famous Chef Haller supervised the kitchens. Its simple elegance reflects Escoffier's influence.

Exhibit 1.1 White House Dinner Menu

Courtesy of Chefs Haller and Bender of the White House

Dinner

Johannisberger
Klaus   Timbale of Seafood White House
1970   Fleurons Dorées

              Châteaubriand Béarnaise
Louis Martini   Pommes Soufflées
Cabernet Sauvignon
1968   Artichokes Andalouse

              Bibb Lettuce Salad
                  Brie Cheese
Dom Pérignon
1964
          Fresh Peaches Glacées Monticello
                Sauce Framboise

            THE WHITE HOUSE
            Tuesday, July 24, 1973

FOOD SERVICE IN THE UNITED STATES

The Early Years

During colonial times in the United States, foods served to those away from home were served much the same way as in Europe. For a considerable period of time, travelers were cared for at roadside inns, some of which still exist. Coffeehouses operated in New York, Philadelphia, Boston, and other large cities. Taverns and *eateries* (*beaneries* in Boston) also served food. Some clubs existed that also served a fairly high standard of food, usually of a local character.

Institutional Feeding

Orphanages, hospitals, prisons, and other institutions cooked food in quantity over fireplaces or over beds of coals. A form of cooking sometimes called "ground" cooking was also used to cook foods. A fire was built in a hole in the ground containing some stones or in a clay or brick oven and when they were very hot, the fire was put out, the food was put in, and the oven was closed or the hole covered, and the food cooked for a long time in the stored heat.

Some universities had a dining service where the students came to eat family-style. Food was brought to the table in serving dishes and the students passed the food. This service style is still used today in some schools—the U.S. Naval Academy is one such place. Other schools offered table service. These dining rooms were often called *commons*. Still other schools had small apartments for the students and each student brought a cook from home, usually a slave, who would cook and care for the student. These quarters still stand on the University of Virginia campus, designed by Thomas Jefferson.

Hotels Appear

With the continued growth of the United States, a need arose for hotels, which began to appear in the larger cities. In 1818, New York City had eight hotels. By 1846, there were more than 100. In 1850, Chicago boasted 150 hotels. Some of these hotels were built to provide great luxury. Famous chefs were brought from Europe, along with their staffs, to cook for guests. The Astor House in New York City, the Brown Palace in San Francisco, the Butler in Seattle, and the Palmer House in Chicago were as elegant and fashionable as any hotel operated by Ritz and Escoffier. Many of these hotels became the cultural and social centers of the cities where they were located.

The Gold Rush to California and later gold discoveries in Montana and elsewhere, along with the discovery of silver lodes in Colorado and Nevada, drew many people to the west. Many became wealthy and could then afford fine dining.

After the Civil War, railroads were rapidly built all over the country. In communities served by railroads, small hotels were built near railroad stations to feed and shelter travelers. Restaurants also opened, but these were patronized largely by affluent people or those away from home for a short period of time.

Dining Trends

The trend to elegance and luxury found in the best hotels also began to appear in restaurants. Lorenzo Delmonico (1813–1881) started his famous restaurant, Delmonico's, near Wall Street in New York City for the financial tycoons there. It developed an international reputation. He and his brothers started other restaurants in New York City, beginning what was probably one of the first restaurant chains. However, the era of the working class was approaching in the United States, and with it a need for a type of food service that did not have the elegance, fashion, or high cost of operations, such as Delmonico's.

At the turn of the century, people began to leave their homes to work in factories, office buildings, stores, hospitals, schools, and commercial centers. They needed meals, particularly lunch, and many coffee shops and restaurants sprang up, including Child's, Schrafft's, and Savarin. Popular foods were served at nominal cost. Horn and Hardart, a cafeteria system, introduced the *nickelodeon* automatic food service. Food portions were loaded into small compartments, some of which were heated by steam. Patrons would insert the required coins and a door would open to allow removal. When the door closed, it locked again, and empty compartments would be replenished. In some factories and office buildings, employee feeding took place on a restricted basis.

Other changes were occurring. The average American began to have more disposable income. The automobile arrived, giving the population much more mobility. Working hours were shortened, providing more leisure time. Electricity became available on a wider scale. Foodservice operations now could have refrigerators and freezers rather than iceboxes. Mixers, dishwashers, and other electrical equipment became available, reducing many laborious tasks in the kitchen.[3]

Postwar Expansion

After World War II, the foodservice industry began to grow rapidly. While the normal rate of growth in retailing during that time was about 6 percent per year, the foodservice industry saw an annual 10 to 11 percent growth. Some of this growth was prompted by the expansion of institutional feeding. Factories and office buildings put in their own foodservice units for workers. In 1946 the Federal Government passed the National School Lunch Act, which started a vast school feeding program. Colleges and universities put in extensive dining services. Dietitians, trained to operate food services, began to be sought out, not only by health services, but by commercial operations, such as Stouffer's. Margaret Mitchell, a vice-president and one of the dominant forces behind Stouffer's, was herself a dietitian. Cornell University, under Professor Howard Meek, introduced the first hotel school, which branched out into restaurant and institutional curricula, and later added tourism.

Vast hotel chains were being formed, with Ellsworth Statler leading the way. People began to eat out, not only as a necessity, but because they wanted recreation, entertainment, and a change from eating at home. The desire was not just for food to satisfy nutritional and hunger needs, but for an environment that would help meet social and psychological desires.

Fast Food and Chains

Two very important changes occurred simultaneously and were related. These were the development of the *fast-food*, or *quick-service*, concept and the birth of multiple-operation foodservice groups, or *chains*. The first of the units serving food that could be prepared and eaten quickly were the White Castle hamburger units, which appeared in the 1930s. The idea grew slowly until after World War II. Then in the late 1940s and 1950s, many were started. They were immensely popular, serving an item that had wide acceptance at a nominal price with rapid service. Another item that found acceptance as a quick-service entree was chicken. To Americans on the go, fast food was an affordable luxury. Vast chains, such as Kentucky Fried Chicken, built by Colonel Harlan Sanders, and McDonald's, led by Ray Kroc, soon appeared all over the country, and were faced with competitors seeking to break into this lucrative market. The low price and lower margin of profit per sale was compensated for by big volume. A limited menu made it possible to simplify operations and use personnel of limited experience and skill in food preparation and service. This segment of the industry has grown tremendously, to the point that the National Restaurant Association says it makes up about 25 percent of all commercial foodservice units. The quick-service segment's percentage of entire industry sales is much higher than that.

The type of ownership of the industry started to change as well. While the single, independent unit still predominates, its significance in the foodservice industry decreased in comparison to the influence exerted by corporations.

CONTINUAL GROWTH

In a period of about 40 years, the foodservice industry has changed from a rather small one in our total industrial economy, to one of our major ones. Growth and changes in feeding habits will not stop. They will continue, and eating away from home should become an even more important factor in the lives of people than it is now. Some say that in the not too distant future, we will be eating more than 50 percent of our meals outside the home. If past growth reflects the future, this seems quite possible.

SUMMARY

The seeds of our foodservice industry were sown many centuries ago when a cluster of cave dwellers gathered together and cooked food over an open fire. Many ancient cultures had foodservice operations that served food to travelers, prepared foods for feasts, and served meals to ordinary people at public gatherings. During the Middle Ages, monasteries maintained quantity cooking and service and even acted as hostelries for travelers. Inns and taverns also opened in cities and along travel routes. People of wealth and royal blood had kitchens and dining areas designed to serve food in quantity, and many of their best cooks advanced our knowledge of food preparation and service.

The restaurant industry really began in Paris just after the French Revolution and rapidly spread throughout Europe. An aristocracy of wealth appeared and provided patronage for fine, elaborate restaurants, clubs, and hotel dining services.

The development of the foodservice industry in the United States did not occur to any degree until after the Civil War. Until that time, it functioned on the limited scale that was typical in Europe. As the United States started to industrialize, people had more discretionary income, and they began to want food away from home. Along with the coming of a vast network of railroads across the nation came a demand for hotels offering meals, as well as lodging. After World War I, factories and office buildings began to provide meals for workers. A large number of cafes, restaurants, and cafeterias began to appear in highly populated areas. School lunches started in 1946 as a federally sponsored project.

After World War II, the foodservice industry leaped forward. One of the reasons for this was the introduction of the quick-service operation, in which certain foods could be offered at moderate prices. These establishments became a significant segment of the foodservice industry. With continued development and the increase of chains and franchises, the foodservice industry has developed into one of the largest industries in the nation. The growth of this huge industry is expected to continue. Chapter 2 will discuss both the present and future of the foodservice industry.

QUESTIONS

1. What was the significant contribution made to food service by the ancient Greeks? By the Romans? By Europeans in the Middle Ages?

2. What characterized French cuisine during the reigns of Henry II and Henry IV? Of Louis XIII and XIV?

3. What were the significant contributions made to food service by Carême? By Escoffier?

4. What historical events and forces led to the rise of hotels and restaurants in the United States?

2

Profile of the Modern Foodservice Industry

Outline

Objectives

After reading this chapter, you should be able to:

1. Characterize various types of foodservice operations.

2. Differentiate between commercial operations, institutional operations, transportation food services, health services, clubs, military feeding, and central commissaries.

3. Identify economic and social trends likely to impact the future of the foodservice industry.

INTRODUCTION

The foodservice industry consists of many diverse operations that provide food and drink for people away from home. This somewhat simplistic definition covers a wide variety of operations, types of service, and markets. The industry is huge; in 1990 it was made up of 721,299 operations and in 1993, it was projected that the sales value of the food and drink served would total nearly $267 billion. (See **Exhibit 2.1**.) It hires more people than any other industry in the world. It is estimated that this industry serves about 25 percent of the food consumed in this country. Today, food service is one of our largest industries, ranking among the top ten.

The foodservice industry has been one of our country's most consistent growth industries. After World War II, the industry, then relatively unimportant in our economy, started to grow rapidly. By 1970, it was doing over $40 billion a year in sales. This growth continued. **Exhibit 2.2** shows the total sales per year from 1970 to 1990 and the percent change from 1971 to 1990. The projected sales in 1993 show a continued growth.

A DIVERSE INDUSTRY

The types of units differ greatly from each other in the food and drink offered and in their preparation and service. They serve different clientele, merchandise their items differently, and run their businesses differently. Yet they all exist to serve market needs and patron desires in food and drink.

Eating and drinking establishments make up most of the units in the industry and do most of the sales, having 375,951 units in 1990 (52 percent) and in 1993 are projected to do about $180 billion (50 percent) of the sales. At one time, food contractors lagged behind in total sales, but in the last several decades have gradually made a larger contribution to them, projected in 1993 as $16 billion, or 4 percent, of all sales. Lodging food services will probably do about the same amount of business. The group called retail hosts follow in projected sales, $10 billion or 3 percent. Institutional foodservices or Group II in 1990 numbered 173,047 units (24 percent) are projected to do nearly $29 billion, or 7 percent, of total sales in 1993. Military food services, or Group III, was projected in 1993 as doing 0.3 percent of the business, or $1.1 billion dollars.

INCOME AND COSTS

Few foodservice operations operate successfully if their combined food, beverage, and labor costs are above 65 percent—the most common division being 35 percent food and beverage, and 30 percent labor. Operations with higher costs that operate well are usually subsidized in some way. This 65 percent percentage was not always the rule. At one time, the combined total could be 75 percent and still leave a profit, but taxes and other costs have risen considerably.

Exhibit 2.1 Foodservice Industry Food and Drink Sales Projected through 1993

	Number of Estab-lishments	1990 Estimated F & D Sales ($000)	1993 Projected F & D Sales ($000)	1990–1993 Compound Annual Growth Rate
GROUP I—Commercial Foodservice[1]				
Eating Places				
Restaurants, lunchrooms	163,314	$ 76,072,427	$ 83,526,004	3.2%
Limited-menu restaurants, refreshment places	149,246	69,458,199	80,240,752	4.9
Commercial cafeterias	7,543	4,345,213	4,548,083	1.5
Social caterers	1,285	2,239,820	2,705,529	6.5
Ice-cream, frozen-custard stands	13,546	2,111,214	2,569,423	6.8
Total Eating Places	38,724	$ 154,226,873	$ 173,589,791	4.0%
Bars and Taverns	39,227	9,212,061	9,269,387	0.2
Total Eating and Drinking Places	375,451	$ 163,438,934[2]	$ 182,859,178	3.8%
Total Food Contractors	15,739	$ 14,149,055	$ 16,376,167	5.0%
Lodging Places				
Hotel restaurants	16,532	$ 12,907,190	$ 14,645,498	4.3%
Motor-hotel restaurants	1,748	545,255	542,913	−0.1
Motel restaurants	8,828	819,750	785,465	−1.4
Total Lodging Places	27,108	$ 14,272,195	$ 15,973,876	3.8%
Retail-host restaurants[3]	107,807	$ 9,887,729	$ 11,151,430	4.1%
Recreation and sports[4]	14,447	2,916,332	3,188,944	3.0
Mobile caterers	4,134	844,452	891,185	1.8
Vending and nonstore retailers[5]	1,760	5,574,428	6,054,200	2.8
TOTAL GROUP I	**546,996**	**$211,083,125**	**$238,494,980**	**3.9%**
GROUP II—Institutional Foodservice—Business, educational, governmental, or institutional organizations that operate their own foodservice				
Employee foodservice[6]	7,717	$ 1,985,115	$ 1,894,697	−1.5%
Public and parochial elementary, secondary schools	95,883	3,700,454	4,128,626	3.7
Colleges and universities	2,719	3,970,343	4,534,887	4.5
Transportation	133	1,235,459	1,538,086	7.6
Hospitals[7]	6,603	8,967,767	10,067,221	3.9
Nursing homes, homes for the aged, blind, orphans, and the mentally and physically disabled[8]	29,164	3,913,090	4,123,434	1.8
Clubs, sporting and recreational camps	13,156	2,155,987	2,363,016	3.1
Community centers	16,297	688,909	863,695	7.8
TOTAL GROUP II	125,826*	$ 26,617,124	$ 29,513,662	**3.5%**
TOTAL GROUPS I & II	722,822	$237,700,248	$266,008,642	**3.6%**
GROUP III—Military Foodservice[9]				
Officers' and NCO clubs ("Open Mess")	700	$ 733,277	768,808	1.6%
Foodservice—military exchanges	556	379,365	386,463	0.6
TOTAL GROUP III	1,256	$ 1,112,642	$ 1,155,271	**1.3%**
GRAND TOTAL	724,078	$238,812,891	$267,163,913	**3.8%**

FOOTNOTES:
1. Data are given only for establishments with payroll.
2. Food and drink sales for nonpayroll establishments totalled $5,004,228,000 in 1990.
3. Includes drug and proprietary store restaurants, general-merchandise-store restaurants, variety-store restaurants, food-store restaurants, grocery-store restaurants (including portion of deli merchandise line), gasoline-service-station restaurants, and miscellaneous retailers.
4. Includes movies, bowling lanes, and recreation and sports centers.
5. Includes sales of hot food, sandwiches, pastries, coffee, and other hot beverages.
6. Includes industrial and commercial organizations, seagoing and inland-water-way vessels.
7. Includes voluntary and proprietary hospitals; long-term general, TB, mental hospitals; and sales or commercial equivalent to employees in state and local short-term hospitals and federal hospitals.
8. Sales (commercial equivalent) calculated for nursing homes and homes for the aged only. All others in this grouping make no change for food served either in cash or in kind.
9. Continental United States only.
*The Figures in this column, reported in 1992, reflect reporting changes by the Bureau of Census. Included in the total, but not shown in Group II, are 4,129 penal institutions.
SOURCE: The National Restaurant Association, Washington, DC, and the Bureau of Census.

Exhibit 2.2   Sales 1970–1990 and Percent Change 1971–1990 in the
Foodservice Industry

Year	Total Sales (000)	Percent Change
1970	$ 42,779,550	
1971	46,069,750	7.7%
1972	49,930,480	8.4
1973	56,321,683	12.8
1974	62,866,913	11.6
1975	70,313,255	11.8
1976	78,379,710	11.5
1977	86,833,688	10.8
1978	97,615,162	12.4
1979	109,576,421	12.2
1980	119,616,722	9.2
1981	131,399,046	9.8
1982	140,437,079	6.9
1983	151,618,538	8.0
1984	164,181,308	8.3
1985	173,664,165	5.8
1986	185,114,930	6.6
1987	199,706,509	7.9
1988	213,855,955	7.1
1989	226,699,296	6.0
1990	238,812,891	5.3

SOURCE: Foodservice Numbers, National Restaurant Association, Washington, DC, 1992.

Exhibit 2.3 shows the division of income and costs for four types of operations. Note that only in cafeterias is the combined food and beverage cost up to 35 percent. The others are lower and this trend is typical of today's operations. To remain profitable, the combined food-beverage cost is often lower than 35 percent. Note also in two operations that the labor costs are above 30 percent. This too represents a trend. Labor costs are gradually encroaching upon profitability, and foodservice operators are trying to cut food and beverage and other costs to make up for it. Operations with a limited-menu and no table service do best in profitability, indicating that when labor can be reduced, it is easier to make a profit.

Combined food, beverage, and labor costs are often higher than 65 percent in institutions that do not need to make a profit. Also, other costs are often not as great. Costs such as music, entertainment, and marketing usually are nonexistent, and rent, if charged, is lower and repairs and maintenance less. Commercial food services have the expense of maintaining attractive, well decorated surroundings, with suitable furnishings, linens, and tableware. Some need a wait staff to serve patrons. All these factors are usually added costs in institutions.

Nevertheless, the cost squeeze has also hit institutions and many find they are challenged to operate successfully under the monetary restrictions imposed. In fact, some, like hospitals, are looking to their food services to become revenue producers to help pay expenses elsewhere.

Notice how beverages give significant dollars for full-menu and limited-menu tableservice and only a small amount for the other two types. Predictions are that alcoholic beverage sales will drop, but probably not as fast as in recent years. Since beverage sales are usually more profitable than food sales, this means another squeeze on profits.

Undoubtedly in the future, foodservice management will be increasingly challenged to make a profit. It is expected that the foodservice industry will become more competitive, and this, together with rising costs and customer resistance to paying more, will require highly competent management to ensure success.

Exhibit 2.3   The Restaurant Industry Dollar**

Figures represent percent of each dollar spent

	Full-menu, table service	Limited-menu, table service	Limited-menu, no table service	Cafeteria
Where It Came From*				
Food Sales	79.7	84.4	97.3	95.0
Beverage Sales	18.1	13.9	2.2	3.1
Other Income	2.2	1.7	0.5	1.9
Where It Went*				
Cost of Food Sold	27.6	30.0	31.6	33.8
Cost of Beverages Sold	5.1	3.8	0.6	1.2
Payroll	28.3	25.0	24.1	31.1
Employee Benefits	4.5	3.2	2.8	4.3
Direct Operating Expenses	6.5	5.4	6.4	5.7
Music and Entertainment	0.6	0.5	0.1	0.1
Marketing	2.2	3.2	4.2	2.7
Utilities	2.8	3.0	3.3	2.3
Administrative and General	3.7	3.4	2.1	3.7
Repairs and Maintenance	1.9	1.7	1.7	1.5
Rent	4.9	5.5	6.5	4.1
Property Taxes	0.6	0.5	0.6	0.4
Other Taxes	0.4	0.8	0.5	0.2
Property Insurance	0.9	0.9	0.7	0.5
Interest	0.9	0.9	1.1	0.7
Depreciation	2.5	2.4	2.3	2.5
Other Deductions	0.3	0.3	0.4	0.1
Corporate Overhead	1.9	2.1	3.1	2.8
Net Income Before Income Taxes	4.4	7.4	7.9	2.3

*All figures are weighted averages.

**Based on 1991 data.

SOURCE: Foodservice Numbers, National Restaurant Association, Washington, DC, 1992.

SEGMENTS OF THE FOODSERVICE INDUSTRY

Before a menu for a particular operation is written, the menu planner should know the characteristics of the operation, so it can be written to please guests and meet the needs of the operation. In writing these menus, the planners must use all the technical and other information discussed in this text, as well as their own experience. Proper control of costs must be observed; the physical presentation of menu items and menu makeup must be adequate; the planner must remember to include items that are looked upon as healthful foods; and the goods needed for menu items must be available at a proper cost. While these are not discussed in detail in the presentation of the various operating units that follow, they should be remembered. Unless all of this is done, the menu will fail. A menu cannot do some things well and do other things poorly. All links in the chain must be strong.

Commercial Operations

The commercial segment is the largest division of the foodservice industry and is responsible for most of the sales. The commercial category includes any type of operation that sells food and beverages for profit. The operation could be a stand-alone foodservice unit or part of a larger business, which is also designed for profit.

Commercial feeding operations include the following types of units: eating places, bars and taverns, food contractors, lodging places, retail hosts, recreational and sports centers, vending retailers, and mobile caterers.

Restaurants and Lunch Rooms

By far the largest group of units in the foodservice industry is restaurants and lunch rooms, comprising approximately 32 percent of the total number of commercial foodservice units in the industry. Some of these are fine-dining restaurants with seated service, where the average check is $25 or more. Sometimes these restaurants are referred to as "white tablecloth" operations or "expense account" restaurants because they attract business executives entertaining clients and business associates.

Some of these units offer entertainment. They generally have a low customer turnover rate, with two seatings per dining period usually being the maximum. They generally offer lunch and dinner. Wine and other alcoholic beverages are usually offered in a menu separate from the food menu. While food cost in a fine-dining operation may be average, labor cost is usually high, and it must compete for a limited number of customers.

The consumption of alcohol in this country is dropping. In 1981, it peaked at 2.76 gallons of alcohol per person per year over the age of 14. In 1988, this had dropped to 1.94 gallons. Beer and wine have held fairly steady in consumption per person, but that of spirits has dropped. The cost of insurance has also dipped into profitability. New court decisions on third-party liability in serving alcoholic beverages, as well as tremendous fines, have made insurance companies raise their rates to a point where some operations cannot afford it. The foodservice industry has had to cope with this drop and try to better merchandise lighter alcoholic drinks and non-alcoholic drinks to make up for the loss. It also has set up training programs on how to safeguard against serving alcohol to minors, known alcoholics, and those who might be intoxicated. The beverage industry has also addressed the problem. Advertising programs, such as Anheuser-Busch's "Know when to say when," Miller's "Think when you drink," and Coors' "Please drink safely," are examples of how the beverage industry is trying to encourage responsible drinking. Federal and state governments have also stepped in and through regulations have tried to warn individuals of the health hazards involved in consuming excess alcohol. This, plus an increasing awareness on the part of the public of the harm that alcohol can do, has resulted in this drop in alcohol consumption, and brought about a drastic change in how operations serving alcohol must meet the problem.

The term *lunch room* in this group may be somewhat misleading. So-called lunch rooms may also serve breakfast and dinner, but usually their main income comes from the midday period. These operations may depend largely on office, shopper, and other drop-in trade in heavy foot-traffic areas. They are often single units, although chains such as Marriott's may operate lunchrooms. The menu is simple, and may include light meals along with sandwiches, soups, salads, and beverages. Some lunchrooms may offer alcoholic beverages, but most do not. Some serve wine or beer only. Because of their patrons, they may also stress fast service. People shopping or on their lunch hour often have little time and do not want to dally at their meals.

Family Restaurants

Family restaurants are those that cater to a more casual trade, emphasizing food for the family or other groups. Many do not serve alcohol, since some families with young children will not patronize operations that do. If alcohol is offered, the menu may only include beer and wine or a limited selection of mixed drinks. The food menu will offer more popular foods, such as hamburgers, sandwiches, and "specials" (plates or meals for a moderate price). Some family operations compete for the family lunch trade that wants food such as that served in quick-service operations. Family operations expect a better turnover rate than that in fine-dining establishments; 3.5 turnovers per meal may be ideal. These operations are apt to be located in or near residential areas where the average income per household is either above average or moderate. Prices will be moderate. These facilities generally offer seated service, but may serve cafeteria or buffet style. Because children are a significant part of the family restaurant's market, a children's menu is usually available.

California-menu Food Services

Another type of restaurant is based on the *California-menu* concept. The California menu (so called because it originated there) offers breakfasts, lunches, dinners, snacks, and other foods, all on one menu, so patrons can get almost any meal they want, at any time of the day. Counter service may also be a significant part of this type of operation. These operations may be open 24 hours a day. Prices are as low as possible, and the lower profit margin is offset by high volume and turnover. These operations are usually located in high-traffic areas.

Limited-Menu (Quick-service) Restaurants

About a third of the commercial foodservice segment is made up of *limited-menu* or, quick-service restaurants. These operations have only a few items on the menu and the service is fast. Some specialty units serve only one or two main items. Most use a menu that is permanent and offer no items that change daily. Volume is emphasized and prices are low. Fast turnover is required to make a profit.

Quick-service operations try to have a quick seat turnover rate and serve a simple fare that is quickly prepared, served, and eaten. Many do a large take-out service.

Many popular items, such as pizza, hamburgers, chicken, sandwiches, salads, soups, snack items, and ice cream desserts, may be offered on the menu along with carbonated beverages. Few limited-menu operations serve alcohol. Most have a la carte items only, but some also offer a limited amount of table d'hôte items, which can be whole meals. A number of these operations may have seated service using tables and booths. No tablecloths or cloth napkins are used. Many items are prepared for carryout.

Quick-service menus are changing; many new units now have menus that emphasize pasta, Mexican foods, and other ethnic dishes. Many items offered contain more healthful foods with less fat and calories.

Drive-ins are included in the limited-menu category. Pickup windows may be used for car service, or the operation will be so constructed that patrons can park their cars and receive service from a counter for carryout.

Many limited-menu units are owned by chains or are a part of a franchise operation. The number of limited-menu operations has grown faster than other types of operations and should continue to do so. This is most apt to come from the growth in the number of quick-service operations that offer ethnic foods.

Commercial Cafeterias

In cafeterias, patrons go to counters where hot and cold foods are offered, select the food, and then take it to a table to eat. A menu board lists the offerings; and items may be marked with their prices according to where the items are placed. Foods are usually simple and the prices are usually low, reflecting the lack of seated service. Alcohol usually is not offered. Payment may be made at the counter at the end of the service line or as the patron leaves the operation. In some operations, especially those catering to families and the dinner trade, a worker may be at the end of the counter after all selections are made to carry the patron's tray to a desirable dining spot. This person may also serve water. Condiments and napkins may be on a table in the dining area so patrons can serve themselves. Dining utensils are usually prewrapped in cloth or paper napkins or placed in containers at the serving counter so guests may select their own. Entrees are often foods that hold well in a steam table. If steaks and other grilled items, which do not hold well are on the menu, employees may cook these to order. When such an order is taken, the patron is given a number or some other type of identification. The patron then chooses a table, and a worker brings the specially ordered item to the table.

Patrons may or may not remove their soiled dishes and trays after eating. Commercial cafeterias usually depend on a high volume and a fast turnover, and are located in high-traffic areas.

Social Caterers

Catering enterprises prepare food and beverages in a central kitchen often to take somewhere else for service. They cater to such occasions as picnics, weddings, bar and bat mitzvahs, meetings, banquets, office parties, and so forth. Others cater only small group or individual orders. The catering business has not grown as fast as the rest of the commercial segment, probably because other kinds of food service have entered into competition with them. Restaurants, some supermarkets, and even quick-service operations have moved into catering to increase their profits.

Some caterers allow customers to order food by phone and then come in and pick up their orders. These caterers differ from takeout units in that they provide a more complete service.

In some cases, a caterer may be invited to bid for an event, and the patron will select from a group of bidders. This could be for a special occasion or some permanent kind of service, such as catering for a nursing home. In most cases, the client furnishes the space, eating utensils, tables, and chairs. In some instances, the caterer must provide everything. Sometimes the caterer may also furnish an orchestra, sound system, or other items. Since the need for service varies, the payroll may be flexible; only a few full-time, permanent employees may be kept on. The volume of business can vary from providing food for a few people to providing a banquet for more than a thousand people in a convention center. Some caterers may restrict their business to small business parties, teas, or simple buffet dinners. Some caterers work out of their homes.

For catering to be successful, there must be a continuous market for it, and the operation must be properly promoted by advertising. One of the best advertising media for caterers is word-of-mouth by patrons and others who have been to a well-catered event.

The prices for catered events are usually higher than those for regular food and drink offered by a restaurant. The amount of equipment that must be kept in stock, the cost of transportation, and the nature of the business make this necessary. The products offered must be suitable for preparation, holding, packaging, transporting, and serving. The food must be attractive and kept and served hot or cold, according to service and sanitation requirements.

Frozen Dessert Units

Frozen dessert units have become very popular. Often these are part of a franchise or chain. Menus are restricted generally to the frozen dessert and perhaps some simple beverages, but in some menus, sandwiches, salads, and other simple foods are obtainable. Usually no alcohol is served. The turnover in seats (if the establishment provides any) is usually fast, and the operation should be located in places where there is a considerable amount of foot traffic. Some do well in large shopping center complexes. Takeout service is almost always provided. Some operations take orders for specially prepared frozen desserts, such as decorated birthday cakes made of ice cream or other special desserts prepared for holidays.

Bars and Taverns

This group consists of bars and taverns operated as independent free-standing units. It does not include bars, lounges, and other alcohol-dispensing units operated in conjunction with another type of foodservice operation. Total sales in 1993 were approximately $9.3 billion, about 3.5 percent of the sales of the entire food and beverage industry.

Most bars and taverns are single-owner or family-run units. The trend toward chains and multiple operation formation has not been as great in this segment of the industry as it has been in other segments.

Bars and taverns may serve food—sandwiches, snacks and other light items—but this is normally limited to merely what is necessary to attract customers. More and more bars are offering unique or special appetizers to attract patrons. The cost of goods sold is usually lower than that of a food service; labor costs are also lower, so the profitability margin may be better for bars than for food services. (The average cost of goods sold usually runs from 20 to 25 percent in bars and taverns and from 35 to 45 percent in food services.)

Bars and taverns often build reputations as social gathering centers and sometimes provide recreation, such as pool, TV, sports events, video games, and other attractions. Special drink promotions are common. However, because many states now have *dramshop laws* making bar owners, managers, and servers liable for alcohol-related injuries to third parties, "happy hours" and special promotions that encourage patrons to drink more, have all but disappeared. Nonalcoholic and low-alcohol drinks, as well as "designated-driver" programs, are being promoted more often.

Bar and tavern owners and operators are worried about the future because of the growing emphasis on stricter enforcement of dramshop laws. Because of very heavy court judgments, insurance rates for operating bars and taverns have risen to almost prohibitive levels.

Food Contractors

The different types of food contractors can be discussed together since their modes of operation are similar. A food contractor is paid to take over the food service of an operation for a fee, a percentage of sales, a share of the profits, or another financial arrangement. Both commercial and noncommercial organizations use contract foodservice companies. Manufacturing and industrial plants are the biggest customers of foodservice contractors. Other users include hospitals, schools, colleges and universities, airlines, and sports centers.

When an operation turns over its foodservice management to a contractor, it usually does so because its major business purpose is not food service. Nevertheless, they want their units professionally run and staffed. Often a professional food contractor with trained employees and experience can do a better job than the owner. Experts in many fields of foodservice operation are on the staff at the central office of the contractor, and they are valuable resources when problems arise; these individuals are not available to the independently run food service. The food contractor often has a much better system of production, purchasing practices, and accounting skills than is available to nonexperts.

The amount of subsidization a contractor gets from the contracting company varies. In rare cases, the contracting company may subsidize the entire project and pay the contractor a fee for operating the unit. This is rare, however, and the practice of subsidization may run from complete to none at all. The frequency of what is done seems to follow a normal curve with some subsidization occurring in most cases.

The practice of companies charging nothing for foods served in their own food services is also ending. Companies that once gave free meals to employees have had to end that practice.

One of the unique problems in contract foodservice management is that the unit manager usually has to satisfy two bosses: the home or central office and the client company. This can complicate the management process and divide management's emphasis and loyalty. However, it can also act as a stimulus by ensuring adherence to management procedures as set by the contract manager responsive to the client.

Each different type of operation requires different contractor services. Contracted food service is often run as a cafeteria. Industrial or office food services may have executive dining rooms with fine seated service, and a cafeteria for employees. Industrial and office contractors also may provide food and drinks for breaks, meals, and special occasions. They may operate over a 24-hour period to serve three shifts. Others may close down their regular foodservice areas and operate from vending units during slower hours. Health facilities must emphasize nutrition and diet. Hospitals often have a cafeteria for employees, a doctors' dining room, a coffee shop for visitors, and, possibly, a dining room for nurses.

In some very large offices, factories and health complexes, contractors such as McDonald's, KFC, and Burger King have been invited in to operate units. They are now even moving into companies and hospitals. They often receive good patronage because the service is fast and the foods are well known.

School food services in elementary and high schools have a strong nutritional emphasis, and have to conform to nutritional and other standards established by the federal government if they are participants in the general meal pattern program or the milk program. A school may have separate dining rooms for faculty and staff members, in addition to student cafeterias. Some caterers and chains have entered the school lunch program. Many school districts have had to retrench and reduce subsidization of their foodservice programs. Today a food service may be required to break even after paying for lights, janitorial services, and some other expenses. Usually no rent is paid, but in some cases it is. College and university foodservice operations may include residence hall cafeterias, student center coffee shops, and vending operations.

Companies contracting with recreational and sports units have a wide variety of requirements. There may be cafeterias, bars, refreshment stands for fans, and clubs for exclusive groups or members of a recreational association. Alcoholic beverages may be provided.

Contractors may also be expected to cater parties, meetings, and other affairs sponsored by a client company. Contractors usually seek out professionally trained managers. Each year large food contractors, such as Marriott and ARA, visit schools where foodservice management is taught to recruit graduates for trainee positions. Many large contractors have well-structured systems for training and a career development plan, in which the trainee may start out as an assistant manager and move up to full management later.

The service of food by contractors for transportation operations, especially airlines, has become a significant business. Organizations such as Hosts, Marriott, and Dobbs may serve thousands of meals a day from one contractor commissary. The meals are packaged so that hot foods can be heated, cold foods kept cold, and the complete meal assembled during service by the flight attendants. Carbonated and alcoholic beverages are usually provided. Special meals are prepared for first-class passengers. On many flights passengers are offered a menu choice.

Lodging Places

The food and beverage department of a hotel is often a complex system from which a number of different types of food services are operated. They may include a coffee shop, banquet facilities, snack bars, bars, a nightclub, a fine dining room, specialty restaurants, room service, a cafeteria, and even an employee dining room.

A hotel foodservice department is usually managed by a food and beverage manager responsible for seeing that the operation keeps adequate records and makes a profit. A chef may be responsible to the food and beverage manager, or to the manager or assistant manager of the hotel. A maitre d'hôtel may be in charge of the better dining areas, but a host or hostess might be responsible for service in a coffee shop. A banquet or catering manager handles banquets or special parties. A steward may work with the chef in preparing menus, setting up order requirements, and seeing that linens and silver are properly handled, stored, and accounted for. A steward may also be in charge of storage spaces for food, equipment, and other supplies. The hotel sales department should work closely with the food and beverage department, since this department is usually responsible for making arrangements for special catering and other functions, such as meetings and conferences.

Many hotels operate on the continental system, in which an *executive chef* manages operations with a *sous chef* and *chefs du parti* doing the actual food production. The operation is somewhat complex because of the variety of food that must be prepared and the number of different dining areas that must be served. Much food preparation occurs in a central kitchen, which is distributed to the various serving units. Thus, a sandwich grill might get many of its sauces, soups, salads, and other foods from the central kitchen, preparing only sandwiches or grilled items in the grill area.

Many hotel dining rooms stress luxury-type foods and serve alcoholic beverages and wines. Table d'hôte and a la carte menus are often combined. The menu usually features a wide variety of food. Service should be consistent with the menu. Even a hotel's coffee shop can be fairly luxurious, although it may have a different service and offer simpler foods than those served in the main dining room.

Many lodging units cater to conventions, parties, meetings, receptions, and other occasions. This service may be elaborate and may require a special staff. Banquets must be handled with high efficiency and speed. A special kitchen may prepare a large part of the banquet, but the central kitchen can be called upon to supplement many items. Since banquet service may be sporadic, a list of people who can be called on to work as servers, buspersons, and even cooks must be maintained, or the hotel must have a contract with a union or other labor source for its short-term needs. There are many people in the foodservice industry who work only for banquets and are available on call.

Hotels frequently have a problem in that many of the guests who have rooms do not eat at the hotel, especially lunches and dinners. The reason given for this is that customers prefer to eat elsewhere for a change or think the food at restaurants is better or costs less. Thus, many hotels are challenged both to attract their in-house customers and bring in outside trade through creative menus and promotions.

Lodgings generally do more to emphasize their food and beverage business than they did in the past. The reason is that the food and beverage department is now seen as an additional source for revenue and profits. In some hotels and motels, the food and beverage income can be almost equal to that from rooms. Thus, we see many lodging units with elaborate facilities for conventions, meetings, and special events. These can bring in considerable revenue in food and beverage sales, as well as help fill the rooms.

Hotel food services have not led the market in acceptance of more mod-

Exhibit 2.4 Summary of Hotel Revenues, Costs, and Expenses

Revenues

Rooms	64.1%
Food	21.9
Beverages	6.1
Rental from stores, etc.	2.1
Telephone	2.0
Other	3.8

Costs and Expenses

Salaries, benefits and meals	30.1%
Operating expenses	23.7
Cost of sales	8.2
Energy costs	3.6
All taxes	3.4
Management fees, insurance, rent, interest, depreciation, amortization, other additions	31.0

Figures courtesy of the American Hotel and Motel Association, Washington, DC.

ern forms of foods. Some today still cut their meats from carcass or whole-sale cuts. However, there is a growing interest in convenience and preportioned foods.

Exhibit 2.4 is a summary of percentages of income and expenditures that might be considered typical for a hotel.

Retail Hosts

About 60,000 food services are operated in retail establishments, such as drug, department, variety, grocery stores, and in conjunction with gas stations.

Department stores emphasize food for shoppers and usually do well with the lunch trade. Many department stores are diversifying their foodservice operations. Some have salad bars and yogurt stands in addition to their regular dining rooms. They may also have an upscale dining room as well as a moderately priced coffee shop. Often variety stores have counters where fountain items and light meals are served.

Foodservice operations often are found in stations on highly traveled routes. Travelers on these roads find it convenient to get car service and a meal or snack at a single stop. Many interstate highways have such operations, which may be operated by food contractors. Service station units must gear their operations toward families with children, business travelers, and truck drivers.

Grocery stores and convenience stores have become increasingly competitive with foodservice operations, especially since some of the large supermarket chains have found such diversification profitable. Since many groceries already operate bakeries and delicatessens and often sell other prepared foods, it is only a short step to serve these foods to customers. Today one can walk into a supermarket and see a long row or several rows of prepared meats, salads, sandwiches, soups, and desserts attractively arranged and ready for purchase. Often customers supplement their purchase with items picked up off the grocery shelves. As a result, one can get adequate food at a price that one could not get it for in a foodservice operation. However, well-prepared foods and excellent service continue to be a differentiating factor.

Some supermarket stores operate catering businesses as well. Many convenience stores are expected to compete directly with quick-service operations.

Recreational Food Services

Recreational food service is a $3.2 billion market with a growth rate of approximately 3 percent per year. The recreational field consists of sports stadiums, coliseums and arenas, municipal convention centers, concert facilities, amusement parks, pari-mutuel racetracks, expositions, carnivals and circuses, zoos, botanical gardens, state and national parks, and roller and ice-skating rinks.

The basic menu is a concessions type, which generally is a low-cost, high-profit menu. Foods include hot dogs, popcorn, ice cream, soft drinks, and, in some cases, beer. Some facilities also have full-service dining rooms, cafeterias, and coffee shops.

In 1992, there were 14,447 food services in recreational facilities with over 200,000 employees, of which 10 percent were management and supervisors. This segment also employs many people part-time during peak seasons.

Large industrial caterers may operate by contract to provide for the foodservice needs of convention centers or sports arenas. They usually have an office at the location and operate the business from there. Snack foods, carbonated beverages, hot dogs, peanuts, popcorn, and alcoholic beverages are typical fare. Meal service may also be available in dining areas. Some, such as at racetracks, may offer elaborate meals. Often, service personnel circulate in the stands and sell snack items. Counters where patrons can purchase items are located in selected areas.[1]

Mobile Caterers

Prior to World War II, there were few mobile caterers, other than street ice cream on routes in the summer. During World War II, trucks, vans, and other mobile units began to visit factories and construction sites to sell hot and cold food. Some even cooked food to order. Today the mobile catering business is a growing part of the foodservice industry. Most of the sales are divided among industrial plants (60.8 percent), construction sites (24.4 percent), and office buildings and complexes (12.6 percent), with the remainder (2.2 percent) at parks, recreational areas, and special events.

Mobile caterers may be corporations (67 percent), individually owned (21 percent), or partnerships (12 percent). A corporation usually hires people to operate its trucks, but it may lease its trucks to individuals, who then take a percentage of sales. Some also sell the food to them and charge a percentage of sales to operate the route.

The typical mobile catering firm has 17 trucks, and each truck stops at an average of 21 locations a day. Routes are subject to pirating. To hold a business, the route operator must come on a regular basis and provide good service. Some routes may have up to 40 or 50 stops on a 15- to 20-mile run, but many individuals operate shorter routes. Some routes have only a few stops, since enough business may be generated to give a satisfactory return. Most routes are not more than 20 to 30 miles away from the pickup spot. A good route should generate at least $500 to $800 in an eight-hour run. Such a route may require 10- to 12-hour workdays, since the truck must be cleaned, serviced, and loaded, in addition to being operated over the route. Some routes may operate every day, but many operate only five days a week, serving workers who are at the stops only on week days.

The food must be of acceptable quality and moderately priced. The foods should be those that are satisfactory for such service and hold well. Usually, the same foods that are easily machine vended are sold in a mobile unit, although the mobile unit may be more flexible and be able to sell a wider variety of foods. Box lunches, cold and hot drinks, sandwiches, hot lunches, coffee, desserts, bagged goods, candy, salads, crackers, and cookies are all sold.

Sanitation is important in mobile catering, and many foods will have to be kept under refrigeration or frozen. Hot foods must be kept at or above 140°F (60°C) until they are sold.

Vending

Vending foodservice operations continue to grow in popularity. Schools, industrial plants, and colleges and universities are big users of vending equipment and service. Figures on actual vending sales may be somewhat misleading since many sales are reported as sales of other foodservice operations and totaled in their own sales. About 25 percent of vending companies own their own commissaries, and some do catering as well as service vending machines. Some may even service cafeterias and other kinds of operations.

Of the operators offering vended foods, menu items include sandwiches (70 percent), pastries (29 percent), casseroles and platter foods (7 percent), and salads (6 percent). A central commissary should produce sales of not less than 500 to 600 food items per day to be efficient. Otherwise, purchasing from outside units is best. Foods for vending can be obtained from purveyors, wholesalers, or from other vending operators.

More than 20 percent of in-plant feeding services are operated completely from vending machines. For in-plant needs, the food must be substantial and popular with workers. Fresh, high-quality foods should be available from vending units. As with foods for mobile catering, sanitation is an important factor in selecting, preparing, and holding the foods for vending.

Vended foods may require a substantial investment in machines and distribution equipment. A simple candy, pastry, or other machine needing little or no refrigeration may cost $1,000 or more; one that dispenses hot beverages or soup, or refrigerates or holds frozen foods, may cost two or three times more. Service attendants also raise labor costs. Normally, from five to eight years are required to recover the cost of a machine. Food cost may be as high as 65 percent and labor and commissions 21 percent. **Exhibit 2.5** indicates average operating ratios typical of vending companies.

If a vending operation, or any other food service, transports foods across state lines, the place where these foods are processed must meet federal standards for food production facilities and sanitation.

Institutional Feeding

The institutional segment consists mainly of noncommercial and commercial private and public organizations that operate food services in support of the actual purpose of the establishment. They are involved in some of the same types of operations as are enterprises discussed under commercial feeding that *do not* use food contractors to manage their foodservice operations. Many hospitals and nursing homes manage their own foodservice operations, as do many elementary and secondary school systems, colleges and universities, and prisons. Private clubs and camps are also part of the institutional sector.

Employee Feeding

Contract feeders in manufacturing and industrial plants and office buildings do about twice as much business as privately owned industrial and commercial units. Public school systems, colleges and universities, hospitals, and other institutions also have employee feeding programs, and many of these will be managed by contract feeding companies. Seagoing ships and inland waterway vessels make up the rest of the employee feeding division.

Employee feeding programs are increasing in popularity as more workers recognize the value and convenience of eating where they work. Employee feeding operations are getting into the breakfast trade. They are also emphasizing more healthful and nutritional foods that are low in fat and calories. More and more, employee feeding trends reflect those of the commercial feeding sector.

Employee feeding programs usually consist of cafeterias, vending operations, and executive dining rooms. Some dining operations may be subsidized by the employer. Attempts are made to keep food costs and prices low to encourage employees to stay on the premises for lunch and for breaks. If meal prices are very low, the foodservice operations may be considered part of the employee's benefit package.

Exhibit 2.5 Average Vending Profit and Loss for All Companies with Sales over $1 Million (1992)

RETAIL SALES	100.0%
Cost of sales	45.4
Gross profit	54.6
PAYROLL EXPENSES	
Route and location	9.3
Maintenance and repair	1.7
Warehouse	0.5
Supervisory	2.9
Administrative and all others	4.5
Fringe benefits and payroll taxes	5.0
Sub-total PAYROLL EXPENSES	23.9
OPERATING EXPENSES	
Commissions to locations	8.9
Depreciation—vending equipment	4.7
Depreciation on buildings	0.2
Depreciation on vehicles	0.7
Other depreciation	0.6
Rent and lease costs—vending equipment	0.4
Rent and lease costs—buildings	0.9
Other rent and lease costs	0.2
Sales, use of occupational taxes	3.8
All other taxes except income and payroll taxes	0.6
Vending machine maintenance and repair costs	1.2
Accountability	0.3
Vehicle expense	2.1
Insurance premiums	1.0
Other operating expenses	3.3
Sub-total OPERATING EXPENSES	28.9
TOTAL EXPENSES	52.8
OPERATING PROFIT	1.8
Parent company overhead allocation	(2.1)
Interest expense	(0.9)
Other income	2.9
PROFIT BEFORE INCOME TAX	1.7%

Figures courtesy of the National Automatic Merchandising Association, Chicago, Illinois.

Educational Feeding

Elementary and Secondary Schools

About 92,000 elementary and secondary schools and 2,500 public and private colleges and universities belong to the educational feeding group. Noncontract educational feeding accounts for about 0.6 percent of the total dollar sales of the foodservice industry. However, this does not reflect the value of federally donated foods used in the program.

Most elementary and high schools belong to the school lunch program. The National School Lunch Program was established by federal law in 1946.[2] The program is administered by the U.S. Department of Agriculture, which distributes funds and surplus foods on the basis of the number and circumstances of the participating children in each state. The program has two objectives: 1) to offer a market for agricultural products; and 2) to serve nutritional foods to school children at low or no cost. In addition, the USDA administers the Special Milk Program, whereby a school gets a cash refund from the government for each half pint of milk it purchases for a child.

To obtain cash and surplus foods, a school system must provide each student with foods in compliance with a school lunch *meal pattern*. The meal must contain a certain amount of food to qualify for subsidy from the federal government. The foods required under the original law have been changed somewhat. Butter, once required, no longer is; to reduce the amount of fat on the menu, many schools do not serve butter or margarine. Desserts and rich foods are also discouraged. A variety of foods of different nutritive values must be served, for a total of five foods, for the school to be reimbursed by the federal government. Bread alternatives may include whole-grain rice or pasta. Either flavored or unflavored milk may be offered, but unflavored fluid low-fat milk, unflavored skim milk, or buttermilk must be available. Low-salt or even no-salt foods are encouraged.

The foods prepared for the federal program are generally simple and plain. They should have high popularity with children, who have extremely sensitive food tastes and habits.

Today, the school foodservice system is deeply ingrained in our educational system. It is a tremendous force in providing adequate nutrition to many children in this country.

Colleges and Universities

Residence halls, student unions, and other college and university food services can be huge operations doing millions of dollars of business. Residence halls may be operated on a closed board plan that provides three meals a day to students at an established rate. Students are charged for all meals regardless of whether they eat them. Many schools have modified this program and provide fewer meals at a standard board rate. These schools allow the students to select the meals they wish and to pay individually for them. Some others have worked out plans in which only a specific number of meals are purchased during the week.

Foods must be popular with students. Some food services offer natural or vegetarian foods. Pastas, pizza, seafood, and a variety of ethnic food items are popular. In general, today's college students are more sophisticated and have more varied tastes than students in previous decades. As with school food service, the frequent use of casseroles and the like has declined. The food must still be nutritious and provide adequately for dietary needs.

Most college and university food services are cafeterias, with students serving themselves beverages, bread, butter or margarine, desserts, salads, condiments, silverware, and napkins. For this reason, many foods may have to be preportioned and dished. Students may also bus their own trays from their tables to dishwashing areas.

In addition to the main cafeteria, a school may operate snack bars, a coffeehouse, a faculty club, and a faculty dining room. These will usually be typical of commercial counterparts, but slanted in price and ambience to suit campus needs. Faculty clubs must provide quality foods for parties, meetings, and receptions. Alcoholic beverages may be sold in some. Faculty clubs frequently resemble regular social clubs. They may even have recreational facilities.

Usually a central department operates all food services on the campus. Registered dietitians may be on the staff to see that menus are balanced and nutritionally adequate. A regular staff of cooks and other personnel is maintained, along with numerous part-time student employees.

Colleges and universities are finding that they must compete with off-campus foodservice alternatives more directly than they did in the past, by combining marketing and merchandising.

Transportation Feeding

Airline feeding is the largest transportation foodservice, doing close to a billion dollars in sales by about 133 companies. Ships, buses, and railroads make up a smaller percentage of sales in this group.

Airline Feeding

In many respects, a large kitchen producing airline foods is like a central commissary, but with some very significant differences. Timing demands are tremendous. Foods must be ready as needed. Thus quick production, plus rapid transportation to the planes, is required. Often, an incoming plane needs to be ready for takeoff in about 20 to 30 minutes. This means that a rapid system for unloading used food items and loading on new must be worked out. The delay of a plane because food is late is a serious problem. However, foods cannot be produced too far in advance, or quality and safety may be lost. There is a need to develop maximum efficiency in work methods, and many units now use automation and labor- and time-saving methods.

A production center may produce foods for one or several airlines. A local foodservice company may set up a central production unit to sell meals and operate the airport food services. As an alternative, a large airline may operate its own production center and provide foods for other airlines.

Often an airline uses a cycle menu—a menu that repeats at regular cycles. A six-day cycle prevents frequent passengers from getting the same foods if they travel a certain day of the week. Each airline has its own standards and own menus, with some now having meals (often snacks) that never change. Food standards and food specifications are usually tightly written directives that leave the producing unit little leeway to use a different item. The menus vary depending on the length and type of the flight.

Several menus may be required for the same plane: for example, a choice for first-class passengers, a menu for coach class, plus any special dietary items ordered by passengers. Thus, if there are a large number of planes to be loaded in one day, there may be a set number of foods to produce at one time. Usually production centers are advised 14 to 30 days in advance that a plane must be loaded, but the actual passenger count is not given until several hours before flight time. Often, though, there is a preliminary count available approximately 24 hours or more before. Special meals must be ordered 24 hours in advance, but some planes are able to accommodate requests just before loading because they carry special foods for this purpose. This is possibly due to the limited menus now served on most flights.

Each plane may also require its own type of dishes with accompanying equipment. It is not unusual for a large center to produce 6,000 to 8,000 meals a day with only a limited number of common items used for all planes. In addition, alcoholic and nonalcoholic beverages, ice, water, tea, coffee, milk, napkins, nuts, and other items are provided.

Because of the large inventory of different kinds of dishes, tableware, equipment, and other items, the production center must have considerable storage space for holding items for each airline. Transportation of foods and equipment to and from the center to planes must also be well organized. The operation of a food production center for airlines is quite complex.

Good flexibility must be established. Changes can occur rapidly, and the center must meet them. For example, a plane may be routed to a different airport and have to be loaded there.

The federal Public Health Service has jurisdiction over sanitation on public transport carriers moving across interstate lines, and the rules are stringent. No food or beverages returned on one plane can be used on another, unless they are packaged items, such as canned soda-pop, bagged pretzels or nuts, or bottled alcoholic beverages. Sanitation standards for the facilities, equipment, workers, and work methods are quite high. Besides meeting federal standards, an operation often must meet those of the local authorities.

With the deregulation of the airlines, a number of "no frills" airlines entered the field. Often these airlines offered only packaged snacks or beverages. Passengers were even encouraged to bring their own foods. This trend caught on with the major airlines and now many airlines entail a lighter meal—a sandwich, a piece of fruit, cookies, a sweet, or crackers and cheese. It is rare to see a regular meal served; this is done when airlines meet stiff competition from other airlines and food is then used as a means of attracting and holding passengers.

Railroad and Bus Food Services

Railroad feeding today is very different from the past, when passenger trains served meals in dining cars that competed in quality and service with the best restaurants, and terminal stations provided food service that ranged from quick-service to fine-dining units. Today there are fewer passenger trains, and many on short runs serve only sandwiches or other fast foods. However, others serve meals that are reminiscent of the past, with gourmet-type offerings, fine service, and excellent decor. Most of these trains make longer trips and also have a snack bar offering lighter foods.

"Luxury ride" trains with accompanying fine dining stop to pick up diners and move much slower than commuter trains. Obviously this type of foodservice operation must maximize sales to pay for itself.

Normally, railroad food services are not very profitable, but government railroad subsidies are substantial and can enable some operations to break even or lose only a small amount.

Bus terminals are busier places and normally have quick-service operations. Some also have coffeehouses. Bus travel has not slowed as much as railroad travel, and so has been able to support food services better. Only rarely will any kind of food or beverage be sold on board the bus, except at stops where vendors may board the buses and sell snack foods and drinks.

Health Services Feeding

Within the foodservice industry, the health service category includes nursing homes; homes for the aged, blind, mentally and physically handicapped; and homes for orphans. Hospitals, nursing homes, and long-term care facilities all provide some dietary food service. Hospitals do more than $10 billion worth of business a year, while nursing homes and others do more than $4 billion. Together these health service foodservice operations do about 5.3 percent of the total sales in the foodservice industry.

Hospitals

A hospital's food service is usually directed by a professional with a college degree in foodservice management or an administrative dietitian with a degree in dietetics. Dietitians are certified by the American Dietetic Association. Some hospitals use a professional foodservice manager to administer the different food services, and dietitians to handle dietary concerns. A chef or food production manager works under the director of the hospital's food service. Hospital food is generally simple, but good quality. The nutritional value of the food and sanitation are vital considerations in production.

Most hospitals prepare a general menu from which patients on nonrestricted diets select the foods they desire. Modified diets, such as low-sodium, are adapted from the general menu. For this reason, a general menu must be planned with a view toward its being used for modified diets. However, food choice should not be dictated by this consideration alone.

Most hospitals use a cycle menu. Since patients' stays are usually short, most hospitals find they can operate with a rather short cycle. The food must be nourishing, simple, and not too highly seasoned.

Some hospitals use a cook-chill method in which food is cooked in batches enough for two or more meals. After cooking, they are packaged and rapidly chilled, then stored to be withdrawn as needed at a future date. The food is then reheated and served. This method reduces labor and waste, and, when done properly, gives adequate quality food.

The method of delivering and serving the food to patients may vary. Some hospitals have *centralized services*, where foods are dished up in the central production area and then sent to patients. Various methods of keeping the food hot or cold are used. Some hospitals have trayveyor systems that deliver food to the various floors in a short time. Others use insulated carts in which hot or cold food is loaded and sent to floors for delivery. A hot *pellet* (a round piece of metal weighing about a pound) may be put under dished food to keep it at a desirable temperature. Also available is an insulated server in which hot or cold foods can be kept with little or no loss of temperature for several hours. Thermalization units can be used that heat foods quickly for service. Microwave ovens also can be used to heat foods.

With the increasing use and availability of cook-chill, quick-frozen, convenience, and preportioned foods, many newer hospitals are developing decentralized foodservice systems. Only a limited amount of bulk preparation occurs in a central area. This is then sent to the various pantries on individual floors where these foods are combined with others to make patient meals. Thus, a foodservice may purchase all of its salad greens ready-to-use. Frozen entrees may also be purchased. These foods will then be sent in the proper amount to the smaller pantries where final preparation occurs. Some pantry staffs wash the dishes and do a great deal of the cleanup. Foods in these pantries may be heated by microwave, quartz (infrared), or conventional ovens.

Hospitals serve patients who are ill and, consequently, under considerable emotional stress. While the food may be of good quality, patients may be dissatisfied with it because of their own physical or emotional condition. The food becomes a "whipping boy" on which the patient takes out his or her fears and frustrations. Because of this, many hospitals now recognize the need to "sell" patients on the food, just as commercial units do. Food should be attractive, properly garnished, served at the right temperature, and have good form, color, texture, and flavor. While patients may have little choice as to their food, every attempt should be made to cater to patients' personal tastes. For this reason, more and more hospitals today run special menus and promotions.

Long-term Health Facilities

Long-term care facility foodservice operations are much like those in hospitals, but may not have the wide number of modified diets, although many patients in nursing homes will be on some special type of diet. The food must be nutritious and fairly simple. Many older people and people with long-term illnesses have problems eating, so much of the food must be soft, and suitable for easy chewing and swallowing. However, special soft and bland diets should be prepared only for those who must eat them, while others can have more normal, textured food.

Most long-term facilities operate on low budgets. The foodservice department must, therefore, watch its costs. A foodservice manager or supervisor will have the responsibility for direct operations management. Dietitians may act as consultants, calling once a week or sometimes as seldom as once a month. Thus, responsibility for management may rest on an individual who has little foodservice management or dietary training.

The equipment and layout of the foodservice unit may not be designed for maximum productivity. Because of this, menus and the foods that can be produced must necessarily be restricted. While the food should be simple and close to what patients are used to, it should not lack variety. With a little care, even low-cost foods can be highly varied, interesting, desirable, and nourishing.

Clubs

Club food services usually emphasize luxury-type foods. Clubs serve members who use the club for enjoyment, relaxation, or to entertain guests. However, some also offer quick-service food in addition. Food quality must be high. The food and service must give pride to members and impress guests who eat there. The market is usually restricted to members and guests.

In addition to parties, social clubs may serve breakfast, lunch, and dinner. Many such clubs exist in urban areas, and they may provide rooms for resident members. Serving meals and catering to events are usually big sources of revenue. Many clubs sell alcoholic beverages.

Country clubs are social clubs, but usually have recreational and sports facilities, such as pools, tennis courts, and golf courses, in addition to the food services. Club food services may vary from fine dining to snack bars.

Most clubs have a wide fluctuation in the amount of business done. At times they will be extremely busy, with every food service operating at full or even greater capacity, while at other times, little or no business will be done. This makes it difficult to schedule production and labor. The menu must include food items such as steak or chicken that can be quickly prepared to meet a sudden surge in business. Some convenience items must be available so they can be used quickly if the demand arises.

Club food services must endeavor to attract members. A meal featuring ethnic foods, a fashion show with a luncheon, dances, and golf tournaments may be used to draw in members.

Military Feeding

The value of food served to military personnel at posts and in other military units is not included by the National Restaurant Association in its classifications. The only sales that are included are those in officers' and noncommissioned officers' (NCO) clubs and in military exchanges.

Military-feeding operations have gone through major changes and will continue to change. These changes reflect the changes in the troops in the post-Vietnam and Cold War era. There are more married enlistees than ever, and military commanders consider the stability of those families critical to reenlistment. The trend in military clubs is moving away from operating them as drinking places and toward using them as family centers and fitness clubs.

Post exchanges (large variety stores on a military base or post) continue to offer quick-service options, snack bars, and sometimes coffee shops.

Feeding the troops is still a priority, and in this area the changes are consistent with changes in the commercial feeding segment. The food is still substantial but more healthy than in the past. More selections are offered. Also, quick-service units are springing up on military bases and posts, offering even more variety.

Central Commissaries

The production of central commissaries in our classification is included in the different types of units served by them. However, since these commissaries are specialized kinds of food production operations, they merit separate discussion.

Chain and large foodservice operations use central commissaries to produce much of the food they sell. School systems are presently using them. Some large food services, such as Horn and Hardart, Howard Johnson's, and Horn's, have a substantial quantity of their foods produced in them. These foods are shipped to satellite units where they are reprocessed and served.

Some central commissaries may receive only large shipments and then reship the food items to individual units in smaller lots. Michigan State University's central commissary acts as a warehouse and breakdown center where fresh vegetables, groceries, meats, and other supplies are received, broken down, and reshipped to campus units. Another central commissary in the city of Los Angeles school district does this, but prepares basic dry bakery mixes, pudding mixes, and sauce mixes, in addition to reshipping other items. The advantage in such a system is that lower prices can be obtained since the central commissary can qualify for brokerage rather than wholesale prices.

Other central commissaries may prepare entrees, meats, salads, vegetables, desserts, bakery items, and soups ready for use. These may be shipped portioned or in bulk lots to be processed by the satellite. The foods may be shipped frozen, chilled, or cooked and ready-to-eat.

A central commissary is not a kitchen as much as a factory in which foods are quickly mass-produced on assembly lines. Special equipment must be used. Some foods are cooked in huge steam-jacketed kettles holding 2,000 gallons or more of food. The food is also cooled down in these kettles by shutting off the steam and running refrigerated glycol or water into the jacket. Huge electric stirrers must be used to move the food while cooking and cooling. Special pumps and other units must be used to put the food into the kettles and remove it. Highly sophisticated packaging machines must also be used.

Some food services are becoming disenchanted with central commissary production because cost savings are not substantial. Some chains have shut down their units. However, the use of commissaries to prepare food for school systems and other institutions continues.

THE FUTURE OF FOOD SERVICE

The foodservice industry operates in an environment facing economic and social changes. The foodservice industry is also dynamic, and forces within the industry will generate change. **Exhibit 2.6** lists some of the broad predictions made in the National Restaurant Association's study, Foodservice Manager 2000.

Exhibit 2.6   Highlights of Foodservice Manager 2000

- Competition in the foodservice industry will be more intense at the turn of the century, but growth is expected to continue.
- Major foodservice chains will increase their share of both sales and units.
- Independent operators and entrepreneurs will be the main source of new restaurant concepts.
- The foodservice industry will have an increased need to train and develop its employees, with hotel, restaurant, and institutional degree programs becoming more comprehensive.
- Productivity will be emphasized, but the industry problem with employee turnover will still remain an issue.
- Higher tax levels for both individuals and businesses will be in effect.
- Restaurant design will be more flexible and incorporate a wide variety of technological advances.
- Nutritional concerns will be critical at all types of foodservice operations, and food flavors will be important.
- Service will become a more important point of differentiation.
- Environmental concerns will receive increased attention.
- The foodservice industry will become more international, with U.S. operators entering new foreign markets and foreign operators penetrating the U.S. market.
- AIDS and an aging population will be among the top social/ethical concerns.
- Consumers will spend a greater portion of their food dollar away from home.
- More restaurants will be leasing rather than owning both land and buildings.
- Payroll and benefit costs will consume a larger portion of the restaurant industry's sales dollar.
- The year 2000 and beyond will see the foodservice industry putting as much effort, talent, and money into its managers as customers because managers represent the ultimate key to success.
- A foodservice manager at the turn of the century will have to be either Superman or Wonderwoman.
- 2000 will be the dawn of a new professionalism for the restaurant manager.
- Foodservice managers in 2000 will continue to be faced with the same challenges they are faced with now.
- The restaurant manager in 2000 will be a coach, facilitator, and cheerleader, rather than a director.
- Changes to the foodservice industry and the manager's job in 2000 will occur so fast that only those who are prepared will prosper—everyone else will merely survive.

Forces of Change

The Economy

The recession of the early 1990s left permanent scars in the economy. Competition among producing nations has become fierce. While the foodservice industry will face tremendous economic and competitive challenges, it will continue to grow. The biggest gains will most likely take place in quick-service, health facilities, contractors, retail hosts, vending, and take out.

The commercial segment of the foodservice industry—by far the greatest part of the industry—is very dependent on the amount of disposable income consumers spend. This is expected to slow down to an increase of 2.4 percent per year in the year 2000, down from a 2.7 percent growth in 1985.

The Social Pattern

The Bureau of Census predicts that while the U.S. population will increase, there will be a change in the makeup of its age groups. Birth rates will be slowed. The percentage in the total population of people under 18 will decrease as well as the percentage of people 18 to 34. The percentage of those between 35 and 49 will increase substantially, and there will be a significant but smaller increase in the percentage of people over 50. We have about 30 million people in the population today over 65. By the year 2000 there will be over 50 million.

The makeup of our social living structures affects the industry's economy. Family-style units profit in a stable population group. Couples and singles usually patronize a different type of unit and eat a different kind of food. The number of married couples with children will fall from half to nearly a third of family groups. There will be an increase in married couples without children, and a large increase in the number of single people with children. These figures probably indicate a decrease in the number of births per year, unless those having children increase the number they have. However, family size has been shrinking. The fact that people live longer and the increase in the number of senior citizens, as noted above, also influences the way population growth affects the industry.

This change in our population will mean that the kinds of operations and kinds of foods needed to satisfy patrons will change. **Exhibit 2.7** compares family compositions of 1970 to those of 1990.

Ethnic differences will also play an important part in dictating styles of operation and the kinds of foods served. Because of the emphasis on healthful foods, certain ethnic foods which seem to be healthful will become more popular.

The Labor Force

The industry workforce will change because of the way our population is growing. The white population will increase at a rather slow pace while the African-American population will grow twice as fast, and the pace of growth of Asian and Hispanic groups will be three times as much. Furthermore, the

Exhibit 2.7   Family Composition in the United States

Families have become more diverse over the past two decades

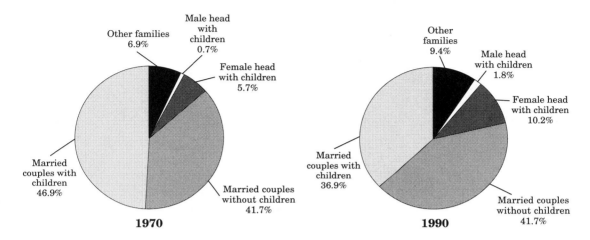

1970

Other families
6.9%

Male head with children
0.7%

Female head with children
5.7%

Married couples with children
46.9%

Married couples without children
41.7%

1990

Other families
9.4%

Male head with children
1.8%

Female head with children
10.2%

Married couples with children
36.9%

Married couples without children
41.7%

SOURCE: Bureau of the Census, U.S. Department of Commerce.

makeup of people immigrating into this country will change. Most European immigrants will come from southern Europe, but the bulk of new immigrants will be Asian and Hispanic. The percentage of the labor force made up by men will decrease; women are expected to make up over 47 percent of our national workforce. However, these general statistics will be even greater in the foodservice industry. The National Restaurant Association and others predict that the percentage of non-Hispanic whites working in our industry will drop substantially, to be replaced largely by African-Americans, but more substantially by Asians and Hispanics. Women will make up over 65 percent of the foodservice work force. Challenges in handling a multicultural group of employees will be multiplied; and the need to introduce more training programs will increase.

The predictions are also that with the increasing number of immigrants working in the industry, training needs will increase. A large number of walk-in workers have little or no work experience and must receive their training on the job. This will be an ongoing challenge to foodservice employers.

Hospitality schools will also have to change their programs to produce supervisors, managers, and others who direct operations who are knowledgeable about marketing, human resources management, and computer systems. The skills involved in "managing diversity," will have to be taught.

The Labor Department's Commission on Achieving Necessary Skills (SCANS) has said that "fewer than half of today's young adults have the basic skills needed to be work-ready."

Because of a smaller number of employees to fill the available jobs, we will see strong competition in the labor market. As a result, it will benefit foodservice operators to hire qualified senior citizens and people with disabilities to get the employees they need.

There is also a trend toward flexible hours, adapting jobs to suit the ability of employees to perform them, and meeting governmental regulations regarding the use of such employees.

Many hospitality programs must recognize the new needs, but the industry itself will also have to change its training programs. Professional associations must change their programs also to meet these new conditions so those now employed in the industry will be able to meet future demands.

Healthful Foods

Consumers today are much more aware of the relationship between their state of health and what they eat. This has had a great impact on the foodservice industry. Patrons today want more fresh vegetables and less fatty meats and foods; fish and poultry are more in demand. Many menus now offer special items to meet the demand for healthful foods. (This topic is covered more thoroughly in Chapter 10.)

Employee Turnover

As noted, the foodservice industry has more people on its payroll than any other, employing nearly 7 million full-time and 2 million part-time employees. At one time or another, one out of every four people in a household will work in the industry. Employment time is shorter than in many other industries, because it is often a means of livelihood while one prepares for a career in another area. This is a contributing factor to the high labor turnover. In some operations the turnover is over 100 percent per year. Another reason for the turnover is that the industry pays low wages; some employees are paid below the minimum wage because tips are considered a part of the total wage. Yet another reason is the long or irregular hours demanded of some employees.

Turnover is costly; it costs money to hire replacements and train them. Often the replacement employee, new to the job, lacks the proficiency in doing the job of the former employee. For instance, if it costs $300 to replace a worker and the operation makes a 5 percent profit, $60,000 in sales are required to make up for this cost.

The foodservice industry realizes its problem and has taken steps to try to reduce its turnover. The advantages of industry careers are stressed and many try to compete with other industries to pay wages that attract good employees. However, according to predictions, the labor turnover problem will remain.

Government Regulations

For many years the foodservice industry was largely ignored by governments at both federal and local levels. Laws and regulations that the government made that did affect it were those made in general for all industries. Laws such as those that established minimum wage rules, child labor laws, and the Occupational Safety and Health Act (OSHA), and laws regarding the employment of people with disabilities, income tax, and unemployment benefits are examples of this detached regulation. However, during the past few years, state and federal governments have singled out the foodservice industry for special regulation.

The majority of the laws that affect foodservice operators directly are written at the state and local levels. These include truth-in-menu laws, laws requiring nonsmoking sections in public dining areas, sanitary regulations, third-party liability (dramshop) laws, and liquor laws.

The federal government has also become interested in foodservice industry practices in recent years. Tip-reporting regulations under the tax code requirements predominantly affect foodservice employers and employees. Further government regulation has resulted from changes in U.S. immigration policies.

Certainly, in the future we will see further direct government regulation of the foodservice industry. The National Restaurant Association, state restaurant associations, and other groups representing the foodservice industry are aware of this and are active in political and legal areas. Among the issues that will continue to affect the foodservice industry are continued heavy regulation of liquor sales and service, including tighter dramshop laws, and truth-in-menu regulations regarding additives and preservatives, and possibly laws restricting their use.

Foodservice Industry Trends

Trends within the foodservice industry itself are important to watch if one is concerned about growth. These include changes in patron preferences, menu trends, and the availability of new convenience foods.

Among the menu items that have grown in popularity are breakfast items, quick-service ethnic foods, healthful foods, light entrees, and gourmet items. Operators who are aware of the differences between menu trends and menu fads will consider national trends in light of local tastes and eating patterns.

Growing consumer interest in convenience has resulted in the entry of retail operations into the foodservice field. This is one of the fastest-growing segments of the foodservice industry, and growth is expected to continue.

The need for the industry to reduce costs—foodservice prices have been increasing faster than food for the home, sharpening the competition of the home-cooked meals with the foodservice industry—has brought about such changes as more self-service, takeout, partial meals, and menu items not easily prepared at home.

The demand of consumers for more healthful foods has been felt by the industry, which has taken steps to meet the demand. Many food services are trying to emphasize health in menu items. Some are even hiring professional dietitians as consultants to help them do this and also to assist in the preparation of some of the more simple special diets.

One specific area of substantial growth, takeout business, can be a major part of almost any type of foodservice operation. The National Restaurant Association says that the increase in working women, singles, childless couples, and two-income households has led to an increase in foodservice takeout sales and that this growth is likely to continue. Working women are responsible for much of the growth in the takeout business. Snack foods, partial meals, and gourmet dishes are all popular. The market is divided into consumers who buy foods to take to eat during the work day and consumers who purchase food to take home. There is a difference between the foods desired. The first group of buyers wants snacks, light lunches, and other items that provide nourishment during work hours. The second group buys a complete or partial meal, and may be more interested in gourmet meals, especially items they would not fix at home.

Technology

Technology will continue to change the industry, not only because of the continued production of convenience foods that reduce labor in the operation, but also because of more modern equipment, facilities, and modes of operation. The availability and cost of energy will also influence the foodservice industry and will help shape its future.

Looking back 50 years and comparing production and service then and now, we recognize that vast changes have occurred. Foods 50 years ago were neither as fresh nor as sanitary as they are today. Our grading standards and our ability to hold foods safely were not as good. Many foods now come to operations processed to such a degree that less labor is needed to get them ready for service. Many different kinds of cooked foods, ready for service, are on the market. Frozen foods, as we use them today, are less than 50 years old.

More than 60 years ago, food services began to use mechanical dishwashers and mixers. Coal, wood, and fuel-oil ranges and ovens were common in comparison with the thermostatically controlled units in almost universal use today. There were no electric meat saws, cubers, or grinders. Steam-jacketed kettles and pressure cookers were just appearing. The modern deep-fat fryer was unknown. Potatoes and other vegetables and fruits were prepared by hand. Technology has taken us a long way.

Foodservice operators are now demanding more energy-efficient appliances and more convenience foods preportioned for quick production and service. Improvements in packaging should help increase the shelf life of many food items. The *aquaculture* or farm-type raising of fish and shellfish is improving the prices and availability of such items. The *hydroponic* growing (growing plants in water rather than soil) of vegetables will also be more common.

Perhaps one of the biggest changes is occurring in the way we are packaging our foods, and this will continue. Today we can use *controlled atmosphere packaging* which seals in atmosphere around the fresh fruit or vegetable and keeps freshness for a much longer time. New labeling laws will make it possible for consumers to know more about what they are buying so they can better evaluate healthful qualities. New fat substitutes in foods give flavor without the calories and cholesterol. New non-caloric sweeteners have been produced, which are even more sweet and leave less aftertaste than non-caloric sweeteners containing phenylalanine.

The computer has potential for application in all areas of food production and service. In the near future few operations will be without some sort of computer application. Not only can it be a factor in simplifying internal operations, but its expanded use by other organizations, such as banks and suppliers, could "network" a number of operations, including bank deposits, reorders, and credit checks. Use of the computer in foodservice will be discussed in Chapter 13.

In the next 50 years, we can look forward to even greater technological progress because we have far more technology available to improve food production than ever before.

SUMMARY

The foodservice industry is marked by wide diversity in operating units and by yearly sales that make it one of the largest industries in the nation. The three major divisions are: 1) commercial feeding operations that account for 88.5 percent of total foodservice sales; 2) institutional operations, contributing 11.1 percent; and 3) the military feeding segment, which accounts for 0.4 percent of sales. Eating places do most of the business in the first group, consisting of restaurants, lunchrooms, limited menu operations, commercial cafeterias, social caterers, and frozen dessert stands. Bars and taverns that are not a part of another foodservice operation do about 4 percent of the total sales in the commercial feeding category. Contractors in the commercial group do about 6 percent of all foodservice business. Lodging places do about the same. Food services in retail units, recreation and sports facilities, mobile caterers, and vending units account for the rest of the sales in the eating places group, about 7.7 percent.

Employee feeding, schools, transportation, health facilities, clubs, and community centers are in the institutional group, doing about 48 percent of the total institutional sales. The military feeding facilities consist of officers' and NCOs' clubs and military exchanges.

About 25 percent of the total meals consumed in this country are eaten away from home. This amounts to 42 percent of what Americans spend on food. Typical restaurant food costs are about 35 percent of sales and payroll and employee benefits costs around 30 percent. The average industry profit is generally small, being from 3 to 7 percent.

The type of ownership in the foodservice industry has had a gradual change. At one time the industry was dominated by family-owned single units, but this started to change after World War II. Today, while independently owned units still predominate, the percentage has dropped considerably. Quick-service chains and franchises within a corporate structure have begun to take over the sales of the industry and promise to grow at a rapid rate in the future.

The foodservice industry is the biggest employer in this country, including both full and part-time employees. Turnover is very high at all levels. Training of these employees and others already in the industry will be necessary to improve the quality and quantity of the labor supply.

Trends in the U. S. social structure and economy influence the foodservice industry. Perhaps one of the largest factors has been the growth in the number of women working outside the home, who eat out more and have more discretionary income to spend when they do. Another factor in our social structure is the growth in the number of single people, and the fact that people are marrying later and having fewer children. The size of households is smaller, with more and more families headed by single women. These factors bring more people out to eat and affect the type of foodservice operations these groups patronize. The growing number of retirees is also a factor, having implications for the foodservice industry not only in menu planning, but also for the labor supply. With the decline of the population of the number of teenagers, retirees represent a readily available and, many times, more reliable labor supply.

Evidence of industry change that can influence the foodservice industry includes economic conditions; government control; changing social patterns; the interest of people in nutrition, value, and diet; the high employee turnover rate in the industry; the advent of the computer; and the popularity of convenience foods. Technology will continue to affect the future of the foodservice industry. New methods of packaging, holding, and portioning foods will help keep costs low and preserve quality for consumers. Computers are the major technological boon to the foodservice industry. They can be used in some way in almost every operation.

QUESTIONS

1. How are foodservice labor requirements likely to be changed by technological advances in the future?

2. How are changes in the population likely to affect the foodservice industry in terms of the menu? Of labor?

3. Describe some of the trends in consumer preferences that will affect menu planning.

4. Contrast the major differences in commercial and noncommercial/institutional feeding services in terms of goals, menus, and people served.

5. How do government regulations currently affect the foodservice industry? How might they affect it in the future?

3

Planning a Menu

Outline

Objectives

After reading this chapter, you should be able to:

1. Identify and characterize various menus used in the foodservice industry.

2. Explain what a meal plan is and how menus may be developed for them.

3. Identify the basic organizational structure of a menu.

4. Identify tools needed to plan menus.

5. Compare and contrast institutional and commercial menus.

INTRODUCTION

For foodservice consumers, a menu is a list, often presented with some fanfare, showing the food and drink offered by a restaurant, cafeteria, club, or hotel. For the manager of a foodservice establishment, however, the menu represents something significantly more: It is a strategic document that defines the purpose of the foodservice establishment and every phase of its operation.

In considering the menu, we may think of it generally in two ways: first, as a working document used by managers to plan, organize, operate, and control back-of-the-house operations, and second, as a published announcement of what is offered to patrons in the front of the house. In its first model it serves a variety of functions: as a guide to purchasing; as a work order to the kitchen, bar, or pantry; and as a service schedule for organizing job duties and charting staff requirements in all departments. In the second case it is a product listing, a price schedule, and the primary means of advertising the food, beverages, and service available to guests.

A good menu should lead patrons to food and beverage selections that satisfy both their dining preferences and the merchandising necessities of the operator. It can serve as public notice of days and hours of operation, inform patrons of special services available, narrate the history of the establishment and significant material concerning its locale; and may even be used to inform patrons of new ways to enjoy the dining experience, including descriptions of unusual or exciting dishes, drinks, or food techniques. The importance of this selling opportunity makes designing a menu that sells critical.

Selling is a goal not only of commercial operations but of noncommercial and semicommercial institutions as well. For instance, a hospital menu must offer items and present them in a manner that pleases patients and leads to favorable impressions. The same applies to other institutional menus. All menus should be an invitation to select something that pleases.

WHAT IS A MENU?

As far as we know, the first coffeehouses and restaurants did not use written menus. Instead, waiters or waitresses simply recited what was available from memory. Some Parisian operations had a sign board posted near the entrance, describing the menu for the day. The maitre d'hôtel stood near the sign and, as guests arrived, described the various offerings to them and took their orders.

Eventually, some restaurants in Paris originated the custom of writing a list of foods on a small sign board. Waiters hung this on their belts to refresh their memories. As menus became more complex, and more items were offered for sale, this method became too confusing—both to the patron and to the servers—and written menus entered into general use. Grimod de La Reyniere, an 18th-century gourmet who outlived both Louis XVI and the French

Revolution, noted that many restaurants handed out bills of fare for patrons to take home with them, both as souvenirs and as advertisements to bring in more business. It was at the time of Napoleon that the restaurants in Paris began to reproduce private gourmet dinner menus for use in the public eating rooms. The elaborate menus written traditionally for the great banquets of the nobility thus found their way into the hands of the emerging middle class.

The word *menu* comes from the French and means "a detailed list." The term is derived from the Latin *minutes*, meaning "diminished," from which we get our word *minute*. Based on this, perhaps, we can say that a menu is "a small, detailed list."

Instead of *menu*, some use the term *bill of fare*. A *bill* is an itemized list, while *fare* means food, so we can say the term means "an itemized list of foods." This seems to be just another way of saying the same thing—*menu*.

The Purpose of the Menu

The job of a menu is basically to inform—inform patrons of what is available at what price, and also to inform workers of what is to be produced. But it is much more than that. The menu is the central management document around which the whole foodservice operation revolves.

"Start with the menu" is a familiar byword of the foodservice trade. The menu should be known at the initial stage when planning a foodservice enterprise because it describes the very nature of the undertaking and the scope of the investment.

Management professionals have known for many years that in order for a company to succeed, it needs to have a clear idea of where the company is headed and how it plans to get where it wants to go. This process is known as long-range or *strategic planning*. In addition to developing strategic plans, management must also create short-range or *tactical plans* that define how the various parts of the organization must function in order to achieve strategic plans.

One of the first activities a manager must perform is to create a *mission statement* or statement of purpose for the organization. The mission for a school district's food service might be to provide wholesome, nutritional meals to students from a variety of economic circumstances and faculty during the school year. A commercial operation's mission might be to serve unique Mexican food at moderate prices to customers of all ages. Once the mission statement is developed, the organization must develop objectives or goals the establishment wishes to attain. These may be expressed as *profitability objectives* (written in specific numbers), *growth objectives* (addition of units), market share objectives, or any number of other objectives. **Exhibit 3.1** shows a list of common organizational objectives.

Organizational objectives are turned into specific strategic plans that answer questions concerning exactly how the company intends to fulfill its

Exhibit 3.1 Common Organizational Objectives

Type of Objective	Sample Objective
Diversification	Operate sit-down only, takeout only, and mixed units.
Efficiency	Operate using skilled workers and automated processes where possible.
Employee welfare	Provide a workplace free of sexual harassment that encourages maximum growth.
Financial stability	Maintain key financial ratios in accordance with internal standards.
Growth	Increase sales at a rate of 10 percent per year.
Management development	Train, develop, and provide opportunity for committed employees to become senior corporate managers within ten years.
Market share	Enter and compete in markets where the company is likely to have the major market share.
Multinational expansion	Operate throughout North America and Japan.
Product quality and service	Serve wholesome, nutritious foods in a friendly, home-like environment.
Profitability	Operate with an average profitability of 30 percent over total sales.
Social responsibility	Hire and train economically disadvantaged people in the community.

mission and objectives. Managers often create these plans after studying environmental conditions. The business environment a foodservice establishment finds itself in may be relatively stable and risk-free. More often, though, the environment is one of frequent change and high risk. Patrons' desires change rapidly, while vigorous competition is a constant challenge. Working within these environmental constraints, the manager must develop a strategy to accomplish the objectives found in the mission statement. An example may be the task of converting a productivity objective into a strategy for increasing worker efficiency coupled with a strategy for increasing equipment efficiency.

The next stage in planning is developing the financial plan. This is a complicated activity, whose details are beyond the scope of this book. Successful managers usually consult with a Certified Public Accountant or other knowledgeable financial advisor when formulating these plans. A numerical "road map" of the future is helpful in many ways, so this important area of planning should not be overlooked. Without long-range financial direction, managers are without a way of measuring operational success.

Related to the financial plan is the establishment of operating budgets. Successful managers perform this task regularly. Budgets are usually created on an annual basis, and are usually expressed in terms of monthly increments. More detailed information on this topic is found in Chapter 14.

Remember that no manager is so clever or so knowledgeable that he or she can do all of this work alone. A management team, composed of people highly qualified in many skills, will usually be more effective than one manager working alone. While the foodservice industry is one of the few remaining industries where individual achievement is both possible and highly prized, most successful individuals learned to listen to suggestions from others before making the final decisions on their own.

Who Prepares the Menu?

Because the menu is the essential document for successful operation of the establishment, menu planners must be highly skilled in a number of areas. They must know both the operation and the potential market. They should know a great deal about foods; how they are combined in recipes, their origin, preparation, presentation, and description. They must also understand how various recipes can be combined, which menu items go together, and which do not. Planners must also be aware of how operational constraints, such as costs, equipment availability, and the skills of the available labor, affect the final menu selection. They must be able to visualize how the menu will appear graphically, what styles will look good, and which may be inappropriate for the particular operation. Finally, planners must be skilled at communicating successfully with patrons through the menu

If all of the above requirements seem daunting, perhaps there is a way to compensate. One key skill in managing is the ability to work in groups. Perhaps a management team is the answer (in even a small establishment the cook and host can meet). While no one person in the organization may possess all the skills required to write the perfect menu, it is likely that a group can be formed whose membership combines all of the skills mentioned. Group preparation of the menu has one additional advantage, it gets the various members of the operational staff into a receptive frame of mind, anticipating the changes about to be implemented.

Menu planning is a time-consuming and detailed task, and should not be done quickly or haphazardly. Treat menu planning for what it is—the most critical step in defining the operation.

Tools Needed for Menu Planning

What are the tools needed to prepare a menu? First, a quiet room where one can work without disturbance. A large desk or table is needed so materials can be spread out. These include a file of historical records on the performance of past menus, a menu reminder list, a file of menu ideas, and sales mix data indicating which items may draw patrons away from specials the operation wants to sell. A list of special occasion and holiday menus should be on hand. Costs and the seasonality of possible menu items should also be available.

Market Research

Market research is the link between the consuming public and the seller. This link consists of information concerning the public's buying preferences and how well the seller's business meets those preferences *as viewed by the potential buyer*. Formal market research is a scientific process of collecting data, analyzing the results, and communicating the findings and their implications to the seller. Anyone planning a menu is well advised to use as many forms of market research as possible. The more specific the research (for example, research concerning a specific group of potential patrons in a specific geographic location), the more reliable the results. At the minimum, the menu planner should take advantage of information available from marketing research firms. The federal government, financial newspapers and magazines, stock and investment firms, and many other large companies all provide the results of their market research. Trade associations, such as the National Restaurant Association and state associations, constantly produce market research reports that can be very useful in determining market trends.

Market studies have always been expensive. Traditionally, therefore, only the largest hospitality companies and chains could afford to conduct their own studies. However, it is beginning to be more feasible for smaller organizations to conduct market studies. An operator might, for example, commission a local college or business school to conduct market research. Advertising agencies can sometimes conduct a useful study for just a few thousand dollars. Operators also can conduct studies personally.

A key element of a market study is to determine exactly what kind of information is needed. If a menu planner wants to create a menu that will increase sales from existing customers, then the market data should be gathered only from that group. On the other hand, if the menu planner is attempting to draw in new customers, then that group should be targeted.

The next key element is to decide how the research will be conducted. Methods include conducting interviews, mailing out questionnaires, observing customers, and holding focus groups. Each is useful in eliciting specific kinds of information.

The questions asked of research subjects can be either open-ended or closed. An example of a closed question, which requires only a one-word answer, is "Do you prefer seafood or steak?" An open-ended question, which requires that the respondent supply a longer answer, might be "What are the most important factors that help you decide where to eat out?"

The information obtained through market research must coincide with other menu planning factors, such as purchasing costs and staff capabilities.

MENU PLANNING FACTORS

A new menu should be planned sufficiently in advance of actual production and service to allow time for the delivery of items, to schedule the required labor, and to print the menu. Some menus must be planned six or more months before use. Operational needs will dictate how far in advance of use new menus should be prepared.

Number of Menus

A number of menus may be needed by a single operation. A large hotel might need several different menus for different dining areas and specialty events. Some operations may need even more. Menu needs will differ with differing types of enterprises. Atmosphere, theme, patrons, pricing structure, and type of service must all be taken into account.

TYPES OF MENUS

A La Carte Menu

An *a la carte* menu offers food items separately at a separate price. All entrees, dishes, salads, and desserts are ordered separately; the patron thus "builds" a meal completely to his or her liking. A la carte menus often contain a large selection of food items and, consequently, often lead to increased check averages. Commercial operations often find this menu type highly profitable, provided they can keep food spoilage, which can result from the large number of offerings, under control.

Table d'Hôte Menu

The *table d'hôte* menu groups several food items together at a single price. This often can be a combination, such as a complete meal of several or more courses. Often there is a choice between some items, such as, between a soup or salad or various kinds of desserts. This type of menu often appeals to patrons who are unfamiliar with the cuisine offered by the establishment. It is an excellent way to introduce the new patron to fine dining as perceived by the establishment. Another advantage of this type of menu is the limited number of entrees that must be produced. These menus can combine wine selections with each course, further enhancing the dining experience, especially for those hesitant to order wine. Very often a la carte and table d'hôte menus are combined.

Du Jour Menu

A *du jour* menu is a group of food items served only for that day. (*Du jour* means "of the day".) The term is most often associated with the daily special, the "soup du jour" being one example. Again, these items often are combined on a la carte and table d'hôte menus. One profit-boosting technique is to offer daily specials that use foods purchased at a reduced price or to use surplus goods.

Limited Menu

A *limited* menu is simply one on which selections are limited in some way. Often associated with quick-service operations or cafes, the limited menu allows the manager to concentrate his or her efforts in training, planning, and calculating food cost or other menu analyses. Cost control is one very important benefit available to operators using limited menus. These menus do not look different from those previously mentioned with the exception of offering fewer choices. This is not entirely a new concept; a restaurant in Paris operated from 1729 to the 1800s offering only one menu item, chicken, cooked in several ways.

Cycle Menu

A *cycle* menu refers to several menus that are offered in rotation. A cruise ship, for example, may have seven menus it uses for its seven-day cruise. At the end of the seven-day cycle the menu is repeated. The key idea here is to inject variety into an operation catering to a "captive" patronage.

Some hospitals might use only a three-day cycle. When patron stays are fairly long, such as in nursing homes, prisons, or on long steamship journeys, the cycle must be longer. Some operations of this type may have four cycle menus for a whole year that change with the seasons of the year to allow for seasonal foods as well as menu variety. **Exhibit 3.2** shows a high school's cycle menu for one month. It is important when using a cycle menu over a long period to rotate Sunday and holiday selections since people seem to remember what they had to eat on Sundays and holidays. Holidays require special meals to mark the occasion.

California Menu

The *California* menu, called that because it originated there, offers breakfast, snack, lunch, fountain, and dinner items that are available at any time of the day. (See **Exhibit 3.3**.) Thus, if one patron wants hot cakes and sausage at 6:00 PM and another patron wants a steak, french fries, and a salad for breakfast, each is accommodated. It is typically printed on heavy, laminated paper so it does not soil easily. Many hotel roomservice menus are based on this design as well.

THE MEAL PLAN AND THE MENU

Menu planners must keep in mind that there are two things a patron decides when selecting a meal from a menu. The first is what the sequence of foods will be, and the second is which items will be selected. The meal planner must do the same: 1) decide on courses and their sequence, and 2) establish the specific foods in each course.

Exhibit 3.2   Cycle Menu

Courtesy of Lane Technical High School, Chicago, Illinois

CHICAGO PUBLIC SCHOOLS DEPARTMENT OF FOOD SERVICES
High School Lunch Menu
May

Wk	MONDAY	Portion	TUESDAY	Portion	WEDNESDAY	Portion	THURSDAY	Portion	FRIDAY	Portion
1	CHICKEN ENCHILADA Extra Cheese Refried Beans Corn on the Cob Peanut Butter Brownie Low Fat Milk 5–3	2 1 oz 1/2 c 1/4 c 1 ser 1/2 pt	TURKEY CHOP SUEY W/ VEGETABLES Fried Rice w/ Eggs Fresh Apple Croissant Low Fat Milk 5–4	1 c 1/2 c 1/4 c 1 1/2 pt	SPAGHETTI W/ MEAT SAUCE & CHEESE Steamed Broccoli Pear Halves Garlic Bread Low Fat Milk 5–5	1 c 1/2 c 1/2 c 1 1/2 pt	CHICKEN FAJITA W/ TORTILLAS (2) Carrot Sticks Blueberries w/ Whipped Topping Low Fat Milk 5–6	3 oz 6 1 oz 1/2 pt	FISH PORTION W/ BUN W/ CHEESE Mixed Vegetables Rosy Applesauce Raisin Spice Bar Low Fat Milk 5–7	2 oz 1 oz 1/2 c 1/2 c 1 ser 1/2 pt
2	SLICED TURKEY W/ GRAVY Whipped Potatoes Seasoned Green Beans Bread Slice Peanut Butter Brownie Low Fat Milk 5–10	3 oz 1/2 c 1/2 c 1 1 ser 1/2 pt	BEEF-R-RONI Peas & Carrots Frozen Juice Cup Hot Corn Bread Low Fat Milk 5–11	1 c 1/2 c 1/4 c 1 1/2 pt	CHICKEN NUGGETS Tator Rounds Coleslaw Croissant Low Fat Milk 5–12	8 1/2 c 1/4 c 1 1/2 pt	BBQ PORK W/ BUN Glazed Carrots Fresh Apple Sweet Potato Pudding Low Fat Milk 5–13	#8 scp 1/2 c 1/2 c 1 1/2 pt	CHICKEN PATTIES OR MACARONI & CHEESE Steamed Broccoli Pear Halves Bread Slice Low Fat Milk 5–14	2@1.5 oz 1 c 1/2 c 1/2 c 1 1/2 pt
3	CHILI W/ BEANS & CHEESE Buttered Corn Cherry Apple Juice Saltine Crackers Peanut Butter Cookie Low Fat Milk 5–17	1 c 1/2 c 6 oz 8 1 1/2 pt	TURKEY EGG ROLL W/ SWEET & SOUR SAUCE Fried Rice w/ Eggs Seasoned Green Beans Fresh Apple Low Fat Milk 5–18	1 1/2 c 1/2 c 1/2 c 1/2 pt	SUPER DELUXE BURGER W/ BUN Cole Slaw Chilled Peaches Low Fat Milk 5–19	3.5 oz 1/2 c 1/2 c 1/2 pt	MEAT LOAF W/ GRAVY Whipped Potatoes Garden Peas Croissant Raisin Spice Bar Low Fat Milk 5–20	4 oz 1/2 c 1/2 c 1 1 ser 1/2 pt	ITALIAN SAUSAGE W/ SAUCE Mixed Vegetables Sweet Potato Pone Hot Roll Low Fat Milk 5–21	3 oz 1/2 c 1/2 c 1 1/2 pt
4	CHICKEN NUGGETS W/ BBQ SAUCE Rotini Pasta Salad Mixed Vegetables Frozen Juice Cup Hot Roll Low Fat Milk 5–24	8 1/2 c 1/2 c 1/4 c 1 1/2 pt	SAUSAGE & CHEESE PIZZA Onion Rings Tossed Salad Raisin Spice Bar Low Fat Milk 5–25	1 sl 1/2 c 1/2 c 1 ser 1/2 pt	HAM & CHEESE ON CROISSANT Vegetable Soup Fresh Orange Peanut Butter Cookie Low Fat Milk 5–26	1 sl 1/2 c 1/2 c 1 ser 1/2 pt	BAKED CHICKEN Glazed Carrots Tossed Salad Hot Biscuit Low Fat Milk 5–27	3 pcs 1/2 c 1/2 c 1 1/2 pt	HOT TAMALES W/ CHILI Buttered Spinach Pineapple Orange Juice Drink Low Fat Milk 5–28	2 1/2 c 1/2 c 6 oz 1/2 pt
5	MEMORIAL DAY (HOLIDAY) 5–31		CHICKEN ENCHILADA Extra Cheese Tossed Salad Chilled Peaches Peanut Butter Cookie Low Fat Milk 6–1	2 1 oz 1/2 c 1/2 c 1 1/2 pt	SUBMARINE SANDWICH ON CROISSANT Chicken Vegetable Soup Fresh Apple Low Fat Milk 6–2	3 oz 1 c 1/2 c 1/2 pt	TURKEY EGG ROLL Sweet and Sour Sauce Fried Rice w/Eggs Broccoli Chilled Peaches Low Fat Milk 6–3	1 pkg 1/2 c 1/2 c 1/2 pt	CHILI W/ BEANS & CHEESE Corn on Cob Mixed Fruit Croissant Low Fat Milk 6–4	1 c 1/4 c 1/2 c 1 1/2 pt

Exhibit 3.3 California Menu *Courtesy of IHOP, Glendale, California*

These two factors make up the *meal plan* or the manner in which foods are grouped for particular meals throughout a day. The typical American meal plan is three meals a day, with about a fourth of the day's calories eaten at breakfast, a third at lunch, and the balance at dinner, although some may reverse the lunch and dinner percentages. For a table d'hôte menu, some knowledge of the meal plan is required, even for partial meals. On an a la carte menu, a meal plan is not needed since the patron establishes one by selecting the items.

In this country, food patterns have been changing. Some menus may be written for a four- or five-meal-a-day plan. This gives a greater division of calories but the same total amount in a day. Most meal plans call for all the food to be consumed within a ten-hour period, but if a snack is served at night, the fasting period may be less than 14 hours.

Staying too strictly with a meal plan can become monotonous, so it is recommended that a plan be varied occasionally. Thus, a supper of vegetable soup with crackers, large fruit plate with assorted cheeses, bran muffins and butter, macaroon cookies, and a beverage may be a relief from the often consumed meat, potatoes, and gravy dinner. **Exhibit 3.4** shows a breakfast meal plan and a menu based on it.

Exhibit 3.4   Breakfast Meal Plan and Menu

Meal Plan	**Menu**
Fruit or juice	Orange, grapefruit or tomato juice
Cereal	Dry cereal or oatmeal, milk
Entree	Eggs any style or ham timbale with light cheese sauce
Bread	Bran muffins or toast
Beverage	Tea, coffee, or cocoa

Menu Organization

Menus usually group foods in some order in which they are intended to be eaten. Typical menus begin with appetizers and end with desserts. Several sample courses are shown in **Exhibit 3.5**.

Within the entree category, it is usual to split the various food offerings into the following categories: Seafood and Fish, Meat (beef, lamb and pork), Poultry (chicken, duck, etc.) and Others such as pasta or meatless entrees.

Each menu category should offer choice. It is important to note that the foods within a major category must differ in style of preparation. For example, every entree should not be fried. You will notice in the exhibit that various

Exhibit 3.5   Sample Menu Organization

Coffee Shop	**French Restaurant**	**Hospital**	**Family Dining**	**Steakhouse**
Appetizers and side dishes	Hors-d'oeuvre	Appetizers and soups	Appetizers	Appetizers
Salads	Potages (soups)	Salads	Soups	Soups and salads
Sandwiches	Salad	Entrees	Salads	Entrees
Hot entrees	Sorbet	Vegetables	Entrees	Side dishes
Fountain items	Entrees	Desserts	Side dishes	Desserts
Desserts	Plateau de fromage (cheese platter)		Desserts	
	Entremets (small desserts)			

preparation methods are used such as poaching, roasting, grilling, frying, and baking. While it may not be feasible to include all methods of preparation, a menu heavily weighted toward one method or another will be unbalanced. Only in an operation specializing in one preparation style is repetition recommended.

It is often said that variety is the spice of life. It certainly is the key to creating a menu that sparks patrons' interest and encourages them to come back again and again. The variation of cooking methods is a subtle form of variety. The variations in tastes and textures are less subtle. It is important that foods vary from spicy or hot to bland or mild. Even the most adventurous tongue needs a rest, which is why some dinner restaurants are serving an intermezzo course (often a fruit sorbet) between courses. Both spicy and hot dishes can appear on a menu. (Hot dishes cause burning on the tongue, while spicy items incorporate complex flavors.)

Various cooking methods will affect menu items' texture as much as their ingredients.

Variety extends to the visual as well. There is a saying that people "eat with their eyes." Chefs have been concerned with balancing color as well as texture. Whether an ingredient is cut, ground, minced, cubed, sliced, pared, or kept whole affects its visual appeal as well as its "mouth feel." Even the use and kind of garnish can distinguish items and make an otherwise common dish seem exotic.

How Many Menu Items?

The number of menu items found on menus varies greatly, from the simplest limited menu operations (one operation in London has only one choice each for appetizers, soup, salad, entree, and dessert) to Chinese menus offering many choices. Management usually wants to limit the number of offerings in order to reduce costs and maintain good control. The patron may desire fewer items also. Some studies have shown that people who are confronted with a large number of choices tend to fall back to choices they have made before.

The key word in choosing the items for a menu is balance. There must be a balanced selection that allows for different tastes. It is necessary to balance selections within food groups. Thus, a lunch menu might offer a minimum number of appetizers, say two juices (one fruit and one vegetable), a fruit, and a seafood cocktail. This minimum offering could be expanded on the dinner menu into choices of both hot and cold appetizers. Gourmets may substitute a hot seafood appetizer for the traditional fish course.

The number and kinds of soups also depend on the meal period. Lunch patrons may wish to have a bowl of hearty soup such as vegetable or beef and rice, or a combination cup of soup and half a sandwich. A recent trend has been toward cold soups. However, the dinner patron may want soup as a beginning for a large meal. This patron may wish to have a light appetite-stimulating soup like a consommé or bouillon. The balance with the amount of food offered with the rest of the meal must be struck between light clear soups, purees, and bisques, and the heavier chowders and stew-like soups.

The typical menu has at least five or six entrees. Theme operations, such as a seafood restaurant, naturally will specialize in certain entree categories. They must still offer some alternative dish; for example, a seafood restaurant may offer a non-seafood item for those patrons who will not (or cannot) eat seafood but who are with a party that does. Non-meat items (like pasta or vegetable dishes) are increasingly being found on menus. If balance is required, the entrees should be divided among beef (more than 50 percent of the meat consumed in this country is beef), pork and ham, poultry, lamb and veal, shellfish, fish, egg dishes, cheese dishes, and non-meat main dishes. If only two food items appear on the menu they may both be beef (one roasted and one a steak dish) or one beef and one of the other meat categories. If two fish or shellfish items appear, they should be quite different, such as a lean, white-fleshed fish like a sole or flounder, and a fatter one such as salmon.

If one is limiting the entrees to five or less, it is best to remember that quantity is no substitute for quality. A few items prepared and served with absolute perfection is as good or better than a dozen mediocre items.

The ideal menu must also provide for balance and variety in the vegetable, sauces, and starch dishes as well. The vegetables must be chosen to complement the entree choices. Thus on a menu in which there is ham, chicken, or turkey an offering of sweet potatoes or yellow winter squash will complement the meal. Potatoes, rice, wild rice, polenta, and other starches are today becoming an important part of a menu.

When selecting vegetables, as with all menu items, an eye must be given to the flavors, colors, and texture contrasts. Popular vegetables like asparagus, peas, string beans, and carrots should be offered, but for variety's sake it may be wise to include one or more exotic vegetables as well. Variety can also be achieved by using different cooking methods, or serving some vegetables raw. Vegetables can be creamed, deep-fried, au gratin, baked, mashed, pureed, diced, julienned, made into fritters, or served with a variety of sauces like honey mustard, hollandaise, tomato, or cheese.

Again, variety must not be carried to extremes; three to five starches, and five or so vegetable dishes are more than sufficient for most menus.

The number of salads offered as meal accompaniments (as opposed to salads as main dishes) has been constantly decreasing. For many years table d'hôte meals included a choice of several salads. Now the typical menu includes only one or two salads, usually a tossed green salad, or a special salad like a Caesar salad. However, as more people strive for a healthy lifestyle, many menus are offering several generous-portioned salads as main courses; seafood, egg, fruit, and chicken salads are common. Variety is achieved, not only in ingredients—arugula, endive, spinach, artichokes, hearts of palm, nuts, seeds, patés, and edible flowers are just some of the creative ingredients being used—but also by offering a variety of salad dressings, featuring flavored vinegars and oils, honey, cheese, and mustards. The self-serve salad bar trend has crested as more operators become concerned with the labor and food costs associated with salad bars as well as heightened fears concerning the potential health risks associated with self-serve environments.

Another trend in menus has been to offer fewer dessert choices but to make those items offered more elaborate. Some operators see dessert as a low-profit area and confine the choices to an ice cream or sherbet dish. Others see dessert as a selling opportunity, where desserts can be coupled with unusual after-dinner drinks to generate sales. The dessert course must be treated as seriously by the manager as any of the other food courses. One way to free up tables for other diners is to offer dessert in a separate room. Several operations have turned this into a very profitable way to keep diners on site and spending additional dollars on after-dinner drinks.

We look at breakfast menus last. This important meal is characterized by high volumes and low profits. The public seems to have a clear idea of what it is willing to pay for breakfast, and operators emphasizing this meal period are often caught in the price trap. While there is no study to support the idea, it may be conjectured that the reason for this price problem is that breakfast, more than any of the other meals, consists of food items that patrons regularly prepare at home. This knowledge of the costs and skills required may cause a patron to develop firm attitudes concerning what is a fair price to pay for breakfast.

One way to boost check averages is to offer breakfast items that the public cannot relate to their at-home cost. Elaborate breakfasts or unusual breakfast combinations may be the answer to this dilemma. An analysis of 50 breakfast menus from hotels around the country showed that the average breakfast menu offers about 100 choices. There are usually five to ten juices, five or more fruit dishes, a hot cereal, and a dozen or more cold ones offered with and without a variety of toppings. One may find eggs cooked in perhaps four to six different ways (there are about 100 ways to cook an egg in formal French cooking). Meat dishes may include hams, steaks, bacon, sausages, and other meats. French toast, pancakes, toasts, and rolls may add another five to ten items to the menu, with side dishes increasing the menu size even further. Finally there are the requisite beverages from coffee and tea to milk shakes, herbal teas, and vegetable shakes.

It is possible to limit the breakfast menu to perhaps 30 or 40 items, but many menu planners feel the need to offer more.

MENUS FOR VARIOUS MEALS AND OCCASIONS

Many operations have one menu that covers choices for the three meals of the day with the times of availability included. Other operations have separate menus for each meal, and still others have separate menus for special occasions and parties. The types and number of menus needed will vary from one operation to another.

Each operation must rely on patron preference, costs, and operational goals to dictate what items should be included on each menu. The following section should serve as a guide to meeting general menu requirements.

Exhibit 3.6 Breakfast Menu

Courtesy of Bob Evans Farms, Columbus, Ohio

BREAKFAST

Eggs

Start the day right with your favorite breakfast. Served with your choice of buttermilk biscuits, wheat or white toast, or one blueberry or Country Morning muffin.

Early Riser · Two eggs any style, with choice of bread _____ $1.99

Daybreak · Two eggs any style, with sausage patties or links or thick-sliced bacon and your choice of bread _____ $3.69

Rise and Shine · Two eggs any style, with sausage patties or links or thick-sliced bacon, home fries and your choice of bread _____ $4.69

NEW! Country Skillet · Hot from the skillet. A layer of eggs, with home fries, Bob Evans Farms' sausage, country gravy and shredded cheese. Served with your choice of bread _____ $4.79

NEW! Border Skillet · Hot from the skillet. A layer of eggs, Bob Evans Farms' sausage, diced potatoes, green and red peppers, onions, mild picante sauce and shredded cheese. Served with your choice of bread _____ $4.79

NEW! Country Fried Steak and Eggs · Our famous country fried steak topped with country gravy served with two eggs any style, home fries and your choice of bread _____ $5.99

Homestead Breakfast · Two large eggs, choice of Bob Evans Farms' sausage patties or links or thick-sliced bacon, sausage gravy, home fries and your choice of bread _____ $6.29

You may substitute **egg beaters** *on any egg combination for an additional* _____ $.40

Omelettes

Served with our home fries and your choice of buttermilk biscuits, wheat or white toast, or one blueberry or Country Morning muffin.

Sausage & Cheese · Featuring our own Bob Evans Farms' sausage _____ $4.49

Western Omelette · Diced ham, onions, green peppers and sharp American cheese _____ $4.49

Ham & Cheese Omelette · An all-American favorite _____ $4.49

You may substitute **egg beaters** *on any omelette for an additional* _____ $.40

© 1993, BEF & OFR, Inc., 1 11/92

Hotcakes with Strawberry Topping

It's the tops

Border Skillet

Get that great wake-up taste

Hotcakes & Such

These complete breakfasts are served with warm syrup and margarine. Low calorie syrup and real butter available upon request.

Hotcakes · Three buttermilk hotcakes served with your choice of thick-sliced bacon or sausage patties or links _____ $3.69

French Toast · Thick-sliced, dipped in cinnamon batter, served with your choice of thick-sliced bacon or sausage patties or links _____ $3.69

Fried Mush · A Bob Evans' Special Recipe. Three slices, fried golden brown and served with your choice of thick-sliced bacon or sausage patties or links _____ $3.69

Blueberry Hotcakes · Full of blueberries. Served with your choice of thick-sliced bacon or sausage patties or links _____ $4.20

Hotcakes & Eggs · Three buttermilk hotcakes and two eggs any style, served with your choice of thick-sliced bacon or sausage patties or links _____ $4.79

The Tops · Juicy strawberry topping crowned with whipped topping or delicious cinnamon apples on your choice of hotcakes or our classically prepared French Toast. Served with your choice of thick-sliced bacon or sausage patties or links _____ $4.90

Bob Evans' Own

Sausage Gravy & Biscuits · With home fries _____ $3.79

Border Scramble · A large flour tortilla filled with sausage, fresh vegetables and potatoes. Topped with Texas-style chili and melted cheese _____ $4.59

The Lighter Side

Try one of our lighter alternatives for breakfast. They'll satisfy you without slowing you down.

Fruit Bowl · Half a melon filled with fresh mixed fruit and two Country Morning muffins. Fruit selection will change seasonally to give you the best available _____ $4.99

Oatmeal Breakfast · **QUAKER** Oatmeal, orange juice and blueberry muffin. Until 11 A.M. Brown sugar available upon request _____ $3.19

egg beaters **Breakfast** · With fresh sliced tomatoes and wheat toast ___ $2.40

A La Carte

One Fresh Egg · Any style _____ $.69
Grits · Southern style Until 11 A.M. _____ $.69
Home Fries _____ $1.19
QUAKER **Oatmeal** · Served with milk. Until 11 A.M. Brown sugar available upon request _____ $1.59
Toast & SMUCKERS Jelly · Choose white or wheat bread _____ $.99
Two Hot Buttermilk Biscuits _____ $.99
Two Blueberry or Country Morning Muffins _____ $1.69
Breakfast Fruit _____ $1.80 (seasonal fresh fruit)
Breakfast Fruit Bowl · Half a melon filled with seasonal fresh fruit _____ $3.30
Hotcakes · Three hotcakes with warm syrup _____ $1.99
Golden Brown Waffle · With warm syrup _____ $1.99
French Toast · Dipped in cinnamon batter. With warm syrup _____ $1.99
Fried Mush · Three slices with warm syrup _____ $1.99
Blueberry Hotcakes · Three hotcakes with warm syrup _____ $2.50
Sausage Gravy _____ $1.89
Bob Evans Farms' Sausage · Patties or links _____ $1.80
NEW! Bob Evans Farms' Smoked Sausage · Our larger 5 oz. link ___ $2.10
Honey-Cured Ham _____ $1.80
Bacon · Three thick-sliced strips ___ $1.80
Sausage Gravy & Biscuits · With two buttermilk biscuits _____ $2.79

Breakfast Menus

Some breakfast menus are printed on the regular menu, while others appear as separate menus. An example of a breakfast menu is shown in **Exhibit 3.6**. A California menu that offers breakfast during all hours of operation may list the breakfast on a side panel or in a special space. Some have breakfast items on the back of a placemat. A children's breakfast menu may be offered in some units.

Both a la carte items and table d'hôte breakfasts should be on a breakfast menu. Table d'hôte offerings should list a *continental breakfast* that includes a juice (usually orange), a bread item (usually a sweet roll or toast, but a croissant is common), and a beverage (usually coffee). It should also list heavier breakfasts. A juice or fruit may or may not be included with these. Meat, eggs, or other main dishes will be accompanied by toast, hot breads or rolls, and perhaps hashed brown potatoes or grits (in the South). Hot cakes or waffles are served sometimes with bacon, ham, sausage, or even an egg. A beverage is usually included with these breakfasts.

The offerings of table d'hôte breakfasts should be balanced. A familiar one includes eggs fixed any style and priced for one or two eggs. Omelets or eggs with bacon, ham, or sausage are other offerings. Egg-white omelets are becoming common. Meats alone may also be offered. A pancake and a waffle breakfast offering is usual. Sometimes a corned beef hash main dish with or without poached eggs, steak plain or with eggs, creamed chipped beef, or other main dishes may be on table d'hôte listings. Items such as shirred eggs with chicken livers, Huevos Rancheros, Eggs Florentine, or other "occasion" foods can be included, depending on the type of operation. Specials, such as a low-calorie breakfast, a steak-and-egg breakfast, a high-protein breakfast, or a child's breakfast may be offered. Remember to also have something low-calorie, low-fat, low-cholesterol, or low-salt that guests might want.

Table d'hôte and similar breakfasts that bring in a higher check average should be in the most prominent place on the menu. These higher-income items should also be given as effective a presentation as possible, with large type, bracketing, and effective description.

Numbering breakfasts on a large menu makes them easier to order, both for the patron and the server. Specialties, such as a variety of syrups, jellies, and jams, may serve to encourage choices of desirable menu items.

The menu order for breakfast items is usually as follows.

1. Fruits and juices
2. Cereals
3. Eggs alone or combined with something else
4. Omelets
5. Meat and other main dishes
6. Pancakes, waffles, and french toast
7. Toast, rolls, and hot breads
8. Beverages

Side orders must be placed in available space. On the a la carte menu, items should be grouped together in the same order.

Breakfast menus should cover less space than the other meal menus and usually should have larger type, because people are not yet awake. Do not list items only as "juices" or "cereals," but list each offering separately. Also list essential information, such as how long breakfast is served and special breakfast facilities.

Special breakfasts may have to be catered. A wedding breakfast may start with champagne, silver gin fizzes, a fruit punch, or juices. A fresh fruit cup is often served as the first course. If not, then a fruit salad or molded gelatin salad is appropriate. A typical main dish is served with a high-quality sweet roll. Eggs Benedict would be suitable for the early party-type breakfast, or eggs with sausage, ham, or bacon. An omelet of some type would be suitable. If the affair is held late in the morning, the main dish can be creamed chicken, sauteed ham and mushrooms, or creamed sweetbreads and ham in a patty shell with a few green peas. A beverage choice is offered. If wine is served at the table, it is usually a chilled white or a semi-dry rosé.

Buffet breakfasts are popular. Some may be offered to allow guests to quickly obtain what they want and leave. Many people at conventions or meetings are in a hurry and may patronize the foodservice operation if they feel they can get what they want quickly. Some who usually skip breakfast may still be enticed to come in and get a quickly served buffet continental breakfast.

A buffet breakfast for more leisurely dining may be much more elaborate and feature a wide choice of juices and fruits; cold items, such as cheese, sliced baked ham, lox and bagels, chopped chicken livers, even salads; and hot dishes, such as scrambled eggs, assorted breakfast meats, chicken livers and mushrooms, pepper steaks, corned beef hash, creamed chipped beef, and different kinds of omelettes. Side dishes, such as hashed brown potatoes or grits, can be included. Assorted hot breads and sweet rolls are offered, along with a beverage choice. The drink is often poured at the table by servers, the guests selecting the other foods they wish at the buffet. On the most elaborate buffets, a dessert may be offered. Depending upon the occasion, champagne or alcoholic beverages may be provided. Wine service may be offered with a white wine (not completely dry) or a rosé.

A *hunt breakfast* is an elaborate buffet that may include broiled lamb chops, steaks, roast beef, grilled pork chops, pheasant, hare, venison, or other items. A hunt breakfast originated as a meal before or after a hunt and was intended for hearty eaters leading a vigorous life—they had to eat that way.

A *chuck wagon breakfast* should feature sourdough hot cakes, steaks, eggs, hashed brown potatoes, and perhaps freshly cooked doughnuts. Grits or biscuits can be substituted for the breads. (A chuck wagon is the meal wagon that was used to feed cowboys when they were away from the ranch.)

A *family-style breakfast* is one in which the food is brought to the table and guests serve themselves.

Group breakfasts should be planned carefully. Eggs and other breakfast items cool rapidly. Do not attempt difficult egg preparations, such as omelets or Eggs Benedict, unless they can be prepared and served properly. Toast is difficult to serve because it gets cold and chewy quickly. Hot breads, such as biscuits, muffins, and cinnamon rolls, are easier to handle. American service is usually used, but Russian service is sometimes also used (see Chapter 12).

Brunch Menus

A brunch menu should combine items usually found on breakfast and lunch menus and provide for substantial meals. (See **Exhibit 3.7.**) A fruit juice or fruit should be offered. The main dish should be substantial—omelets; creamed chicken on toast points; a soufflé; a small steak with hashed brown potatoes; chicken livers and bacon; or a mixed grill of lamb chop; sausage, bacon, grilled tomato slice, and potato. Hot breads and a beverage choice should be offered, and vegetables can be served. A fruit salad or molded gelatin salad filled with fruit is a favorite.

Luncheon Menus

Luncheon menus may contain a wide assortment of foods, from complete table d'hôte meals to snacks. Offer a wide number of a la carte items with combinations, such as a sandwich and a beverage, or a cup of soup, salad, and dessert with beverage. A few casserole dishes can be offered. Items such as sandwiches, salads, soups, and fountain products can be stressed. A lunch menu can more easily feature economical purchases than the dinner menu.

Many units have modestly priced items and attempt to cover costs with volume and fast turnover. Occasion foods—specialty items created to enhance a special occasion—may be profitable, if especially slanted to the trade. Executives and expense account patrons may wish more elaborate menus. Thus, a club, better hotel, or fine restaurant that they patronize may feature a higher priced list for lunch. Alcoholic beverages may or may not be offered.

Lunch menus should have permanent a la carte offerings on the cover, but may also present daily offerings. The permanent menu will offer sandwiches, salads, fountain items, and desserts. Flexible menus are more typical of lunch than any other meal. Inserts or table displays may be used to call attention to specials.

Lunches for groups usually are complete meals. Clubs or organizations may meet at lunchtime, and a main dish with vegetables, salad, dessert, and beverage will be included. A first course will be included for a more elaborate luncheon. Party or occasion foods may be offered, but since most diners have little time, the menu must allow them to eat quickly, have time for scheduled events, and get back to work. However, if the luncheon is to last for a longer period and features an important speaker, the group may want to have more luxury-type food. The foods should fit the occasion and the particular group.

Exhibit 3.7 Brunch Menu

Courtesy of The Ritz-Carlton, Chicago, Illinois

THE RITZ-CARLTON
CHICAGO
A Four Seasons Hotel

The Dining Room
Sunday Brunch Buffet

Array of Breakfast Pastries
Large Assortment of Different Salads
Smoked Salmon Station
Smoked Trout
Shellfish on Ice
Pates and Terrines
Omelette Station
Waffle Station
Eggs Benedict
Poached Fish in Wine Sauce
Baked Salmon in Puff Pastry
Chicken Stir Fry
Roasted Prime Rib
Assorted Fresh Vegetables and Potatoes
International Cheese Display
Fresh Fruit
Extensive Pastry Buffet
Coffee or Tea

Children's Buffet available for kids 12 and under

Adults - $31.00   *Children - $15.50*
Seating times are at 10:30 a.m. and 1:00 p.m.
Reservations are recommended.

160 East Pearson Street • Chicago, Illinois 60611-2124 • USA • Telephone (312) 266-1000
Hotel FAX (312) 266-1194 • Executive Office FAX (312) 266-9501

Afternoon Menus

Many operations have little or no business in the afternoon following lunch. To bring in business, a different menu can be designed with specials to catch the afternoon and shopper trade. These menus should appeal to people most likely to eat out in the late afternoon—retirees, shoppers, artists, students, and homemakers. The foods should be snack-type with considerable occasion appeal, different from the usual menu. Thus, after the lunch-hour rush, an operation might put on a special menu with small sandwiches, desserts, fountain items, fruit plates, cookies, and pastries.

Many people can be induced to eat dinner early if a lower-priced menu is offered. A variety of items should be included; along with one or two light desserts.

Dinner Menus

The dinner menu usually has more specialty items than others and attempts to feature more occasion foods. The menu must be carefully directed to patrons.

The typical American meal plan of a main dish, potato, vegetable, salad, dessert, and beverage is probably most appropriate for the family market, though some variation of it is probably appropriate in all operations. (See **Exhibits 3.8** and **3.9**.)

This traditional family dinner is as well liked as it once was; however, families often cannot eat together, so meals like pizza or hamburgers might be in order. However, for the usual family dinner meal, a soup, fruit cocktail, juice, or other appetizer may be served as a first course. Regular meats such as steaks or roasts are popular but other kinds of meat, chicken and other poultry, fish and shellfish should also appear. Interesting casserole dishes, Italian pastas, and some specialty foods may also be offered.

Families dining out very often know exactly what they want from any menu. Familiar items, such as mashed potatoes, macaroni and cheese, and chocolate cake are often appealing.

Menus are also needed that feature moderately priced items for those who want convenience foods rather than the luxury type. Some individuals who live in modest housing or patrons eating in a downtown cafeteria will not have much to spend but will want enough to eat. Some operations may find this type of trade a satisfactory source of revenue.

In attempting to develop memorable dinner menus, it is important to remember that service and decor are as essential as food. Complete follow-through on *all* details of an idea is a requirement. Too many menus attempt to create a food *atmosphere* on the menu only to have the rest of the performance a dismal failure, or vice versa. The operation must be constantly watched to see that there is complete follow-through. If a menu features Mexican, Greek, or other ethnic foods, the cuisine should be absolutely authentic. Research is necessary to verify authenticity, yet modification may also be needed to suit the nonauthentic palate. A very hot Indian curry served with Bombay

Exhibit 3.8 Dinner Menu

Courtesy of Shaw's Crab House, Chicago, Illinois

Soft Shell Crabs	Royster With the Oyster	Private Party
—From Virginia—	—Oyster Hour: 4:30-6:30, Mon-Fri—	—Facilities Available—
May 15—Sept. 15	Blue Crab Lounge	See Manager

WELCOME TO SHAW'S

Our commitment to quality is a source of pride at Shaw's. We have exact standards of freshness and we work with oyster growers, distributors and fishermen to insure that we receive the highest quality in seafood.

PROPRIETORS

Kevin Brown   Chef Yves Roubaud   Stephen LaHaie

REGIONAL OYSTERS

–See Daily Specials for Today's Selections–

Eastern (Crassostrea virginica)

Long Island Sound . . . . Connecticut
Malpeque . . . . Prince Edward Island, Canada
Caraquet. . . . . New Brunswick, Canada
Chincoteague Salts . . . . Virginia
Cotuit. . . . . Massachusetts
Wellfleet . . . . Massachusetts
Pemaquid . . . . Maine

European Flats (Ostrea edulis)

Wescott Flats. . . . . Washington
Casco Bay Flats . . . . Maine

Olympia (Ostrea lurida)

Grown in the Bays of Southern Puget Sound

Kumamoto (Crassostrea gigas var. kumomoto)

Grown in Northern California & Washington

Pacific (Crassostrea gigas)

Totten Inlet. . . . . Washington
Malaspina . . . . British Columbia
Fanny Bay . . . . Vancouver Island, Canada
Hamma Hamma . . . . Washington
Hog Island. . . . . California
Pearl Point. . . . . Oregon
Rock Point. . . . . Washington
Shoalwater Bay . . . . Washington
Coromandel . . . . New Zealand
Tomales Bay . . . . California
Wescott Bay Selects . . . . Washington
Crescent Beach. . . . . Washington

Chilean (Ostrea chilensis)

Chiloé . . . . Chile

OYSTER ACCOMPANIMENTS

Oyster-Friendly Wines

A selection of dry, crisp, clean-finishing wines are available by the glass or bottle to complement Shaw's oysters.

Or try a malty beer from our list below.

BEER

–DRAUGHT–

Anchor Steam   Guiness Stout
Bass Ale   Harp
Samuel Adams

–BOTTLED–

Amstel Light   Miller Lite
Heineken   Pike's Place Ale
Michelob Dry   Point Special
Miller Genuine Draft   Budweiser
Samuel Smith's Nut Brown Ale   Beck's
Clausthaler—non-alcohol   Rolling Rock

BOTTLED WATER

La Croix   Evian
Canadian Spring Berry

FRESH OYSTERS

On The Half Shell . . . . 6.95 ♥
  Daily Regional Varieties, Shucked to Order
Oysters Rockefeller. 6.95
Pan Fried Pacific Oysters. 6.95

SEAFOOD APPETIZER PLATTERS

–serves two–

Cold Combo—Shrimp, Oysters, Clams, & Blue Crab Fingers. 14.90
Hot Combo—Mini Crab Cakes, Popcorn Shrimp, & Calamari 12.90

(additional servings available)

COLD APPETIZERS

Blue Crab Fingers. 4.95
Topneck Clams, Half-Dozen. 5.95
Charred Sashimi Tuna 6.95
Shrimp Cocktail (in shell) 7.95

HOT APPETIZERS

Escargot, Garlic Butter. 5.95
Steamed Blue Mussels . . . . 4.95 ♥
French Fried Calamari 4.95
Popcorn Shrimp. 6.95
Baked Clams Casino. 6.50
Shaw's Crab Cake 7.50

SOUPS

	CUP/BOWL
Seafood Gumbo.	2.50/3.95
New England Clam Chowder	2.50/3.95
Soup of the Day.	2.50/3.95

SALADS

Shaw's Caesar Salad 3.95
Mixed Greens 2.95
Cole Slaw. 1.95
Iceberg Wedge 2.50
Sliced Tomato & Onion. 2.50
Boursin Cheese with Mixed Greens 3.95

Dressings: 1000 Island, Mustard Vinaigrette, Italian, Maytag Blue Cheese, & Ranch

VEGETABLES

–serves two–

Creamed Spinach 2.50
Baked Ratatouille en Casserole. 2.95
Steamed Fresh Broccoli . . . . 2.50 ♥
Steamed Green Beans . . . . 2.25 ♥
Green Beans and Mushrooms 2.50
Steamed Carrots . . . . 2.25 ♥
Carrots and Mushrooms 2.50

POTATOES & RICE

–serves two–

Hashed Browns. 2.50
Hashed Browns w/Onions 2.95
Au Gratin Potatoes 2.95
Boiled Red Potatoes 1.95
Cajun Rice 1.95
Four Grain Wild Rice. . . . . 1.95 ♥
–single–
Charred Baked Potato. 2.50

Cigar and Pipe	All Major	Margarine
—Smoking—	—Credit Cards—	—And Salt Substitute—
In Bar Only	Accepted	On Request

Exhibit 3.9 Dinner Menu

Courtesy of Charlie Trotter's, Chicago, Illinois

* * *

<u>*GRAND MENU DEGUSTATION 75.00*</u>

Smoked Maine Salmon with Petite Lobster-Tomato Salad & Chilled Smoked Salmon Broth
or
New York State Foie Gras & Oxtail Terrine with Arkansas Short Grain Rice Salad,
Sherry Wine Vinaigrette & Yellow Bell Pepper Juice

Grilled Hamachi with Peeky Toe Crab & Cardamom Infused Carrot Juice
or
Potato Wrapped Veal Sweetbreads with Soy-Bacon Vinaigrette & Shiitake Mushroom Essence

Hawaiian Spot Prawns & Hand-Harvested Sea Scallop with Spring Pea Shoots, Cashews
& Spicy Coconut Milk Broth
or
Belgian Endive, Frisee, Roasted Hazelnuts, Goat Cheese, Japanese Pears & Dried Mission Figs

Gulf of Maine Swordfish with Carmelized Walla Walla Shallots, Artichokes,
Olive Oil Poached Tomato, Basil & Black Olives
or
Duck Confit with Lamb's Tongue, Mushroom & Pig's Feet Ragout
& Szechwan Peppercorn Infused Reduction

Spicy Seared Yellow Fin Tuna with Morel Mushrooms, Black-Eyed Peas, Sweet Peas,
Celery Root Coulis & Veal Stock Reduction
or
Texas Baby Antelope Saddle with Rosemary Polenta, Ratatouille
& Thyme Reduction

* * *

This Evening's Progression of Desserts

duck and all the side dishes may be delicious to one who knows this food, but it could be a disappointment to one who isn't familiar with it.

Foreign foods have become popular and help give menu interest and variety. If offered, make them correctly with high quality ingredients. An important consideration in featuring many foreign foods is that they usually do not require the most expensive ingredients. Thus, they may be more profitable to serve than some American foods. The fact that these foods are not normally a part of our diet makes them good occasion foods. Novelty can also be achieved by unique service.

It is becoming more and more common on table d'hôte meals to omit appetizers and desserts and have these selected from a special menu. **Exhibit 3.10** shows an attractive dessert menu. Furthermore, many operations today serve the salad as a first course, making it fairly substantial, and then omit the salad with the main course.

Formal Dinner Menus

Very few formal dinners are served today that follow the traditional French style of three settings with a progression of courses for each setting. People now find it difficult to eat this much food. Even a more simple formal meal can be exhausting unless properly planned. Portions for a formal dinner should be adequate but restrained. The food should be selected to give a progression of flavor sensations, avoiding any heavy sweetness until the very end of the meal to "silence the appetite."

A formal meal should give time for the guests to appreciate the food and service and to converse. The most formal meal today usually does not have more than eight courses.

The first course of a formal meal can be oysters or clams on the half shell, a seafood cocktail of some type, a canapé, or fruit, such as melon or mango. Some may omit this course if cocktails and appetizers are served before the meal. Soup is the next course, and this should be quite light, such as a consommé, bouillon, or a light cream soup. On all courses, garnishes are important and may be the only item accompanying the food.

The fish course comes after the soup, followed by the poultry course. The roast or joint, with perhaps potato and vegetable, is the next course. The salad course is next, followed in turn by cheese and then the dessert course. In some formal meals an ice cream or sherbet (sorbet) may come right after the roast course. The meal may end with demitasse coffee, nuts, mints, and bonbons.

Wines and alcoholic beverages for this type of meal should be selected carefully. Cocktails made from spirits, such as martinis, manhattans, or scotch and sodas, blunt the taste buds. Aperitif wines, such as Dubonnet or cocktail sherry, are usually better before meals. Nevertheless, many Americans prefer the former. The trend, however, is toward moderation. Sweet wines and drinks should be avoided, except at the end of the meal, where a sweet dessert wine may be served with the dessert or sweet liqueurs after the dessert.

Exhibit 3.10 Dessert Menu

Courtesy of Bakers Square Restaurants and Pie Shops, Matteson, Illinois

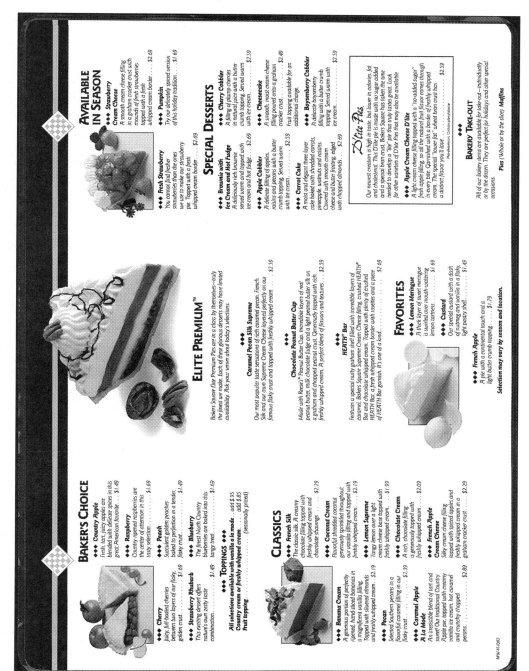

BAKER'S CHOICE

◆◆◆ Country Apple
Fresh, tart, juicy apples are blended with delicate spices in this great American favorite. . . . $1.49

◆◆◆ Raspberry
Country ripened raspberries are the center of attention in this tasty selection. . . . $1.69

◆◆◆ Cherry
Juicy, full-bodied cherries between two layers of our flaky, golden crust. . . . $1.69

◆◆◆ Peach
Succulent golden peaches baked to perfection in a tender, flaky crust. . . . $1.49

◆◆◆ Blueberry
The finest North Country blueberries are baked into this tangy treat. . . . $1.69

◆◆◆ Strawberry Rhubarb
This exciting dessert offers nature's own zesty taste combination. . . . $1.49

◆◆◆ TOPPINGS ◆◆◆
All selections available with vanilla a la mode . . . add $.95
Country cream or freshly whipped cream. . . . add $.85
Fruit topping . . . . (seasonally priced)

CLASSICS

◆◆◆ French Silk
The classic silk. A creamy chocolate filling topped with freshly whipped cream and chocolate shavings. . . . $2.29

◆◆◆ Coconut Cream
Flavorful shredded coconut generously sprinkled throughout our vanilla filling and topped with freshly whipped cream. . . . $2.19

◆◆◆ Banana Cream
A generous portion of perfectly ripened, hand sliced bananas in a magnificent vanilla filling. Topped with slivered almonds and freshly whipped cream. . . . $2.19

◆◆◆ Pecan
Selected Southern pecans in a flavorful caramel filling in our flaky crust. . . . $2.39

◆◆◆ Caramel Apple A La Mode
An irresistible blend of tart and sweet! Our traditional Country Apple pie, topped with creamy vanilla ice cream, hot caramel and crunchy chopped pecans. . . . $2.89

◆◆◆ Lemon Supreme
Tangy lemon over a light cream cheese base topped with freshly whipped cream. . . . $1.99

◆◆◆ Chocolate Cream
A rich, chocolate filling is generously topped with freshly whipped cream. . . . $2.09

◆◆◆ French Apple Cream Cheese
Silky cream cheese filling topped with spiced apples and freshly whipped cream in a graham cracker crust. . . . $2.29

ELITE PREMIUM™

Bakers Square Elite Premium Pies are in a class by themselves—truly the finest we make. Each is one of those glorious desserts may have limited availability. Ask your server about today's selections.

◆◆◆ Caramel Pecan Silk Supreme
Our most popular taste sensations of rich caramel pecan. French Silk and our own Supreme Cream Cheese layered perfectly on our famous flaky crust and topped with freshly whipped cream. . . . $2.59

◆◆◆ Chocolate Peanut Butter Cup
Made with Reese's® Peanut Butter Cup. Incredible layers of real peanut butter, milk chocolate fudge and a light peanut butter silk on a graham and chopped peanut crust. Generously topped with rich freshly whipped cream. A perfect blend of flavors and textures. . . . $2.59

◆◆◆ HEATH® Bar
Features a special nutty graham shell filled with incredible layers of caramel, Bakers Square Supreme Cream Cheese filling, crushed HEATH® Bar and chocolate whipped cream. Topped with plenty of crushed HEATH® Bar, a fresh whipped cream border with rosettes and a piece of HEATH® Bar garnish. It's one of a kind. . . . $2.69

FAVORITES

◆◆◆ Lemon Meringue
A thick layer of sweet meringue is swirled over mouth-watering lemon tartness. . . . $1.69

◆◆◆ Custard
Our special custard with a dash of nutmeg and vanilla in a flaky light pastry shell. . . . $1.49

◆◆◆ French Apple
A pie with a continental touch and a light butter crumb topping. . . . $1.79

Selection may vary by season and location.

AVAILABLE IN SEASON

◆◆◆ Strawberry Cream Cheese
A smooth cream cheese filling in a graham cracker crust with mounds of fresh strawberries topped with a fresh whipped cream border. . . . $2.69

◆◆◆ Pumpkin
Try our delicately spiced version of this holiday tradition. . . . $1.69

◆◆◆ Fresh Strawberry
You cannot find fresher strawberries than the ones we use to make our strawberry pie. Topped with a fresh whipped cream border. . . . $2.69

SPECIAL DESSERTS

◆◆◆ Brownie with Ice Cream and Hot Fudge
A deliciously rich brownie served warm and topped with ice cream and hot fudge. . . . $2.69

◆◆◆ Apple Cobbler
A delicate filling of apples, raisins and pecans with a butter crumb topping. Served warm with ice cream. . . . $2.59

◆◆◆ Carrot Cake
A moist and elegant three layer cake baked with shredded carrots, pineapple, walnuts and raisins. Covered with smooth cream cheese and butter frosting, edged with chopped almonds. . . . $2.69

◆◆◆ Cherry Cobbler
A filling of plump cherries in natural juice with a butter crumb topping. Served warm with ice cream. . . . $2.59

◆◆◆ Cheesecake
A smooth, moist cream cheese filling poured onto a graham cracker crust. . . . $2.49
Fruit topping available for an additional charge.

◆◆◆ Boysenberry Cobbler
A delicate boysenberry filling with a butter crumb topping. Served warm with ice cream. . . . $2.59

D'lite Pies.

Our newest creation is high in taste, but lower in calories, fat and cholesterol. This D'lite pie is made with no sugar added and a special bran crust. Bakers Square has taken the time needed to develop a "lite" pie that truly tastes great. Look for other varieties of D'lite Pies that may also be available.

◆◆◆ Apple Cream Cheese D'lite
A light cream cheese filling topped with a "no-added-sugar" fresh apple filling, so all the natural fruit flavor comes through in every bite. Garnished with a border of freshly whipped cream. The special "lower-fat" wheat bran crust has a distinct flavor you'll love. . . . $2.59

PhenlAlmanmm, "Dietary phenyllalanine"

BAKERY TAKE-OUT

All of our bakery items are available for take-out—individually or by the dozen. They are perfect for holidays and other special occasions.

Pies (Whole or by the slice) **Muffins**

MN-H-097.

A wine such as dry sherry may be served with the first course and with the soup. A light, white dinner wine would typically follow with the fish and poultry. A full-bodied dry red wine is served with the main course. A very good dry red wine may be served with the cheese, followed by a light-bodied but refreshing sweet dessert wine. The tendency in formal meals is to limit the number of wines. As few as one or two wines may suffice.

A properly planned formal dinner should compare with a symphony or concerto. It should have different movements and themes in the foods and wines. The progression of themes should lead to a taste climax and then gradually recede in intensity as other foods follow. There are places in the meal where the foods should be modest, quiet, and subtle in flavor; and in other places the food and flavor should stand out in a loud crescendo. Each course should lead into the next, and the meal should be a continuity of related taste themes just as a good symphony has continuity of musical themes.

Lightness and delicacy should be the motif of the appetizer and soup. Both should be refreshing and somewhat zestful to whet the appetite. They should be a good introduction to the foods to follow. The fish course should be bland but sufficiently pronounced to give contrast with the courses that preceded it and with the more pronounced flavors in the poultry course that follows. The poultry course should be light and delicate. The roast can be a red meat, and should be the peak of the meal. At this point, flavor values are more pronounced, but excessive richness, sweetness, or sharpness in flavor should be avoided.

The salad should be a relieving course. Its cool crispness and slightly tart flavor should be delicate and possess a distinctive quality, giving a respite from the heavier foods that have gone before. The Italians say the salad should "clean the palate and the teeth." Any oiliness or sharpness in flavor should be avoided. The tangy cheese course that may follow the salad should renew the jaded palate and set it properly for the concluding course—a sweet dessert. This should be light and delicate, and not too sweet. It should end the meal with some finality, but not on a heavy note.

The most formal meals are served without bread or butter. Salt and pepper are not on the table. In fine commercial dining rooms, bread and butter, salt and pepper, and ashtrays are often found on the table.

A less formal dinner may have only three to five courses. The first course can be a fruit cup, juice or seafood cocktail, melon, canapé, oysters, or clams, followed by a soup and then a fish course. Or there can be either an appetizer or a soup and no fish course. The main course is next, accompanied by a potato and vegetable and, often, a salad. A dessert follows. Rolls and butter are usually also served.

Evening Menus

Some places operate after dinner hours. This may be to catch those who are out at the theater, an athletic event, or some other attraction, or it may be that there is a good trade potential for night workers. Some operations may attempt to attract business with entertainment that may either be quite elaborate, such as a night club, or quite simple, as a juke box for dancing. Still others may be simple places that function more as social gathering places with limited menus. It is possible to combine night customers, with separate areas for those who want entertainment and those who only want food.

Many operations remove specials and table d'hôte dinners from the a la carte dinner menu and offer customers a selection of a la carte items on their evening menu. Some may "pull" the whole dinner menu and have another completely different evening menu emphasizing snack foods, such as hamburgers, milk shakes, pies, cakes, and fountain goods. Such a menu may be desirable to reduce the need for a large kitchen staff after dinner hours. In this case, most menu items are available up front where servers can get them. If an operation is near a theater or similar entertainment area, the menu should emphasize good desserts, specialty coffees, and perhaps light supper items.

A good analysis of the desires of the market and its potential should be made if one hopes to draw a trade that seeks entertainment as well as food and drink. The menu should then be designed to meet the demand for the appropriate kind of entertainment rather than attempting to create a demand. The menu should be supported by proper emphasis on props, such as servers' uniforms, dishes and glassware, table decorations (candles, vases, flowers), lighting, and entertainment.

Special Occasion Menus

Quite a few hotels, clubs, and restaurants are able to develop a substantial party and catering business. This can be profitable and considerably supplement overall income.

The special occasion menu must be planned in detail to suit the occasion. While there is a general pattern to events such as wedding receptions, buffet dinners, and cocktail parties, each should be characterized by its own special arrangements. Thus, some menus may have to be planned for a special occasion and not used again. Some events will be quite formal, while others will be very informal. The menu should carry out the spirit of the theme. Creativity and ingenuity are required. Color, decor, props, foods, and service should be combined to give correctness and novelty to the occasion.

A menu for a party should be carefully analyzed to see that it does not make excessive demands on servers, dishware, or equipment. The foods selected should be easy and fast to serve and be kinds that can stand delays in service and stay sanitary and of good quality. They should be suitable for the occasion.

Party Menus

A wide variety of parties may be served by a catering department. These may be as simple as punch for a dance or coffee for a meeting. Others may provide a simple dessert before a bridge game or a fashion show. Others may cater formal luncheons or dinners.

Party menus will vary according to the event, and thus there may be constant change. However, some operations pre-plan menus and have these available for clients when they call to discuss an event. This helps to standardize production and allows an accurate calculation of costs. If a special menu has to be developed, the individual planning the menu and establishing the price should know the complete costs so that an adequate price can be charged.

Most operations doing party business use standard printed forms for details. (See **Exhibit 3.11**.) The number of copies distributed may vary, and each operation will have its own special procedure. It is important that all departments affected have a coordinated plan and that the system work smoothly. There are many details in planning parties. Party business can be profitable, but it is very demanding of personnel. Good use of forms and procedures and a smooth, efficient system can do much to add to profits and make party business less demanding.

Some food services have catering departments that do considerable amounts of business and set up a sales office to handle booking arrangements. They often have preplanned menus with prices for patrons. It may be necessary to quote a tentative price at first and then later, when menu and service costs can be more accurately determined, set a firmer price. Catering menus can be developed for breakfasts, continental breakfasts, buffet breakfasts, luncheons, luncheon buffets, dinners, buffet dinners, receptions, holiday celebrations, cocktail parties, birthdays, weddings, liquor (spirits), and wine lists; prices can be established for shows and for entertainment. **Exhibit 3.12** is an example of a catering menu selected for a dinner party held in someone's honor.

Tea Menus

There are both high and low teas. A low tea might be simply tea, served perhaps with lemon, milk, and sugar. A more elaborate tea would add a simple dessert item or cookies, mints, bonbons, and nuts; a still more elaborate one might add a frozen dessert and fancy sandwiches. Often a tea is served from a table with the beverages served by an honored host or hostess at one end of the table and coffee served at the opposite end by another honored host. These hosts are usually changed at set times. The placement of the tea table should be considered carefully because traffic can be a problem.

A high tea is somewhat like a meal. It is served late in the afternoon and is more substantial than a low tea. It is often used as a light meal between lunch and a late evening dinner. It is most frequently served in homes, and in some luxury hotels.

A tea may be used as a reception event for a speaker, followed by a talk in a room nearby. It can also be used to honor individuals or an event.

Exhibit 3.11   Typical Catering Form

BANQUET PROSPECTUS

Name of Organization _____

Address _____ Phone _____

Nature of Function _____

Day _____ Date _____ Time _____

Room _____ Rent _____

Name of Engager _____

Address _____ Phone _____

Responsibility of Party _____

Price per Person $ _____ Gratuity: _____ Minimum Number Guaranteed: _____ Maximum Attendance: _____

FOOD MENU	BEVERAGE MENU
	Cash: _____ Charge: _____
	Corkage: _____
	Room for Bar: _____
	Open: _____ Close: _____
	Bartender Charge: _____
	Minimum Charges (4 hrs): _____
	Types of Beverages: _____
	Staff:

Table Arrangements: _____ Set Up By: _____ Head: _____

Flowers: _____ Centerpiece: _____ Checking: _____

Ticket Table: _____ Blackboard: _____ P.A.: _____ Stage: _____

Lectern: _____ Screen: _____ Piano: _____ Music: _____

Cigars: _____ Cigarettes: _____ Platform: _____ Dance Floor: _____

REMARKS: _____ **COMMENTS BY PARTY:** _____

Copies to:

❑ Customer ❑ Chef   **Date Booked:** _____

❑ Catering Office ❑ Houseman

❑ Maitre D' ❑ Bar

❑ Accounting   BY _____

Exhibit 3.12 Catering Menu

Courtesy of Blue Plate Catering, Chicago, Illinois

Dinner Menu

Passed Hors d'oeuvres

Fillet of Beef Bruschetta
Slice tenderloin of beef on a garlic crouton
with a remoulade sauce and a mixed pepper garnish

Endive Spear with Gorgonzola and Walnuts

Artichoke Strudel

*

First Course

Fresh Buffalo Mozzarella
with
Red and Yellow Beefsteak Tomatoes
Served on a bed of raddichio and boston lettuces
with a pesto vinaigrette

Entree

Broiled Whitefish with Lemon Chive Butter
Garnished with fresh chive and lemon zest

Fresh Steamed Asparagus
With a balsamic cherry tomato relish

Three Grain Pilaf
Wild rice, brown rice and bulgar cooked in a
rich chicken stock and seasoned with fresh herbs

Dinner Rolls
Thyme and onion muffins
Au Pain French dinner rolls
Served with butter

*

Dessert

Feuillite of Fresh Mixed Berries
with
Champagne Sabayon

Coffee Service
Regular and decaffeinated Caravelli coffees,
tea, cream, sugar and sweet & low

27.00 per person

Reception Menus

Receptions resemble teas but may feature alcoholic beverages. A wedding reception usually has a punch made of fruit juice, brandy, and champagne; although almost any other drink combination would be satisfactory. At some receptions, cocktails with canapés, hors d'oeuvres, and other tangy foods may be served. These may be picked up by guests at a buffet or they may be passed among guests. When passed, the service is called "flying service," from the Russians who originated the service and called the trays of foods carried around "flying platters."

It is usual to estimate that each guest will eat two to eight pieces of food at such gatherings. The type of function, its length of time, and the variety of food offered will affect the amount of food required. Bowls of dips and platters of crisp foods, such as pickles, olives, or crudites, that are easy to replenish may assist in giving flexibility. Some operations plan a runout time and toward the end of service leave only a few foods remaining. The number of drinks served may also vary. Men usually consume, on the average, two to four alcoholic drinks per hour of service, and women one to three. Again, the occasion decides but on the average the number consumed is falling. Light wines, beer and non-alcoholic drinks are to be included.

Since the preparation of a large quantity of fancy canapés, sandwiches, and hors d'oeuvres can require much labor, ways should be found to reduce preparation time by purchasing items such as tiny pre-baled puff shells or other items that can be filled and made to look as if they were prepared on the premises. A tray of canapés or fancy sandwiches need not have every item on it highly decorated. If a few fancy ones are properly spaced among plain ones that take little labor to produce, the effect is still appealing.

Buffet Menus

Originality in buffet menu items should be sought; too many foodservice operations today provide little in the way of novelty. They may use kidney bean and onion salad, pickled corn, whole or sliced pickled beets, or fruit gelatin salads made with canned fruit cocktail. This may be fine if other, more unique foods are served with them. Otherwise, patrons may find the buffet resembles a home-style potluck buffet.

The effectiveness of a buffet depends almost wholly on the originality and presentation of the food. If these are not emphasized, the purpose is lost. Foods that look tired or that are excessively garnished, off-color, or messy will not satisfy guests.

The number of foods to put on a buffet can differ with the occasion and the meal. For a simple meal, only a few items may be used along with rolls and butter, beverage, and dessert. A dessert buffet may be only a dessert and beverage. A slightly more elaborate luncheon buffet may have four to six cold foods, including appetizers and salads, several hot entrees with a vegetable and perhaps a potato dish, a selection of bread or rolls and butter, and perhaps several desserts. There may be 20 or more cold foods on an elaborate buffet, eight or more hot entrees, a number of different hot vegetable dishes, potatoes, a variety of hot breads and rolls, and various cakes, puddings, pies, and other desserts.

The number of items and their presentation will dictate the degree of elaborateness. Certainly an overabundance of items is a mistake and can lead to waste. The purpose of a buffet is to give guests the feeling that they can help themselves as much as they desire, but it should not lead to waste.

Some buffets require particular foods. A *smorgasbord*, the Swedish buffet, must have pickled herring or other fish, rye bread, and *mysost* or *gjetost* cheese, in addition to many cold foods; hot foods, such as *lefse* and Swedish meat balls; and a dessert, such as a pancake in which lingonberries are rolled. Cold foods are eaten before the hot ones. Dessert is served last with coffee. A true smorgasbord usually includes *aquavit* or *schnapps* (Swedish liquers) served in tiny glasses.

A Russian buffet should have caviar served from the table center, either from a beautiful glass bowl or from a bowl made of ice. Dark rye bread and butter must accompany it. The other foods should be typical of a buffet.

A Russian buffet includes small glasses of vodka. The use of buffets for breakfast has been mentioned, and additional material will be found in the discussion on service in Chapter 12.

MENUS FOR PATRONS' SPECIAL NEEDS

The menu planner must focus closely on the patrons to be served. Special menus may have to be developed to meet the special tastes of specific groups. Restaurants and institutions that serve the elderly or the very young may want to consider how to meet the desires and needs of these groups, either with the regular menu or by developing a new one.

Children's and Teenagers' Menus

Menus for young people are generally limited because youngsters usually lack food experience and tend to stick to a small number of food selections that they know and like.

Small children tend to have smaller appetites. While the food selections for children should vary, the portions should be small. Teenagers often have hearty appetites and usually are hard to fill up. Therefore, the teenage menu should be filling as well as appealing.

A highly visible, entertaining menu appeals to children and makes them feel they are getting special attention. Colorful menus, perhaps with reproductions of animals or cartoon characters (you may need permission for the latter) will appeal to young children. **Exhibit 3.13** shows an appealing children's menu. If the menu is planned to entertain and keep the child busy working at some puzzle, drawing, or reading a cartoon, the child will be quiet and not annoy other guests.

Offering children's food on the regular menu is often not as successful as having a special menu. A special menu is advantageous to the operation as well as to the child. That is because with a regular menu parents may be tempted to share their own food with children and not order anything special for them. If a moderately priced child's menu is available, it leads to the child selecting his or her own food, and the total size of the guest check is increased.

The child's menu should limit selections to favorites, because confusion results if too many items are offered. The wording should be simple and straightforward. Following through on a theme is a good way to introduce interest. A menu that gives the child something to do that can be taken home—or an operation that gives a child a gift—is a big help in winning young customers.

Exhibit 3.13   Children's Menu

Courtesy of Red Lobster, Orlando, Florida

REDS TREASURE MEALS ™

JUST FOR KIDS 10 AND UNDER

ALL MEALS ARE SERVED WITH A FRESHLY TOSSED GARDEN SALAD, COLESLAW OR APPLESAUCE, HOT CHEESE GARLIC BREAD AND ONE OF THE FOLLOWING: FRIES   FRESH BROCCOLI   BAKED POTATO   RICE PILAF

HAMBURGER OR CHEESEBURGER $3.39

SPAGHETTI WITH CHEESESTICKS $3.39

FRIED SHRIMP $3.99

POPCORN SHRIMP AND CHEESESTICKS $3.99

CHICKEN FINGERS AND FRIED SHRIMP $3.99

SHRIMP ON A STICK $3.99
Twin skewers of grilled shrimp served over rice pilaf

POPCORN SHRIMP $3.39
Bite size shrimp lightly breaded and fried

FRIED CHICKEN FINGERS $3.99

Red Lobster/A

100% Recycled Paper

Some operations give a child something that is one of a group of items, such as a cartoon glass. Then the child wants to return to the operation to complete the set.

The selections offered on a children's or teenagers' menu should also be set for the geographic location and/or ethnic base. Some Mexican foods that are successful on a Texas menu may not be successful on a Wisconsin menu. A menu offering Cuban and South American items that is popular in Miami, Florida, might not be popular in Portland, Oregon. It is a case of suiting a menu to patrons, something covered more thoroughly in Chapter 4.

Senior Citizens' Menus

Many operations can sell successfully to senior citizens, especially by offering discounts during slow periods and using the menu as a marketing tool. Senior citizens generally eat less than younger adults, so food portions for menu items should be smaller. In some areas seniors may be on fixed incomes so, for the most part, prices should be moderate. A few seniors will not chew well and soft foods should be included on the menu. In a recent Gallup survey of a group over 65, 20 percent were on some sort of diet. Thus, a menu that offers items that are low-fat, low-calories, and low-sodium will likely satisfy most senior dietary needs.

It is helpful to know something about the background of seniors who patronize an operation. For example, if they are of Germanic stock from a rural area in Wisconsin, they will probably enjoy things like chicken, pork, liver, sausage, sauerkraut, and other similar items. Knowing customers is the first and most important step to satisfying them.

MENUS FOR NONCOMMERCIAL AND SEMICOMMERCIAL ESTABLISHMENTS

Noncommercial and semicommercial operations will have menu requirements that differ from those prepared for full commercial operations. If the operation is institutional, and the patrons are a "captive market," the menu must be evaluated, based on the fact that most patrons will eat two or more meals a day at the facility. This means that nutritional needs of patrons must be considered along with their preferences.

Institutional Menus

Commercial operations are in business to make a profit. Institutions usually are not. They often operate from a budget that indicates the limits of expenditures, and they try to keep within these limits. *Breaking even*—bringing in enough sales to cover costs—is often the goal of an institutional operation. Most institutional food services work with a cost per meal allowance or a per-day allowance. A hospital will have a cost per bed per day. Hospital budgets for operating the entire department usually take about 12 percent of the hospital's expenditures.

Many institutional menus do not have to merchandise or sell to the extent that commercial operations do, since they have a built-in clientele. Many patrons in institutions do not see the menu, since it is written for the foodservice staff only. Some menus will not have a selection. Others will offer slight variations in the basic menu, such as a choice of dessert or beverage. Institutional operations that have to compete with commercial establishments may have to do some merchandising. In any event, dull menus are not a necessary characteristic of institutional operations.

Nutritional considerations about the food served are important; however, these will depend on whether patrons must get all their meals from the operation or eat there only occasionally. If they dine there less often and have other options, the nutritional consideration becomes less important, although still a factor. Certain patrons will be on special diets, and this will have to be considered.

Whether patrons eat in the institutional food service all the time or just sporadically, it is important to have good variety in the foods and avoid too much repetition. Long-term cycle menus are best for institutional operations. To break monotony there should be occasional meals that feature such themes as "Night in Venice," "Circus Days," "Old-fashioned Picnic," and so forth. Such menu breaks build interest, and patrons look ahead to such events. It is also important to occasionally break the meal plan and offer items different from the typical groups of foods served.

Most institutional menus are built around the three-meal-a-day plan. Breakfast is a fruit or juice, cereal and milk, a main dish such as eggs and/or meat, hot cakes, Danish pastry, toast or bread with margarine or butter, jelly or jam, and beverage. Lunch may include an entree, vegetable, salad, bread and butter, beverage, and dessert, or be smaller, including only a soup, beverage, and dessert. The institutional dinner may have a first course, such as an appetizer or soup, followed by a main dish with vegetable and potato or other starchy food, a salad, bread and butter or margarine, a dessert, and beverage. There is usually a 10-hour span between breakfast and dinner and a 14-hour fast between dinner and breakfast, unless a snack is served in the evening.

Some institutions find that a four-meal or five-meal plan is more suitable for patron needs. In the four-meal plan, a light continental breakfast is served at 7:00 AM. A substantial brunch follows it at 10:30 AM. At 3:30 PM, the main meal is served, followed by a light supper in the evening.

The five-meal plan is similar, with a continental breakfast at 7:00 AM, a brunch at 10:00 AM, a light snack about 12:30 or 1:00 PM with the main meal following between 3:00 and 4:00 PM. A light snack is served between 6:30 and 8:00 PM.

The four-meal or five-meal plans may reduce the labor required in the kitchen since the two big meals of the day are close enough together for one shift to prepare them. The other meals are light enough to be prepared by skeleton crews.

Some hospitals also find that the four-meal or five-meal plans permit patients to be gone for early morning examinations without losing out on a full meal. Even though the patient has had to miss breakfast, he or she can return to the room when one of the heavier meals of the day is being served.

Not all attempts to change to a four-meal or five-meal plan have been successful. The failures have usually been ones of planning. It is essential that the plan be thoroughly discussed with staff members who may be affected. The plan must have the complete support of the staff and solid backing from the administration. Communication of the plan and a complete discussion of the advantages and disadvantages should occur well in advance of implementation.

The change must consider every factor. For instance, a large state mental hospital changed to a five-meal plan and found that the patients felt they were not getting a breakfast because cereal was not a part of the first meal served. Adding either cold or hot cereals to the continental breakfast resulted in eliminating most complaints. In implementing these four-meal or five-meal plans in health institutions, the amount of sugar, flour, and fat should be watched. Sweet rolls or other breakfast pastries and evening snacks such as cookies, cakes, or other rich products cause undesirable weight gain and result in a failure on the part of patients to eat adequate amounts of other essential nutrients.

Planning Institutional Menus

It is best in planning the institutional menu to work with a sheet large enough to hold the menu for an entire period, usually a month. Obviously, if the menu is to run for a long period, such as three months or more, this cannot be done. The proper headings should be set up with days, dates, and meals designated by columns and rows.

Most planners start with the main dishes for a meal, beginning first with dinners, then lunches, and then breakfasts. Balance and variety must be sought between days and also between the meals in a day. The frequency of the types of meats to use should be established, and a table can be set up for this. For instance, in a week, beef, pork or cured pork, poultry, fish or shellfish, and a casserole dish should each be served only once. These may be varied with an occasional selection of variety meat, veal, lamb, or sausage, and eggs, cheese, or other nonmeat dishes. Similarly, a table may be set up to indicate the frequency desired for various vegetables and other foods. A frequency table can also be set up for breakfast and lunch items.

After the main dishes are selected, the vegetables and potato, or other starch items, are added, followed by salads and dressings. Again, these must be balanced against the various foods used in a day and from day to day. Breads for each meal, desserts, and beverages can follow in that order. After adding these major items, the planner may select the breakfast fruits and cereals.

After this, the menu should be checked to see that balance has been maintained, nutritional needs met, cost restraints not exceeded, and other factors, such as balanced use of equipment and skill of labor, considered. If modified diets based on this general menu are required, they should be planned by someone trained in nutrition.

Different institutions will need different menus to suit varying operational requirements and meet patron demands. Regulatory agencies and other outside influences may also affect menu planning.

Health Facilities

A great number of menus will be required to meet the needs of various kinds of health facilities, such as hospitals, convalescent centers, nursing homes, and retirement homes, in which there may be available nursing and medical care.

Hospitals must provide food for staff, nurses, doctors, visitors, and catered events, as well as patient meals. Different menus will be required. Some of these menus will be typical of those in other food services. Generally, only patient menus will differ.

A hospital's dietary staff will first prepare a general or *house* menu. This includes what foods will be served at a particular meal on a specific day. The planner must keep in mind that from this menu will be prepared the various diets the hospital must serve. The dietitian goes through this general menu selecting items, changing them, or substituting others to meet dietary requirements. It takes an experienced, skilled person to modify a general diet. For instance, if a hospital put the items in **Exhibit 3.14** on the general menu, the dietitian would modify the menu for the various patient diets.

In the diabetic diet the cranberry jelly, potatoes and dressing, glazed onions, and coconut cream pie might not be allowed. The sherbet and baked apple sweetened with an artificial sweetener probably would be allowed. Some carbohydrates would be allowed on this menu because even the most severe diabetic must still have some carbohydrates. The amount of calories allowed in the other choices on the diabetic menu would also be evaluated.

For a low-fiber diet, the dietitian would eliminate the bran muffin and would scrutinize the fiber content in the vegetables and salad, substituting something else if it is considered too high. The baked potato would be served without the skin.

A diet of soft foods would probably require the cook to process the turkey or lamb chop by chopping them up. The salmon might still be served whole because it flakes easily. The broccoli might be finely chopped, and the tomatoes might not appear in a salad but as a cooked vegetable.

A low-fat diet would substitute plain lemon juice for the lemon butter. The butter on the broccoli and that added to the carrots would be omitted, and the glazed onions might not be permitted because they are usually glazed in butter or margarine. The butter would be omitted from the menu and a low-fat French or other dressing would be substituted for the regular French dressing. The sherbet or the apple would probably be allowed.

Menu planning for other health facilities may follow that of a typical hospital, with a general menu being written and modified diets taken from

Exhibit 3.14   Typical Hospital Menu

Roast Turkey, Cranberry Jelly

Vegetable Plate with Lamb Chop

Poached Salmon Fillet, Lemon Butter

Spaghetti Tettrazini

Mashed Potato   Baked Potato   Cornbread Dressing

Buttered Broccoli   Glazed Onions   Pureed Carrots

Sliced Tomato Salad, French Dressing

Soft Diced Vegetables in Aspic, Mayonnaise

Bran Muffin   Parkerhouse Roll

Butter

Sherbet   Coconut Cream Pie   Baked or Fresh Apple

it. However, if only a few in the institution need special diets, the general menu would be written and special foods provided for those few. These foods could come largely from the general diet along with some specialized items.

Retirement homes may provide three meals a day, but some do not. Retirees may live in small apartments, which have facilities for preparing meals. Usually two meals a day are prepared there by the retirees. Thus, the foodservice facility may serve only one meal; this is often a heavy meal at noon or dinner. Patrons often need assistance during the meal. When full nursing care is given and the patron is confined to his or her rooms, a meal service might resemble that of a hospital or even hotel room service. In many retirement homes there will be a small coffee shop that serves breakfast, lunch, dinner, and snacks. Some operations may cater special events for retirees and their guests. Theme meals such as those mentioned earlier are also very popular with retirees and help to give a feeling of change and variety.

Business and Industrial Feeding Operations

A factory or other in-plant food service or one in an office building may have to have several kinds of dining services. There may be an executive dining room where top executives can meet at mealtime, bring guests, and have meetings over a meal. A staff dining service and sometimes a coffee shop are also used. Meals are usually paid for by the employees, but at a marked-down rate because of employer subsidization. Some serve the meal free. Metropolitan Life Insurance was one of the leaders in providing meals under dietary supervision to employees. If a cycle menu is used, it must cover a fairly long period because patrons probably eat there regularly. Worker dining units are often cafeterias. Snacks, sandwiches, salads, beverages, entrees, vegetables, potatoes, breads, and desserts are served. Some foodservice operations may offer breakfast and lunch, and a few executive dining rooms may even serve dinner for late evenings.

Normally, a menu board in the cafeteria announces offerings and prices. A set meal only may be served, and no menu is prepared for patrons. The full-service dining rooms usually have printed or written menus.

College and University Food Services

Many college residence halls have cafeterias. Self-bussing is usual. Some residence halls have foods priced individually or together in a table d'hôte menu, and the students pay for the foods chosen. Other students may be on a board plan where the meals for a period are paid for at a set rate. There is usually no credit for missed meals. Some have systems that combine the two features, with the student purchasing a block of tickets and using these occasionally. The menu must reflect such conditions.

Students are usually young and active and often want substantial meals. They will ignore foods that are not popular, and there may be a limited number of foods that they will eat. Some students still try to live on hamburgers, pizza, sodas, and french fries. Most residence hall units bow to student demands and serve what they want, hoping that in some way the student will get the nutrition needed. In other cases, students will demand natural or healthful foods, and these will have to be on the menu. Student wants vary and it is important to try to meet nutritional needs and student desires for quality, while providing variety as well.

Many colleges and universities operate student unions. A variety of food-service operations can exist here, including snack shops, quick-service operations, seated-service dining rooms, and even banquet and catering facilities. The menus must satisfy the students' culinary desires and, usually, meet a limited budget. However, these now may even be a part of a fixed residence hall menu.

Many campuses also have a faculty club or dining center. Usually the club's big meal is lunch, but some offer dinners. A few may have bars. Prices must be modest, and often the college or university subsidizes the operation by providing space and equipment and even some occupancy costs. These clubs are usually operated like other clubs, and promotional programs will be a part of the merchandising system to bring in members. A faculty dining center differs from a club in that it does not require membership but is open to all faculty.

Elementary and Secondary School Food Services

Elementary schools usually are on the federal school lunch program. If so, a meal following the general meal pattern will be served. (Some schools may be only on the federal milk program.) Many school systems are now computerized and feed a large number of children. Others serve children from diverse racial, religious, and ethnic backgrounds and their menus should reflect this patronage.

In secondary schools, students either pay for foods as they get them or purchase tickets to exchange for meals. Because of the preferences of teenagers for special foods, secondary schools may often serve popular as well as nutritious foods. For a variety of reasons, many secondary schools try to prevent students from leaving the grounds to seek meals elsewhere, such as nearby quick-service outlets. Some have "closed campuses," and the students are forbidden to leave during lunch.

At some schools, such as military academies or religion supported schools, students live on campus. These are usually for older children and teenagers. The menus for these children should be planned with strong consideration given to their nutritional needs, since they will eat most of their meals in the school food service. The foods should also be those young people like. The service may be cafeteria- or even family-style, where foods are brought to the table in dishes and passed around. Some provide table service.

Many elementary, secondary, and private schools will have faculty dining rooms. For the most part, the foods will be somewhat similar to those served to students but modified for adult tastes. These foods may also be supplemented by other offerings, or there may be a completely different menu from that for the students.

Miscellaneous Institutional Food Services

There are many kinds of institutions, such as orphanages, prisons, associations, and religious and charitable groups, that provide food for people. Often these units function on a very limited budget. There may be no payment by the patrons. Either the government or the operation may provide the funds. In general, the provisions presented previously for institutional menu planning will apply.

THE FINAL STEPS IN MENU PLANNING

Once the various marketing, operational, and strategic decisions have been made, the pricing of the menu may begin. This is covered in more detail in Chapter 6. In addition, operators must continually research the popularity of menu items. Customer feedback is essential. The menu that was ideal for the establishment in the spring may be a real turn-off in the fall. Menu analysis, which will be discussed in Chapter 8, is the key to heading off such marketing disasters. Financial considerations, covered in Chapter 14, must also be considered.

SUMMARY

The task of planning and writing a menu is a daunting one. The most successful operations seem to have a menu that is "right"; that is, a menu that fits the operation. That does not happen by accident.

The menu should be thought of as the single most important document that defines the purpose, strategy, market, service, and theme of the operation. It should help "sell" items to patrons, and offer choices that will please a variety of tastes.

Before a menu can be planned, managers must develop a *mission statement* for the operation. This statement sums up the ultimate purpose of the operation, such as to provide high-quality, mid-priced food to a family market, or to provide three daily wholesome and nutritious meals to hospital patients. Next, managers set the objectives the operation is to attain. These can be in the form of profitability objectives, growth objectives, and market share objectives, among others. These objectives are used to develop *strategic plans* for the ongoing growth of the business.

A long-range financial plan is necessary before the menu can be developed. These long-range financial objectives are used to create budgets that must be followed by owners, managers, and supervisors.

One of the first decisions the menu planner (or menu planning team) must make is the number of menus an operation will use. This decision is based on the mission and scope of the operation.

Next the type or types of menus to be used is decided. Menus fall in the following categories:

- *A la carte* menus, which offer foods separately at separate prices
- *Table d'hôte* menus, which group several items together at a single price
- *Du jour* menus, which change daily
- *Limited* menus, which offer only a few selected items
- *Cycle* menus, which rotate after a set amount of time
- *California* menus, which offer items from all meal periods at all times of the day

Menu planners must take into account the meal plan to be followed—one that will fit the needs of most patrons. Each meal—breakfast, brunch, lunch, dinner, and evening meals—and each type of operation has a typical meal plan that leads to a fitting menu organization for the operation. Each course of the meal plan, such as Entrees, is normally divided on the written menu into subcategories, such as Fish and Seafood, Meat, Poultry, Pasta, and Meatless Entrees.

It is essential that patrons be given a variety of choices within each category and subcategory on a menu. Menu planners should vary flavors, textures, and cooking preparations as much as possible to please guests. This variety will also dictate the number of items included on the menu.

Breakfast menus are often associated with low prices and low profits unless care is taken to offer unique items to guests. Planners should strike a balance between items that patrons expect to find and those that will spark interest. *Brunch menus* traditionally combine items from both the breakfast and lunch menus. A *lunch menu* should offer guests items that are light enough, priced moderately enough, and prepared quickly enough for people who have to get back to work. (Leisurely items should also be available for people out on special occasions.) *Afternoon menus* are intended to attract people with free afternoons—retired persons, shoppers, artists, students, and homemakers—and typically offer sandwiches, fountain items, fruit plates, and pastries and desserts.

Dinner menus normally require the most elaborate dishes, organization, and variety. Of all menus, dinner menus should reflect the atmosphere, decor, theme, and patronage of the operation. *Formal dinner menus* follow the traditional courses included in classic French menus. They are appropriate for very formal occasions and may follow some—not necessarily all—classic French customs. *Evening menus* cater primarily to theater-goers and others who are out for the evening. They typically offer such items as hamburgers, fountain items, and desserts. *Special occasion, party,* and *reception menus* must fit the occasion and specific clientele of the event. Every effort should be made to make the meal a very unique experience for guests. *Tea menus* can range from simply tea and a light snack to an elaborate combination of teas, sandwiches, and pastries.

Buffet menus rely as much on presentation and service as they do on the food served, and the food itself should be unique. A traditional Swedish *smorgasbord* must have pickled herring, rye bread, Swedish cheeses, meat balls, a traditional dessert, such as lingonberry pancakes, and small glasses of aquavit or schnapps. A traditional Russian buffet includes small glasses of vodka, caviar, and dark rye bread.

Special considerations must be taken into account when planning menus for specific groups of people. Children's menus should include a manageable number of simple items that will appeal to children. The menu itself should be fun for young diners. Menus for teenagers should include filling items that will appeal to teenage tastes. Many older guests will appreciate menu items that reflect dietary concerns, such as those low in fat, cholesterol, salt, and sugar. Softer textures and mild flavors might also be appropriate.

Menus for *institutional operations*—hospitals, nursing homes, schools, universities—require some special menu planning considerations. While commercial operations are in business to earn a profit, institutional food services often have as their goal to *break even*, or earn enough in sales to cover all costs. (If a not-for-profit organization does earn more than it spends, that money must go back in the business rather than being paid out to stockholders.) Since many institutional operations have a "captive" clientele, they are more driven to offer nutritious and varied menu choices.

Business and industrial food services must plan menus that will induce workers to stay on the premises rather than taking their business outside the office or factory. The types of food served should reflect the tastes of the patrons. College and university food services must please young people and their tastes. Elementary and secondary school food services, whether or not they follow the federal government's school lunch program guidelines, are obligated to offer children nutritious meals at costs their families can afford.

QUESTIONS

1. Collect five menus from different types of operations. Which type of menu is each one? Are items on each menu organized well? Are there too many items? Too few items?

2. For each menu type below, discuss the types of operations in which they are appropriate, the tone they set, and the markets to which they normally appeal.

A la carte	Limited
Table d'hôte	Cycle
Du jour	California

3. What typical items do consumers expect to find on a breakfast menu? On a brunch menu? On a lunch menu? What specialty items have you seen on these menus that balanced expected items?

4. What are some of the important factors to consider when developing a children's menu? A menu for teenagers? A menu for senior citizens?

5. How is planning and developing an institutional menu different from developing a commercial menu? How is it similar? What are the *specific* considerations involved in developing menus for business and industry operations? For colleges and universities? For elementary and secondary schools?

4

Considerations and Limits in Menu Planning

Objectives

After reading this chapter, you should be able to:

1. Identify the major constraints in menu planning (cost, personnel, food availability, and patron preferences and needs) and recognize why they must be considered in menu planning.

INTRODUCTION

The creator of a new menu almost never has a free hand in developing the menu. Constraints are placed on the development from various constituencies, including customers, owners, investors, lenders, suppliers, employees, and regulators. Like a politician, the menu planner must be able to address the concerns of these constituencies while not seeming to pander to one group at the expense of another. Thus, the menu developer must take into account the financial constraints placed on the foodservice facility (like limits to equipment purchasing, or required minimum net return on investment) from the lenders and investors while attempting to maximize menu choice and variety within the limits of current employee abilities and training. This balancing act is a fine art, and may be what distinguishes the truly great foodservice operator from the merely competent.

Let us look at the various forces that tug at the creator of a new menu. These forces, when in balance, pull the foodservice operation down the road to success. When one or more factors are neglected or slighted, the disharmony created is as annoying as one singer in a chorus who sings flat. A menu must be in tune with all of the constraining factors.

What is the perfect balance? **Exhibit 4.1** shows the forces that effect the menu and that, when in harmony, create exceptional menus.

PHYSICAL FACTORS

The menu must be written to fit the physical operation; that is, the facilities must be capable of supporting production of menu items of the right quality and quantity, and the menu must not be written so as to allow some of the facility to be overburdened while other parts are underused. A menu featuring a dinner of baked ham and escalloped potatoes, candied squash, baked tomatoes, corn bread, and chocolate cake may sound appealing, but it places too much demand on the ovens and underutilizes other equipment. This sample menu also places too much demand on too few personnel; perhaps the fry cook may wish to take this night off. Such failure to take into account physical factors may result in service breakdowns (such as making patrons wait while the over-busy oven has room enough to cook the meal.)

Equipment and Facilities Available

Clearly, some thought must be given to what equipment is on hand (or could be reasonably purchased). Menus must be planned to suit equipment capacity. A 20-gallon steam kettle is capable of producing only 16 gallons of soup. Similarly, a 24-by-36-inch griddle can produce a maximum of 80 orders of pancakes (at three cakes per order) in an hour. Planning for production of 100 orders per hour plus bacon, ham, hash browns, or eggs is another example of a failure to consider equipment limitations.

The time required to process foods through the equipment must also be considered. Using the soup example from before, to plan for more soup than

Exhibit 4.1 Considerations in Designing a Menu

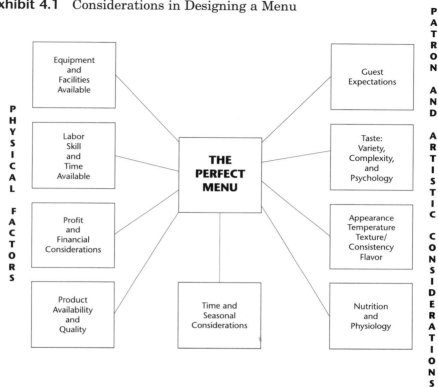

the capacity of the steam kettle (say, having a menu with only one soup item on it and more than 16 gallons of soup served per meal period) means the soup must be cooked in batches. If you are cooking two batches of soup, why not have two different soups on the menu? Similarly, one must consider whether there is even enough time to cook more than one batch of soup before the meal is to begin. Workbenches, mixers, ovens, sinks, cooking ranges, and other equipment can handle a limited amount of work in a given time. (Not to mention the cooks who can process food only so fast.) If a menu planner asks for more than the kitchen is able to produce, the whole system might collapse because employees cannot meet quotas if they have to wait for equipment to become available.

Storage capacity also must be considered when planning a menu. Refrigerated, frozen, and dry storage areas must accommodate foods both before and after preparation. A menu that overburdens storage abilities is disastrous for sanitation and cost reasons.

The menu planner can often alleviate equipment overload by getting input from production personnel. Planning or procedural changes regarding equipment use can often overcome perceived limitations. For instance, a seeming lack of griddle space may be overcome by cooking hashed brown potatoes in an oven and finishing smaller portions quickly on the griddle. A stew could be cooked in a roasting pan in the oven just as easily as on top of the stove. A change in the menu can avoid overload problems by using alternative cooking methods (a double bonus, as this also increases menu variety). This is a perfect example of why the menu planner must be familiar with cooking methods and preparations.

Naturally, equipment overload can often be reduced by buying preprepared, or *convenience* foods. Many planners find that they can considerably extend the production capacity of the kitchen by purchasing this kind of food. Convenience foods have the advantage of overcoming deficiencies in labor skills as well. But nothing is free, and convenience foods may add considerably to the operation's food cost and might not offer the appropriate quality.

Of course, the menu planner's equipment considerations do not end in the kitchen. Service equipment is also a consideration. A dining area can support service for only a given number of people; and many believe that the quality of service begins to deteriorate whenever the room nears capacity. The kind of service offered matters as well. Full continental service, complete with flambé dishes prepared tableside, requires more square feet per guest than would a cafeteria-style operation. A service with numerous courses or one that requires long periods of time between ordering and serving can greatly affect the capabilities of a given space to accommodate a given number of people. Too many menu selections can also slow down service, both because of the time it takes patrons to make up their minds, and the time it takes to serve them. Even the type of staffing—experienced servers versus part-timers, how they are organized (teams versus individual servers), and what levels of expertise they bring to the job—all have an effect. These considerations must be taken into account by the menu planner. Most importantly, the menu planner must maintain a certain continuity. The service area's decor must match the menu's theme.

LABOR CONSIDERATIONS

Labor constitutes one of the single largest expenses in most foodservice operations. Just as the equipment, furnishings and fixtures are assets, the smart modern manager will think of labor as a valuable asset. Just as we don't abuse the equipment by demanding more than the capacity of the griddle, so, too, we must be careful not to exceed the capabilities of our people. Unlike equipment, however, people have the capacity to learn. A good training program can teach new skills (and, hence, new capacities) to an employee. The menu planner must know what skills people possess in order to: 1) create a menu that requires labor skills currently possessed by the people; 2) not to create a menu which does not underuse employees' skills.

Training of labor can overcome the first problem, at some cost in terms of money and time. It takes time to train a person in new skills, and that time must be allocated from an already busy schedule. Also, training costs money. Even with on-the-job training the operator must realize that the person being trained and the person who is doing the training will work at a much slower pace during the training period than they may be expected to do once the trainee has been trained. By conducting a *skills inventory*—an assessment of the skills employees currently possess—the menu planner can create a menu that minimizes the amount of training and retraining required, and hence reduce the cost of implementing a new menu and the time it will take before the staff is operating as efficiently as possible under the new menu.

Underusing employees' conversely, will most likely lead to boredom. Studies have consistently shown that bored employees are less productive and more prone to absenteeism and turnover than are employees whose jobs provide challenges and are interesting. Similarly, many operations note that on slow nights they often have more problems and employees seem less coordinated than on busy evenings. The essential question is why pay a person who has more skills than you need? In simple economic terms, it makes sense for the menu planner to write a menu that uses as many skills as possible.

The menu planner must also consider the most effective use of employee's time. If equipment is unavailable or inefficient, valuable labor is wasted. The menu planner must seek to avoid bottle-necks in production when writing the menu.

Before a food item can be placed on a menu, its availability must be known. It makes little sense to have a dish listed on the menu that is unavailable. This only causes aggravation on the part of the patron and the server. Menus planned to last a long time must be careful to avoid too many seasonal items. One way of getting around this is to list a product group with the words "in season". For instance, breakfast menus usually offer some kind of fresh fruit, so the listing could be "melon, in season" or "seasonal melon." In the United States, many food items are available year-round. But even these items often have very different prices and quality at different times of year. Cost and, often, profitability are important considerations.

Often seasonal availability or price fluctuations can be overcome by volume purchasing. For instance, beef is often cheaper in early winter as the ranchers thin their herds. Buying large quantities and freezing them for later use will save money and ensure a constant supply of these items throughout the year. However, the costs of freezer storage, interest on the investment, and other elements must also be covered.

One subject whose importance cannot be overstated is that of food quality. Nearly every food item has a season in which its flavor, color, and texture are at their peak. Menu planners working in operations whose patrons are expecting a high level of quality must be especially sensitive to seasonal and quality constraints.

A menu should maximize revenue and minimize costs. Even in a nonprofit operation like a school or hospital there are cost and budgetary restraints that a menu planner must weigh when creating the perfect menu. These are discussed fully in Chapters 5 and 6.

PATRON AND ARTISTIC CONSIDERATIONS

The menu must fulfill the patron's physiological, social, and psychological needs—especially when it comes to food. To plan a menu that adequately does this requires a considerable amount of knowledge and ability.

Guest Expectations

Often what a guest expects from a menu is unknown, even to the guest. Marketing experts use a variety of techniques to measure guest expectations. They may survey guests (or potential guests), either by telephone or through some written survey form. They may interview selected guests, either individually or in focus groups. However it is done, the goal is to encourage patrons to reveal their innermost thoughts and desires. This process is inexact, though it can help foodservice managers spot trends and have at least an idea of what patrons expect.

There is a very important difference between customers' *needs* and their *wants*. A need can be either a *physiological need*, such as the need for liquid when one is dehydrated, or a *perceived need*, such as a "need" to own a new television set. Perceived needs are quite strong, and many industries successfully cater to these needs. The wine industry, for instance, has experienced poor overall sales in recent years, yet premium wine sales remain strong. Perhaps some of this strength is due to a perceived need on the part of some wine drinkers to project a certain image. Wants are often expressed through impulse sales. A patron may be quite full after a large meal, but a dessert cart display may spark a desire within the patron to order something which surely cannot fulfill a physiological (and probably no perceived) need. The menu should try to satisfy both customer needs and customer wants.

In an attempt to satisfy their guests, foodservice operations have invoked ad campaigns saying everything from "You deserve a break today" to "Sometimes you have to break the rules." These slogans appeal to people's vague needs and expectations for satisfaction. When these needs and expectations cannot be satisfied or when they are in conflict—such as when a guest wants a hearty breakfast of eggs, bacon, toast smothered in butter, and milk, but also wants to reduce cholesterol, the menu planner must make the best effort possible toward meeting patrons needs, but of course, one can't satisfy all of them.

Variety and Psychological Factors

One theory of human behavior, called Hedonism, states that people try to maximize pleasure and minimize pain. Certainly maximizing pleasure as it relates to food means maximizing sensory input. This can be done by varying taste. Just as film makers have found that with each new thriller they must create more and more elaborate special effects, so too do menu planners find that they must have greater variety in their menus if they are to spark patrons' interest. There is a physiological reason for this: the brain reacts to new situations with much greater interest than to similar or routine situations. Just as we spend much time thinking about how to dance the latest step and almost no time thinking about how we place our feet when we walk down the street, we spend more time savoring and thinking about new taste combinations than we do when we are eating something common.

At the same time, too much variety, like too much ice cream, can cause dissatisfaction. Patrons must feel that there are items on the menu with which they are familiar, especially those who are slow to experiment. However, even these common items can be prepared exceptionally well or in an unusual way. The sizzle platter (a metal plate that is heated in a broiler and causes food to sizzle when served) offers little added taste to fairly common menu items, but the unusual presentation has been used for years to add variety to menus.

There are other ways that food can meet people's psychological needs. Hunger creates anxiety and restlessness that eating quiets. This property of food is often called its *satiety value*. Some people overeat when they are frustrated or disturbed. The satiety or peaceful feeling they get from food tends to quiet and soothe them.

College and university students often show distinct ties between frustration and food. Arriving at school in the fall, most students' spirits are high and they enjoy their new experiences. At this time, the food is considered good. (This is the time for the foodservice department to save money on its budget.) However, as the newness wears off, students miss home and loved ones more. The rigors of classes, assignments, term papers, and examinations begin to create problems and frustrations, and students begin to take out their frustrations on the food they are getting. Food riots can even result. It is no coincidence that troubles on campus rise with such pressures. Students don't realize that the food they once liked now is cause for great dissatisfaction. (This is now the time to put the money previously saved on the budget into better food.)

The ties between food are even more apparent in prisons or reform institutions. For example, one prison riot was traced to the fact that the foodservice operation ran out of fried chicken for its weekend special and had to substitute another entree.

Many otherwise well-balanced adults have the same reactions. A business executive at a club may find the food totally unacceptable while others at the table enjoy it. The problem may be that frustrations at the office did more to ruin the person's appreciation of the food than the chef, the waiter, or anything else the club did.

Many times institutional food of much higher quality than individuals get at home is criticized for its quality because diners miss the home atmosphere, family, or friends. People learn to eat amid familiar surroundings. There is comfort and security in eating at home. This security and comfort is deeply ingrained and is tied to food. These feelings have been built up over a long period of time. Then, when an individual must eat elsewhere, away from his or her loved ones, there is insecurity, loneliness, and a desire for familiar things associated with food. So it is not always the food that is lacking in quality but environmental factors associated with it. An individual who is hospitalized and ill has little appetite anyway; under the stress of illness and the loss of familiar surroundings, it is not surprising that the hospital's food is often not liked.

Fact and fancy are frequently interwoven in our notions about food. Thus, some individuals eat certain foods because they feel they are beneficial. For instance, many feel they must eat the foods they associate with home in order to stay healthy. Others believe that raw oysters stimulate the sex drive, while saltpeter (potassium nitrate) depresses it.

Food can also have deep religious significance. Unleavened Passover bread (matzo) and kosher foods have deep religious meaning for Jews. Many Seventh Day Adventists and Roman Catholics will not eat meat at certain times. The fact that food and drink may have deep religious significance for some people should be respected.

Appearance, Temperature, Texture, and Consistency

People use senses other than their taste buds to evaluate food. It is often said that people "eat with their eyes," so visual factors may take precedence in creating appealing food. Certainly we often see a dish well before we can smell it. Smelling the aroma actually stimulates our appetite. Once we taste a food, its temperature, texture, and consistency help determine whether we like it. Since the menu planner's goal is to provide the patron with maximum pleasure, making the food appealing is a key part of creating a menu.

Appearance includes things like color, form, and texture (in its visual sense). Colors like red, red-orange, butter-yellow, pink, tan, light or clear green, white, or light brown are said to enhance the appeal of food while purple, violet, yellow-green, mustard yellow, gray, olive, and orange-yellow do not. Colors naturally associated with foods are appealing while colors associated with spoilage or unnaturalness are not. But the chef as artist does not stop here. Contrasts in acceptable colors should be sought. A myriad of bright color in a fruit cup or salad can heighten interest. Freshness in color (what an artist calls "vibrancy") is important, while unnatural combinations or too vivid colors should be avoided.

The form taken by the food is also important. There should be an interesting assortment of forms or shapes on a plate. Variations on a plate, like a slice of baked ham dressed with a small quantity of light brown raisin and shredded pineapple sauce, diced beets with a light gloss or sheen of butter, and mashed sweet potatoes graced with a small spray of parsley will achieve a difference in form and color that is agreeable. But too many mounds, cubes, balls, or similar shapes can cause loss of appeal, just as a picture that is "too busy" may distract from its central theme.

It is also important to have foods of different heights. While this may not be possible to do on one plate (or may cause one plate to become "busy"), it can be achieved by having different heights on different foods. Thus, a salad can be in a deep bowl, or a dessert can be in a parfait glass in order to give contrast to the relatively flat entree plate. Tall garnishes (provided they do not overpower the dish) can also be used to give height to a plate.

It is important that at least some of the foods served retain their natural shapes. Too much pureed or chopped food can resemble baby food. This does not mean that planners should avoid interesting or novel presentations, but they should be sure not to get carried away.

Texture, such as that of kiwi fruit or fork-split English muffins, provides pleasant visual experience. A glistening or shimmering food is often more appealing than a dull one. Butter or other oil coatings, aspics and jellies, and egg liaisons all provide a shimmer.

The creative use of garnishing provides important visual activity, and having different garnishes for different food items is one sign that the menu planner has really put thought into planning the perfect menu.

The *flavor* of food is distinguished primarily by its aroma or odor. While our taste buds can distinguish only four tastes—sweet, sour, bitter, and salt— our noses can distinguish among different aromas with incredible accuracy. The great chef Escoffier was said to have made omelets by stirring them with a fork on which a clove of garlic was impaled. The taste of garlic was so minor, yet so compelling that he single-handedly introduced this "forbidden vegetable" into haute cuisine.

Which flavors are pleasing or disagreeable differ with individuals. Naturally, we are more pleased with flavors with which we are familiar. The intensity of the flavor is also subject to individual preference. Intensity or "sharpness" may be an acquired taste. One may dislike sharp cheeses until one becomes used to the flavor, then one may cherish the flavor. There is a saying about olives that one must eat seven of them before one can appreciate their distinct flavor.

Our senses are sharpest around the ages of 20 to 25 and after this they slowly decline. Actually, there is a spot devoid of taste in the middle of the tongue which grows in size as we age, perhaps from the ingestion of hot or cold foods which kill off the nerve endings. Thus as people age, they may seek out more intensely flavored foods. Because the sweet-and salt-sensing nerves deteriorate first, older people lose their ability to taste these first.

An interesting phenomenon associated with flavor and taste is that some people cannot identify different food items by taste alone; they must see the food while tasting it. This may be why food displays engender such a favorable response from patrons. Certainly the display of foods at a buffet or in a salad bar is apt to stimulate the appetites of many patrons.

Another aspect of taste is the texture and consistency of food. Cooking food breaks down cell walls within the food, softening the texture. Unless carefully monitored, this can result in mushy, overcooked food. *Texture* is the resistance food gives to the crushing action of the jaw. Texture contrasts bring variety to the menu. A crisp salty cracker contrasts nicely with soups; chewy turkey meat is complemented by soft mashed potatoes.

Consistency refers to the surface texture of food. Okra can often have a slimy feel or consistency. Mashed potatoes made without enough liquid have a grainy, pasty consistency that is unappealing. Years ago we drastically overcooked vegetables; for instance, at the turn of the century, most recipes called for cooking asparagus for 40 minutes in water and baking soda. Most people today would find this most unappealing.

Finally, taste is a function of temperature. Serving cold foods cold and hot foods hot not only helps ensure sanitation and food quality, but also can give a pleasing temperature contrast to a meal. Mixing hot and cold foods in a meal provides further contrast and variety. A small cup of cold cucumber salad is an excellent contrast to a hot Indian curry. By serving hot foods hot and cold foods cold, we are not simply providing variety, we are showing the patron that we really care.

Time and Seasonal Considerations

A menu planner is very much constrained by the time of day that the menu will be for. A menu with traditional breakfast items on it will find little appeal at dinner time, except as a novelty. Others menu items are identified with certain times of the year. Others are associated with certain holidays, for example turkey and its fixings with Thanksgiving and Ham with Easter. These items can be put on menus long before and after the specific date of the holiday. Some items are associated with the four seasons. A winter menu may have a very different selection of salads, for example, than might a summer menu. Also, we would expect fewer salad offerings in winter but more soup offerings, especially up north. In sunny Florida and California, we tend not to have this constraint. In fact, tourists tend to enjoy the surprise of seeing summer salads available in the dead of winter.

RATING FOOD PREFERENCES

Patron's food preferences must be considered when planning menus. People are influenced in their preferences by food habits acquired over a long period. Studies have been made of what foods individuals most prefer. These may be helpful to menu planners, but what people say they prefer is not always what they select from menus. The military asked what its personnel said they preferred and, then, in a further study, found that there were significant differences between what people said and what they actually selected. (See **Exhibit 4.2.**)

The Taste Panel

Many operations use taste panels made up of their own personnel to taste various dishes—which might be placed on menus—to see if the item has good enough appeal to warrant featuring it. Often score sheets are used with the tasters rating factors such as flavor, consistency, temperature, color and others

Exhibit 4.2   Food Preference Questionnaire

FOOD PREFERENCE QUESTIONNAIRE

Now I am going to ask you to rate the food you just ate. For each food, will you tell me if you liked it extremely, liked it very much, liked it moderately, liked it slightly, neither liked nor disliked it, disliked it slightly, disliked it moderately, disliked it very much, or disliked it extremely. This card has a list of these ratings. (Interviewer circle number.)

a.	What main dish? _____	1	2	3	4	5	6	7	8	9
b.	Any other main dish? _____	1	2	3	4	5	6	7	8	9
c.	Vegetables? _____	1	2	3	4	5	6	7	8	9
d.	Drinks? _____	1	2	3	4	5	6	7	8	9
e.	Breads or cereals? _____	1	2	3	4	5	6	7	8	9
f.	Potatoes or starches? _____	1	2	3	4	5	6	7	8	9
g.	Salads? _____	1	2	3	4	5	6	7	8	9
h.	Soup? _____	1	2	3	4	5	6	7	8	9
i.	Desserts? _____	1	2	3	4	5	6	7	8	9

For breakfast, ask only for main dishes, beverages, breads and cereals, and fruits.

Overall, how would you rate the meal you just ate, using the same scale? (Circle)

1   2   3   4   5   6   7   8   9

How did this meal compare with other Army meals you have had?

❑ Much better?   ❑ About the same?   ❑ Much worse?
❑ A little better?   ❑ A little worse?

Respondent's name _____   Number _____

Interviewer _____

SOURCE: United States Army

with a scale of 0 to 9. The individual scores are totalled to see how well each dish did. If there seems to be a problem, individual scores can be checked as well as the scores for specific factors to see why a dish might not score well. Often scores are interpreted as follows:

9: Like extremely

8: Like very much

7: Like moderately

6: Like slightly

5: Neither like nor dislike

4: Dislike slightly

3: Dislike moderately

2: Dislike very much

1: Dislike extremely

0: Discard

Not all individuals have a good sense of taste, so panel members should be selected carefully. Some lack good taste perception, lacking in the ability to distinguish subtle differences of one or more of the four basic tastes: sweet, sour, bitter, and salt. They might have poor flavor memories so they cannot carry over flavors to evaluate differences between two or more samples. Smokers often have taste problems. Alcohol dulls the taste, as can a cold, fatigue, and stress.

A young person may not be as good a judge as an older one, because flavor identification requires experience. Older people often have more experience, but may lose good taste perception.

Taste panels are best conducted at 11:30 AM and 4:30 PM, when people are apt to be most hungry. The room in which the taste panel works should be quiet and comfortable. Each judge should have a separate place in which to taste and score, unless a panel discussion is desired as the tasting goes on. A score sheet is shown in **Exhibit 4.3**.

Where only flavor, consistency, texture, and temperature are being evaluated, judges may be blindfolded and asked to judge a food without being able to see it. Often the elimination of appearance can make quite a difference in what a judge thinks of a food. The saying, "We eat with our eyes" is often proven in such a test, since a food found not too appealing when tasted and seen, may be quite acceptable when one does not see it. However, the opposite result can also be true.

Sometimes guests are given complimentary samples to see how well they like new items. Sampling is usually not as formal as a taste panel, and guests may simply be asked if they like it or not.

Exhibit 4.3 Scoring Rice Pudding

Date _____	**ITEM: OLD FASHIONED RICE PUDDING**	Menu No. <u>512</u> Scorer <u>LHK</u>

Characteristic to Score	Score (0 to 9)	Comments
Flavor	6	Little eggy; may have been baked at too high a temperature; either lower temperature or bake in pan of water.
Color	8	Good; also good sheen.
Texture	5	Slightly watery and some openness showing some syneresis. Rice soft and visible in grains.
Form	8	Good; soft, yet solid. Holds shape.
Temperature	7	Served at room temperature; try chilled or try slightly warm.
Consistency	6	Slightly tough perhaps because of too high a baking temperature or too much heat.
Total Score	40	

General Comments:

Cut down on baking temp. and bake in another pan of water; try reducing eggs & replacing with yolks to tighten up more and retard breakdown.

PATRON EXPECTATIONS

When most patrons look at a menu they conjure up specific images of what they expect. They should not be disappointed. If the menu item is accompanied with a short description, this can help in indicating what it is. Service personnel can also do much to indicate this.

The purpose of a menu is to communicate to the patron what is offered and, in commercial operations, the price. Menu terms should be simple, clear, and graphic, presenting an exact description of what the patron is to get. Patron expectations and what is served should coincide. The patron may misinterpret unclear terms. Or, the menu writer may mean one thing, but the patron may interpret it differently, especially if there are regional meanings applied to cooking terms or certain food flavors. There should be no ambiguity or confusion. Nor should descriptions be overstated.

If foreign words are used, the writer must be sure they are explained and understood by patrons. An explanation may be given in English below a term. *Keep the language simple* is a cardinal rule in menu planning.

Restaurant critic, John Rosson, has said that readers should be able to read menus quickly and understand what the terms mean.[1] He discourages the use of ambiguous terms, such as "meats dressed with the chef's special sauce" or, for a pie, "(made from) a secret family recipe, handed down from generation to generation" saying that they seem phony and may even be insulting. Rosson advises the use of descriptions that clarify without being overdone. Terms that mean little or nothing to the average diner should not be used. Examples are items called "The Navajo Trail" and "The Ocean Blue." The first might involve beef and the other fish, but they could just as easily be a Mexican platter and a plate of tempura seaweed. The item's name should leave little doubt as to what will be served.

When a menu says the steaks come from prime beef, this means the beef grade is prime and not a lower grade. A bisque is a cream soup flavored with shellfish, yet one company producing canned soup named a product "tomato bisque," which is essentially false. Every menu planner should be sure of the terms used and what they mean when they are put on the menu. Too much license is frequently taken in the use of terms when writing menus. Selecting words to describe a food and give it glamor must be done carefully. To try to make a curry sound more exotic by calling it "Curry of Chicken, Bombay," without using the typical ingredients that a curry from Bombay, India, would have, is not encouraged. The right curry seasoning, accompaniments (especially the small, dried fish called Bombay duck), and other factors should be a part of the menu item.

Often menus present the name of the item in large letters and then give a description in smaller letters, as in **Exhibit 4.4**. Further clarification of the dish might also come from the server, who might explain that the rice is served as a mound in the middle of a large bowl containing the gumbo. (The method of item presentation will be discussed further in Chapter 7.)

Exhibit 4.4 Menu Description

SHRIMP GUMBO WITH RICE

A thick soup made of shrimp, tomatoes, okra, and other vegetables delicately seasoned with filé, a seasoning containing ground sassafras leaves, served over a mound of fluffy rice.

Truth-in-Menu Standards

In some cities and states, *truth-in-menu*, or *accuracy-in-menu* laws govern menu descriptions. These laws are the results of governmental interest in menu irregularities, such as indicating one item on a menu and actually serving another. These irregularities are perceived as *misrepresentations,* which may benefit the operator at the expense of the consumer. Some of these laws are state interpretations of Food and Drug Administration standards. They act as guides to menu planners when it is time to write the menu.

The federal government's Pure Food, Drug, and Cosmetic Act of 1938 forbids the use of any pictorial or language description on a container that misrepresents the contents. No grade or other term can be used that is not representative of the product. For example, if a label says, "Georgia's choicest peaches" and the peaches are not graded at least Choice, the product is considered mislabeled because of the similarity of the terms *choicest* and *Choice.* If any nutritional claim or nutrient value is given, the claimed value must be a part of the food. (For more on truth-in-menu guidelines, see Appendix A.)

The federal government also has developed *standards of identity* that define what a food must be if a specific name is used for it. For example, food labeled as egg noodles *must* contain at least 3.25 percent dry egg solids. If the word *cheese* is used, the product must contain 51 percent or more of milk fat, based on the dry weight of the product. The term *cheese food* must be used for food that cannot meet this regulation. Standards of identity exist for all foods except those considered common, such as sugar.

Many states have adopted laws that clarify federal standards.

Menu Pricing

Menus must often be priced to meet patrons' expectations. Some patrons are very price conscious and a menu must meet their expectations of perceived value. Most patrons want to get the most for their money. The price paid should represent an adequate value in patrons' minds, and they will not be happy if they do not feel the value is there. However, menus must also be priced to cover costs in institutional operations and ensure profits for commercial ones. Since pricing is such an important subject, it will be discussed in depth in Chapter 6.

SUMMARY

The perfect menu is one that weighs the various constraining factors to menu design and ideally balances them. Many of the factors involved in menu planning seem contradictory. Like a good politician, the menu planner must produce a solution that keeps everyone happy. Patron needs and desires must be balanced against the needs of the owners to make money. Equipment constraints must be balanced against the need for a variety of choices. The skills and abilities of the staff must be balanced against the desire by the patron for new and interesting choices.

QUESTIONS

1. What are some personnel considerations that will affect the success of a menu?
2. Why might a patron who orders a meal of broiled chicken, mashed potatoes and gravy, and a fruit cup in a restaurant not like the same meal when in a hospital?
3. Why is it important to know whether a menu can help satisfy the physiological, psychological, and social needs of patrons?
4. Look at an actual menu's items and descriptions. Are explanations adequate in predicting what will be served? How do items served together complement each other?
5. Name five important considerations discussed in this chapter that anyone planning a menu should give special emphasis. Why did you select these and not others?

❦ 5 ❦

Cost Controls in Menu Planning

Objectives

After reading this chapter, you should be able to:

1. Explain how cost factors affect menu planning.

2. Describe how food and labor costs can be ascertained and controlled.

3. Describe cost control factors unique to commercial operations or nonprofit institutions.

INTRODUCTION

Of all the limitations placed on menu planners, costs are probably the most challenging. Normally, menu planners are concerned mostly with food and labor costs. But other costs are also important, such as the cost of energy, equipment, nonfood supplies, and storage costs. Whenever possible, the menu should reflect the overall costs of running an operation, whether the operation is institutional or commercial.

The menu planner has to know the operational costs to stay within a price budget or cost allowance. The costs of running a commercial operation must be more than covered in the budget if a profit is to be made. Cost is also the basis for pricing many menus. If costs are not known, selling prices are difficult to determine. The planner of the institutional menu who pays no attention to costs is flirting with disaster. This is because institutional or noncommercial establishments usually must operate within a budget, and costs are tightly controlled.

OBTAINING OPERATIONAL COSTS

All costs must be known to be controlled. Managers must identify costs, determine their magnitude and frequency, and then, if they are too high, take steps to reduce them. It is important to recognize that locating such information is not, in itself, a control. It only indicates that control is needed. Such information about costs indicates a symptom, not a cure. Reports such as budgets, daily food cost reports, precosting sheets, financial statements, and payroll figures are tools used by foodservice managers to analyze data and root out any food-cost problems.

Once a menu is planned, priced, and analyzed, it can be implemented, and a series of operational functions can be set in motion. These functions are purchasing, receiving, storage, issuing, preparation/production, service, and cleanup. During each of these steps, controls must be established to assure that only planned costs occur and that the menu price or meal charge, if any, gives the desirable return. Today computers can be used to do much of this.

In the *purchasing* function, the proper kind of food and its cost, quantity, and quality must be determined and the right supplier found. If the wrong kind, quantity, or quality of food is bought at the wrong cost, the menu will not have the desired end result.

Efficiency during the *receiving* is essential to see that exactly what was ordered is obtained. This also starts a series of accounting and inventory steps that are important to cost control.

Controls must be placed on *storage* procedures so there will be no loss as a result of spoilage, contamination, or theft.

Product *issuing* must be exact to control costs of foods moving into preparation or production.

Preparation and *production* are usually controlled by standardized recipes and proper application of procedures. Careless acts such as leaving potatoes too long in a peeler or overcooking a roast results in loss of product quality and waste.

Calculating Food Cost

Two food cost figures are often used. One is the *total* or *overall cost of goods sold,* or *total food cost.* The other is a food cost for individual menu items or for a group of menu items. Both have different uses.

Total (Overall) Cost of Goods Sold

Total or overall food cost is usually stated as both a dollar figure and as a percent of total sales. The dollar value is most often calculated from beginning and ending inventory and total food purchases, as shown below. The percent can be calculated from this total figure, if the total sales for the same period are known.

Beginning inventory	$ 62,016.25
+ Purchases plus transportation, delivery, and other charges	+ 113,183.22
Total food available for period	$ 175,199.47
− Ending inventory	− 59,866.21
Total food cost	$ 115,333.26

To find the total *food cost percentage*, divide the total food cost by total sales.

$$\frac{\text{cost of good sold (food cost)}}{\text{total sales}} = \text{food cost percentage}$$

If total sales were $350,000, then the food cost percentage would be 32.95 percent ($115,333.26 ÷ $350,000 = 0.32952, or 32.95%).

The total food cost can also be obtained if a *daily food cost report* is maintained. The cost of goods sold and food cost percentage are kept from the start of the period, accumulated up to the last day of the period. The *daily food cost* is obtained for this report by totaling the value of issues from storerooms and adding direct deliveries. Suppose issues total $12,212.34 and direct deliveries (direct from receiving dock to the production area for use) are $900.87; the total food cost is $13.113.21 ($12,212.34 + $900.87). If sales for that day are $45,840, the food cost percentage is 28.6 percent ($13,113.21 ÷ $45,840 = 0.2860). Comparative data is also usually given such as food cost a month ago, a year ago, etc. **Exhibit 5.1** shows part of a daily food cost report.

Exhibit 5.1 Daily Food Cost Report with Comparative Data

Date	Direct Purchases	Storeroom Issues	Total Food Cost		Sales		Food Cost Percent	
			Today	To Date	Today	To Date	Today	To Date
5/1	$159.15	$545.68	$704.83		$2,113.23		33.4	
5/2	206.22	611.17	817.39	$1,522.22	2,844.11	$4,957.34	28.7	30.7
5/3	185.34	589.13	774.47	2,296.69	2,788.10	7,745.44	29.6	

	Food Cost Percent			
	Last Month		Last Year	
	Daily	Accumulated	Daily	Accumulated
4/1	31.2	30.8	32.3	31.8
4/2	32.1	31.0	31.9	31.7
4/3	33.0	32.6	32.1	31.8

If the labor cost is included, the word *labor* is added to the title and similar figures showing labor cost are presented. The report is usually compiled by the food and beverage or accounting departments; it takes someone with experience and time to compile it. Copies go to management of the operation, management in the foodservice department responsible for food cost (and labor cost, if compiled), and to accounting, if compiled by the food and beverage department.

An even more complex daily food cost report can be prepared by breaking down food cost into different categories, such as dairy, fish, meats, and bakery. This helps pinpoint food cost production problems by showing which category is out of line. A total overall figure is also given.

Sometimes a similar dollar and percentage figure are obtained in advance of actual operation by *precosting*, or estimating future costs. If management knows that daily sales average $35,000 and makes the estimate for 30 days, then total sales will be $1,050,000. A menu is planned to run a 30 percent food cost, where projected total food cost is $315,000. Precosting figures helps managers in overall planning. For instance, suppose a large chain is planning to run a special on prime rib, but wants to estimate what the impact on food cost will be if the ribs jump in cost by $0.05 a pound. The result can be seen by making the proper calculations.

Another way of precosting is called *averaging*. It is only helpful in giving a figure on food cost when a limited menu is used and the menu is separated into very similar or like items in each group of items. To average, one should have a good idea of what the sales mix is on the sale of various items sold. One must also know the food cost percentage for each member of a group of menu items. **Exhibit 5.2** shows how to find the overall food cost for one day's sales. Note that once one has the percent of dollar sales for each category

Exhibit 5.2 Averaging Food Costs

Item	Sales	Percent of Dollar Sales	Percent of Food Cost
Hamburgers	$ 875	40.8	39.0
Milkshakes	410	19.1	32.0
French fries	550	25.6	27.0
Beverages	312	14.5	30.0
Total	$2,147	100.0	

Then, the following calculation can be made to get average or overall food cost:

Hamburgers	$0.408 \times 0.39 = 0.159$
Milkshakes	$0.191 \times 0.32 = 0.061$
French fries	$0.256 \times 0.27 = 0.069$
Beverages	$0.145 \times 0.3\ \ = \underline{0.044}$

0.333, or 33.3% Overall food cost

The steps in making this calculation are:
1. Predict total sales and the percent contribution each item or group makes to sales.
2. Calculate the food cost percentage for each item or group.
3. Multiply each item's or group's percent food cost times its percentage of sales.
4. Total these results for an average food cost percentage.

and its percent food cost, the calculation is merely one of multiplication and addition.

Often in *budgeting*, we estimate future total food cost. This may be done based on previous figures, or a percentage of a specific allocation of funds. As an example of the first, a hospital knows that its food cost runs $6.25 per patient-day, and based on an estimate of the number of patients expected during an operating period, makes the calculation $6.25 \times 350,000 estimated patient-days = $2,187,500 total food cost budgeted. For the second, an example might be where a prison allocates in its budget $4,000,000 to the foodservice department for operation for one month. Historically, the department knows its food cost is usually 55 percent, labor 28 percent, and other expenses 17 percent. The total food cost allocation is therefore $2,200,000 (0.55 \times $4,000,000).

The simplest way of compiling total food cost is the *spindle method*. Here a food service takes all purchase invoices, tacks them onto a spindle, and adds them up later, the total becoming the food cost. While only an approximation, because it does not consider foods in inventory, it gives management a ball park idea of the total food cost, especially if kept over a substantial period of time. **Exhibit 5.3** shows how such a simplified method works out, giving both dollar values and percentage values based on sales.

Exhibit 5.3 Approximate Daily Food Costs and Percentages

Date	Sales		Food Purchases		Food Cost Percent	
	Today	To Date	Today	To Date	Today	To Date
Oct. 1	$ 882.75		$254.16		29	
Oct. 2	901.30	$1,784.05	312.86	$ 567.02	35	32
Oct. 3	792.45	2,576.50	301.20	868.22	38	34
Oct. 4	922.20	3,498.70	295.18	1,163.40	32	33
Oct. 5	1,006.10	4,504.80	452.13	1,615.53	45	36
Oct. 6	831.35	5,336.15	286.17	1,901.70	34	36

Individual or Group Item Food Cost

The cost of food items may be obtained from: 1) the purchase price of foods purchased per portion or per item; 2) calculations based on the number of portions derived from a single purchase unit; 3) recipe costing; and 4) yield tests.

Calculating Portion Cost

It is relatively easy to find the cost of a food portion if it is purchased on a portion basis. For example, if five 10-ounce sirloin steaks are purchased for $22.50, it is easy to determine that the portion cost is $4.50. This simple calculation is often used.

Calculating Portions Obtained

When a unit that contains a specific number of portions is purchased, the portion cost is obtained by dividing the cost of the unit by the number of portions. This is simple, except when there are food losses to calculate and additions in weight because of added ingredients, absorption, or other factors. In such cases the percent of loss or decrease must be considered if an accurate food portion cost is to be obtained.

For instance, if a case containing six #10 cans of peach halves costs $47.40, the cost per can is $7.90 ($47.40 ÷ 6 cans = $7.90). If there are 35 peach halves per can, the portion cost is $7.90 ÷ 35 peach halves, or $0.23 per half.

Allowing for cooking loss in cost calculations can complicate the job. If preblanched frozen potato strips cost $0.30 a pound and they lose a third of their weight in frying, the cost per pound of finished potatoes is $0.45 ($0.30 ÷ 67% yield (0.67) = $0.45). The cost of the frying oil absorbed must also be considered; most frozen preblanched potatoes absorb about 6 percent of their weight in oil. Thus, 1 pound of finished potatoes has about an ounce of new frying oil in it (16 oz × 0.06 = 0.96 oz).[1] If the cost per pound of frying oil is $1.00, 1 ounce costs $0.06 ($1.00 ÷ 16 oz = $0.062). Thus, for 17 ounces of finished product—16 ounces of potatoes and one ounce of fat—there is a cost of $0.45 + 0.062, or $0.51. An ounce then costs $0.51 ÷ 17 oz, or $0.03 per ounce. If a 2-ounce portion is served, the cost per portion will be $0.06.

Recipe Costing

If used correctly, a standardized recipe will give a known quantity and known quality of food. It should name all ingredients and the amount of each that is needed. It is then easy to calculate the cost of each ingredient and add up these costs to get a total food cost for the recipe. Since a standardized recipe gives the *yield* or resulting number of portions, all one has to do is divide the yield into the total cost to get a *yield cost* or *portion cost*. **Exhibit 5.4** shows a standardized recipe costed out. In some cases, an added cost of 2 percent of the total ingredient cost is added to the ingredient cost to pay for the cost of seasonings, frying fat, and so forth. Other operations add up to a 10 percent additional cost for seasonings, frying fat, garnish, or crackers.

Exhibit 5.4   Standardized Recipe Costed Out

Barbecued Spareribs
Yield: 10 portions
Portion: ½ **lb**

Ingredients	Amount		Ingredient Cost	Portion Cost	Method
Hoisin sauce	2 oz	57 g	$3.12/pint*	$ 0.39	1. Combine all the ingredients in a large bowl.
Bean sauce	2 oz	57 g	2.47/pint	0.31	
Apple sauce	2 oz	57 g	2.38/gal	0.07	2. Score the ribs with a sharp knife. Place the ribs in the marinade. Marinate them for at least 4 hours at a product temperature of 45°F (7.2°C) or lower in refrigerated storage.
Catsup	5 oz	142 g	3.16/gal	0.25	
Soy sauce	2 oz	57 g	1.56/pint	0.20	
Rice wine	4 oz	114 g	9.89/gal	0.62	
Peanut oil	3 oz	85 g	4.43/gal	0.21	
Red food coloring (optional)	½ oz	14 g	1.29/8 oz	0.08	
Ginger, minced	1 oz	28 g	3.49/lb	0.22	3. Place the ribs in a smoker at 425°F (220°C) for 30 minutes. Reduce the heat 375°F (190°C) and continue smoking the ribs for 50 minutes.
Scallions, minced	8 oz	226 g	2.12/lb	1.06	
Garlic cloves, minced	6 oz	170 g	2.29/lb	0.86	
Sugar	4 oz	114 g	1.64/lb	0.41	
Salt	1 oz	28 g	0.96/lb	0.06	
Pork spareribs, trimmed	5 lb	2.27 kg	2.36/lb	11.80	4. Brush the honey on the ribs during the last 5 minutes of smoking. Final internal product temperature must reach 150°F (65.5°C) or higher.
Honey	8 oz	226 g	4.21/gal	0.53	
					5. Slice the ribs between the bones and serve.

*16 ounces = 1 pint

Reprinted with permission from *HACCP Reference Book.* Copyright © 1993 by The Educational Foundation of the National Restaurant Association. Recipe originally adapted with permission from *The New Professional Chef, Fifth Edition.* Copyright © 1991 by the Culinary Institute of America. Published by Van Nostrand Reinhold, NY.

It is usual to round off ingredient costs to the nearest cent. Portion costs are usually carried out to $^1/_{10}$ of a cent. Many operations have a practice of pricing out all recipes and then checking these every six months to see whether they are accurate. Some simplify a recalculation every six months by comparing it to the *national price index*. If the index rises or drops a specific percentage, the total recipe cost is raised or lowered by this percentage and the portion or yield cost is recalculated. Even using this method, it is advisable to do a complete revision every year.

It is often necessary to combine portion costs. While a steak may cost $3.10 if it is served with a salad, french fries, roll and butter, and beverage, these must be added to the steak cost to get a cost for the entire menu item. Often, the exact cost of all added food is calculated and added to give the total cost. Some operators simply calculate the average cost of extras and add this figure to similar items.

When patrons help themselves at a salad bar, there may be some question as to how to cost out a meal. The usual procedure is to keep an account of the cost of foods in the salad bar and keep another count of patrons served from it. Dividing the number of patrons into the total cost of the salad bar will give an average cost per patron. This is then added to the basic entree cost.

Conducting a Yield Test

A *yield test* is made to see how much edible food is obtained from raw, unprocessed items, plus cost per portion. Often those making the test must know the amount of product obtained in some common measures or containers. Some of these are given in Appendix B along with the amount in some common measures frequently used in yield testing.

Making a yield test may be simple or complex. A simple example is where a menu planner wants to know the food cost of a 2-ounce portion of cranberry sauce, if the cranberries are purchased fresh. Five pounds of cranberries costing $4.70, five pounds of sugar at $1.25, and 1 quart of water are used; thus, the cost is $5.95. The yield test shows that the yield is 11 lb, 12 oz, or 188 oz, or 94 portions. The cost of a 2-ounce portion is therefore $0.063 ($5.95 ÷ 94 = $ 0.063). (Since only the food cost is desired, the cost of labor, heat energy, etc., is not added in.)

A more complex yield test occurs often in cutting out meat portions, where fat, bone, trim, and other items are obtained in addition to the desired portions. A cutting shrink also occurs. **Exhibit 5.5** shows the results of a cutting test made on a No. 180 boneless strip loin to get boneless strip steaks. Note the by-products, including the suet, have a value that must be deducted from the original cost. In this test, the cost of the labor is included so the buyer can get an idea of the cost per 10-ounce steak to compare with already cut 10-ounce steaks that might be obtained instead.

In some cases, evaporation and trim contribute to weight loss. It is therefore wise to not always take the original purchase price as the cost of the item in a yield test, but to take the cost of the item as it goes into the test.

Exhibit 5.5   Precooking Yield Test on Boneless Strip

Boneless Strip, No. 180, 12 lb, $3.80/lb				$45.60
Yield:				
Trimmed meat	16 oz	$2.60/lb	$2.60	
Suet	12 oz	0.08/lb	0.06	
Cutting loss	4 oz			
	32 oz (2 lb)			2.66
Strip steaks: 10 lb, or 16 10-oz steaks				$42.94
Cost of labor @ $0.30/lb				3.00
Cost of steaks				45.94
Cost per lb				4.59
Cost per 10-oz steak				2.87

Getting a product down to its *edible portion* (EP) state from its *as purchased* (AP) state in yield tests does not always produce the ultimate *as served* (AS) cost. Thus, if a No. 180 boneless strip were trimmed of 12 ounces of fat before roasting, the total cost upon use would be $45.60 − $0.06, or $45.54. A 25 percent shrink occurs during roasting, and there is a further 5 percent carving loss when the meat is portioned for service. The yield cost of a 6-ounce AS portion would be:

12 lb − 12 oz fat = 11 lb 4 oz or 180 oz × (100% − 25% shrink) = 135 oz

135 oz × (100% − 5% cutting loss) = 128.25 oz = 21.4 6-oz portions

$$\frac{\$45.54 \text{ cost of meat}}{21.4 \text{ portions}} = \$2.13 \text{ per portion}$$

Once yields are known, menu planners may not need to repeat them again and again. However, some products can produce very different yields when they are used from time to time. For instance, very young, tender spinach cooks down to a much smaller quantity than older spinach with coarser leaves and texture, so it is wise to make spot checks.

OBTAINING LABOR COSTS

As mentioned previously, labor cost is a major factor in menu planning for both commercial and noncommercial operations. Finding the right quantity and quality of employees at the right cost is a challenge to all foodservice managers.

The menu planner must also be aware of labor cost constraints. Labor costs can be high if the menu requires elaborate preparations. Also, menu items that are complicated to prepare require skilled labor, which is not always readily available. Scheduling is another factor not easily controlled by the menu. Rather, it is controlled by forecasting how many patrons can be expected for various meal times.

The labor factor can prove less of a constraint if good hiring procedures are used and thorough training programs are implemented.

Monitoring Labor Costs

The menu planner has considerable control over how much labor must be used in food preparation and, to a degree, how much may be used in service. If some foods on the menu require complex prepreparation and production labor, the cost goes up. Simple preparation will save on labor. It is also possible to use purchasing to reduce labor needs. Purchasing frozen instead of fresh leaf spinach can save on washing the latter, and buying shelled rather than unshelled walnuts also saves labor.

Convenience foods can be used to reduce labor needed to produce menu items. In a number of cases, the products are as good or even better as products made from scratch. The foods also standardize quality and often standardize portions. However, the food cost of the convenience product is often higher than that of the similar products made on the premises, and menu planners must evaluate this extra cost to see whether the convenience product is within cost restraints. Besides labor saved by the convenience product, menu planners also need to add in the cost of energy and perhaps other costs that enter into the preparation of items.

Managers must always keep an eye on service requirements. Certain menu items require much more labor than others. Some items require more tableware and so increase not only service time but also the time needed to wash and put away extra dishes.

Labor cost is made up of wages, salaries, payroll taxes, employee meals, and other costs and benefits. Normally, labor cost for a commercial operation is calculated as a dollar cost and then stated as a percentage of sales. For instance, if labor is \$665 and sales are \$2,500, the labor cost is 26.6 percent of sales (\$665 ÷ \$2,500 = 0.266 × 100 = 26.6 percent). Often other factors, such as the labor cost per meal, per individual item, per patron served, or the average labor cost per employee may be required to accurately determine total labor costs. Many institutions that do not work on percentages use a dollar labor cost per meal or per patron.

Different kinds of labor costs will be determined. *Direct labor cost* is the cost directly involved in producing, serving, or otherwise handling a menu item. We often calculate the direct labor cost in producing a particular food item and combine this with food cost to get what is called a *prime cost*, or total cost for preparing a menu item.

Labor cost can vary in food services. Some clubs have a labor cost that is more than 50 percent of sales because they must have considerable labor on hand, regardless of whether members are there or not. A takeout unit, however, may have a labor cost of 15 percent. Deciding what is proper must, therefore, be left up to each manager.

In some cases, instead of using a labor cost figure stated in dollar values, a figure representing items produced per hour of labor is used. This is often used by hospitals. Thus, if a small hospital in one week used 5,664 hours of labor to produce 1,416 meals, the meals produced per labor hour used would be 4 (5,664 ÷ 1,416 = 4). However, other types of units—and even some hospitals—might want to know how many units of a particular menu item are produced per labor hour. Thus, if a pantry worker produces 60 sandwiches in 4 hours, the worker productivity figure in making sandwiches is 15 per labor hour used.

CONTROLLING COSTS

For any type of foodservice operation, controlling costs is vital. Generally, both commercial and noncommercial operations budget costs. They have slightly different reasons for doing so, but cost control is vital to the success of the menu. If labor and food costs consistently cannot be controlled, the menu may not be right for the facility.

Institutional Cost Control

Nonprofit operations usually do not use a percentage of food cost for information and control as much as commercial ones do. When they do calculate a percentage of raw food expenditures against income or the budgeted allowance, the food cost frequently runs 50 percent or more of total costs. This can happen when some institutions are subsidized and costs other than those for food and labor may be minimized.

Cash Budgeting

Normally, institutional food services, such as hospitals, operate on budgeted cash allowances per meal, per bed, or per person per day for an established period. Amounts in dollars are budgeted for food, labor, and other costs. These will usually be allocated for a month, year, or some other set period and then be broken down into an allowed cost per day for food, labor, and other costs. For instance, suppose a yearly allowance of $3,555 per person is made for food and all other costs. This allowance is broken down as food, 50 percent; labor, 34 percent; and other costs, 16 percent. The budget will then allow $9.74 per day for food and other per-person costs divided for spending as $4.87 for food, $3.31 for labor, and $1.60 for other costs. This daily cost might be further divided, as shown in **Exhibit 5.6**.

Exhibit 5.6   Daily Per-Person Food Allowance

	Breakfast	Lunch	Dinner	Total
Food (50%)	$1.08	$1.08	$2.80	$4.96
Labor (34%)	0.75	0.75	1.75	3.25
Other (16%)	0.40	0.40	0.73	1.53
Total (100%)	$2.23	$2.23	$5.28	$9.74

An institution might divide the $9.74 equally between the three meals of the day, for an allowance of $3.25 per meal. This might be broken down per meal to $1.65 for food, $1.01 for labor, and $0.59 for other costs. The annual allowance would be $3,555, with $1,759 allocated for food, $1,176 for labor, and $416 for other costs per person.

Commercial Cost Control

Commercial food services usually operate on a cost allowance based on a percentage of sales. Often, a food cost allowance may be 35 percent of sales or of the selling price, and the labor cost allowance 30 percent of sales or the selling price, for a combined 65 percent. Many authorities agree that exceeding 65 percent may spell trouble for an operation. Some even recommend that the combined percentage allowance be lower because of the consistent rise in the percentage of other costs, such as for supplies or rent. **Exhibit 5.7** shows a profit-and-loss statement for a commercial operation. While food and labor costs fall within the norm, other costs do not, and the profit is low (1.4 percent). Other costs, some beyond the control of the menu planner, are eating up the profit.

Precosting has become one way in which the menu planner can check to see how a menu might do. The menu can then be changed if the precosting information does not give the desired answer. Good precosting requires a good forecast of the sales for menu items—this forecast is often called the *sales mix*—and then a precise indication of costs for these menu items. Some operations are able to use precosting to make quite accurate forecasts of what will happen.

With the increased use of computers, the process of precosting has been simplified. The computer can do much of the detailed work and come up with a fairly good prediction of what will occur. There are a number of precosting programs available to foodservice operators. (The use of computer precosting is discussed in Chapter 13.)

Controlling Food Costs

There are a number of factors that can cause high food costs. Improper purchasing, poor inventory control, inaccurate forecasting, waste, a lack of portion control, poor receiving procedures, a failure to follow standardized recipes, poor production procedures, a lack of good selling and service, poor security, and improper selection of menu items can all cause undesirable food costs.

Forecasting

Forecasting is a necessary step in menu planning. After menu items are selected, it is helpful to forecast how many of each will sell. This way the planner can forecast whether the menu will make the necessary profit for a commercial operation or satisfy the budgetary needs for an institutional food service.

There are rhythms in patronage in almost every type of food service. For example, payday may bring out a lot of workers; there is always less illness

Exhibit 5.7 Profit-and-Loss Statement

Sales				
Food	$366,412	73%		
Bar	138,222	27		
Total sales			$504,634	100.0%
Cost of sales				
Food	$128,944	35%		
Bar	29,978	22		
Total cost of sales			$158,922	31.5%
Gross profit			$345,712	68.5%
Operational expenses				
Wages	$151,402	30.0%		
Vacation and retirement	10,093	2.0		
Payroll taxes	5,407	1.0		
Employee meals	10,067	2.0		
Salaries	12,617	2.5		
Supplies	15,008	3.0		
Maintenance and repair	7,511	1.5		
Laundry and uniforms	11,608	2.3		
Advertising	2,418	0.5		
Dishes, glassware, etc.	7,710	1.5		
Heat, light, and power	15,001	3.0		
Office expenses	7,065	1.4		
Total operational expenses			$255,547	50.6%
Occupancy expenses				
Capital costs (interest, mortgage)	$ 15,140	3.0		
Rent	35,327	7.0		
Insurance	2,487	0.5		
Depreciation	20,187	4.0		
Taxes	10,008	2.0		
Total occupancy expenses			$ 83,149	16.5%
Total operational and occupancy expenses			$338,696	67.1%
Net profits	$ 7,016	1.4%		

on that day, and in-plant or office foodservice operations can increase production. College dormitories often are nearly empty on weekends with students going home or eating out. Resorts and operations on well-traveled highways can plan for an increase in business during summer, when vacations start, or when holiday travel begins.

Hospitals can expect lower counts just before a holiday because patients delay entering so they can be home on that day. A race track can expect a capacity crowd on the day of a big race, and a stadium will expect one on the day of a big football game. People tend to eat out more on certain holidays than on others. Mother's Day is a big day for many foodservices, while Christmas is not; many close for the latter. There is also a rise and fall in business done by days of the week, depending on location and patronage. Forecasting in these cases is somewhat simplified, but it is always somewhat uncertain. Some software forecasting programs are available for the computer.

A calculation can be made based on the *probability* of increased or decreased patronage. For instance, suppose a club is running a six-day bridge tournament. The club has presold 350 tickets, and the maximum number of patrons the operation can serve per day is 600. The manager estimates the number served per day between 350 and 600. The manager then estimates the probability of each number actually being sold. (These probabilities must add up to 100 percent.) Each estimate of people served is multiplied by its probability to arrive at an average factor. These factors are averaged out to the number most likely to be served each day, in this case 470. These numbers are plotted on a *probability chart* as shown in **Exhibit 5.8**.

If a manager can get some kind of firm base or estimate, it is easier to make a good forecast. In the example, there was a base of 350 tickets to use. An airline has a passenger count based on ticket sales; a banquet manager will have a reservations count as well as experience on what to expect as far as no-shows and walk-ins.

Weather can affect a probability forecast. For foodservice operations in busy shopping areas or near large office buildings, a clear, warm, bright day can bring people out. If it is cold, rainy, or snowing the place may be almost empty.

Promotions can also act to swell volume. A drive-in may offer a bargain price for several days on a product, and the manager should know that the operation will have to gear up to take care of it. A hotel may have a special promotion in its dining areas, offering an early bird price between 4:30 and 6:30 PM. It has to be prepared to handle the increased business such a promotion may bring in. The problem is, of course, to assess *how well* the promotion will work. To hold a promotion, have it work—in terms of increased patronage—and then not be able to handle the business properly can be as effective in *turning away* business as a well-handled promotion can be in creating it.

Exhibit 5.8 Probability Chart

	Maximum Number Served	Probability	Average Factor
Day 1	600	10%	60.0
Day 2	550	15%	82.5
Day 3	500	20%	100.0
Day 4	450	25%	112.5
Day 5	400	20%	80.0
Day 6	350	10%	35.0
Totals	2,850	100%	470.0

The menu planner should realize that good forecasting is necessary to indicate how much food should be produced. Poor forecasting can cause over- or underproduction. Overproduction results in waste and loss; underproduction means that some patrons may be denied something they want.

Portion Control

Controlling the size of portions can control food costs. Management is responsible for establishing portion size for the menu item and seeing that this portion is served.

There are standard portions for many different foods. For instance, a standard portion of vegetables is usually 3 ounces, or about one-half cup. An oven-baked potato, or a portion of mashed potatoes, is usually 5 ounces. A standard portion of gravy is usually 2 ounces. Meat portions will vary according to the type of operation and meat. Normally, menu planners calculate 3 portions to the pound AP of a roast that has some bone in it. This gives about three 3-ounce portions. If dressing is served with the meat, the meat portion may be only 2 ounces, with 2 or 3 ounces of dressing. Ground meat items usually give 4 portions to the pound AP and an AS weight of about 3 ounces per portion.

A table of standard size portions is usually found in many of the standard recipes used by food services.[2] Foodservice operations should also compile their own lists and see that employees follow them. Portion sizes can be indicated on production schedules, recipes, or service charts.

There are many ways to achieve the right size portions. Items can be dished into standard cups or dishes, or a portion scale can be used. Portioning tools, such as scoops and ladles, can also be used to control portion size. The size of the scoop indicates how many portions the scoop gives *per quart* when it is full and level. Thus, a No. 12 scoop (2 2/3 oz) will give 12 scoops from a quart, if full and level. When speed is important in dishing, employees may not take the time to see that a scoop is full and level. For this reason, it is better to use a smaller scoop, let it be rounded, and obtain faster portioning. Actually, if rounded just slightly, the portion in a No. 12 scoop is about 3 ounces. A slightly rounded basting spoon also gives about a 3-ounce portion and is good for dishing vegetables. Ladle sizes are usually numbered by the ounces they contain when full and level. There are also standard measures that can be used. Sometimes it is useful to work with volume, not weight measure, in portioning.

Individuals who work in food production should be trained to watch portioning and see that the right number of portions is prepared. Some operations have stainless steel measuring rods that, when inserted into a steamjacketed kettle, indicate the number of gallons in the kettle. Thus, if an operation plans to have 400 portions of soup, each portion to be 8 ounces, the rod should show at a certain mark that there are 25 gallons of soup in the kettle. Since evaporation can occur in cooking, this measure should be made just before service. Some operations install mechanical measuring devices that measure and shut off automatically.

Pan weights should also be carefully worked out for proper portions of specific items. Suppose chicken pie is to be dished into 12-by-20-inch steam table pans, topped with biscuits, and baked. Each portion is to be 6 ounces, topped with a small biscuit; 32 portions are to come from each pan. Panning instructions should indicate that 1½ gallons of pie mixture (6 quart-ladles full) are to be put into each pan, topped with 32 biscuits in four columns and eight rows.

Some panning instructions in recipes may be stated in weights. If this is so, then it is wise to stamp metal pans with their weight so that employees know the net weight of the pan when filled. Sometimes an average weight is taken for a certain type of pan and used as a preproduction weight. Thus, a 17-by-25-inch roasting pan may be stamped "4½," indicating that it weighs 4½ pounds. If 20 pounds of au gratin potatoes are to be baked in such a pan giving 40 8-ounce portions, the pan after filling should weigh 24½ pounds.

As much as possible, foods should be marked or scored to indicate portions. Thus, if food in a 12-by-12-inch pan is to be cut into four columns and six rows, markings should be put on the food before or after baking. For instance, a pie crust can be marked lightly before baking to indicate cutting into four columns and six rows. There are many food markers available for use in cutting pies and cakes.

Hidden factors can disrupt portioning. While a No. 12 scoop gives 12 scoops per quart of solid material, such as pudding, it will not give this in ice cream or sherbet because these pack in the scooping. Instead of 12 scoops per quart, one is more apt to get 7.

Items can lose weight and volume in cooking or baking. One may think there are 3 gallons of sauce in a kettle, because that was the original volume, but it might be only 2½ gallons because of the evaporation loss. There is usually a 4 to 16 percent baking loss in baking bread or cakes. Thus, if a baker expects to have a loaf of bread weighing 16 ounces, the pan weight of the dough must be 18 ounces.

Selecting Items to Meet Cost Needs

In planning a menu, one may wish to have a certain item on the menu but find that it cannot be included because it is too high in price. Often, an adequate, similar substitution can be made. The substitution should be appropriate to the operation and maintain patron value perception. For example, instead of sirloin steak, a cafeteria menu planner might offer a Swiss steak. (For a steakhouse, however, such a substitution will probably not be possible.) It is also possible at times to reduce other costs associated with the item. A less expensive garnish or sauce may bring about the desired change. If the item is combined with other foods, as on a table d'hôte menu, lower-cost foods to serve with the item can be selected.

Many menu planners work with lists of suggested menu items that have been grouped according to cost. If one needs to have an item in a particular cost range, one can find the group in such a list and select one of the items. Sometimes it is possible to call a purveyor and see if something is on the market that meets not only the need, but also the price restriction. Thus, one may wish to put lemon sole on the menu, but the price may be too high. An inquiry may find that petrale sole or sand dabs would be an adequate substitute.

Usually, item selections needed to meet costs require balancing one cost against the other to get the best possible trade-off. For example, one may have an item on the menu that costs a bit more than desired and balance it with a lower-cost item. One must be sure in doing this that the two items balance out in popularity with guests as well. If the selections are swayed to direct sales toward the higher-food-cost item and the lower food cost one is neglected, the menu planner is in trouble.

Controlling Labor Costs

Labor costs are usually controlled by allocating a specific amount of labor per unit produced, per number of meals per day, per hour, per covers served, or per dollar sales. Commercial operations try to allocate labor costs as a certain percent of sales. Forecasts of labor needs are often made based on expected business. From this a labor budget can be made. *Scheduling* is a crucial step in controlling the amount of labor used. Some operations try to improve labor productivity so they can hire fewer people and still get the same results. This requires good selection, training, and motivation of employees.

The amount of labor used is usually obtained from a *time sheet* on which employees sign in and out. This may be verified by a department head or supervisor and then sent to payroll. (See **Exhibit 5.9**.) The time clock is another device used. At the end of each pay period, the cards can be gathered and sent to payroll.

Computers can be used to record employees' actual work time. The computer can also be used to identify the code number of the employee checking in, the code number of the job, the pay for that job, the deductions, so it accumulates employee hours and can come up with final payroll calculations. With a printer the computer can also prepare payroll checks.

Some operations allocate payroll dollars or hours on the basis of dollar sales. **Exhibit 5.10** shows the dollar sales for a week in an operation's dining and bar areas. One hour of labor is allocated for every $25 in sales, and a payroll dollar allowance is made at $3.50 per hour.

Sometimes an allocation may be made on the number of positions for every dollar amount of sales. For instance, for every $75,000 in sales per year, one position is allowed. (A job position may mean more than one employee.)

Some units allow one worker per a specific number of check covers. For instance, there may be one server for every 20 to 25 breakfasts or lunches served and one for every 15 to 20 check covers at dinner. Donald Greenaway, a former executive vice president of the National Restaurant Association and a hospitality instructor, advised that a host or hostess should be able to take care of 200 people at a meal, and a cook should be able to prepare 100 meals during an eight-hour shift.

Exhibit 5.9   Sample Time Sheet

DAILY TIME SHEET

Department _____

| No. | Name | Time | | Hours | | Wages | | Rate | Other |
		In	Out	Reg.	O.T.	Reg.	O.T.		
1									
2									
3									
4									
5									
6									
7									
8									
9									
10									
11									
12									
13									
14									
15									
16									
17									
18									
19									
20									
21									
22									
23									
24									
	STAFF ALLOWANCE								
	TOTALS								

Total Wages $ _____   Dept. Head _____   Day _____ Date _____ 19 __

Exhibit 5.10 Labor Allocations by Dollar Sales

Unit and Meal	Sun 9/10	Mon 9/11	Tues 9/12	Wed 9/13	Thurs 9/14	Fri 9/15	Sat 9/16	Weekly Total
Dining Room								
Breakfast	$150.00	$ 185.00	$ 190.00	$ 195.00	$ 195.00	$ 215.00	$ 280.00	$1,410.00
Lunch	120.00	180.00	175.00	210.00	210.00	225.00	235.00	1,355.00
Dinner	220.00	300.00	335.00	365.00	365.00	385.00	400.00	2,370.00
Total	$490.00	$ 665.00	$ 700.00	$ 770.00	$ 770.00	$ 825.00	$ 915.00	$5,135.00
Labor Hours	20.00	26.00	28.00	31.00	31.00	33.00	37.00	207.00
Payroll	$ 70.00	$ 94.50	$ 98.00	$ 108.50	$ 108.50	$ 115.50	$ 129.50	$ 724.50
Catering								
Breakfast	$160.00		$ 20.00	$ 40.00	$ 40.00		$ 30.00	$ 290.00
Lunch		$ 130.00	40.00	40.00	60.00	$ 40.00	100.00	410.00
Dinner	20.00	50.00	25.00	40.00	120.00	410.00	260.00	925.00
Total	$180.00	$ 180.00	$ 85.00	$ 120.00	$ 220.00	$ 450.00	$ 390.00	$1,625.00
Labor Hours	7.00	7.00	3.00	5.00	9.00	18.00	16.00	65.00
Payroll	$ 24.50	$ 24.50	$ 10.50	$ 17.50	$ 31.50	$ 63.00	$ 56.00	$ 227.50
Bar								
Total Sales	$120.00	$ 250.00	$ 325.00	$ 270.00	$ 300.00	$ 375.00	$ 400.00	$2,040.00
Labor Hours	5.00	10.00	13.00	11.00	12.00	15.00	16.00	82.00
Payroll	$ 17.50	$ 35.00	$ 45.50	$ 38.50	$ 42.00	$ 52.50	$ 56.00	$ 287.00
Total Sales	$790.00	$1,095.00	$1,110.00	$1,160.00	$1,290.00	$1,650.00	$1,705.00	$8,800.00
Total Labor Hours	32.00	44.00	44.00	47.00	52.00	66.00	69.00	354.00
Total Payroll	$112.00	$ 154.00	$ 154.00	$ 164.50	$ 182.00	$ 231.00	$ 241.50	$1,239.00

Formulas have been developed from which staffing requirements can be established. As previously noted, one of the most common standards used today for noncommercial operations is the number of meals produced per labor hour used. (See **Exhibit 5.11**.) If an operation produced 15,000 meals in a month and wanted to produce 4 meals for every hour of labor used, 3,750 hours of labor would be allocated.

The quantity of labor used between service and back-of-the-house areas varies for different types of operations. A cafeteria or buffet operation often uses less labor for service than a full-service restaurant or club. Some full-service restaurants have found that an allocation of seven hours for back-of-the-house compared to ten hours for service is adequate, but no standard can be set precisely; every operation should work out its own formula.

Some operations develop labor budgets that allocate a given number of hours for various departments per period. Thus, a small food service could allow 739 hours for a month as follows: chef and manager, 162; first and second cooks, 244; assistant cooks or helpers, 275; consulting dietitian, 16; kitchen or lunchroom workers, including dishwashers and storeroom personnel, 26; and accounting, 16. Some may allocate labor on the basis of a percentage for

Exhibit 5.11   Average Number of Meals Produced per Labor Hour

Type Operation	Meals Produced per Hour
Hotels and clubs	1.25–1.75
Restaurants	1.50–3.00
Cafeterias	3.50–8.50
School lunches	11–13
College dormitories	11.5
Hospitals	3–6
Nursing Homes	5
Large State Hospitals	11.6

various types of workers. For example, in an institutional cafeteria, management may get 10 percent of the total hours; service and cashiers, 20 percent; clerical and accounting, 3 percent; food production, 44 percent; janitorial and cleanup, 12 percent; maintenance, 3 percent; and miscellaneous, 6 percent. If a labor budget is set up, it should be extremely flexible and allow for shifting labor between departments.

Formulas used to allocate labor can give broad estimates of requirements. In 1950, John F. Johnson developed a formula for staffing cafeterias that indicated that the number of employees on the staff (Y) equaled 2.99 plus 0.82 times the number of thousands of meals served per month (X). In this formula, $Y = 2.99 + 0.82X$.[3] Thus, a cafeteria serving 90,000 meals in a month would be allocated $2.99 + (0.82 \times 90) = 76.79$ employees. Some hospitals find that a better formula for them is $Y = 2.99 + 0.9X$.

This allows for the additional labor used to handle special diets and meal deliveries. Paul Broton, using Johnson's technique, developed formulas for hotels, clubs, schools, and hospitals, as follows.

Hotels	$Y = 2.34 + 2.2X$
Clubs	$Y = 2.34 + 2.2X$
Schools	$Y = 6.44 + 0.92X$
Hospitals	$Y = 4.01 + 1.08X$

Broton indicated his formulas were for full-time employees working a combined average of 206 hours per month.[4]

In allocating labor, it is necessary to differentiate between the number of employees on the payroll and the number of positions allowed. There will be more employees on the payroll than allowed positions because a single position frequently must be filled by more than one person in the seven days of the week, and because of the various shifts. Say, for instance, that an operation requires 56 labor hours to cover one shift position. This means that 1.4 employees must be on the payroll to cover it ($56 \div 40$ hours per week = 1.4). However, this does not provide for days off, holidays, or vacations, so it is usual to have 1.5 to 1.6 workers on the payroll to cover a seven-day position. Many employees work about 232 days a year, or about 64 percent of 365 days. Some operations allow 1.1 workers on the payroll for a five-day (40-hour) position to cover sick leave, absenteeism, and vacations.

In too many food services, scheduling and forecasting the required amount of labor are poorly done. Few make attempts to ascertain whether the labor scheduled is needed or whether more or less might be required. Fewer make evaluations on whether it is effectively used. This never translates to effective cost control.

Schedules for workers are used for different purposes. One type shows when workers are to be on the job and is usually called a *work schedule*. A second type shows days off or when vacations are to be taken, and a third shows the production tasks for workers on the job. It is possible to combine the first and last types.

A work schedule should identify each employee and indicate time at work for a specific period. This is done differently, depending on the type of schedule and the particular operation. A production work schedule frequently shows:

- Period covered
- Work to be done
- Who does the work
- Amount to produce
- Recipe to use
- Portion size
- Meal or completion time required
- Comments
- Slack-time assignments

Operations should use whichever schedules serve their needs; several are shown here that illustrate this diversity. **Exhibit 5.12** shows a production schedule for an institutional operation; it could be used, with some modification, for a commercial unit. Sometimes a schedule is set up that does not indicate hours to be worked, but work to be done. Thus, management does not set the time that the worker can put in, but sets the work or goals to be accomplished. **Exhibit 5.13** shows such a work schedule by assignment. A typical schedule for work in a commercial dining room—with workers assigned by station—is presented in **Exhibit 5.14**. **Exhibit 5.15** is a time-line schedule developed for an institutional foodservice with a number of dining services. A count of patrons in an operation at a certain time and an estimate of the labor needed can result in what is termed a *bar schedule graph*. This shows when certain employees should be on the job. By taking a look at such a bar graph and looking at the patron count, one can note quickly whether there is a sufficient number of workers when most of the work must be done.

Exhibit 5.12 Production Schedule

Date _____

Meal and Item	Worker	Amount	No. Portions	Portion Size	Comment
Breakfast					
Tomato Juice	F	12 46-oz	87	6 oz	Do Tues PM
Pineapple Juice	F	1 No. 10	12	6 oz	Do Tues PM
Prunes	F	2 No. 2½	16	3 prunes	Do Tues PM
Oatmeal (R-1)	B	4 gal	60	1 c cooked	
Dry Cereals	F	(Assorted)		1 pkg	Send to floors
French Toast	B		84	3 half slices	
Syrup	G		84	1 packet	
Butter	G		84	1 pat	
Coffee (G-2)	B	4 gal	60	1½ c	Send in pitchers
Milk	G	138½ pt.		½ pt.	

Other assignments

Morning

Clean refrigerators 1 and 3 and storeroom.

Pre-prep: Wash lettuce and separate leaves for dinner salads.
     Peel 40 lb AP potatoes for dinner.
     Make cream sauce for croquettes for Thursday (2 gal) (C-11 recipe).
     Pick over split peas for Thursday lunch soup.
     Take turkey meat from bones stored in refrigerator 2.
     Check salad dressings and make up those necessary.

Lunch

Exhibit 5.13 Work Schedule by Assignment

Date _____

Assistant Cook	Cook's Helper	Pantry and Baker
Make coffee and hot cereal	Pick turkey meat from bones	Put ice into bins
Prepare french toast (B-8)	Pare potatoes	Cut butter and margarine
Prepare cream sauce	Wash lettuce and fix leaves	Help dish breakfast
Mash potatoes	Help dish breakfast	Make and dish up lunch
Cook green beans	See cafeteria counter is	Salads
Help dish lunch	properly filled	Make 3 pans cornbread (S-10)
Help clean refrigerators	Prepare 1½ qt diced pepper	Make 2½ gal hot cake
Help clean storeroom	Chop 1 c pimiento	Batter for Thurs. breakfast (S-8)
Do pre-prep as instructed for	Clean up cafeteria counter	Make lemon pudding (R-15)
next day	Make gelatin salads for night	Dish pudding
Bread mock chicken legs	Help clean refrigerators and	Set up gelatin salads
Get vegetables ready for	storeroom	Help dish lunch and supervise
dinner	Help set up lunch counter	lunch counter
Pan baked potatoes and get	Do preparation as instructed	Do preparation for apple
ready for baking	Help dish up lunch	pie for Thurs.
	Clean lunch counter	Clean own unit and do own
	Do pots and pans as required	pots and pans
	Clean cook's shelves	Make 10 dozen muffins for
		dinner (S-17)

Exhibit 5.14   Commercial Operation Schedule

GOLD ROOM SCHEDULE

Morning Shift 7 to 3:30	Station	Afternoon Shift 3:00 to 11:30
Alice Tilton	1	G. Smith
Bert Sivay	2	Gloria Rutter
Sylvia Tubbs	3	Cora Spotler
Rosy Stephan	4	Julia Dilan
Grace Abrams	5	Mabel Morris
Mary Cowder	6	Silvia Field
E. Turner	7	Helen Peller
Bess Manor	8	Mary Sage
Marie Scott	9	closed
Clara Tourney	10	closed
Sam Baker	1, 2 & 3	Teddy Holt
Mike Benner	4, 5 & 6	Arsis Virune
Gary Dentor	7, 8 & 9	Stan Stanford (7 & 8 only)
Sandra Holman 11–3:30	11	closed
Phyllis Lock 11–3:30	12	closed
T. Crane 11–3:30	14	closed
Barry Tucker 11–3:30	11, 12 & 14	closed

Date ___ Feb. 20 ___   Signed ___ George DiNatale ___

Exhibit 5.15 Time-line Schedule

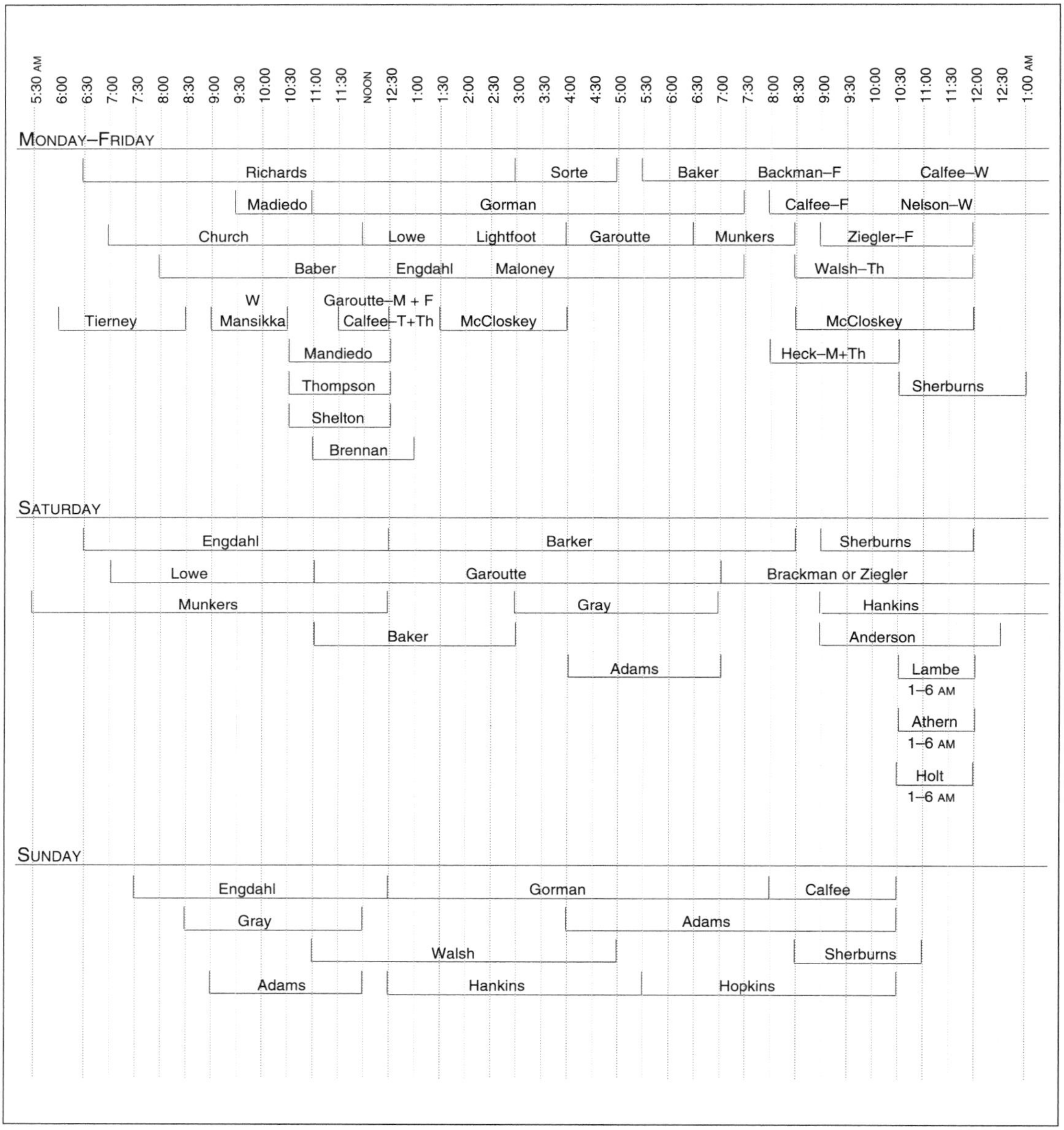

It is extremely important that employees be properly informed of days off and when they can expect to take vacations. Employees have the right to know at least a week ahead which days they can be off to arrange personal time. Nevertheless, days off should be guided as much as possible by business activity and operational needs. Workers must be there when the work is there. However, management should attempt to keep scheduling as flexible as possible so that workers can, in times of personal need, take time off.

Planning vacations should be done with care. There are certain times when labor requirements may be less, and this is the time to schedule vacations. It may be possible, with proper planning, to take care of much vacation time without having to hire additional labor. Planning ahead can do much to please workers and keep the operation running smoothly.

There are state and federal regulations that control the number of hours that teenagers and, at times, children can work. The type of work performed may also be controlled.

The number of hours worked will be controlled and all hours worked over a total time must be paid in overtime. There are different overtime rates and, in scheduling employees, it is important to avoid overtime payment, especially at high penalty rates. Workers should not be allowed to be absent from the job and then, later, attempt to qualify for overtime because they worked special days. Good control of scheduling can do much to reduce loss from manipulation by employees.

Forecasting labor requirements can be very valuable. Management can usually work with department heads to establish accurate labor needs.

After actual events have ocurred, it is always necessary to compare forecasted and actual figures. Too much labor may have been scheduled, or not enough, or perhaps it was not used to the best advantage. There will always be a range of error; but if there is accurate historical information (for example, on business trends, advance reservations, house occupancy, bookings, local or regional events, and other factors, such as the season or internal needs), error can be reduced if the forecast is evaluated afterward.

Exhibit 5.16 shows a form used to budget labor. Whoever is responsible for assigning labor fills in the sheet and sends in a copy to a supervising office. Then the actual time used is shown on a revised sheet. If there is too great a difference, the person responsible for the labor assignment must explain the discrepancies.

Improving Productivity

Authorities agree that high labor waste occurs in food services and that more emphasis should be given to improving the use of labor. At the present time, programs for doing this are directed toward four areas: hiring and training, using labor-saving devices and foods requiring less labor to prepare, improving layouts, and improving forecasting and scheduling of labor.

Many operations use poor methods in selecting employees, with the result that they get employees who do not have the requisite skills, knowledge, or motivation to do an adequate job. Furthermore, after hiring inadequate

Exhibit 5.16 Labor Forecast

			Monday			Tuesday			Wednesday			Thursday			Friday			Saturday			Sunday			Totals	
EMPLOYEE'S NAME	Classification	Rate	From To	hrs.	COST	From To	hrs.	COST	From To	hrs.	COST	From To	hrs.	COST	From To	hrs.	COST	From To	hrs.	COST	From To	hrs.	COST	HRS.	COST

WEEKLY LABOR SCHEDULE AND FORECAST

WEEK BEGINNING _____
DEPARTMENT _____
PREPARED BY _____

(USE SEPARATE SHEET FOR SUMMARY)   (REPORT DUE IN AUDITING—4 PM THURSDAY PRECEDING WEEK)

TOTAL FORECAST
ACTUAL

employees, these operations do little to see that they become more effective employees.

Attention must be given to hiring practices that minimize problems and fill positions with those likely to do the best job. A *job specification* is written to indicate the qualifications, skills, and experience of employees hired for a specific position. This should be used in interviews and for seeking potential employees to improve the selection process. The specification usually covers the job and some of its work requirements, skills, education, and knowledge required.

A *job description* should be written for each position to indicate the tasks of each position. This should be shared with employees during their orientation, during which employees become oriented to the company, position, supervisor, and co-workers.

Training can also do much to improve job performance. Employees should be given the opportunity to learn on the job or take classroom or correspondence courses to become better employees and of more value to the company.

Job evaluations assist management and employees in knowing how well employees are performing and what might be needed for improvement.

Most workers have never been taught how to make their jobs easier yet more productive. Efficient workers often become so because they are basically efficient by nature and learn the shortcuts quickly. However, workers can be taught how to work more efficiently. By planning work, arranging work areas to be more efficient, and reducing motions and energy in work, managers can increase their employees' productivity while reducing turnover. The field of knowledge on how to improve jobs is called *work simplification,* or *human engineering.* Food services that have worked to improve conditions frequently find that not only does productivity increase, but so does employee morale. Considerable material on this subject is available for use in food service.

Other Controls

Managers should continually examine the nature of all fixed operational costs. Some costs thought to be fixed may be what are called *programmed costs* (that is, they may be only programmed into the operation), and these sometimes can be controlled or changed. For instance, the cost of electricity, water, heat for cooking, or the cost of cleaning supplies may be programmed into operation as fixed costs, but if lights are turned off more frequently, supplies are used properly, leaking faucets are fixed to reduce the use of hot water, and broilers, griddles, and steam equipment are turned off when not in use, some of these costs may be reduced. A small change may make a considerable difference in the amount required to pay for these fixed costs.

Budget Costs

Many food services prepare *budgets* to act as guides to direct operations and indicate cost allocations. The budget shows expected income and how it will be spent. Budgets should be based on *realistic expectations* and not hopes. Budgets should be flexible enough to adjust to changing conditions, but only up to a point. If changed too often, a budget becomes *subject to* operating conditions rather than *controlling* them. Some operations have budgets based on variations in income and costs.

Ration Allowance Budgeting

In some cases, an institution may modify a cost allowance by setting up a food allowance per day or per period for a specific quantity of foods from different food groups. This allowance is based on the quantity of food from each group required to provide each individual with an adequate diet. Thus, for each person, a specific grain amount; milk or its equivalent; fish, poultry, or meat; vegetables; and fruit is allowed per day, per week, per month, or per period. The cost of each of these food groups is determined, and the total becomes the cost allowance per person. American military services operate on such a system. It is usually called a *ration allowance.* In many states, tax-supported institutions, such as hospitals and prisons, use the ration system.

Some ration allowances are based on weekly allowances developed each year by the United States Department of Agriculture (USDA) based on current prices. There are three levels for these allowances: low, moderate, and liberal. Most state institutions use the low-cost plan but some, such as California, add a bit more meat to give palatability and acceptability. When a ration system is used, only the cost of the food is obtained. Other costs, such as those for labor, must be added to food costs to get total operation costs.

The USDA operates the school foodservice program and recommends that a General Meal Pattern meal contain servings of meat or a meat alternate, vegetables and/or fruits, bread or a bread alternate, and milk. (See **Exhibit 5.17**.) School food services are actively trying to reduce fats and use sodium and sugar in moderation in the student diet, and menus have reflected this change.

Experience is helpful in establishing what a budget should be, but the budget should not be based on performance alone. Using past figures may compound past mistakes and faulty calculations. Previous budgets should be guides only, used to indicate what costs were under past conditions. If a budget is based on the past, it may be good for past conditions but not necessarily for the present.

Today many operations wipe out past budget figures at the beginning of a new period and start fresh. They first project expected conditions and make up budget figures based on them. The method of not using any past figures in budget planning is called *zero-based budgeting*. If such a budget is well researched and the information is presented with alternatives for action, management has a better chance of evaluating factors regarding menu planning and other issues requiring management decision. For instance, if budgetary projections are properly made, it may be much easier for a manager to decide whether it would be a better idea to purchase all bakery goods or to remodel the bakeshop.

SUMMARY

One of the most important factors in menu planning is *cost*. It is important after establishing a price on a menu to see that both food and labor costs are covered.

All types of operations must control costs. Commercial operations must do so to attain a healthy profit. Noncommercial operations must cover costs, usually to stay within a budget. Food costs may be affected by factors outside the food buyer's control, such as weather, labor strikes, and demand. Yet the operator can control costs by using methods such as forecasting sales, controlling portions, and deliberately selecting items to meet cost needs.

Labor costs are controlled partly by external factors, such as labor demand and minimum wage laws. However, improving productivity is an internal way the operator can control costs. Careful scheduling is crucial.

Other costs, such as for energy and cleaning supplies, should be evaluated to see how they can be controlled.

Exhibit 5.17   School Lunch Patterns for Various Ages and Grades

The U.S. Department of Agriculture recommends, but does not require, that schools adjust portions by age/grade group to better meet the food and nutritional needs of children of all ages. Groups I through IV are minimum requirements to the age/grade groups specified. If no adjustments are made, the Group IV portions should be served to all children.

COMPONENTS		Minimum Quantities				Recommended Quantities[2]
		Preschool		**Grades K–3**	**Grades 4–12[1]**	**Grades 7–12**
		ages 1–2 (Group I)	ages 3–4 (Group II)	ages 5–8 (Group III)	age 9 & over (Group IV)	age 12 & over (Group V)
Meat or Meat Alternate	A serving of one of the following or a combination to give an equivalent quantity:					
	Lean meat, poultry, or fish (edible portion as served)	1 oz	1½ oz	1½ oz	2 oz	3 oz
	Cheese	1 oz	1½ oz	1½ oz	2 oz	3 oz
	Large egg(s)	½	¾	¾	1	1½
	Cooked dry beans or peas	¼ cup	⅜ cup	⅜ cup	½ cup	¾ cup
	Peanut butter or other nut or seed butters	2 Tbsp	3 Tbsp	3 Tbsp	4 Tbsp	6 Tbsp
	Peanuts, soy nuts, tree nuts, or seeds, as listed in program guidance, meet no more than 50% of the requirement and must be combined in the meal with at least 50% of other meat or meat alternate. (1 oz of nut/seeds = 1 oz of cooked lean meat, poultry, or fish.)	½ oz = 50%	¾ oz = 50%	¾ oz = 50%	1 oz = 50%	1½ oz = 50%
Vegetables and/or Fruits	Two or more servings of vegetables or fruits or both to total	½ cup	½ cup	½ cup	¾ cup	¾ cup

SPECIFIC REQUIREMENTS (Meat or Meat Alternate)

• Must be served in the main dish or the main dish and only one other menu item.
• Vegetable protein products, cheese alternate products, and enriched macaroni with fortified protein may be used to meet part of the meat/meat alternate requirement. Fact sheets on each of these alternate foods give detailed instructions for use.

SPECIFIC REQUIREMENTS (Vegetables and/or Fruits)

• No more than one-half of the total requirement may be met with full-strength fruit or vegetable juice.
• Cooked dry beans or peas may be used as a meat alternate or as a vegetable but not as both in the same meal.

(Continued)

Exhibit 5.17 School Lunch Patterns for Various Ages and Grades *(continued)*

			Minimum Quantities			Recommended Quantities[2]
			Preschool		Grades K–3	Grades 4–12[1]	Grades 7–12
COMPONENTS			ages 1–2 (Group I)	ages 3–4 (Group II)	ages 5–8 (Group III)	age 9 & over (Group IV)	age 12 & over (Group V)
SPECIFIC REQUIREMENTS — Servings of Bread or Bread Alternate • At least ¹/₂ serving of bread or an equivalent quantity of bread alternate for Group I, and 1 serving for Groups II–V, must be served daily. • Enriched macaroni with fortified protein may be used as a meat alternate or as a bread alternate but not as both in the same meal. **NOTE:** Food Buying Guide for Child Nutrition Programs, PA-1331 (1984) provides the information for the minimum weight of a serving.	A serving is: • 1 slice of whole-grain or enriched bread • A whole-grain or enriched biscuit, roll, muffin, etc. • ¹/₂ cup of cooked whole-grain or enriched rice, macaroni, noodles, whole-grain or enriched pasta products, or other cereal grains such as bulgur or corn grits • A combination of any of the above		5 per week	8 per week	8 per week	8 per week	10 per week
SPECIFIC REQUIREMENTS — Milk The following forms of milk must be offered: • Whole milk • Unflavored lowfat milk **NOTE:** This requirement does not prohibit offering other milk, such as flavored milk or skim milk, along with the above.	A serving of fluid milk		³/₄ cup (6 fl oz)	³/₄ cup (6 fl oz)	¹/₂ pint (8 fl oz)	¹/₂ pint (8 fl oz)	¹/₂ pint (8 fl oz)

[1] Group IV is highlighted because it is the one meal pattern which will satisfy all requirements if no portion size adjustments are made.
[2] Group V specifies recommended, not required, quantities for students 12 years and older. These students may request smaller portions, but not smaller than those specified in Group IV.

SOURCE: U.S. Department of Agriculture

QUESTIONS

1. A takeout operation has the following in dollar sales, percent of dollar sales, and food cost percentage for the listed items. What is the average food cost?

Item	$ Sales	% of Sales	% Food Cost
Pies	$ 750	17.0	30
Cakes	622	14.0	28
Entrees	1,341	30.3	38
Snacks	812	18.4	27
Beverages	891	20.2	29
	$4,416	99.9	

Average food cost = _____

2. Determine the portion cost for each of the following.

   a. 24 apples per box; one box costs $12.82;

   portion cost: _____

   b. Cake a la mode:

   16 portions per cake; cost per cake $4.76;

   portion cost: _____

   Ice cream, 40 scoops per gallon; 5 gallons cost $27.40;

   portion cost: _____

3. A leg of lamb weighs 10 pounds. It is boned, rolled, roasted, and carved. The losses are boning and rolling, 35 percent; cooking shrinkage, 30 percent; and carving loss, 5 percent. What is the amount of servable meat after carving? How many 3-ounce portions are obtained?

4. According to Johnson and Broten, if a club served 14,820 meals in a 30-day period, how many employees should be allocated to the payroll?

5. Food cost is $864.22 and sales are $2,564.22. What is the food cost percentage?

6. A white sauce recipe calls for the ingredients listed below. What is the total food cost, and the cost per portion if 100 2-ounce portions are obtained?

Flour, all purpose	1 lb 9 oz	$0.24
Margarine	3 lb	0.99
Milk, whole	6¼ qt	3.75

6

Menu Pricing

Outline

Introduction
Value Perception
Pricing Psychology
Market Research
Economic Influences
Pricing Methods
    Pricing Based on Costs
        Derived Food Cost Percentage
        Pricing Factor or Multiplier
        Variable Cost Pricing
        Prime Cost Pricing
        Combined Food and Labor Costs
        All or Actual Cost Pricing
    Gross Profit Pricing
    The One-Price Method
    Marginal Analysis Pricing
    Cost-Plus-Profit Pricing
    Minimum Charge Pricing
        Cover Charge
    Pricing Based on Sales Potential
    Non-Cost Pricing
        Pricing Based on Tradition
        Competitive Pricing
        What the Market Will Bear
    Pricing Aids

Objectives

After reading this chapter, you should be able to:

1. Discuss several theories of menu pricing.
2. Characterize the most common pricing techniques used in the foodservice industry.

INTRODUCTION

After a menu is planned, each item on it has to be priced. There are a number of items to be considered in pricing, including the market, type of operation, and costs. The market is a major factor in pricing. Some patrons want only low prices; others seek moderate ones; some will be willing to pay higher prices. *Perception of value* will also vary from patron to patron; it is sometimes difficult to meet the desires of each group. Many operators use a "what the market will bear" approach to pricing. However, such a simplistic strategy may not meet operational needs and may drive patrons to competitors.

Prices must cover costs. This requirement is essential for both commercial operations and institutions that charge for meals but do not operate for profit. However, noncommercial operations may seek supplemental help from government or charitable contributions to balance losses. Commercial units do not have this insurance and will pay the consequences of faulty pricing.

Different kinds of operations use different markups. A *markup* is the difference between the cost of a product and its selling price. Some operations can use a low markup and depend on high volume to give an adequate income with which to operate and make a profit. Others will use a higher markup and require a lower volume to attain a profit. Menu prices must not only cover the costs of food and labor but must often include other significant cost factors such as atmosphere, rent—especially in a prime location—and advertising.

VALUE PERCEPTION

Value perception, or what patrons think of the desirability of a product compared with its menu price, is an important factor in menu pricing, since prices largely influence patrons' thinking about the value of menu items. A high price may be associated with high quality and a low price with lower quality. Some people want to go to a place where prices are high. A salesperson may take potential customers to a luxury restaurant to impress them with a lavish display and hope this will transfer into a sale. The menu must tie in with any attempt to present high prices and luxury by using proper menu wording and item presentation.

The way patrons perceive value is often manipulated favorably by getting buyers to think there is something special about a product that competing products do not have. We call this development of special, unique characteristics in a product *differentiation*. If a product can be favorably differentiated, buyers will want it rather than a competing product, and the seller has better control of the market and pricing. Through good advertising, buyers can be persuaded that it is better in some way than competitive products.

Food services can differentiate products and services in various ways. Often several special items on the menu can do the trick, such as a special, thick cut of roast beef, a marvelous dessert, or a unique cocktail. Location, atmosphere, and decor are also used to differentiate one operation from another. A smiling host or hostess to greet guests can differentiate the service from that of a competing operation. When a food service achieves differentiation, patrons may pass up competitors, going a long way just to eat at a particular place.

PRICING PSYCHOLOGY

Studies have been made on how menu planners set, and how patrons react to, menu prices. Menu planners usually try to avoid whole numbers and try to shade numbers just below them. A price of $6.95 or even $3.99 is perceived as less than $7 and $4. Number "5" is the most-often used ending digit. Some authorities say that a price ending in .99 is more suited to quick-service menus, and 0 and 5 as ending digits suit full-service menus better.

Price length also has importance; many menu pricers hesitate to use four-digit prices if they can avoid it. They feel that a price of $9.95 is better than $10.95, that three digits appear as a much lower price to patrons than four.

Patrons tend to group prices by range and think of them as single-figure amounts. For example, prices from $0.86 to $1.39 are considered to be about $1.00; from $1.80 to $2.49, about $2.00; and from $2.50 to $3.99, about $3.00. Prices from $4.00 to $7.95 are thought of being about $5.00. Instead of raising a price into the next full price range, the menu planner may try to hit the upper limit of the range the present price is in. That is, instead of raising a menu price from $2.25 to $2.55, the planner may raise it to $2.45. A price of $7.75 is preferable to $8.25 because the former is in the "about $5" range and the $8.25 is in the "about $10" range.

Patrons do not seem to like wide ranges in menu prices. They want prices grouped together within the price range they want to pay. If too wide a price range occurs, patrons will tend to select the lower-priced items.

Price increases are not always viewed in the same way by patrons. A price increase from $5.95 to $6.25 is seen as a bigger jump than from $6.25 to $6.75.

Some operations find that patrons resist buying after a certain price is reached. A Montana restaurant built as a stockade and located on a high mountain pass found there was resistance to any dinner price above $10. Items priced below $10 were popular. Items over that were not. To resolve this, the table d'hôte meals were dropped and all items were listed a la carte at seemingly lower prices. The highest priced steak with a salad, potato, and roll and butter was $8; a popular Trappers Stew was priced at $6.50; and so on. If patrons wanted appetizers, soup, or desserts, they paid extra. The strategy worked. Most checks now came to more than $10 per person. The $10 wall was broken.

MARKET RESEARCH

Market research should point out what kind of market exists and what consumers will pay. If a gourmet restaurant opens, it must be located where it will attract customers with money. Adequate market information can lead to greater precision in setting prices. A *base price* and *top price* can be defined and the menu planned to work within this range.

ECONOMIC INFLUENCES

A variety of methods is used to price menus. Many managers calculate their costs as a percentage of sales and then calculate the selling price. Others base selling prices on factors other than costs.

Foodservice operators should be aware that laws of economics and commerce work both to the benefit and harm of businesses. The two most basic economic laws affect every operation: 1) when supply is limited, prices tend to rise, and when supply is plentiful, prices tend to drop; and 2) when demand is high, prices rise, and when demand is low, prices drop. Thus, every menu planner should try to plan menus that create a high demand. Operations that can restrict supply are few, but when they can, they have a chance to charge enough to make a good profit and still hold their business. Dropping prices may create more demand, while raising them may reduce it. Some operations reduce prices and hope to increase demand and, while making a smaller profit, make it up with increased volume. Some others raise prices, reducing demand but earning a greater profit. The south Florida area has a large demand for food and housing during the winter months and many operations do well as a result. Many restaurants have waiting lines for lunch and dinner. In the summer, both tourists and residents leave, and many operations drop their prices, cut their staffs, and retrench in every way because of the lack of demand. Some even close.

A smart menu planner knows that when the supply of an item is plentiful, costs will be low, and a better profit made. Thus, in the late spring and early summer, lamb is plentiful, relatively inexpensive, and of good quality and, therefore, a good menu item. Turkey is plentiful in the late fall and early winter. When the smelt run is on in the Great Lakes, local foodservices offer them as "all you can eat" menu items. This promotion works well.

If possible, menu planners should be sure that there will be an adequate supply of all menu ingredients. Sometimes, an item is on the menu and the price of the items used for it become so costly that the item is served at a loss. Often such an item is removed from the menu. Some prices, such as those for fresh fish and seafood, vary so much that a menu planner lists only "market price," indicating the price will depend on the operation's cost.

Competition can reduce the number of patrons coming to an operation. Some may try to increase demand by dropping prices. However, this can be dangerous, because if competitors also drop their prices, both fight for the same demand, earning less from it.

Advertising and special promotions create demand. When a big-name star appears in a Las Vegas casino, food, beverage, and room prices may rise because the demand for them is high. Many operations put on special promotions to create a higher demand during certain periods. A quick-service chicken operation may advertise a special price on a bucket of fried chicken during a slow period. Such a promotion not only increases demand but also introduces the product to people who might not otherwise become patrons.

When forces of supply and demand increase and decrease in relation to increases and decreases in prices, the market is called *elastic*. If it does not, it is *inelastic*. If patrons pay no attention to prices and purchase items regardless of price, or refuse to purchase others even when prices drop, the market is said to be *inflexible*. However, if patrons increase demand when prices drop, and decrease demand when prices rise, the market is called *flexible*. A market where neither the price, nor supply and demand are changing is called *steady*.

A menu pricer should know whether a market is flexible, inflexible, or steady, and how patrons are likely to respond to price changes. Often a test can be made by changing prices briefly to test patron response. The test should be repeated several times over a period.

Thus, menus must reflect and take advantage of the influence of economic laws. A menu is one of the best contacts a food service can have with its patrons. It can help create demand and take advantage of the flow of supplies.

Pricing Based on Costs

One of the most common methods of pricing is for the planner to list costs of the food for each item on the menu—using methods discussed in Chapter 4—and then mark up the final figure to obtain a selling price. For instance, if an a la carte item has a food cost of $2 and the operation wants a 40 percent food cost percentage, the selling price would be $5 ($2 ÷ 0.40 = $5). If the operator wants to maintain a 40 percent food cost in relation to sales, all foods would be marked up by dividing food cost percentage into food cost.

The disadvantage of this method is that it assumes that other costs associated with preparing menu items remain the same with every menu item. On the contrary, menu items vary considerably in the cost of labor, energy, and other factors needed to produce and serve them.

For instance, a steak is on the menu for $16.95 while a pasta dish sells for $11.95. The labor cost to make a portion of pasta is $1.10, and the labor cost to prepare the steak is $0.97. The pasta's labor cost is 9.2 percent of the selling price and the steak's is 5.7.

Assuming other costs have the same ratio to food cost for each menu item is a mistake. This leads to undesirable pricing that fails to cover costs on some items and can work against the sale of others. Costs must still be a paramount factor in pricing, and all costs—not just one or two—should be considered.

Pricing experts also claim that food cost pricing does not work because many foodservice operators do not know *all* their costs. These critics point out that many hidden food costs, such as spoilage, are not determined.

Derived Food Cost Percentage

The most common method is to use a *derived food cost percentage*. Simply divide the dollar cost of the food by the desired percentage (food cost ÷ food cost percentage). If a menu item has a total food cost of $2.73, and the operator wants a food cost percentage of 35 percent, the calculation is $2.73 ÷ 0.35 = $7.80.

Pricing Factor or Multiplier

Sometimes managers may convert a desired food cost percentage into a *pricing factor* or *multiplier*. For this, one divides the desired food cost percentage into 100 percent. This formula gives a factor by which a food cost is multiplied to get a selling price. For instance, suppose a food's cost is $2.73 and the desired food cost percentage is 35 percent; 100% ÷ 35% = 2.86, and 2.86 × $2.73 = $7.81, the selling price. (See **Exhibit 6.1**.) If a manager uses a food cost percentage plus other cost percentages, a multiplier can be calculated and used. Thus, if an operator wants a multiplier based on a combined food and labor cost of 65 percent, the calculation would be 100% ÷ 65% = 1.54. If the combined food and labor costs were $5.20, the selling price would be 1.54 × $5.20 = $8.01, probably set at $8.00 or $7.95.

Variable Cost Pricing

A *variable food cost pricing* method is sometimes used for a la carte menu items. For instance, an operator may assign food cost markups for menu items, as shown in **Exhibit 6.2**. This variable pricing can also be used to arrive at

Exhibit 6.1 Pricing Factors (Multipliers)

Food Cost %	Factor	Food Cost %	Factor	Food Cost %	Factor
20	5.00	30	3.33	40	2.50
21	4.76	31	3.23	41	2.43
22	4.55	32	3.13	42	2.38
23	4.35	33	3.00	43	2.32
24	4.17	34	2.94	44	2.27
25	4.00	35	2.85	45	2.22
26	3.85	36	2.78	46	2.17
27	3.70	37	2.70	47	2.12
28	3.57	38	2.63	48	2.08
29	3.45	39	2.56	49	2.04
				50	2.00

Exhibit 6.2 Variable Cost Markups

Appetizers	25%	Beverages	40%
Salads	40	Desserts	35
Entrees	35	Breads and butter	30
Vegetables	40	Miscellaneous	35

Exhibit 6.3   Table D'hôte Meal Costed Out

	Food Cost	**Allocated Menu Price**
Tomato juice cocktail	$0.14	$ 0.56
Salad	0.48	1.20
Entree	2.84	8.11
Vegetables	0.94	2.35
Roll and Butter	0.27	0.90
Dessert	1.24	3.54
Beverage	0.46	1.15
Total Food Cost	$6.37	$17.81

table d'hôte menu prices. Using the food costs in **Exhibit 6.3** and the percentages in Exhibit 6.2, a table d'hôte meal can be priced out.

Labor costs also can vary with different menu items. In these cases, menu items are divided into high (H), medium (M), and low (L) labor costs. Different percentages of food costs are then assigned to these. For instance, for high-labor menu items, a food cost of 25 percent is assigned; for medium, 35 percent; and for low, 40 percent. **Exhibit 6.4** indicates how the pricing of three items turns out compared with an overall price based on a 33.3 percent food cost only calculation. This method weighs food cost and allows the price to reflect the influence of labor as a cost.

Prime Cost Pricing

A selling price can be based on a dollar *prime cost value* divided by a cost percentage or multiplied by a factor. Prime cost is raw food cost plus *direct labor,* or labor spent in preparing an item. Thus, if food cost is $1.00 and direct labor $0.25, prime cost is $1.25. An operation that wants a 35 percent food cost and a 10 percent direct labor cost has a prime cost percentage of 45 percent.

Direct labor time is usually obtained by timing work. A selling price based on prime cost is obtained by establishing a desired combined food and direct

Exhibit 6.4   Selling Costs Based on Various Labor Costs

Item	Labor Requirements	% Food Cost Assigned	$ Food Cost	Selling Price Based on Labor and Food Costs	33.3 % Selling Price
Stew	H	25	$1.10	$4.40	$ 3.67
Steak	M	35	3.20	9.14	10.67
Milk	L	40	0.17	0.43	0.57

labor cost percentage. Suppose 45 percent is the desired prime cost percentage and a cook takes 1.5 hours to make a recipe that gives 60 portions. The food cost of the recipe is $126.56. The cook is paid $5.75 per hour; 1.5 × $5.75 gives a direct labor cost of $8.62, which, added to $126.56, gives a prime cost of $135.18. The prime cost per portion is then $135.18 ÷ 60 portions = $2.25. The selling price would be $2.25 ÷ 0.45 = $5.00.

Combined Food and Labor Costs

Prices may sometimes be based on a combined food and labor cost percentage. For instance, if one wants a 35 percent food cost and a 30 percent labor cost, the combined cost would be 65 percent. If food cost for an item is $2.11 and all labor costs are $1.60, then using these figures the selling price would be ($2.11 + $1.60) ÷ 0.65 = $5.71. For this method, it is necessary to use a dollar value for labor cost that is based neither on a percentage of the selling price nor on a percentage of sales. It has to be a labor cost that is specific for the item.

All or Actual Cost Pricing

Sometimes a method called by several different names—*all cost, actual cost,* or *pay-yourself-first*—is used in operations that keep detailed and accurate cost records. Costs are divided into food, labor, and operating cost units. A dollar value and the desired food and labor costs are obtained for each item. A desired profit percentage is also established. **Exhibit 6.5** illustrates how this method is used to price a dinner choice on a menu. Selling price equals 100 percent; desired profit equals 10 percent; food cost equals 35 percent, or $3.12; labor cost equals 30 percent, or $2.44; operating cost equals 25 percent, or $1.81. The formula is food cost plus labor cost plus operating cost plus 10% profit equals 100% (or selling price). Using these figures, $3.12 + $2.44 + $1.81 = 100% − 10% = $7.37 ÷ 0.90, a selling price of $8.20 is obtained. Again, *actual cost figures must be used*, not percentages based on sales or selling price. This method is useful only with a good cost accounting system. Many smaller food services do not have the accounting system to do this.

Exhibit 6.5 All Cost Pricing

Food cost	35%	$3.12
Labor cost	30	2.44
Operating cost	25	1.81
Total	90%	$7.37
Profit	10	
Total	100%	

Gross Profit Pricing

In this method, a gross profit dollar figure is taken, usually from the profit and loss statement for a certain period. This is divided by the number of guests served during that time to get an average dollar gross profit per guest, as the following example shows.

Sales	$851,322.14
Cost of food	261,110.36
Gross profit	$590,211.78

Suppose the number of guests served during this period was 108,113. The average gross profit per guest is $590,211.78 ÷ 108,113 = $5.46. The dollar cost for an item is then added to this average dollar gross profit to get a selling price. For instance, suppose the food cost for four items was $2.10, $3.13, $2.85, and $4.00. The selling price would then be calculated as in **Exhibit 6.6**.

When using a gross profit average, be sure it includes an adequate profit. If it does not, the desired profit should be added in a dollar value. Thus, if the profit were $0.27 of the $5.46 figure but management wants a per-patron profit of $0.85, about 10 percent of sales, $0.85 – $0.27, or $0.58, is added to the $5.46 figure, bringing the gross profit average up.

Gross profit pricing is a useful method because in many operations the cost of serving each patron is much the same after food costs are considered. It tends to even out prices in a group.

The One-Price Method

In some food services, the overall cost of menu items is the same, such as a doughnut shop where all doughnuts and beverages cost about the same. This is the one-price method in action. The operation can charge just one or a few prices to simplify things. The small differences will usually even out. A nightclub with a cover charge can also use the one-price method because the cost of what is served is nominal when compared to other costs, such as entertainment, music, and decor.

Exhibit 6.6   Gross Profit Pricing

Item	Food Cost	Average Gross Profit	Selling Price
A	$2.10	$5.46	$7.56
B	3.13	5.46	8.59
C	2.85	5.46	8.31
D	4.00	5.46	9.46

Another kind of operation that might charge one price regardless of the item selected is one in which selling food is not a primary purpose. This operation could be a tavern that makes all sandwiches one price. Or it could be a casino, where the objective is to get people in to gamble, and if food at one price helps do that, the operation benefits.

Marginal Analysis Pricing

Retail operations, including food services, may use the *marginal analysis* pricing method. This is an objective method in which the maximum profit point is calculated. The selling price chosen will be the one that establishes this maximum.

Say a quick-service operation wants to set the most favorable price for its milkshakes in order to maximize profit. It estimates that at various prices it will sell a certain number of milkshakes, as shown in **Exhibit 6.7**. Fixed costs are $80.00, and variable cost per milkshake is $0.40. Thus, 100 shakes cost 100 × $0.40 food cost plus $80.00 (100 × 0.40 + $80 = 120).

From the marginal profit column we can see that the best selling price is $1.10 with 410 sold; the next best is $1.20. **Exhibit 6.8** shows how this marginal analysis problem appears in graph form.

The greatest distance between the costs and sales lines is at points *a* and *b*, where 410 milk shakes are sold to bring $451 in sales at a cost of $244, giving a profit of $207.

Cost-Plus-Profit Pricing

In the *cost-plus-profit* pricing method, a food service may decide it needs a standard profit from every patron who enters. The rationale behind this is that every customer who comes through the door costs the operation money, no matter what is ordered. The operation may reason that it wants a set

Exhibit 6.7 Marginal Analysis Projection

Selling Price	Number Sold*	Total Sales	Total Costs	Marginal Profit
$1.50	100	$150.00	$120.00†	$ 30.00
1.40	190	266.00	156.00	100.00
1.30	275	357.50	190.00	167.50
1.20	340	408.00	216.00	192.00
1.10	410	451.00	244.00	207.00
1.00	450	450.00	260.00	190.00
0.90	525	472.50	290.00	182.50

*Estimated from marketing studies or by other means.
†$80 fixed cost + 100 sold × $0.40 each = $120.

Exhibit 6.8   Marginal Analysis Graph

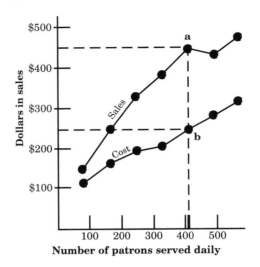

amount of profit from every patron. Therefore, total costs may be calculated and then a set amount added to this. For instance, an operation that wants to make $600 a day in profit may find it has an average of 400 patrons per day. Then, when pricing, the food, labor, and operating costs are added together, plus a $1.50 profit. This covers all costs and should result in the desired profit of $600. Next, an average labor cost value and operating cost value are determined from the profit and loss statement, and both are divided by the number of patrons served in that period. If labor costs, including all benefits, are $80,511, operating costs are $50,336, and 83,001 patrons are served, the average labor cost per patron is $0.97 and the operating cost per patron is $0.61. The selling price calculations for items A, B, C, and D are shown in **Exhibit 6.9**. In this case, the low operating and labor costs give low selling prices. This method tends to even out selling prices.

Exhibit 6.9   Cost-Plus-Profit Pricing

	Food Cost		Labor Cost Per Patron		Operating Cost Per Patron		Profit	Selling Price
A	$2.10	+	$0.97	+	$0.61	+	$0.50	$5.18 (or $5.25)
B	3.13	+	0.97	+	0.61	+	0.50	6.21 (or $6.25)
C	2.85	+	0.97	+	0.61	+	0.50	5.93 (or $5.95)
D	4.00	+	0.97	+	0.61	+	0.50	7.08 (or $7.15)

Minimum Charge Pricing

Pricing based on a minimum price to cover costs and give a desired profit in a commercial operation is much the same as calculating the price based on costs plus profit. The rationale for this method is also much the same. That is, every customer costs a certain amount to serve, and by having a minimum charge these costs will be covered. A hospital or nursing home might use such a method. A private club might have a minimum for certain rooms where food and beverage service is provided. Such a policy is also common in some commercial dining rooms. Pricing may be "arranged" on a menu card to make it impossible to obtain service below a certain price. For instance, the Four Seasons Restaurant in New York City may not want to see a price of less than $15 for lunch. Such operations will test out various luncheon combinations. Whatever menu items produce the desired result will be priced accordingly.

Some operations may state on the menu card that there is a check minimum. If a customer does not order enough food to cover this minimum, the check will still include the minimum payment. Clubs may require that members spend a specific amount during a certain period on foods and beverages so that the foodservice department receives enough income to operate. If the member does not spend this amount during the period, the balance is added to the bill.

Cover Charge

A cover charge is a set price that is added to customers' bills, regardless of what menu items are purchased. This cover charge establishes a base from which costs for space, atmosphere, entertainment, and other costs will be paid. The cover charge is used by nightclubs and other operations where entertainment or dancing may be an attraction.

Pricing Based on Sales Potential

Some menu planners believe that pricing should reflect factors in addition to food and labor costs, including how an item is expected to sell. They divide items into High Cost (HC) or Low Cost (LC), High Risk (HR) or Low Risk (LR), and High Volume (HV) or Low Volume (LV). Thus, one menu item may be labeled HC-LR-HV and another LC-HR-HV. Ratings of LC, HV, and LR are considered favorable, while HR, HC, and LV are considered unfavorable. Eight combinations are possible.

HR-LC-HV	HR-HC-LV	
HR-LC-LV	HC-LR-LV	HV-LR-LC
HR-HC-HV	HC-HV-LR	LR-LC-LV

If a plus (+) is assigned for a favorable factor and a minus (–) for an unfavorable one, the following matrix is obtained, based on the previous combinations.

– + +	– – –	
– + –	– + –	+ + +
– – +	– + +	+ + –

If this formula is used when pricing, the highest markup would be assigned to any item having three minuses or two minuses and a plus, a lower markup to one minus and two pluses, and the lowest markup to the one with three pluses. Perhaps the highest markup would be based on a 25 percent food cost, the next on a 30 percent food cost, and the last on a 40 percent cost. This type of pricing would ensure a profit margin for low-volume, high-cost items. **Exhibit 6.10** shows how an operation might classify items, and then indicate the desired food cost markup.

Non-cost Pricing

A number of methods that are not based on cost are used in pricing menus. Some, such as pricing based on tradition, competition, or what the market will bear, are in this category. Surprisingly, they are used often and, even more surprisingly, are often successful. Some are difficult to use. Finding a price based on what the market will bear is an involved process and takes a lot of testing and observation. Others, such as traditional pricing or pricing against competition, are relatively simple.

Exhibit 6.10   Menu Item Markups

Menu Item	Risk High	Risk Low	Cost High	Cost Low	Volume High	Volume Low	% Markup
N.Y. steak	—		—		+		30
Apple pie		+	—			—	30
Chicken noodle soup		+		+	+		40
Vanilla ice cream		+		+	+		40
Lobster	—		—			—	25
Vegetables		+		+		—	35
Fish	—			+	+		35
Swiss steak		+		+		—	35

These figures can be used to record risk, cost, and volume levels so the menu pricer can properly allocate markup.

Pricing Based on Tradition

Many operations look at traditional prices, often those set by the leaders in a particular market niche. Tradition in pricing may relate not only to a specific price but also to the pricing structure and market. Many operations find they cannot get as high a markup for California wines as they can for European ones, although the California product may be of equal or better quality. Tradition has it that the domestic product is usually lower in price, and, therefore, the pricing structure must be varied to suit this tradition.

Different types of operations will also find that the pricing structure they must follow is one in which a lower markup must be taken than that of another type of food service. Thus, while two operations may sell exactly the same thing, one will be able to set prices on a different basis from the other.

Some operators may find that they have prices established for such a long time that they become traditional with their customers. When they attempt to change these prices, they may meet with very strong sales resistance and customer dissatisfaction. Thus, they may decide not to change the price on a particular item but get a higher markup on other items that are not so restricted.

It is possible for a price to become traditional because a leader in the market charges this price. Thus, an industry leader like McDonald's sees its prices often become traditional among similar operations.

Competitive Pricing

One of the most common pricing methods is to base the price on what the competition charges. While it is wise to pay attention to competitors' prices, it is unwise to base your prices *completely* on them. What the competition charges may bear no relation to your costs. Pricing in this manner wrongly assumes that prices satisfactory for the competition's customers are also satisfactory for your customers. In addition, copying competitors' prices does little to differentiate an operation.

If competitive pricing is indicated by research, a unit should study its own costs to analyze how it can price menu items to produce a more favorable response than that produced by the competition's prices. A competitor's price may be studied to reveal information about the food, labor, and other operating costs. Food and labor are standard commodities that will have a known price. A close scrutiny of these may indicate what the competition might be doing to achieve a favorable price structure. A study of competitive pricing and its effect on one's own business is also warranted. In some cases, prices may have to reflect the influence of competition.

What the Market Will Bear

A method of pricing used by some companies is to design a product and then test market it at a given selling price. The product may be put on several markets at different prices and the reaction of customers studied to ascertain which is the best price.

Marketing specialists state that one of the best routes to success is to develop a product the market wants and then price it so that a healthy profit is made. With proper pricing and strong demand, these specialists say there is a high chance of developing a successful market. They recommended studying the value of the product *in the minds of patrons* and then charging accordingly. Some products may have to be priced only slightly above cost to be accepted by the market; others can have a much higher margin.

Establishing a selling price based on what the market will bear is not just a trial-and-error method; it should be based on sound research. To some extent, prices can be tested to see how well patrons accept them; however, not too much experimentation per item can be done. Perhaps three or four prices can be tested on an item, and then the testing must be stopped. Otherwise, patrons might reject the item because of the instability of the price.

Pricing according to what the market will bear has become a popular method with a number of industries. It is a perfectly legitimate system. If a customer attaches a certain value to a product and is willing to pay a higher price for it, there is no reason why it should not be marketed at that price. Patrons are not interested in what it costs to produce and market an item. They are much more interested in getting something they feel represents a good value for their money. If the price is within the value they have in mind, they are happy. If they feel that a meal priced at $4 is worth $4, even though its cost to the operation is only $2.50, there is nothing wrong with charging $4 for it. However, if a meal costs $4 to produce and patrons consider it worth only $2.50, they will not buy it, even if it represents a lower price than cost.

Success in pricing according to what the market will bear is enhanced if some attempt is made to show patrons the true value of the menu item. It is often difficult for patrons to see the value in atmosphere, service, fine tableware, linens, and foods that are somewhat out of season or brought in at an additional cost. If a way is found to get patrons to understand that these increased costs increase value, they may be willing to pay a higher price. Having a differentiated product is one way of getting patrons to see and appreciate value. The food service with exceptional service, decor, atmosphere, and dining experience, including fine presentation that patrons would not get at home, can make patrons feel they are getting good value for their money.

Pricing Aids

Pricing can be made easier if tables and computer printouts are available that give food costs of various menu items, with prices based on the operation's food cost percentage already tabulated. These types of programs are covered in detail in Chapter 13.

EVALUATING PRICING METHODS

Few operations use only one pricing method. Most use a combination to best meet their needs and those of their patrons. Pricing based only on competition is generally not a good method, but considering the prices of competition when establishing one's own menu prices is advisable. Using a standard markup over an accurate cost determination can give a fairly precise price basis and usually assures an adequate profit or budget performance. However, varying margins over cost based on what the market will bear should also be considered, as should pricing based on volume. Perhaps markups should be varied to promote merchandising and entice patrons with *loss leaders* (items that have a low markup but can bring in extra business). Additionally, various items may be priced to cover the high food cost of items with prices based on local competition. Thus, a quick-service operation may not make as much on its hamburgers and hot dogs as it does on milkshakes, carbonated beverages, and fries, but in the end the achieved sales mix can give a very desirable markup level.

And, finally, *pricing is not something that is done and then is over*. There is a need to evaluate prices constantly, to study how customers react to prices, and to gather data on costs. Too often no follow-up occurs, and when a revision of menus and prices is necessary, there is a lack of adequate information to do a good job. Gathering, compiling, collating, and filing pricing data are as much a part of the pricing function as the establishment of prices.

PRICING FOR NONPROFIT OPERATIONS

The previous discussions on menu pricing for commercial operations are applicable to noncommercial operations, except that most do not need to allow for profit in their prices. They are required to meet costs and perhaps make a slight margin above costs as a safety factor that can be accumulated to bridge times when costs are not covered. Costs may be paid for in part by the patron, with the balance paid by federal and state agencies or charitable donations.

When nonprofit operations price items to break even, accurate cost information must be available from operating records. The information must be timely, so that action can be taken promptly to bring costs into line when they vary from desired levels. Many institutional operations estimate costs for a period and are given an allowance from the total budget to cover this estimate. When costs for a future period must be estimated, information from federal agencies, economic indexes, and economic price predictions of price changes can be used.

Nonprofit operations usually establish prices on the basis of a budgeted amount per meal, per day, per week, per month, or per period. Some nonprofit budgets allow a cash allowance for food, labor, and operating expenses. Other operations may first get a total food allowance for a period, and then a cash allowance is worked out from this. This food and cash allowance system is called a *ration allowance*. (See the discussion on ration allowance budgeting in Chapter 5.)

PRICING EMPLOYEE MEALS

In in-plant and company food services, whether employees pay for meals or the company subsidizes them, costs must be calculated so they are covered.

Employee meals are often considered a benefit and, thus, an operating expense. Therefore, when the cost of food for employee meals is included in the cost of food used, it must be deducted. The value for deducting an employee meal can be based on: 1) the actual cost of the meal, 2) experience, 3) a standard charge made in the area for meals, or 4) an arbitrary amount. The actual cost may be standard menu prices with a discount given to employees. In some areas it may be a practice to deduct a predetermined amount for employee meals, a plan followed by a number of food services. The arbitrary amount may be only a nominal charge but one that the food service thinks is adequate to cover its costs, or at least a major portion of them.

Most operations take their average food cost percentage and use this to arrive at a value for the food used for employees' meals. Thus, if the food cost is 35 percent and a total value of $800.19 is assigned to the employees' meals for a certain period, the value of the food in these meals for that period will be 0.35 × $800.19, or $280.07. When employees eat the same meals as patrons, the cost of employees' meals may be calculated using the following steps.

1. Ascertain the number of employee meals.
2. Calculate the individual meal cost.
3. Consider food for employees' meals as 50 percent of the cost of a meal.
4. Multiply the number of employees' meals by the food cost per employee meal.

For example, say an operation has total costs of $11,400 for 15,571 meals served during the period, with 1,240 of these meals being eaten by employees.

$11,400 ÷ 15,571 = $0.732 per meal
73.2 × 0.50 = $0.366 food cost per employee meal
1,240 × $0.36 = $453.84 total food cost for employee meals

Based on this information, it would be simple to arrive at a nominal menu price. This information will also provide the data for deducting meals as a benefit.

CHANGING MENU PRICES

At times a change in a menu price is necessary. If it is an item that appears frequently on the menu and has good acceptance, repricing may present difficulties. Customers may resent the change and may stop ordering the item to show their displeasure. Sometimes this does not last long, and the item gradually assumes its former importance as a seller.

During periods in which food prices increase rapidly, most customers recognize the need for an operation to increase prices and will accept them.

In periods when prices are stable but some other factor makes a change necessary, customers may not be so willing to accept a price change.

Some operators attempt to change a price by removing an item from the menu for a time and then bringing it back at a new price. If it also comes back in a somewhat new form, or in a new manner of serving and with a slightly different menu name, the price change may be less noticeable. Changes also tend to be noticed less if they are made when volume is down.

Prices are frequently changed when a new menu is printed. In fact, the need to change menu prices may sometimes stimulate a menu change more than the need to change items. Some authorities advise against changing format and prices at the same time, saying that customers will notice price changes *because* of the new format.

Using menu clip-ons removes the need to print new menus just to incorporate new prices, and avoids the needs to cross out old prices to put new ones in. The latter, especially, can give patrons a negative impression.

In some instances, if a general rise in menu prices must occur, an operation may change several items $0.05 or $0.10 each and then let these remain at this price while changing a few others. In this manner prices are gradually worked up to the desired level. This has the disadvantage of giving customers the impression that the menu and its prices are unstable.

Some announcement, on a clip-on or table tent, can be helpful in indicating to patrons why a change in menu prices is necessary. However, this can also have the undesirable effect of calling attention to changes that some customers might not otherwise notice.

Patrons are likely to be especially aware of price changes for popular items. Also, as noted, they are more aware of a change when the dollar price changes than when the cents price does. Rather than changing a dollar amount, it might be wiser to make a price change in cents, or make it gradually.

Only a few items' prices at a time should be changed if prices are changed frequently. More items can be repriced if the change is less frequent. Some say that only two price changes should be made in a year; others feel that only one is advisable. With some items for which prices may have to change frequently, such as lobster or stone crab, it is advisable to list the price as "Seasonable Price" or "Market Price."

Printed menus that rarely change their items offered or format are more difficult to change in price than are blackboards, panels, or handwritten menus. If a menu has a daily insert in which items change daily or frequently, it is easier to make price changes on this than on the permanent hardcover menu. It is not a good practice to cross out an old price and write in a new one. Even whiting out a price and writing in a new one is not recommended.

Specials and highly promoted items are difficult to change in price because buyer attention is often centered on them. They should be dropped from promotion for a time and then reinserted with the prices changed. In all cases, price changes on menu items should end up within the range expected by patrons.

PRICING PITFALLS

All foodservice managers should beware of the following pitfalls committed by inefficient menu planners.

1. Pricing should not be based entirely on just one cost, such as food cost, giving a price that may not reflect actual costs. Other costs vary considerably from a direct relationship with food cost. Thus, pricing only on the basis of food cost can lead to pricing errors.

2. Foodservice pricing should not ignore the economic laws of supply and demand.

3. Value perception on the part of patrons in equating price to value of a menu item should have greater emphasis in pricing.

4. More attention needs to be given to market information in establishing prices.

SUMMARY

Pricing a menu is a complex process, and a number of factors need to be considered when doing it. Anyone pricing a menu should know about and experiment with some of the latest pricing methods, such as marginal analysis pricing and market testing of prices.

Studies have shown that consumers view prices somewhat differently than operators might expect. They want prices grouped within a price range they expect to pay, and resist purchasing items outside this range.

A number of pricing methods are used by the foodservice industry. Probably no one method is used alone, but a combination of them can be used in establishing menu prices.

Patrons will pay only so much for certain kinds of foods in certain kinds of operations, and the menu planner must be sure to meet this restriction. Menu prices are often not easy to change, and planners should be aware of the techniques that make price changes less noticeable by patrons.

QUESTIONS

1. What is a *differentiated* product? What is its purpose? How is it used?

2. A food service wants a 25 percent food cost. What multiplier or pricing factor should be used?

3. The food cost of a table d'hôte group of foods is $8.20, and a 30 percent food cost is desired. What is the selling price?

4. If raw food cost is $1 and direct labor cost is $0.30, what is the prime cost? If a 40 percent price based on this prime cost is wanted, what is the selling price?

7

Menu Mechanics

Objectives

After reading this chapter, you should be able to:

1. Identify the basic requirements to make a menu an effective communication and merchandising medium.

2. Discuss aspects of using type: typeface, type size, line length, spacing between lines and letters, blank space, weight, and type style.

3. Indicate how to give menu items prominence by using displays in columns, boxes, or clip-ons.

4. Indicate how to best use color in menus.

5. Discuss paper use, construction of covers, and other physical factors.

6. Indicate how menus are commonly printed, how to work with professional menu printers, and how to self-print.

INTRODUCTION

Certain mechanical factors must be considered in menu planning. No matter how well the menu is planned and priced, it must also be properly presented so that it is understood quickly and leads to satisfactory sales. *Communicating* and *selling* are the main functions of a successful menu. Good use of mechanical factors will enhance a menu's appearance, make a favorable impression on patrons, and advance the overall aims of the operation.

Professional menu printing companies can be of considerable help in developing a menu that is attractive and achieves its purpose as a merchandising medium. For this reason, the material in this chapter is designed to teach readers how to work with professionals as well as how to do the job without assistance.

MENU PRESENTATION

How a menu is presented is important to most operations. For commercial establishments the menu does much to convey the type of operation and its food and service. If the menu communicates accurately through design and layout, as well as through the copy, it can "sell" the items on it.

While most menus are printed on paper and given to patrons to look at, some might not be presented in this way. A cafeteria menu board may show items for sale and list prices. A quick-service operation might have menu signs or cards on tables. Some operations have hand-written menus to give a homey and personal touch. A menu may be made to resemble a small newspaper and list the latest news along with menu items.

The manner in which menu items are presented should be selected to best meet the needs of the operation. A hospital may have selected menus printed on colored paper, each color indicating a different diet. On some, special instructions concerning selections by patients may be used. The sales department of a hotel or catering department may need a special menu to give to people interested in arranging special functions at the hotel.

Some operations need a number of different menus, such as breakfast, brunch, lunch, matinee, dinner, or evening. A country club may need a menu for its bar where steaks, sandwiches, and snack foods are served; another for a coffee shop or game room; a small snack and beverage service near the swimming pool; and another for the main dining room. A hotel or motel might use a special room service menu. As these menus vary in their purpose and requirements, so must they vary in the manner in which menu items are presented.

The most common menu is the one presented on firm paper, the front being used for some logo, design, or motif. Inside, on the left and right sides of the fold, a la carte offerings (items selected and paid for individually) are listed. The back may also contain a la carte items and alcoholic beverages, or give information about hours of operation and short notes of interest about the operation, locale, or some of the special items served. The items on this heavy paper are permanent.

Exhibit 7.1 A la Carte and Table d'Hôte Entrees

	A la carte	Table d'hôte
Southern Fried Chicken with Country Gravy and Corn Fritter	$ 6.50	$ 8.95
Crab Cakes Mornay en Coquille with Steamed Rice	9.50	11.95
Fillet of Cod en Papillote, French Fried Zucchini	7.95	10.50
Hawaiian Ham Steak, with Mashed Sweet Potatoes	5.95	8.50
New York Strip Steak, French Fried Potatoes	11.50	14.95
Breaded Veal Cutlet, Sauteed Mushrooms, and Baked Potato	5.95	7.95

With the table d'hôte dinner you have a choice of salad or vegetable, beverage, and desert. Roll and butter are served with a la carte and table d'hôte orders.

Often, menu items that change, including table d'hôte meals (foods or meals sold together at one price), are printed on lighter paper and attached to the more rigid menu.

Sometimes menus list two prices for an item, one including the entree as the main dish in a table d'hôte meal, the other offering it a la carte. Even as an a la carte item, it may be served with such foods as bread and butter. (See **Exhibit 7.1.**) While this listing shows about a $2.50 difference between table d'hôte and a la carte items, it is not unusual to see prices between table d'hôte and a la carte vary widely.

Some menus may offer specials. These can be attached as clip-ons or inserts. If they are used, the basic menu should provide space for them. They should not cover other menu items.

Clip-ons or inserts are used to give greater emphasis to items management wants to push. They should not repeat what is on the menu but offer variety. The use of these clip-ons or inserts make it possible to change a permanent menu for weekly specials or holidays. Clip-ons and inserts may be of the same color as the menu, but if special effects and heightened patron attention are desired, the use of a different color can help focus attention on them.

Menu Format

Regardless of how a menu is presented to patrons, certain rules in format should be observed. Wording and its arrangement should be such that the reader quickly understands what is offered. If foods are offered in groups, it should be clear what foods are included. Clarity is promoted by making menu items stand out. Simplicity helps avoid clutter. Foods usually should be on the menu in the order in which they are eaten. An exception might be a cafeteria menu board, listing items as they appear in the line. Some offer cold foods first and hot foods last. This avoids the hot foods cooling off while a customer selects cold foods. Some menus also indicate the location of foods, such as in a takeout operation, where different counters offer different foods, or a cafeteria where patrons move from one section to another to get different foods. In this case, the menu board can be helpful by indicating a counter number or using a diagram to show where foods are found.

Production Menus

Some menus may never be seen by patrons. They are written principally for back-of-the-house workers to inform them about what must be produced. This requires a different form and terminology, selling words and fancy descriptions are not required. The term "carrot pennies," which sounds good on a menu read by patrons, instead will be "sliced carrots." Production information is included, such as the amount to prepare, the recipe number to use, preparation time, distribution to service units, designation of the worker to prepare items, and portion sizes. Service instructions, such as the portioning instructions and the dishes and utensils to use, may also be added.

MENU DESIGN

The design of a menu contributes greatly to its legibility and patron reaction. Therefore, the design should be well planned. Menus, like individuals, should have personalities. They should reflect the atmosphere and "feel" of the operation. The eye should be pleased with what it sees on the menu and patrons should quickly grasp what is offered and the price. The printing and coloring should blend in with the logo or trademark of the operation as well as with the type of establishment. The menu should be to a foodservice operation what a program is to a play or opera—an indication of what is to come. It should be an invitation to a pleasing experience and should not promise too much. Patrons should clearly understand what they are to get and the price they are to pay for it.

Using Type

Typefaces

One of the most important factors in accomplishing a menu's purpose is the style of type, or *typeface*, used. There are many different kinds of type, and some are more legible and more easily and quickly read than others. The type most often used for menus is a *serif* type, or one in which letters are slightly curved. These are some of the easiest types to read. Letters set in *sans serif* type look blocky. (See **Exhibit 7.2**.)

Studies have been made to ascertain legibility, reading speed, and comprehension using different typefaces. Unfortunately, not all of the types that have been studied are used in menus, and some that have considerable popularity in menu use were not included in the studies. Nevertheless, from such studies we can get some idea of the best typefaces to use for menus.

Print comes in plain (regular), bold (heavy print), italics, and script. Any type of italic or script print is more difficult to read than plain type. However, in some cases, these might be preferable to others because of special

Exhibit 7.2 Samples of Type

Serif

Times Roman
Braised in butter and then simmered in red wine with shallots and other herbs, this dish has been for centuries one of the most typical of the Bretony area. Braised in butter and then simmered in red wine with shallots and other herbs, this dish has been for centuries one of the most typical of the Bretony area.

Palatino
Braised in butter and then simmered in red wine with shallots and other herbs, this dish has been for centuries one of the most typical of the Bretony area. Braised in butter and then simmered in red wine with shallots and other herbs, this dish has been for centuries one of the most typical of the Bretony area.

Bookman
Braised in butter and then simmered in red wine with shallots and other herbs, this dish has been for centuries one of the most typical of the Bretony area. Braised in butter and then simmered in red wine with shallots and other herbs, this dish has been for centuries one of the most typical of the Bretony area.

Sans Serif

Helvetica
Braised in butter and then simmered in red wine with shallots and other herbs, this dish has been for centuries one of the most typical of the Bretony area. Braised in butter and then simmered in red wine with shallots and other herbs, this dish has been for centuries one of the most typical of the Bretony area.

Helvetica Black
Braised in butter and then simmered in red wine with shallots and other herbs, this dish has been for centuries one of the most typical of the Bretony area. Braised in butter and then simmered in red wine with shallots and other herbs, this dish has been for centuries one of the most typical of the Bretony area.

Futura
Braised in butter and then simmered in red wine with shallots and other herbs, this dish has been for centuries one of the most typical of the Bretony area. Braised in butter and then simmered in red wine with shallots and other herbs, this dish has been for centuries one of the most typical of the Bretony area.

effects desired. A fine-dining restaurant may want to use these typefaces because they imply elegance in dining. Italic, script, or specialty types can bring on fatigue in reading, but this may not be a factor in short menus.

Type Size

The size of type is important to both understanding and speed of reading. Type that is too small makes reading difficult, but type that is too large takes up too much space; it might actually inhibit comprehension because it spreads the words out too much.

Type size is measured in *points*. There are 72 points to an inch. Thus, 18-point type is nearly a fourth of an inch high. Most menu designers use 10- or 12-point type for listing menu items and 18-point type for headings. This can be varied for descriptions.

Readers have ranked their preferences for type size. Three sizes—10-point, 11-point, and 12-point—ranked together as first choices, followed by 9-point, 8-point, and 6-point. Various type sizes are shown in **Exhibit 7.3**.

Exhibit 7.3   Type Sizes

Point Size	Name
3 $\frac{1}{2}$ point	Brilliant
4 $\frac{1}{2}$ point	Diamond
5 point	Pearl
5 $\frac{1}{2}$ point	Agate
6 point	Nonpareil
7 point	Minion
8 point	Brevier
9 point	Bourgeois
10 point	Long Primer
11 point	Small Pica
12 point	Pica
14 point	English
16 point	Columbian
18 point	Great Primer

Menus printed in a single type size can be monotonous. The sizes are usually varied on a page to give relief. (See **Exhibit 7.4**.) Thus, menu items may be listed in 12-point type, with 9- or 10-point type used for the description just below the item.

Menu headings may be in capital letters in bolder and larger type. Different type from that for the items sometimes may be used, but some mixtures may give an undesirable effect.

At times, to draw attention to an item, larger type is used than that used for regular items. For instance, the menu may use normal-weight 12-point type rather than heavy or light printing for regular items, and then change to a 14-point boldface (heavy) type to give emphasis to a special item. Additional emphasis can be given to an item by placing it in a box and putting an ornamental border around it. (See **Exhibit 7.5**.) If the box is in a different color from the regular menu, the emphasis may be greater.

Exhibit 7.4   Menu Showing Type Size Contrast

Appetizers

Shrimp Cocktail **5.50**
Six ice-cold jumbo shrimp served with tangy cocktail sauce.

Cold Seafood Platter **6.50**
Oysters, shrimp, lobster, and clams served with Brooklyn
Navy Yard sauce or drawn butter.

Steak Tidbits **5.50**
Strips of sirloin breaded, served with marinara sauce.

Chicken Fingers...**4.75**
Fried chicken pieces with blue cheese dipping sauce.

Mozzarella Marinara **4.95**
Fried cheese smothered in marinara sauce.

Arugula Salad **6.95**
Crunchy arugula with mushrooms, red onions,
hearts of palm, and raspberry vinaigrette dressing.

Mozzarella Salad **5.95**
Fresh Buffalo mozzarella, fresh basil, and sliced tomatoes
dribbled with extra virgin olive oil.

Exhibit 7.5   Menu Item Emphasis

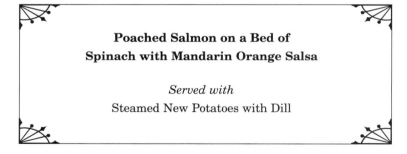

Spacing of Type

Another factor affecting ease of reading and comprehension of menus is the spacing between letters in a word and between words. If letters and words are set too close together or too far apart, reading is difficult. Associated with this horizontal dimension in typography is the width of the individual characters in a particular style of type. They may be condensed (narrow), regular, or extended (wide), and this quality has its effect on readability and the scanning rate. Thus, a condensed word would be printed **"condensed,"** a regular would be printed **"regular,"** and an extended would be printed **"extended."**

Exhibit 7.6 Samples of Leading

Solid

A treat to the palate sends taste buds soaring. A treat to the palate sends taste buds soaring. A treat to the palate sends taste buds soaring. A treat to the palate sends taste buds soaring.

1-Point Leading

A treat to the palate sends taste buds soaring. A treat to the palate sends taste buds soaring. A treat to the palate sends taste buds soaring. A treat to the palate sends taste buds soaring.

2-Point Leading

A treat to the palate sends taste buds soaring. A treat to the palate sends taste buds soaring. A treat to the palate sends taste buds soaring. A treat to the palate sends taste buds soaring.

3-Point Leading

A treat to the palate sends taste buds soaring. A treat to the palate sends taste buds soaring. A treat to the palate sends taste buds soaring. A treat to the palate sends taste buds soaring.

5-Point Leading

A treat to the palate sends taste buds soaring. A treat to the palate sends taste buds soaring. A treat to the palate sends taste buds soaring. A treat to the palate sends taste buds soaring.

Vertical spacing between lines of type, called *leading* (pronounced "ledding", is also important to ease of reading. If no leading is used, the type is said to be set *solid*. The thickness of these leads is also measured in points. **Exhibit 7.6** shows lines set solid and lines with 1-, 2-, 3-, and 5-point leading.

A general rule for easy reading is that leading should be two to four points larger than the typeface being used.

Weight

Weight is a term used to indicate the heaviness or lightness of print. Light print may appear gray, rather than black, and does not stand out well; normal or *medium* is what is normally used on menus; *bold* or heavy print is quite dense; sometimes even extra bold is used. Bold or extra bold weight helps give emphasis, but too much can lead to a cluttered look.

Emphasis can be given and items made to stand out by the wise use of light and bold type. Very light type will not give good emphasis and is sometimes difficult to read. Extra bold type is extremely dark and black. Bold or heavy may be desirable to draw attention but should be used sparingly. Too bold a typeface is not suitable for the menu of a refined, quiet dining room.

(Sometimes a printer may refer to the weight of the type as its color, but this is a term used mostly by professionals.) The light level of an operation must be considered. A restaurant with a low level of light should use a slightly larger, bolder type to keep the menus readable. Light type is best used in an operation with a normal or higher than normal level of light.

Use of Uppercase and Lowercase Letters

Another factor that influences ease of reading and comprehension is effectively combining the use of *uppercase* (capitals) and *lowercase* (small) letters. Uppercase gives emphasis and can set words out more clearly. Lowercase is easier to read. Uppercase is used with lower case to begin sentences, or for proper nouns. It is usually desirable to capitalize all first letters of proper names and main words in item titles on the menu. For instance, the following would be normal: "Top Sirloin Steak Sandwich." Words such as *or, the, a la, in, and*, or *with* are usually not capitalized. Descriptive information, such as "A combination of shrimp, scallops, halibut and oysters in Newburg sauce", will not have capitalized letters, except for the name of the sauce, because it is a proper noun. Uppercase may be used to emphasize words, as in "Includes French Fries, Tossed Green Salad with your Favorite Dressing, and Choice of Beverage and Dessert".

Often menu items are put in large, bold caps to stand out, and lower case type is used for descriptive material below the name of the item, capitalizing only proper nouns and first letters of sentences in the descriptive material. Special effects can be obtained at times by setting all descriptive words in small caps.

Descriptions should be in keeping with the menu theme and set in a typeface compatible with other type on the page. All elements should blend together if a maximum effect is to be achieved.

Special Effects Using Type

The use of type may give special effects. For instance, a nation's script—Javanese, Russian, Greek, Hebrew, Arabic, Japanese, Chinese, Thai—can be used to reflect a restaurant's cuisine.

Page Design

Page layout and design is an essential element of menu development. A good menu will "grab" patrons and attract them to items the operation wants to sell. A poorly designed menu will do the opposite—lead patrons into a maze with more than enough items to confuse them.

The amount of copy on a page affects how quickly a menu can be read and understood. In one study, readers indicated they wanted fairly wide margins and disliked copy that ran too close to the edge of the paper, a warning to menu planners who tend to overcrowd areas. Normally, just slightly more than 52 percent of a printed page has print on it, and slightly over 47 percent is margins. **Exhibit 7.7** shows a page with a black area in the center

Exhibit 7.7 Spacing for Margins

indicating print and margins around it. One would not suspect that the white margin area accounts for nearly half the page. Perhaps, in menu copy, slightly more than this could be covered but not much more. Providing as much margin space as possible without squeezing menu copy should be the objective.

If space is a problem, extra pages should be added rather than crowding a single menu page. A good margin should remain on the left and right sides and on the top and bottom. **Exhibits 7.8** and **7.9** are examples of good use of space in the menu.

Making a menu so large that a patron has difficulty holding it should be avoided. Some operations make menus very large to give the feeling of luxury, but many guests find them difficult to handle. An operation should give strong consideration to the menu size before deciding on a large one. If a large menu must be used, extra panels that fold open should be considered. Separate menus may also be used. For instance, if desserts are not given with the table d'hôte dinner, or if there is an additional group of a la carte desserts, a special dessert menu may be set up, thus saving space on the main menu. Likewise, alcoholic beverages and wines can be on separate menus. A special fountain menu may be placed on tables and counters where customers can find them, leaving the main menu free to offer a more standard list of items.

Exhibit 7.8 Menu Using Space Effectively

Courtesy of Trillium Restaurant, Grand Traverse Resort, Grand Traverse Village, Michigan

Sandwiches

THE DAGWOOD VEGETARIAN SANDWICH 5.95
Avocado, leaf lettuce, sliced low-fat cheese, guacamole, tomatoes, alfalfa sprouts and reduced-calorie mayonnaise on a whole wheat bun.
With Thinly Sliced Roast Beef 6.50

TURKEY PITA POCKET SANDWICH 6.50

CHICKEN SALAD CROISSANT 5.95

CALIFORNIA CLUB SANDWICH 6.25
A triple decker filled with crab salad, Monterey Jack cheese and bacon.

TUNA MELT 5.95
Select white albacore tuna salad served on our homemade sourdough French bread, topped with sliced tomatoes, alfalfa sprouts and melted Monterey Jack cheese.

MARINATED FLANK STEAK 5.95
Thinly sliced marinated grilled flank steak with red and green peppering and bleu cheese dressing on sourdough French bread

SMOKED TURKEY SANDWICH 5.50
With Wisconsin cheddar on a whole wheat bun.

ROAST PORK SANDWICH 6.25
With mango chutney, sliced apples, alfalfa sprouts and brie cheese on whole wheat.

HAMBURGER 5.95
One-half pound of freshly ground burger served on a toasted bun with leaf lettuce, tomatoes and sliced onion. With cheese, add .30.

All Sandwiches include Your Choice of Unsalted Chips or Fresh Fruit.

Pizza Corner

MINI WHOLE WHEAT PIZZA 5.25
Create your own personal pizza with homemade sauce and provolone cheese. Select any three toppings.

Pepperoni Sliced Avocado Sweet Red Peppers
Sliced Tomatoes Black Olives Italian Sausage Red Onion
Smoked Ham Fresh Pineapple Extra Provolone

Each Additional Topping .50

Entrees

All Entrees include Seasonal Fresh Vegetables.

SAUTEED BEEF TIPS 7.50
With fresh black pepper fettuccini and Hungarian paprika sauce.

CHICKEN and WILD MUSHROOM CREPES 6.50
Served with curry cream sauce.

BREADED SHRIMP SAUTEED in GARLIC BUTTER 8.25
Served with dijon mustard sauce.

PAN FRIED SESAME PERCH 8.95

BAKED WHITEFISH, LEMON CAPER SAUCE 6.95

Health Minded

SAUTEED SHRIMP 8.25
Sauteed in virgin olive oil and served with black bean, tomato and Anaheim pepper salsa.
(206 Calories)

GRILLED CITRUS CHICKEN 7.50
With steamed garden vegetables.
(249 Calories)

WHOLE WHEAT PASTA PRIMAVERA 5.50
With tomato basil sauce.
(171 Calories)

VEGETARIAN PIZZA 5.75
Whole wheat crust topped with onion, green pepper, zucchini and fresh herbs.
(283 Calories)

Cold Starters

CHEESE and FRUIT PLATE 2.95
With poppyseed dressing.

FRESH CUT VEGETABLES and SPINACH DIP 3.50

SHRIMP COCKTAIL 7.50
Served with cocktail sauce.

Hot Starters

CHEESE, ONION and POTATO FRITTERS 2.50

BEER BATTERED FRESH VEGETABLES 3.95
Fried and served with dill dip.

HOT ARTICHOKE DIP 3.95
With parmesan bread sticks.

Soups & Salads

BAKED SHALLOT SOUP 2.75

GAZPACHO SOUP 1.95
With cilantro and sour cream.

TODAY'S FRESH SOUP
Cup 1.95   Bowl 2.25

TRADITIONAL SPINACH SALAD 2.50
With choice of dressing.

MIXED GREEN SALAD 2.50
With choice of dressing.

GREEK SALAD 4.95
Mixed greens with Greek olives, feta cheese, garden vegetables and Greek salad dressing.

TACO SALAD 4.50
All of the taco fixings inside a large taco shell with ranch dressing and salsa.

PASTA SALAD 3.95
Rotini tossed with ham and cheddar cheese.

Salad Buffet

THE UNLIMITED TRILLIUM SALAD BAR BUFFET
Sensational selection of garden fresh house made salads, cheese, seafood, fresh produce, pasta and so much more!
Selected as Lunch 6.50
Selected with Sandwiches 4.50

Exhibit 7.9   Menu Using Space Effectively

Courtesy of Coq d'Or, The Drake Hotel, Chicago, Illinois

Exhibit 7.10   Line Length of 24 Picas

Line Width

The width of a line affects reading comprehension. One study found that about two-thirds of menu readers preferred a double-column page to a single-column page. It has also been found that students learn better when reading two column pages. Most readers like a line length of about 22 *picas* (about 3²/₃ inches—there are approximately 6 picas to an inch). Long lines may cause readers to lose their place. **Exhibit 7.10** shows a line length of 24 picas. Most books are printed in columns of line length around 25 picas (about 4³/₁₆ inches), which gives the page only one column.

The eye does not normally flow evenly across a page. It grasps a certain group of words, comprehends these, and then jumps to the next group. If the line is too long, there is a chance of losing the reading place when the eye jumps. Also, too long a line may cause a reader to lose his or her place since the eyes must refocus as the gaze passes from the end of one long line to the beginning of the next line. One menu authority recommends that, rather than putting prices a distance from menu items in a column to the right, prices should be put right next to or directly under the item.

Emphasizing Menu Items

There are a number of ways to emphasize menu items that management wants to sell. An item is set apart by separating it by a bit of space and special type, and then giving some description of the item, as shown in **Exhibit 7.11**. This description can help give emphasis, especially if it is italicized or set in different type. Items can also be shifted slightly for emphasis. Note that when this is done in a column, items will stand out well, as in **Exhibit 7.12**.

In spite of the fact that menu space is valuable, some blank space is needed to set items apart and to avoid having the menu so crowded that the reader is confused. From one-fourth to one-third of the printed area should be blank, in addition to margin space. Headings and lines can be used to indicate separations and help draw attention to items.

The first and last items in a column are seen first and best. This is the place to put menu items one wishes to sell. It is possible to lose items in the middle of a column, so items that management may be less interested in selling, but that have to be on the menu, might be placed here.

Readers tend to skip items. Indenting items presented in a column can help make readers look at all the items in the column. Items too deeply indented, however, are often lost; this is where items are put when one does not wish to give them emphasis. Arranging items in a column from highest

Exhibit 7.11 Item Emphasis

Special Texas Sirloin Steak, Charbroiled **$14.50**
Served with Baked or French Fried Potatoes and a Tossed Green Salad
with your choice of French, Thousand Island or Blue Cheese Dressing

Exhibit 7.12 Emphasis on Columns

FRUITS OF THE SEA

Sauteed English Sole, Almandine with Spinach Soufflé **$14.00**
with Cole Slaw and French Fried Potatoes

New England Crab Cakes with Braised French Garden Vegetables **$13.50**
with Sun-dried Tomatoes and Creamy Basil Dressing

Curry of Shrimp on a Bed of Rice, Chutney Sauce **$16.95**
with Fresh Fruit Salad and Creamy French Dressing

Cold Boiled Salmon with Mayonnaise and Potato Salad **$12.95**
with Sliced Cucumbers in Balsamic Vinaigrette Sauce

in price to lowest, or vice versa, is usually not desirable. People looking for price tend to go to the least expensive one and never look at the others. Mixing up prices makes people look through all the items to see what is there and what the prices are. This is more likely to make even price-conscious buyers see something they find very desirable, and that they will purchase not on the basis of price but on the desirability of the product.

Where the eyes focus is also important in menu design. When patrons open up a two-page menu, their eyes usually go to the right, often to the center of the page or, if not there, to the upper right hand corner of the page and then counterclockwise to the right bottom. If a menu is a single page, readers will tend to go to the middle of the page and then to the upper right, left and down, then across to the lower right, and then up again. **Exhibit 7.13** indicates this eye movement. It is important that items management most wants to sell be put into those positions where readers look first, known as *emphasis areas*. These items need not necessarily be specials, since many people will come in for specials and will hunt for them on the menu.

Color

Besides making an artistic contribution, color can affect legibility and speed of reading. The use of white print on a black background may get more attention than black print on a white background, but it is harder to read. Black on white is read 42 percent more rapidly than white on dark gray, and black type on light color is read less easily than black on white. However, black on

Exhibit 7.13   Menu View

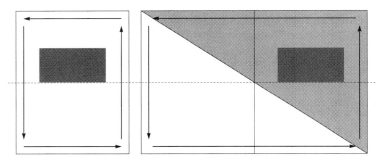

some light colors is about equal to black on white. The results of a test with various colors of paper stock are summarized in **Exhibit 7.14**. The order is from easiest to most difficult in each of the three classifications.

In another test, to ascertain how well different colored inks stood out against various tints, the results shown in **Exhibit 7.15** were obtained. Again the order is from easiest to most difficult to read.

Color and design can enhance a menu and make it a better merchandising tool. Color and design are as important to menus as they are to dinnerware. A large amount of color can run into a sizable cost. Yet, as with china, considerable decorative effect can be obtained with only a small amount of color and design. Similarly, plain-colored paper can achieve good effect and is not too expensive. Some paper has color on one side and white or another

Exhibit 7.14   Color Test Results

Quite Easy to Read	**Fairly Easy to Read**	**Poorly Read**
Black on light cream	Black on light yellowish green	Black on fairly saturated
Black on light sepia cream	Black on light blue green	yellowish red
Black on deep cream	Black on yellowish red	Black on reddish orange
Black on very light buff		
Black on fairly saturated		
yellow		

Exhibit 7.15   Colored Ink Test

Quite Easy to Read	**Fairly Easy to Read**	**Poorly Read**
Black print on yellow	Blue print on white	White print on black
Green print on white	Yellow print on blue	Red print on yellow
Red print on white	White print on red	Green print on red
Black print on white	White print on green	Red print on green
White print on blue		

color on the reverse. As special effects are added, costs increase. Adding silver or gold to a menu can be expensive.

Too much color and design can distract a customer's attention from the menu. Colors that are intense should be avoided unless some special effect is desired. Perhaps a bold color could be used in a club wishing to project a bold atmosphere, but it might not be appropriate in other food services.

Clip-ons can be used to give a different design and color. Some menus may be given additional color by using ribbons, silken cords, or tassels, but these are usually restricted to menus for special dining areas.

The variety of colors in paper suitable for menus is wide, including metallic papers. Since the basic color must serve as a background for the print that describes menu items and lists prices, the print stands out very clearly. Dark browns, blacks, reds, and other deep colors should not be used with dark colored type, nor should light-colored print be used with light-colored paper.

Color can be used for special events and holidays. Mandarin red with black print is appropriate to commemorate a Chinese New Year; a Halloween menu would traditionally use orange and black; black type on emerald green is suitable for St. Patrick's Day.

All colors and designs on the menu should blend with and complement the operation's decor. However, they also can be contrasted with good effect. For example, an outstanding color may be used to give a vivid color splash, just as an interior decorator might use a vividly colored vase to give a highlight to a more subtle color scheme in a room.

Complementary colors are usually those that come from the same primary colors (red, yellow, and blue), but some contrasts between colors coming from different primaries also can be pleasing. For instance, some shades of red and green go well together. While some greens and blues clash, others do not. Knowing how to use colors in design is inherent in some people, but not all. Some menus may seek to achieve a desirable color effect by using colors in stripes, squares, triangles, or circles in some unique pattern. Obtaining a balance takes an ability to blend colors, lightness, and darkness. The services of a menu designer can do much to produce a menu with striking color effects that are in good taste.

Color in pictures results from colored inks used in different combinations. The basic four-color-process inks—black, yellow, magenta, and cyan (bright blue)—will give almost any combination of color desired in printing. A fifth color is sometimes added for special effect.

To reproduce a picture, at least four pieces of film, called *separations*, must be made. This is done by taking all yellow tones in one separation. All cyan (blue) tones are taken from the picture in another separation. All shades of magenta and all blacks are taken in other separations. If a special color effect is wanted, other color separations will be made. When these are printed, the human eye will combine and reproduce all colors in the picture. Sophisticated machines now do separations by laser beam, which gives almost perfect placement of one color over another.

A four-color separation can cost more than $500. However, high quality might be worth the expense. Also, buying a large quantity of printed menus can reduce color costs considerably because the cost is spread or *prorated* over time to bring down the unit cost.

There frequently are other costs in using colored pictures. A photograph must be of good quality—a corned beef sandwich must look like a *good* corned beef sandwich. It is usually worthwhile to pay a professional photographer and perhaps even a food stylist to take photographs.

There are companies that maintain libraries of stock photos. It may be possible to find an appropriate photograph and save the cost of taking a picture. Clip-out sheets can also be used.

Color separations can be "doctored" to enhance colors and make them appear as close as possible to the color of the actual food. Color *proofs* must be checked carefully before any printing is done. Poor color reproductions of food items will ruin an otherwise well-developed menu.

Sketches and line drawings, which may or may not have a background, can also be effective. It is possible to add a color within a line picture to help give color contrast, rather than have the line drawing appear filled with the basic color of the paper. Further emphasis can be obtained by putting the picture in a box. Additional color and design can be obtained with decorative borders.

Paper

The Menu Cover

The paper used for a menu cover should be chosen carefully. First, consider how often the menu will be used. If it is designed to be disposable, such as a menu on a place mat, then the paper can be a lightweight stock. If it is going to be used regularly, a coated grease-resistant stock is important. Texture is also a factor to consider, since customers hold the menu in their hands, which can soil menus.

A heavy paper, *cover stock*, is used for most menu covers. This is usually a paper stiff enough to be held in the hands without bending. It may be laminated with a soil-resistant material, such as plastic. The surface is frequently shiny and smooth, but cover materials may have different textures. Laminated covers last for a longer time than untreated ones, and they are easily wiped clean. The weight of cover stock should be in heavy cover, bristol, or tag stock at least .006 inch thick.

Some operations may use a hard-cover folder in which a menu is placed. Often these are highly decorative and represent a considerable investment. Some may be padded, to give a softness in the hand, and covered with strong plastic or other materials that can give the feeling of silk, linen, or leather. These are often laminated onto base materials. Sometimes a foil inlay is stamped on the front. This is done using heat and pressure to set the inlay in the cover material. Gold, silver, and other colors may be stamped onto covers. Using inlays can be expensive.

When these heavy covers are used, it is possible to use a printed menu inside that will not be too expensive. With such a cover, the menu is usually printed on lighter-weight paper.

Characteristics of Paper

The weight of paper for interior pages can be of a lighter weight than that for covers. Usually, strong, heavy book paper is used. Its finish should be such that it resists dirt. Paper can be given different finishes to make it more suitable for menu use. If novelty or striking effects are desired, some specialty papers can be used. (See **Exhibit 7.16**.) The type of ink and printing process used will also help determine the type of paper used. The operator should also investigate the texture and the opacity of the paper.

Paper Textures

Paper textures can range from slight rises, such as is seen in a wood grain, to a rough, coarse surface. It is possible today to give paper almost any texture desired, even that of velvet or suede. *Opacity* of paper (inability to see through it) may depend on the strength of the ink or the use of color. Heavy ink should be used on highly opaque paper. Some transparency may be desirable for some artistic effects. Most often, a maximum opacity is desirable.

Exhibit 7.16   Basic Paper Terms

Bond paper	Used for letterheads, forms, and business uses
Book paper	Has characteristics suitable for books, magazines, brochures, etc.
Bristol	Cardboard of .006 of an inch or more in thickness (*index, mill,* and *wedding* are types of bristol)
Coated	Paper and paperboard whose surface has been treated with clay or some other pigment
Cover stock	Variety of papers used for menu covers, catalogs, booklets, magazines, etc.
Deckle edge	Paper with a feathered, uneven edge
Dull-coat	Coated paper with a low-gloss surface
Enamel	Coated paper with a high-gloss surface
English finish	Book paper with a machine finish and uniform surface
Grain	Weakness along one dimension of the paper—paper should be folded with the grain
Machine finish	Book paper with a medium finish—rougher than English finish but smoother than eggshell
Matte-coat	Coated paper with a little- or no-gloss surface
Offset paper	Coated or uncoated paper suitable for offset lithography printing
Vellum finish	Similar to eggshell but from harder stock, with a finer grained surface

Menu Shape and Form

The shape and form of the menu can help create interest and sales appeal. A wine menu may be in the shape of a bottle, while one featuring seafood can be in the shape of a crab, lobster, or fish. When using food shapes, however, the shape chosen must be one that is distinctly recognizable to the average diner. A steakhouse bill of fare may feature a menu in the shape and coloring of a Black Angus steer. A child's menu can be in the shape of a clown whose picture is on the front cover. A pancake house can have its menu shaped like a pancake or waffle.

The fold given the menu may also create an effect. Instead of having a right and left side to a cover, a fold may be used that gives a half page on the right and a half page on the left, so that the menu opens up like a gate. If folds are used, the "foldability" of the paper should be investigated; most coated papers crack easily at a fold.

If a special fold or shape is required, a special *die* (a form used to cut out shapes, such as in jigsaw puzzles) may have to be made. This costs money and should be the property of the one who pays for making the die. Also, the film and/or plates used for printing the menu should become the property of the individual paying for them. This must be clearly understood in making the original agreement. In some instances, printers may not be required to give them up unless such an agreement is made beforehand.

Printing the Menu

Development of Typesetting and Printing

Around 700 A.D., the Chinese began the process of setting type. They carved each block of type from blocks of wood, rubbing ink over the top surfaces and blotting them on cloth or paper. In Europe, it was not until the early 1400s when Gutenberg invented movable type on the printing press. Letters were cast in metals and put together to make words, then blotted much like their wood counterparts. This method of hand typing was long and laborious.

The *linotype*, a machine that enabled a person to stroke a keyboard that dropped carved letters into place, made the process faster and easier.

The Modern Printing Process

Today, handset and linotype is seldom done except for special purposes. Typesetting has become highly computerized, and in many instances copy is typed into a computer system. The typesetting program reproduces the type either on transparent film or on photographic paper. A copy of the type called a galley proof or reader proof is made. It is not in pages and is usually in long sheets. This is used to proofread and note corrections. The corrections are made on the computer and either a new galley proof or a finish proof is made. An artist will either take the finish proof and make up the menu pages or they may be made up in the computer with special programs. Page proofs with the illustrations and everything else in place, just as it would be in the final form, must be checked. The page proof is usually a print (similar to a photograph) made from a film. A photographic process is used to make a printing plate from the film once the proof has been okayed. The plate is put onto a press that produces the printed material. Most printing nowadays is produced by the offset method. Ink is applied to the plate, the image is then transferred to another roller, and this image is then "offset" onto a piece of paper. The paper never touches the plate.

Silk-screening is another method of printing. A stencil is made, either photographically or by hand, and applied to a silk screen. Ink is forced through the silk onto the paper. This method produces a very intense, dense image and is often used for metallic inks (gold, silver, and copper). It is usually a hand process and consequently expensive, but the effect may be worth the cost. It is most often used on covers.

Hot foil stamping, *embossing* (creating a raised image with a stamp), and *diecutting* (by which shapes are cut into paper) are other methods of printing and enhancing a menu. As with silk-screening, they are all more expensive to do and the cost must be weighed against the effect produced.

Permanent menus are usually printed in sizable lots. Some large chains using the same menu can have printings in the hundreds of thousands. A single, small restaurant may print only 500, having only 100 with prices and leaving the remainder with the printer, who can add new prices later when more menus are needed. This takes care of price changes. Most printers want a minimum order of 500.

Self-printing

Many operations today print their own menus. This can be done almost as well as a professional printing company and often at a huge savings. Having personal control of menu production has some advantages also. Some large operations set up sophisticated systems and produce remarkable results. However, even with much less equipment and facilities, it is possible to print one's own menus which are adequate for use in the facility. The minimum equipment is usually a computer and a desktop-publishing program with a number of different typefaces and design features. A good laser, color printer is also desirable on which to print camera-ready pages to send to a printer. **Exhibit 7.17** shows an attractive self-printed menu produced on a personal computer.

Working with Professional Printers

Certain companies specialize in assisting food services in planning, developing ideas for, and printing menus. They usually can be extremely helpful in producing an effective menu. Their experience in setting up menus to do the best merchandising job will be greater than that of the individual menu planner, and this experience can be helpful in avoiding mistakes.

Professional menu printing companies exist to do special art and design work. They may blend printing techniques with special effects to make the best possible menu. If special artwork is needed, either the company will have a staff artist to do it or they will know where to find freelance artists. Often,

Exhibit 7.17   Self-printed Menu

Courtesy of Opus One, Detroit, Michigan

Luncheon Orchestrations

Sauteed Lake Perch
Sauce Remoulade.

$12.95

Broiled Great Lakes Pickerel
Served with a leek and horseradish coulis and sour cream.

$12.95

Pan Fried Salmon Cakes
Garnished with asparagus tips.
Sauce Bearnaise.

$11.95

Broiled Halibut
Accompanied with veal bits and haricot vert.
Served with lemon champagne sauce.

$12.95

Spicy Broiled Sea Scallops Shish Kabob
Served over lobster rice and ratatouille.

$13.95

Sauteed Rock Shrimp
Served with oregano-garlic angel hair pasta,
julienne sundried tomatos and poppy seeds.

$12.95

Broiled Breast of Chicken
Served with a honey mustard sauce.

$9.95

Sauteed Breast of Chicken
Topped with a roasted corn and bacon compote and served with
a chicken reduction that is accented with chervil and shallots.

$10.95

Includes the Vegetable or Potato of the Day

using a professional menu printer is just one more facet of producing a successful menu.

SUMMARY

Mechanical factors can be extremely important in making a menu an effective communication and merchandising medium. This, of course, can translate into a profit for the operation.

Dark, simple typefaces are easiest to read, but italic and adorned prints can be used for special effects. The best size print for regular menu items is 10 to 12 points, and headings are usually 18 points.

Usually menu items are typeset in 10- to 12-point type with smaller type right below giving the description. The price should be close to the item, either immediately to the right or underneath, so there is no confusion.

Menus should have about two-thirds to three-fourths of their space covered with print. Some blank space is desirable on a menu. The size of a menu should allow it to be handled easily by patrons. If more space is needed, additional pages should be used, or separate menus might be used for such items as wines, alcoholic beverages, or desserts.

There are many ways to give emphasis to menu items; a change from one size of type to a larger size, for example. Using bold type can make a menu item stand out. Using all uppercase letters will give emphasis. Setting items in a box with an ornamental border and giving enough space around the box to make it stand out can attract patrons to items, as can clip-ons.

Placement of menu items is also important. The most prominent place on a two-page menu is the middle of the right-hand side. The most prominent place on a single sheet is the middle. The top and bottom are the most prominent places in a column. Items can be lost in the middle of a column. It is not desirable to offer menu items in order of price, because price-conscious patrons will quickly go to the lowest-priced items and not look at other offerings. Mixing prices requires price-conscious patrons to hunt and may lead to their selection of higher-priced items.

The printing of menus has become quite sophisticated. The offset method is mostly used to print menus. The use of full-color pictures requires making four-color separations. This can be expensive, but color is a good selling medium.

The contrast between the color of the type used and the background should be considered carefully. If either the type or background does not give a good contrast, the menu is not read as easily and may be confusing to patrons. Color is also important in giving good decorative effect.

Type, color, and other factors designed to achieve harmony must not be mixed together haphazardly.

The papers used for covers should be either bristol, cover, or tag stock and should be surfaced with some kind of soil-resisting substance. Covers should be made of heavy paper covered with a durable coating. Covers can be given very effective decoration by stamping or high-pressure lamination.

The shape and form of a menu should be carefully considered. Often a desirable effect can be obtained by working in the logo of the operation, a trademark, or a major food item sold.

Many operations today have computers and laser printers to print menus. This makes the process much faster as well as giving operators more control over design and content.

QUESTIONS

1. Look at any menu and note its typeface, size of printing, legibility, spacing, use of color, and leading. How effectively are these elements used?

2. Look at the same menu. Where is your eye drawn first? Which items does management want to sell?

3. On the same menu, what do its colors tell you? Does its design match the operation's theme and clientele?

4. What is the difference between manual and cast typesetting/printing, offset printing, block printing, and silk screen printing?

5. What are the advantages of desktop publishing over traditional printing in regard to menus? What are the advantages of traditional printing?

8

Menu Analysis

Outline

Objectives

After reading this chapter, you should be able to:

1. Explain the need for menu analysis before and after putting the menu into effect.

2. Explain the use of subjective evaluation in menu analysis.

3. Explain how the popularity index or sales ratio is used in menu analysis.

4. Explain how to use menu factor analysis to judge menu item popularity.

5. Identify the steps involved in the Hurst method of menu analysis.

6. Explain how the break-even method can be used to indicate what a menu must do to be profitable.

7. Identify other methods used by foodservice operations to analyze menus.

INTRODUCTION

After a menu is planned, priced, and set into the form in which it is to be presented, it should be analyzed to see if it: 1) meets the needs and desires of patrons in the kinds of menu items offered and in price, and 2) meets the needs of the operation from the standpoint of being feasible, profitable, and in line with the goals of the operation. Once the menu items are selected, the menu cannot be considered final until its performance is measured. It is best to do this analysis before printing, since after printing little can be done. However, much analysis depends on operating data the menu generates after use. It is up to managers to strike this balance.

It is necessary to check often to see whether menu items are selling, even in institutional operations. Items should be changed if they do not produce sales.

COMMON METHODS OF MENU ANALYSIS

There are seven common ways to analyze menus each of which will be discussed in detail.

1. A count is kept of items sold per period.
2. A subjective evaluation is conducted, in which the menu is examined by management or by others, such as consultants, skilled in making such judgments to see if it meets certain criteria and standards.
3. A popularity index is developed.
4. A menu factor analysis is created, in which the performance of menu items or groups of items can be judged on the basis of popularity, revenue, food cost, and gross profit margin.
5. A break-even analysis determines at what point a menu will move from a loss to a profit, thus indicating how much must be accomplished in dollar volume and customer count.
6. The Hurst method of menu scoring determines how well a menu scores in sales, food costs, gross profit, and other factors.
7. Goal value analysis evaluates the effectiveness of menu items toward total sales and profits.

Each method can be tailored to meet the needs of individual operations. Any menu can be subjected to all methods, and from each method valuable information may be obtained to make management decisions.

Menu Counts

One method of keeping track of menu item popularity is simply to make a count of items sold. In some menu analysis methods, a count of the actual number of items sold is made so the sales mix is known.

This count may be done by having a clerk, cashier, or another individual take the sales checks and make a hand count tabulation. **Exhibit 8.1** is a sheet used for keeping the sales counts of various menu items for one month. This sheet can indicate to management how well certain items are selling. It also summarizes the sales mix, so that it is available for further menu analysis.

Exhibit 8.1   Monthly Menu Analysis

MONTHLY MENU ANALYSIS																				
Month of _____																				
Date																				
1																				
2																				
3																				
4																				
5																				
6																				
7																				
8																				
9																				
10																				
11																				
12																				
13																				
14																				
15																				
16																				
17																				
18																				
19																				
20																				
21																				
22																				
23																				
24																				
25																				
26																				
27																				
28																				
29																				
30																				
31																				
TOTAL																				

Manual counts have become obsolete in operations using electronic cash registers or computers at the point of sale. By punching a preset key, specific menu items can be recorded during the day and then later tabulated for a total count. Thus, in a matter of a few seconds, a complete printout of the number of items sold is possible. If the food cost is also put into these machines, the food cost for each item sold, the total food cost, the gross profit total for each item sold, and the total gross profit are readily available. Thus, much of the basic work required in some of the menu analysis methods is done by the computer or register. The computer can also do a complete menu factor analysis, calculate a break-even point, or analyze a menu according to the Hurst method, methods that will be discussed later.

Subjective Evaluation

The simplest way to see whether a menu is effective is to evaluate it subjectively by having an independent expert review it to see how well it transmits its message to patrons and predict how well it will perform. If those doing the analysis are expert in menu construction, the opinions will be valuable. If, however, analysis is done by someone who has only a bit of knowledge and who makes judgments purely on the basis of personal views, the evaluation will not be valuable.

Menu authorities have published menu evaluation forms that can be used to evaluate various menu factors important to menu success. (A menu evaluation form is presented in Appendix C.) It is designed for a hospital or industrial feeding unit, but it could serve as a model for many commercial restaurants. Managers should set up a menu evaluation form suited to their specific operation.

The Popularity Index

It may be desirable to know how well menu items or groups of items do in popularity (number of items sold), in generating dollars, in covering food costs, and in the costs of profit.

Menu items within a specific food group can compete against each other for patron selection. One or more items in a group can completely kill the sale of others because of their high popularity. Groups of foods, such as salads and sandwiches, can compete against each other. The relative popularity of separate items and of different food groups should be known so their contribution to the sales mix can be estimated. The potential of the menu as a revenue-producing item and as a means of satisfying customers' desires also can be estimated. A *popularity index* will provide information on this.

Even a noncommercial food service needs to study carefully the popularity of its menu items and groups. Both commercial and noncommercial food services should also study trends in patron selections. For this a continuing record of selections is needed, developed over a period of time. Not all menu items should be expected to have a high popularity. Some items may be placed on the menu because management feels they must be there even though only a few patrons select them.

Some operations compile a popularity index for menu items as follows: 1) a count of separate items is made within the group to be studied; 2) all selections within the group are totaled; and 3) the percentage for each item of the total sold is calculated. The percentage obtained for each item indicates its popularity when competing with the other items *of its group*. **Exhibit 8.2** indicates the results of a popularity index calculation.

A similar ratio can be calculated for groups of foods, such as sandwiches against salads or frozen desserts against bakery desserts. Such information can be revealing. For instance, a calculation may show that the sandwich group is far more popular than salads or that frozen desserts are destroying the sales of bakery desserts.

A popularity index for a single day is usually not informative. It is more valuable when calculations cover a period of 30 days or longer. Item groups may also vary in popularity over a period of time according to how they are combined with others.

The results of popularity index studies should be analyzed carefully. A continued low ratio for an item should be checked. In some cases, a low popularity can be expected. Items are put on the menu even though they are known to have a low or moderate popularity. Thus, herbed rice might have a relatively low popularity index, but if it is selected enough times, it might be well to leave it on the menu for the few patrons who appreciate it. It is also advisable to check the popularity index with the menu price. If lower-priced items are much higher in popularity than the high-priced ones, patrons may be showing price consciousness. A review of pricing and the type of items offered may be advisable.

Popularity figures can be misleading. Any analysis should look beyond the popularity index to see whether some hidden factors are at work, causing an adverse ratio. Most forms used by food services for calculating the sales ratios leave a space for comments so that such factors may be weighed when evaluating the popularity of items. For instance, selections can differ, depending on the day of the week they are offered. Sundays are quite different from other days; Mondays may also be.

Exhibit 8.2   Popularity Index

Item	No. Sold	Popularity, %
New York Steak with Bearnaise Sauce	44	24
Breast of Chicken Nanking	38	21
Broiled Lobster Tails Meuniere	14	8
Roast Pork Loin with Chestnut Dressing	54	30
Lamb Shish Kebob	32	17
	182	100

Special events in a location near the foodservice operation, perhaps in the same building, can influence selections. A concert or convention will affect the selection of items as well as customer volume.

Running out of items may force patrons to take different selections then they would have if the runout had not occurred. Therefore, some record of runouts and times should be maintained.

Weather can affect selections; on a cold day, soup may have a higher selection compared to cold appetizers. Seasons are also influential; fresh strawberry shortcake at a nominal price may have a higher popularity when fresh strawberries are first on the market. A sudden shift in popularity might also mean that a menu item has suffered a variation in quality. Menu placement, presentation on the menu, descriptions, and many other factors must be weighed. **Exhibit 8.3** shows how a record might be kept on one menu item—baked salmon and dressing.

Exhibit 8.4 shows a form for recording data to develop a popularity index for five items served both a la carte and table d'hôte. Total contribution of each to sales, food cost, and gross profit are given. The chef's salad, corned beef, and turkey did fairly well, and the chili-burger held its own. Salmon had an unfortunate day. When records such as this are maintained, it is possible to see how well the five items do when competing with each other, and also to check the accumulated popularity index in column 7.

Some differentiation in counts may be desirable for a la carte and table d'hôte items. This may be done by indicating the number of a la carte and table d'hôte items sold for a single menu item, such as eggplant parmigiana sold alone and sold with accompaniments, as shown in **Exhibit 8.5**.

Exhibit 8.3 Popularity Index Record for Menu Item

BAKED SALMON AND DRESSING
(Item)

Date Served	Forecast	Amount Sold	Sales Ratio	Accumulated Ratio to Date	Contribution to: Sales %	Food Cost %	Gross Profit %
1/25	45	30	⑤ 7.6%	7.6%	7.0	7.2	7.6
2/12	40	38	⑤ 12.4%	10.0%	8.1	7.8	7.9
4/1	40	34	⑤ 10.4%	10.1%	8.1	7.8	7.8
5/20	40	40	⑤ 14.2%	11.4%	8.2	7.9	8.0

Exhibit 8.4 Form for Recording Data for Popularity Index

Date 9/27   Day Friday   Dining Area Cobra Coffee Shop   Weather Rain/Sleet   Special Events _____

Meal Lunch   Total Covers 443   Items Covered Entrees

(1) ITEM	(2) FORE-CAST	(3) À LA CARTE			(4) TABLE D'HOTE			(5) PORTIONS SERVED	(6) % TO TOTAL			(7) POPULARITY INDEX	(8) INDEX TO DATE	(9) QUALITY OF ITEM	(10) COMMENTS
		Price $	FC* $	%FC*	Price $	FC* $	%FC*		FC*	Sales	Gross Profit				
Chef's Salad	60	3.65	1.20	32.0	4.25	1.27	30.0	21/48	23.3	24.7	25.4	17.7	16.0	Good	—
Chili burger	80	2.00	.75	37.5	2.50	.80	32.0	38/52	21.1	20.4	20.0	25.7	22.6	Fair—little runny	Sold out 12:42
Baked Salmon	45	3.20	.85	26.6	3.70	.98	26.5	9/21	7.6	9.4	10.2	7.7	12.4	Poor—too dry	Usually better quality
Corned Beef	80	3.25	1.00	30.8	3.25	1.24	38.1	22/49	22.3	20.3	19.3	18.3	16.0	Good	Sold out 12:50
Hot Turkey Sandwich	100	2.10	.75	35.7	2.60	.82	31.5	48/71	25.5	25.2	25.0	30.6	27.9	Good	Price helps sales
TOTALS	365	—	—	—	—	—	—	138/251	99.8	100	99.9	100.00	94.9	—	—

*Food Cost

General Comments:

After four complaints on
the salmon, it was taken off
the menu.

Compiled by: DSG

(11) ITEM	(12) SALES			(13) FOOD COST			(14) GROSS PROFIT		
	À la Carte	Table d'Hôte	Total $	À la Carte	Table d'Hôte	Total $	À la Carte	Table d'Hôte	Total $
Chef's Salad	76.65	204.00	280.65	25.20	60.96	86.16	51.45	143.04	194.49
Burger	76.00	155.00	231.00	28.50	49.60	78.10	47.50	105.40	152.90
Salmon	28.80	77.70	106.50	7.65	20.58	28.23	21.15	57.12	78.27
Corned Beef	71.50	159.25	230.75	22.00	60.76	82.76	49.50	98.49	147.99
Turkey	100.80	184.60	285.40	36.00	58.22	94.22	64.80	126.38	191.18
TOTALS	353.75	780.55	1134.30	119.35	250.12	369.47	234.40	530.43	764.83

Contributions of items to:

Some operations keep a history of costs and pricing for various items. This record indicates by date the food cost, selling price, and the basis for each, and could be tied in with a popularity index. Changes in any of these factors are recorded. This record allows for an evaluation of costs and selling prices and shows how changes in these factors affected popularity. It also can show if prices are appropriate in various dining areas of a large operation. In some large operations where the same item is sold in different dining areas, prices, and thus popularity, may differ.

The magnitude of a popularity index depends on the number of items against which an item competes. If an item is one of four, and has equal popularity with the others, it would have an expected index of 0.25 (1 ÷ 4). If it is one of five, it would an expected index of 0.20 (1 ÷ 5). Thus, if it is one in four and has a rating of 0.42, 0.17 points above average, it is more than holding its own against the other items. If it has a rating of 0.12, 0.13 below average, it is not.

Exhibit 8.5 Price Comparison Card

PRICE COMPARISON CARD

Item Eggplant Parmigiana   Portion Size 6 oz. A la carte; 4 oz. Table d'hôte

Where Served	Date	Selling Price À la Carte/Table d'hôte		Food Cost À la Carte/Table d'hôte		Accompaniments
Leaf Room	3/8	$8.95	$14.95	$2.44 27%	$3.08 21%	A la carte—bread & butter (b&b) Table d'hôte—minestrone, pasta salad, b&b
Coffee Shop	3/12	$5.95	$7.95	$2.44 41%	$3.08 39%	A la carte—b&b Table d'hôte—minestrone, pasta salad, b&b
Coffee Shop	3/20	$6.95	$8.95	$2.44 35%	$3.08 34%	A la carte—b&b Table d'hôte—minestrone, pasta salad, b&b
Gold Room	3/24	—	$17.95	— —	$3.39 19%	Table d'hôte—minestrone, salad, tortoni pasta, coffee
Leaf Party Room	4/20	$9.95	$13.95	$2.89 29%	$3.24 23%	A la carte—b&b Table d'hôte—minestrone, salad, pasta, b&b
Coffee Shop	4/24	$7.25	$8.25	$2.87 40%	$3.24 39%	A la carte—b&b Table d'hôte—minestrone, salad, pasta, b&b

The Popularity Factor

It is difficult to compare the popularity indexes of items when they come from groups that do not have the same number of items but are in competition with each other. For instance, if an item that is one of a group of four and has a popularity index of 0.25 is compared with an item that is one of a group of five and has a popularity index of 0.20, one might conclude that the first is more popular than the second because it has a higher popularity index; this is not true.

To remove this difficulty, the actual popularity index (A) of an item can be divided by its expected popularity index (E) to get what is called a *popularity factor*.

Thus, an item that is one of five, if competing equally well, would have an expected popularity index (E) of 0.20. If its actual popularity index (A) were 0.20, then the popularity factor would be 1.00 (0.20 ÷ 0.20 = 1.00), or what was expected.

However, if A = 0.25, the popularity factor would be 1.25 (0.25 ÷ 0.20 = 1.25), showing it is more popular than expected. If A = 0.15, the factor would be 0.75 (0.15 ÷ 0.20 = 0.75), less popular than expected.

Using the popularity factor makes it possible now to compare the popularity of items from different-size groups. For instance, we may want to compare the popularity of a sandwich with that of a chef's salad. The sandwich is one of eight items and has an expected popularity index of 0.125, with an actual popularity index of 0.15. The chef's salad, one of a group of five items, with an expected popularity index of 0.20, also has an actual popularity index of 0.15. The popularity factor of the sandwich is 1.20 (0.15 ÷ 0.125 = 1.20) and that of the salad is 0.75 (0.15 ÷ 0.20 = 0.75), showing that while both items have the same popularity index within their groups, the popularity factor shows they differ in actual popularity. Calculating the popularity factor puts each item on the same basis for comparison.

Generally, a popularity factor of more than 1.00 shows the item more than holds its own against others; a factor of less than 1.00 indicates it does not. (There is an exception to this rule—food cost—that is explained in the next section on menu factor analysis.)

Menu Factor Analysis

Menu factor analysis is a way of manipulating data to ascertain how well menu items are doing. It develops *factors* to indicate how an item is doing in: 1) popularity; 2) creating revenue or sales; 3) influencing food cost; and 4) how much it contributes to gross profit. Management can use these factors to make decisions on whether to retain the item on the menu, lower its food cost, or increase its price. Menu factor analysis also permits comparison with other factors.

Previously we saw how a popularity index was calculated as a percent of total selections for a group of menu items. The same kind of percentage can be made for indexing dollar sales (revenue), food cost, or an item's gross profit contribution. Thus, if one menu item has 120 orders out of 480 total sold, has $100 sales out of total sales of $500, a food cost of $40 out of $180, and a gross profit of $60 out of $325, the following indexes can be calculated.

Popularity	120 ÷ 480 = 0.25
Sales	$100 ÷ $500 = 0.20
Food cost	$40 ÷ $180 = 0.22
Gross profit	$60 ÷ $325 = 0.18

In menu factor analysis, these indexes are called *actual indexes* since they are derived from actual sales and profit figures and not projections.

The *expected* index is a hypothetical index based on what management expects or projects an item to do in terms of popularity, dollar sales, food cost, or gross profit. Thus, if an item is one of a group of four menu items and management expects all to compete equally in popularity, sales, food cost, and gross profit, all the expected indexes would be 0.25. Menu items in a group, however, are usually not equally popular, nor do they bring in the same percent of sales dollars or have the same percent of food cost or gross profit. Some menu items are generally more popular than others. In menu factor analysis, therefore, management usually assigns what it expects an item to do in these categories. Thus, if there is a group of four sandwiches, management may think one sandwich should bring in 34 percent of sales, another 24 percent, a third 22 percent, and a fourth 20 percent, rather than each contributing equally at 25 percent of sales. Thus, it is possible to have an *equal* expected index and a *variable* expected index.

To illustrate how such indexes would be compiled, **Exhibit 8.6** gives the *actual* number of sales with its index, the *equal* expected sold with its index, and the *variable* expected sold with its index. Similar data is then given for dollar sales, food cost, and gross profit.

Exhibit 8.6 Food Sales Index

Menu Item	Actual		Equal Expected		Variable Expected	
	Sold	Index	Sold	Index	Sold	Index
Popularity						
Vegetable Pita	140	0.292	120	0.250	150	0.313
Tuna Salad	120	0.250	120	0.250	120	0.250
Grilled Chicken	120	0.250	120	0.250	110	0.229
Smoked Turkey	100	0.208	120	0.250	100	0.208
Total	480	1.000	480	1.000	480	1.000
Sales						
Vegetable Pita	$154	0.312	$125	0.250	$168	0.340
Tuna Salad	120	0.243	125	0.250	119	0.241
Grilled Chicken	120	0.243	125	0.250	109	0.221
Smoked Turkey	100	0.202	125	0.250	98	0.198
Total	$494	1.000	$500	1.000	$494	1.000
Food Cost						
Vegetable Pita	$ 80	0.444	$ 45	0.250	$ 90	0.500
Tuna Salad	40	0.222	45	0.250	40	0.222
Grilled Chicken	30	0.167	45	0.250	25	0.138
Smoked Turkey	30	0.167	45	0.250	25	0.138
Total	$180	1.000	$180	1.000	$180	0.998
Gross Profit						
Vegetable Pita	$ 74	23.6	$ 78.50	0.250	$100	0.378
Tuna Salad	80	25.5	78.50	0.250	74	23.6
Grilled Chicken	90	28.7	78.50	0.250	70	0.223
Smoked Turkey	70	0.223	78.50	0.250	70	0.223
Total	$314	100.1	$314.00	1.000	$314	0.998

Exhibit 8.7   Menu Factor Analysis

Menu Item	Equal Factor	Variable Factor
Popularity		
Vegetable Pita	1.18	0.93
Tuna Salad	1.00	1.00
Grilled Chicken	1.00	1.09
Smoked Turkey	0.83	1.00
Sales		
Vegetable Pita	1.24	0.93
Tuna Salad	0.97	1.00
Grilled Chicken	0.97	1.02
Smoked Turkey	0.83	1.02
Food Cost		
Vegetable Pita	1.74	0.89
Tuna Salad	1.00	1.00
Grilled Chicken	0.67	1.20
Smoked Turkey	0.67	1.20
Gross Profit		
Vegetable Pita	0.74	0.74
Tuna Salad	1.07	1.08
Grilled Chicken	1.14	1.08
Smoked Turkey	0.81	1.00

While close study of these indexes could reveal much helpful information to management, it is even better to use them to create a factor that will make their relationship stand out more clearly. To calculate this factor, the actual index is divided by the expected index (A ÷ E). If this is done by dividing the actual index by the equal expected index, and the actual index by the variable expected index, we get the figures shown in **Exhibit 8.7.**

In menu factor analysis, a factor of 1.00 indicates an item is doing exactly what is expected; a factor of over 1.00 means it is doing better than expected; and a factor under 1.00 means that it is doing worse than expected. However, with regard to food cost, a factor of 1.00 still means cost is as expected, but a factor under 1.00 is good, and over 1.00 is bad. We can now look at these factors and make a quick summary of what management might see in them.

First, for popularity: If we think that all four menu items should compete equally, the vegetable pita sandwich seems to be doing well (1.18), tuna salad and grilled chicken about as expected (1.00), and smoked turkey not as well as expected (0.83).

However, when we look at the variable factors, or what management expects the items to do, we get a different view. Vegetable pita is not doing quite as well as expected (0.93) but it is not so far off for management to be too concerned. Tuna salad is doing what it should (1.00), and grilled chicken is selling better than management expected (1.09). Smoked turkey is doing just what management thought it should (1.00).

Now, for sales: If we look at the equal dollar sales factors, we see vegetable pita is doing better than expected (1.24) and tuna salad and grilled chicken (0.97) are not doing too badly. It is the smoked turkey that is in trouble (0.83). However, this all clears up when we get to the variable factors. Vegetable pita now is not doing what management expected (0.93), while the others are doing as well or slightly better (1.00, 1.02, and 1.02). Perhaps the vegetable pita is not bringing in enough dollars because it is not priced high enough, but a look at its variable popularity factor reveals that perhaps not enough sales are occurring. Could this be because the price is too high? Management would have to consider this.

In equal food cost factors, vegetable pita is clearly not doing what it should (1.74) and is driving food costs too high. The others look good, however; in fact, grilled chicken and smoked turkey are excellent (0.67). When we go over to the variable factors, however, the true story comes out. Management has not expected that item to have the same dollar food cost as the others. Its 0.89 variable factor indicates this. While tuna salad does all right (1.00), grilled chicken and smoked turkey are now down in food cost (1.20). Perhaps management needs to increase their prices to get a better food cost ratio.

Gross profit is the last comparative group. In the equal factor, vegetable pita could do a bit better. Tuna salad and grilled chicken are over 1.00, which means they are doing well. Smoked turkey is not doing as well (0.81), and its *profit margin* or contribution to profit will probably not be as satisfactory. Again, some adjustment takes place in the variable factors. Vegetable pita is now not doing what it should in generating gross profit (0.74). Smoked turkey is doing all right. It is grilled chicken that is carrying the load here, with a variable factor of 1.08 and 1.30.

Menu factor analysis can be a revealing and helpful method for analyzing a menu and indicating, perhaps, what should be done in case of problems with menu items. However, it has its drawbacks. The variable factors are based on what management thinks should be true. Management has to be fairly close in its estimates to the actual situation to make the method valuable. Guesses that are too far from the mark can cause problems. One also needs to remember that these are factors based on percentages that do not always reflect all the conditions. Management must look beyond these factors and weigh other things that should be considered. A study problem using menu factor analysis is given in Appendix D.

The Hurst Method

The Hurst method of analyzing a menu considers the effects on sales of pricing, food cost, item popularity, gross profit contribution, and other factors.[1] It is a tool used by management to evaluate menu changes, such as changes in price, items, and food costs. It is a fairly easy method to use and can be quickly performed from a few statistics easily obtained from accounting data.

To use the Hurst method, management should decide on the period for which the scoring will be done. It can be a single meal or a series of meals for which the same menu is used. The period should be a typical one and not one in which unusual events, such as bad weather or a holiday, would keep patrons away.

Eighteen steps are required to make a Hurst menu analysis. **Exhibit 8.8** indicates where data is placed on the form. The numbers (1) to (18) indicate data for each of the 18 steps in the analysis. (Columns and spaces in Exhibit 8.8 are referred to by "column" or "space" numbers.) While the number of steps may seem formidable, each step is easily done, and they follow each other in a natural sequence.

The exhibit contains figures of a Hurst study for three menu items. (Normally, there would be more, but to simplify the study, only three were used.) The meal covers lunch for two days. Sales in this example are 100 orders of shrimp at $8.00 with a food cost of $2 per serving, 500 orders of beef ribs priced at $13.00 with a food cost of $3.28, and 400 orders of roast turkey priced at $9.00 with a food cost of $2.40. This comes to 1,000 orders for the study group items, but total orders for the period studied were 1,500. By following through on the 18 steps outlined, one can see how a Hurst menu score is compiled.

Steps in Performing the Hurst Menu Analysis

The steps in making a Hurst menu analysis are as follows.

1. Decide on the period and meal to be covered, and the number of items to be evaluated, and fill in the necessary data.
2. Select items that contribute to a major portion of the revenue—all can be included or only the part to be studied. The items selected for special study are called the "study group" in this discussion. Place these items in column 1.
3. Make a count of the number sold for each of the items in the study group. Place the results in column 2.
4. Add entries in column 2 to get the total number of study group items sold.
5. Add to the number of study group items sold (step 4) and all other (nonstudy) menu items sold and place the total on the line for Total Items Sold and in space 11, Total Served.
6. Record the selling price for each item in the study group in column 3.
7. Multiply the number of each study group item sold (from column 2) by its selling price (from column 3) to get the total dollar sales for each item. Record these in column 4.
8. Add column 4 to get the total dollar sales of the study group.
9. Calculate the dollar food cost for each item in the study group. Record in column 5.

Exhibit 8.8 Hurst Menu Analysis

HURST MENU ANALYSIS

Time Period 2 days *(1)*

Meal Lunch

Number of
Items Evaluated 3

Columns	1	2	3	4	5	6
	Menu Item *(2)*	Number Sold *(3)*	Selling Price *(6)*	Total Sales *(7)*	Food Cost *(9)*	Total $ Food Cost *(10)*
	Shrimp	100	$ 8.00	$ 800	$2.00	$ 200
	Beef Ribs	500	$13.00	$6,500	$3.28	$1,640
	Turkey	400	$ 9.00	$3,600	$2.40	$ 960
Totals		1,000 *(4)*		$10,900 *(8)*		$2,800 *(11)*

Total Items Sold 1,500 *(5)*
(Including study items)

Spaces

7	8	9	10	11
Meal Average *(12)* (total column 4 ÷ total column 2)	Gross Profit *(13)* (total column 4 − total column 6)	Gross Profit Percentage *(13)* (space 8 ÷ total column 4)	Gross Profit Average *(14)* (space 7 × space 9)	Total Served *(5)* (total column 2 + others served)
$10,900 ÷ 1,000 =	$10,900 − $2,800 =	$8,100 ÷ 10,900 =	$10.90 × 74% =	
$10.90	$8,100	74%	$8.06	1,500

12	13	14
Percentage of Patrons *(15)* (total column 2 ÷ total items sold)	Menu Score *(16)* (space 10 × space 12)	Comments
1,000 ÷ 1,500 =	$8.06 × 66.7% =	Good weather. Many went out of the building to eat elsewhere.
		(17)
66.7%	$5.37	Compiler LHK *(18)*

10. Get the total food cost of each sale by multiplying the number of each item sold by its food cost. Record in column 6.

11. Add column 6 to get the total dollar food cost for all items.

12. Obtain the meal average—or average selling price—of all items in the study group by dividing the total dollars in sales (the sum of column 4) by the total number of study group items sold (the sum of column 2). Place the result in space 7.

13. Calculate the gross profit and gross profit percentage. Subtract the total food costs for all study group items (sum of column 6) from the total dollar sales of study group items (sum of column 4). Record the difference in space 8. Then divide this difference by the total dol-

lar sales (sum of column 4) to get the gross profit percentage. Record this figure in space 9.

14. Calculate the gross profit average by multiplying the check average (average selling price) in space 7 by the gross profit percentage in space 9. Record this in space 10.

15. Calculate the percentage of customers that select the study group items by dividing the sum of the study group items sold (total of column 2) by the total items sold as compiled in step 5 and recorded in space 11. Record the result in space 12.

16. Calculate the menu score by multiplying the gross profit average (space 10) by the percentage of patrons selecting the study group items (space 12). Record the result in space 13.

17. Make any comments in space 14.

18. Sign and date the form.

Evaluating the Menu Score

One menu score by itself means little. It merely indicates how numbers sold interact with prices, sales mix, gross profit, and food costs. A number of menu scores kept over a period of time must be compiled and analyzed to obtain desirable information on how well a menu is doing. (See **Exhibit 8.9**.) Also, comparing scores with those of other operations is not helpful. There are too many varying factors. Only scores generated internally are good for comparison.

Often a low score is the result of too low a selling price resulting in a low check average, or some items may not be eliciting patron selection. Whatever the cause, management should take steps to correct the situation. The manager may try to reduce food costs and thus raise gross profit, use merchandising to elicit more patron selections, or increase volume. There are many possibilities, and managers should investigate carefully to identify the cause of a low menu score.

Exhibit 8.9   Effect of Price Changes on Menu Score

Item		Selling Price	$ Sales	Total $ Food Cost
100	Shrimp	$ 7.50	$ 750	$ 225
500	Beef ribs	10.00	5,000	2,000
400	Turkey	6.00	2,400	600
Totals	1,000		$8,150	$2,825

Meal average ($8,150 ÷ 1,000)   = $8.15
Gross profit % ($8,150 − $2,825 = $5,325 ÷ $8,150)   =   65%
Gross profit average ($8.15 × 65%)   = $5.30
% Meals of total meals (1,000 ÷ 1,500)   =   66.7%
Menu score (66.7% × $5.30)   = $3.53

A menu planner can use a computer to simulate menu changes before actually putting them into effect. Putting the Hurst method into the computer can make simulation easy, quick, and quite accurate—as long as accurate data is fed into the computer.

Goal Value Analysis

David Hayes and Lynn Huffman have reviewed menu analysis methods using matrix systems, and have proposed the Goal Value method of menu analysis.[2] It is largely a quantitative method. They use a mathematical method of A × B × (C × D) = Goal Value, where A = 1 − food cost percentage, B = volume or number sold, C = selling price, and D = 1 − (variable food cost percentage + food cost percentage) to arrive at a goal index they call the numerical target or score. They then calculate individual values for each menu item and compare each value with the standard to see if it is above or below standard. If it is above standard, it is doing better than average; if below, it is considered poor as a menu item. **Exhibit 8.10** gives the information needed to set up a goal value system for four menu items—chicken, steak, shrimp, and sole.

The following results are obtained on chicken, steak, shrimp, and sole: the average food cost is 35 percent, the average number sold is 17.25, and the average selling price is $8.74. Setting the variable cost at 32 percent, the combined food and variable cost is 67 percent (35% + 32%). Thus, the *goal value standard* for the four items is (1 − 0.35) × 17.25 × ($8.74 × [1 − 67%]) or 32.3. The individual achievement values are shown in **Exhibit 8.11**. Thus, steak and chicken do well, being above the goal value standard of 32.3, while shrimp is below standard and sole does poorly. Chicken is the best performer.

Let us say management wants to remove the sole and replace it with a pasta dish with a selling price of $6.50, a food cost of $1.43 (22 percent) and a variable cost of 32 percent. It expects 20 sales. The total number of covers does not change, so the pasta steals 11 selections from the others. **Exhibit 8.12** shows what might be found. The average food cost is 31.4 percent ($177.70 ÷ $565.70), the average number sold is 17.3 (69 ÷ 4), and the average selling price is $8.20 ($565.70 ÷ 69). The combined variable and

Exhibit 8.10 Data for Goal Value Analysis

Menu Item	Number Sold	Item Food Cost	Total Food Cost	Selling Price	Total Sales	Food Cost Percentage
Chicken	24	$ 1.75	$ 42.00	$ 6.95	$166.80	25%
Steak	20	4.75	95.00	11.90	238.00	40
Shrimp	16	2.60	41.60	7.50	120.00	35
Sole	9	3.65	32.85	8.70	78.30	40
Total	69	12.75	$211.45		$603.10	
Average	17.25	3.19	52.86	8.75	150.78	35%

Exhibit 8.11 Achievement Values

	A		B		C		D		
Menu Item	(1 – food cost percentage)	×	Number Sold	×	Selling Price	×	1 – (food cost percentage + variable cost percentage)	=	Item Value
Chicken	0.75		24		$ 6.95		0.43	=	53.8
Steak	0.60		20		11.90		0.28	=	40.0
Shrimp	0.65		16		7.50		0.33	=	25.7
Sole	0.58		9		8.70		0.26	=	11.8

Exhibit 8.12 Goal Analysis

Menu Item	Number Sold	Food Cost Percentage	Food Cost (in dollars)	Total Food Cost Percentage	Selling Price	Total Sales
Pasta	20	22	$1.43	$ 28.60	$ 6.50	$130.00
Chicken	20	25	1.75	35.00	6.95	139.00
Steak	18	40	4.75	85.50	11.90	214.20
Shrimp	11	35	2.60	28.60	7.50	82.50
Total	69			$177.70		$565.70

food cost is 63.4 percent (31.4% + 32%). The goal value standard is $(1 - 31.4) \times 17.3 \times (\$8.20 \times [1 - (31.4\% + 32\%)]) = 35.62$.

The individual menu item evaluation is shown in **Exhibit 8.13**. Now pasta becomes the best-selling menu item, and steak drops to a level slightly above the standard. Shrimp does poorly.

The goal value method of analysis can be very useful to foodservice operators. However, in these calculations, variable cost remains fixed. In actual practice, it does not. The method can be made more effective if a high, medium, and low variable cost is assigned.[3]

The Break-Even Method

Another way to analyze a menu is to see whether it *breaks even*, or covers all the costs of doing business. This method can be used by both for-profit and not-for-profit operations. If the success of an operation is generally measured in terms of cost control and budget, the break-even method is a good approach. Commercial operations just getting started might use the break-even point. Later, when costs are being covered and profit is steady, the operator may switch to another type of menu analysis.

If the costs of doing business are not covered, there is a loss; if they are more than covered, there is a profit. To know when a menu will break even, one can total all the costs of producing and serving the expected volume of

Exhibit 8.13 Menu Item Evaluation

Menu Item	A (1 – fixed cost percentage)	×	B Number Sold	×	C Selling Price	×	D 1 – (fixed cost percentage + 32%)	=	Item Value
Pasta	0.78		20		$ 6.50		1 – (0.22 + 0.32)	=	46.6
Chicken	0.75		20		6.95		1 – (0.25 + 0.32)	=	44.8
Steak	0.60		18		11.90		1 – (0.40 + 0.32)	=	36.0
Shrimp	0.65		11		7.50		1 – (0.35 + 0.32)	=	17.7

meals and deduct this from the expected income. Thus, if a menu in one day is expected to bring in $6,000 and costs are $5,500, the profit is $500.

At times it is desirable to estimate a break-even point prior to putting a menu into effect. The menu planner may want to know how many dollars in sales a menu must generate before it breaks even and how many guests it must attract to do so; or the planner may want to know how much money the operation must take in to make a desired profit, or how many guests will be required to make this profit.

To calculate a break-even point, three things must be known: 1) the average check; 2) fixed costs in dollars; and 3) the fixed cost percent.

The *average check* is the total dollar sales divided by the number of guests served in a particular period. For example, if sales for a certain period were $100,000 and 10,000 guests were served, the average check was $10 ($100,000 ÷ 10,000 = $10).

Fixed costs are costs incurred regardless of whether a single sale is made. These include rent, administrative expenses, license fees, depreciation, insurance on equipment and other capital values, some labor costs and employee benefits, heat, electrical power, and advertising. They are sometimes called turn-key expenses because as soon as the key is turned in the door in the morning, and before any business is done, they are incurred. The *fixed cost percentage* is the dollar value of fixed costs divided by sales.

Several formulas are used to ascertain at what point break-even occurs. The following symbols are often used.

BE	=	break-even point
FC%	=	fixed cost percentage
FC	=	fixed cost in dollars
AC	=	average check in dollars

A simple formula to determine the break-even point in dollars is BE = FC ÷ FC%. If fixed costs are $232,367 and the fixed cost percentage is 46 percent, the formula is BE = $232,367 ÷ 0.46 = $505,146.65.

The break-even method can also be used to calculate the number of customers needed to cover costs. The formula used to obtain this is BE = FC ÷

(AC × FC%). If the average check is $6.54, BE = $232,367 ÷ ($6.54 × 0.46) = $232,367 ÷ $.015 = 77,198 customers.

To find the dollar sales needed to cover fixed costs and give a desired profit, add into the dollar fixed costs the amount of profit desired, using the following formula: BE = FC + P (profit) ÷ FC%. If the desired profit is $15,000, the calculation is $232,367 + $15,000 ÷ 0.46 = $537,754.34.

If one wants to know how many customers would give this profit, the formula would be BE = (FC + P) ÷ (AC × FC%). This would translate into ($232,367 + $15,000) ÷ ($6.54 × 0.46) = 82,182 customers.

Other Methods of Menu Analysis

Operations often use data and analytical methods of their own to calculate how well a menu might do or is doing. Some like to obtain a computer print-out immediately after a meal to see how well certain menu items did. A printout may also be obtained of how many of certain items each server sold—often called a *productivity report*. Some operations collect the gross dollar sales per seat. Another method might be to check operating figures against a profit or to look at the profit and loss statement.

A daily food cost report, as shown in Chapter 5, acts as a check on how well a menu is doing. It indicates total sales and food cost, and often makes comparisons with other periods so management can see how well the current menu is generating business.

SUMMARY

The final step in menu development is analysis of the menu's results. Menu development is actually a continuous process, and most menu items and prices can never be considered final. Menu analysis provides the operator with an approach for improving a menu's popularity and, in commercial operations, making a profit.

It is important that menus meet cost restraints and make a profit for commercial operations. Menu analysis methods available include making menu counts, using subjective evaluation, the popularity index, menu factor analysis, the Hurst method, and break-even analysis. These methods can be helpful in indicating menu item profitability and item popularity. The use of an outside consultant may also provide this information, as well as indicate how well menu items are presented. Besides the methods detailed here for menu analysis, different operations may use their own individual analytical methods, including analysis of daily computer printouts of sales.

QUESTIONS

1. A vendor offering three main items—hot dog, hamburger, and fried fish sandwich—wishes to make a menu factor analysis to see how well these items are doing. Management expects the following indexes.

Item	Popularity Index	$ Sales Index	$ Food Cost Index	$ Gross Profit Index
Hot dog	0.35	0.38	0.37	0.40
Hamburger	0.40	0.38	0.38	0.35
Fish sandwich	0.25	0.24	0.25	0.26

The following information is available.

Item	Number Sold	Selling Price	$ Food Cost
Hot dog	162	$1.59	$0.21
Hamburger	286	1.89	0.31
Fish sandwich	97	1.79	0.17
Total	545	$5.27	$0.69

Complete the menu factor analysis, and then analyze the findings. (Remember that dollars of food cost are compounded with number of sales of an item, and if the number of sales of an item is high this tends to inflate food cost.)

2. If 123 salmon steaks, 171 beef steaks, 86 broiled chickens, 36 lobster tails, 192 ribs of beef, and 204 seafood casseroles are sold, what is the popularity index for each?

3. Fixed costs are 45 percent of $3,904. Average check is $9.95. What must the dollar volume be to break even? How many customers must be served?

4. Using the Hurst method of analysis, complete the following.

1 Item	2 No. Sold	3 Selling Price	4 Item Food Cost	5 Total Food Cost	6 Total Sales
Chicken	15	$ 9.50	$2.86		
Tuna	16	12.00	3.20		
Fettuccine	14	8.75	2.10		
Scallops	15	11.00	3.07		
Pot Pie	13	10.75	2.03		
Tilefish	11	12.50	2.40		
Pork Chop	12	11.25	2.94		
Calf's Liver	14	10.50	2.88		
Lamb Chops	12	14.00	4.53		

The number of items sold is the total count of entree items for this lunch sold to club members, i.e., 122.

7 Meal Average	8 Gross Profit	9 Gross profit %
$_____	$_____	_____%

10 Gross Profit Average	11 Total Meals Served	12 % of Customers
$_____	_____	_____%

13 Menu Score	14 Comments
$_____	

9

The Liquor Menu

Outline

Objectives

After reading this chapter, you should be able to:

1. Identify the basic requirements for planning a liquor menu.

2. Indicate how the liquor menu can be properly implemented through skilled merchandising and service.

3. Describe how to institute controls to ensure that the liquor menu satisfies guests and meets cost and/or profit goals.

INTRODUCTION

No other phase of food service has changed as much in recent years than that of the service of alcoholic beverages. An organization called MADD (Mothers Against Drunk Driving) has been a big factor in bringing about this change. Irresponsible consumption of alcoholic beverages resulting in social disturbances, deaths, and damage to property, plus the danger heavy drinking can impose on individuals and families, were factors cited by this organization in asking that heavier penalties and more control be put on the sale of alcoholic beverages. As a result, all 50 states passed laws increasing responsibility for damages and injuries related to alcohol sales. Lawsuits that resulted in extremely heavy financial and other penalties caused insurance companies to raise their rates to a point that some operators closed. Third-party responsibility (*dramshop laws*) were established so one serving alcohol could be held responsible for the results. Many food services today have training programs to teach employees how to meet the restrictions of the laws and follow strict operating procedures.

Simultaneously, with this trend (and perhaps aided by it) came a great change in people's drinking patterns. A much larger number of people stopped drinking alcoholic beverages entirely, while others changed to lighter drinks such as beer and wine instead of spirits. In addition, recent medical reports touting the health benefits of drinking red wine have increased sales. As a result, the consumption of wine has increased slightly, beer consumption has held steady, while that of spirits has fallen drastically. Many customers have begun asking for nonalcoholic drinks, and overall the amount of money derived from the sale of alcoholic beverages has dropped significantly.

The requirements for an adequate liquor menu, therefore, have changed. Menus now often feature nonalcoholic drinks and offer a wider selection of beers and wines. A reception may now offer no spirits or mixed drinks. Instead, beer, wine, and nonalcoholic drinks will be offered. Even at banquets, the elaborate use of wines has decreased.

A good liquor menu can help an operation's profits considerably if: 1) merchandising and service personnel promote the sales of drinks, 2) procedures are established to control costs and proper inventory levels are maintained, and 3) the menu includes liquor items that complement the food menu and meet patron expectations.

Much of what has been discussed regarding the planning, pricing, and analysis of food menus can also be applied to liquor menus. However, there are some differences. Usually liquor prices are based on a higher markup than food prices. Also, liquor is often really an accompaniment or an accessory to food, and so more emphasis must be given to merchandising and selling. Finally, control procedures must be tighter in the handling of liquor and income obtained from it.

The factors that affect food menu development (personnel, physical facilities, patron expectations, and costs) also apply to liquor menus, but there is an additional controlling factor. Liquor is regulated by law, and the operation *must observe state regulations for alcohol service*. Certain kinds of liquor can be sold only in certain kinds of places, and a liquor license must be obtained by operators wishing to sell liquor. Purchasing may also be controlled to a point. Taxes may be higher, and certain selling hours must be observed. The law on serving minors is strict and penalties can be severe.

PRESENTING THE LIQUOR MENU

Liquor menus may be presented in several ways. It is not uncommon to see liquor items listed on the regular (food) menu, when only a few beverages are offered. Some institutional menus may offer cocktails and wines this way. Hospitals and nursing homes, for example, may provide wine to patients whose physicians allow it. These may be offered on separate lists or on the regular menu.

Some establishments keep separate liquor menus. A number of these may be used. One may cover drinks such as mixed drinks and cocktails; another will present the wine list, another will offer after-dinner drinks. Yet another will list afternoon beverages, including cocktails; mixed drinks; tall, cool drinks; and dessert-type wines, such as port, Madeira, and muscat. The sales department may have still another—a banquet wine and drink list for use in planning special events with patrons.

No matter what the presentation, it is desirable that the regular menu *announce* the availability of alcoholic beverages. A considerable amount of revenue and profit can be lost if guests don't know about the liquor menu.

Some liquor menus can be quite elaborate and contain a large number of items. If the establishment has a good wine cellar, the wine list will naturally be extensive—it may run several pages. If it does, the pages should be marked so that patrons can quickly find the type of beverage desired. Usually, tabulations on the margins can indicate what each page offers.

It is not usually necessary for a liquor menu to offer a wide assortment of drinks or wines to meet patrons' needs. A simple, well-thought-out assortment can do the job. Just as food menus should be analyzed to see which items move, liquor menus should be reviewed regularly to determine which items are selling. Those items that do not move should be eliminated. A sizable amount of money can be tied up in a liquor inventory, and unless these inventories are turned over fairly often, they can be a hidden expense. (One club found that an enterprising manager had tied up so much money in its wine cellar that it took more than 10 years to work off the inventory built up during his tenure.)

Thus, the rule in planning beverage menus is to keep them simple. However, this is usually easier said than done. There are a certain number of cocktails, highballs, and other mixed drinks that patrons will want *and* expect. If one also wishes to have a wine list that covers dry white wines and red wines (both domestics and imports), sparkling wines, apéritif wines, and dessert wines, the list will be extensive. However, it is best not to offer too much—only those items that meet the requirements should be offered.

Since menu planning for alcoholic beverages is a highly specialized area, it is often advisable to have an expert's advice. Some of the better wine merchants and agents have individuals on their staffs who are knowledgeable in planning liquor menus. Some of the big brewers, distillers, and liquor distributors can also give assistance. Each will have a considerable amount of written material for use in designing an attractive menu. Films and other educational materials are available from these companies.

The presentation of some exotic drinks may take skill to set up. Color may be necessary to enhance the menu, and this may require the advice of an expert in menu planning.

If only one liquor menu is used, careful consideration must be given to presentation of the various kinds of spirits. If a beverage list is a four-page folded menu, some designers advise that the front cover be used for the logo and the back of the first inside page be set in four columns: the two center columns for mixed drinks and the two outer columns for specialty items. On the other inside page, various wines can be offered. If necessary, the back panel can present liqueurs and other beverages.

If only a single hardback card is used, the operation's logo can appear on the front with perhaps a presentation of drinks that the establishment especially wishes to sell; on the back in the center columns cocktails and mixed drinks can be offered. Wines can be in the last column and spirits and liqueurs in the first.

Usually, a liquor menu follows the order indicated in **Exhibit 9.1**.

Because requirements vary greatly, beverage lists should be specifically designed for the individual enterprise. Operations with an ethnic theme or

Exhibit 9.1 Liquor Menu Classifications

Main Classification	**Order within the Classification**
Cocktails	Martinis, Manhattans, Daiquiris, Gimlets, Old-Fashioneds, Whiskey Sours, etc. (The order here is not especially important; merchandising may dictate which order is best.)
Mixed Drinks	Scotch, bourbon, rye, vodka, gin, and other spirits in mixed drinks, such as with water, ginger ale, tonic water; along with tall drinks, such as Tom Collins, etc. (Again, the order is not too important, but since most people prefer scotch, bourbon, or gin drinks, perhaps these could head the list.)
Beers and Ales	List those available in draft or in bottles. Imports are usually listed separately from domestic items.
Wines	Usually, the order of consumption is the order of listing: apéritifs; dry dinner wines, red or white; rosés; sparkling wines; dessert wines.
After-dinner Drinks	Frequently, brandies and some other liqueurs are listed, followed by mixed drinks.

clientele should feature a beverage list consistent with that theme. A German restaurant needs a very different list of wines and beers from those offered by a French or Italian restaurant. A menu featuring Mexican foods may present margaritas prominently and perhaps make a specialty of them. The familiar tequila with a slice of lime and salt is also commonly featured in Mexican operations. Some rich Spanish red wines, such as the full-bodied Marques del Lagar from the Rioja hills or Sangre de Toro (blood of the bull), can be offered, along with one or more of the soft white wines of northern Spain. *Cerveza* (beer) may also be served, perhaps in pitchers or attractive pottery mugs. French restaurants will need a good list of quality French wines. Italian restaurants may feature Italian wines, and may also include a few French and California wines. Follow-through is important in a liquor menu, and some research is necessary to make sure that an item is authentic when it is put on a menu. This also includes offering drinks in traditional glasses or steins.

Prices should be presented clearly for each item or group of drinks. The descriptions, type, and use of color should promote clarity and legibility. (See Chapter 7 for information on menu mechanics.) Effective merchandising is vital.

The Wine List

Eight to ten wines on the menu may be sufficient to satisfy patron desires and meet operational goals. The most fastidious connoisseur may wish to have a longer list, but some operations find that up to four wines are enough. One expert has said that if a wine list is well compiled, a list of 24 to 30 wines should satisfy even the most discriminating individuals in their selection of wines for a meal.

It is becoming more and more common for restaurants to offer a *house wine*, filling a carafe or decanter from bulk stock. Such wines should be of the highest quality. Some operations find that premium wines by the glass are popular with patrons. Frequently, when red and white dinner wines of the house are offered, no other choices are presented. In other operations a house wine plus a list of bottled wines may be offered. (See **Exhibit 9.2.**)

Wine lists are difficult to design. Wine menus should be set up by someone who knows a lot about wines. Certain wines *must* be on the menu, such as white or red dinner wines. Dry wines may have to be from both foreign and domestic sources, depending on the patronage. There is a large variety of wines, such as those from the Rheingau and Rheinhesse in Germany; from the Alsace and Moselle areas nearby; from the Burgundy, Bordeaux, and other wine districts of France; and from many other countries. A complete list can be very extensive, and the individual making up the list should know how to reduce it as much as possible.

A distinction should be made between dinner wines, apéritif wines, sweet wines, and effervescent wines on the menu.

Exhibit 9.2 Wine List

Courtesy of Pops for Champagne, Chicago, Illinois

WINE LIST

White Wines

Corton Charlemagne Olivier Leflaive 1985 ....$78.00

Chablis, J. Moreau les Clos 1986 ....65.00

Chateau la Louviere 1989 (Graves) 48.00

Moet & Chandon, Saran Nature 38.00

Saintsbury Reserve Chardonnay 1990
(Carneros) 38.00

Vernaccia, Teruzzi & Puthod "Terre di Tuffo"
1989 ....36.00

Jermann Pinot Grigio 1991 (Italy) 34.00

Joseph Phelps, Sangiacomo Chardonnay
1989 (Carneros) 29.00

Trimbach Reisling Cuvee Frederic Emile
1988 (France)..29.00

Josmeyer Tokay Pinot Gris d'Alsace 1990
(France)...29.00

Selection du Bois des Dames 1990
Chateau Etang de Colombes, Corbieres................27.00

Chablis Domaine Michel 1991 ....27.00

Pouilly Fuisse, Patrick Javillier 1990 ....27.00

Cambria Chardonnay, Katherine's Vineyard
1991 (Santa Barbara)..25.00

Wente Brothers, Riva Ranch Chardonnay
1990 (Monterey) 23.00

Wehlener Sonnenuhr Riesling Kabinett—Mosel
1990 ....22.00

Louis Jadot Macon Villages Chardonnay 1989............18.00

Chalk Hill Sauvignon Blanc 1991 (Sonoma) 17.00

Simi Vineyard Rose of Cabernet 1990 (Sonoma) 14.00

White Wines, by the glass

Pouilly Fuisse, Patrick Javillier 1990 ....$6.50

Cambria Chardonnay, Katherine's Vineyard
1991 (Santa Barbara)..6.25

Wehlener Sonnenuhr Rielsing Kabinett—Mosel
1990 ....5.75

Louis Jadot Macon Villages Chardonnay 1989.............5.25

Chalk Hill Sauvignon Blanc 1991 (Sonoma) 5.00

Simi Vineyard Rose of Cabernet 1990 (Sonoma) 4.00

Red Wines

Chareau Palmer 1984 (Margaux)...............................$76.00

Chateauneuf du Pape—Chateau de
Beaucastel 1988..44.00

Clos du Bois-Briarcrest Vineyard, Cabernet
Sauvignon 1988 (Alexander Valley) 29.00

Robert Stemmler Pinot Noir 1987 (Sonoma) 29.00

Nalle Zinfandel 1990 (Sonoma) 26.00

Waterbrook Winery Merlot 1990
(Washington State)..25.00

Fisher Vineyard, Coach Insignia Cabernet
Sauvignon 1989 (Sonoma).....................................23.00

Avignonesi-Rosso de Montepulciano
1990 (Italy) 22.00

Chateau Tahbilk, Shiraz 1988 (Australia) 20.00

Bonny Doon, Clos du Gilroy, Grenache
1992 (Santa Cruz) 15.00

Red Wines, by the glass

Waterbrook Winery Merlot 1990
(Washington State)..$6.25

Fisher Vineyard, Coach Insignia Cabernet
Sauvignon 1989 (Sonoma).......................................5.95

Chateau Tahbilk, Shiraz 1988 (Australia) 4.50

Port, Madeira, and Sherry—1.5 oz and 3 oz

1875 Madeira Verdelho D'Oliveiras............$29.00 ....$58.00

1911 Bual Blandy's Madeira ....18.00 ......36.00

Cockburn's Vintage Port 1963.....................12.00 ......24.00

Ficklin Vintage Port 1957............................11.00 ......22.00

Quinto do Noval Vintage Port 1970 ....8.00 ......16.00

Taylor Fladgate 20 year old Tawny ....5.00 ......10.00

Blandy's 10 year old Malmsey Madeira..........4.00 ....8.00

Graham's Malvedos Port 1990 ....4.00 ....8.00

Cockburn Late Bottled Port 1987 (3 oz)........................6.00

Dinner wines should be divided between dry reds, whites, and less dry rosés. Most patrons prefer dry wines, but some may like the small degree of sweetness in a rosé. (It is important that the word *dry* be used to describe a *lack of sweetness*, rather than a quality of sourness, in a wine.)

Whether the wines are domestic (produced in the United States) or imported will depend on patron preferences and availability of items. Preferably, the list should include a selection of both.

Some domestic wines are named after imports they are meant to resemble. One may find on a list of domestic wines such names as Burgundy, Beaujolais, and Chablis. These may not be good representations of the European wines they are supposed to imitate. This will mainly depend upon the type of grape and processing used. A domestic wine bearing a generic name—meaning a specific *kind* of wine from a district or area—such as Burgundy may or may not come from the pinot noir grape grown in Burgundy, France. If the buyer wishes a wine that more nearly resembles the foreign wine, he or she should order a domestic wine bearing the name of the *varietal* (variety of grape) used for that wine. Thus, if one orders a domestic wine named "Pinot Noir," a varietal name rather than a generic name, such as Burgundy, the wine will more nearly resemble a French Burgundy because U.S. regulations require that, when the varietal name is used, 75 percent of the wine must come from that specific type of grape. Similarly, if one wishes a domestic wine resembling a true Chablis, the order should be for a wine labeled "Pinot Chardonnay," the grape used to produce this wine in France. The price of a domestic varietal wine should be higher than a domestic generic one, other factors being equal.

For specialty restaurants, either the menu or the service personnel will indicate the wines offered. A seafood restaurant, for example, should feature white wines, while listing a few reds and rosés. A steak house may reverse this, offering mainly red wines.

Normally, red dinner wines are served at room temperature (about 60°F to 65°F, or 15.6°C to 18.3°C) with red meats; white dinner wines are served chilled (about 45°F or 7.2°C) with seafood or poultry. The custom of serving red wines with red meats and white wines with white meats is fading. Many authorities today say that patrons should select the wine he or she likes. Still, guidelines exist for restaurants that want to stay with the tradition. (See **Exhibit 9.3.**)

If there is a doubt about which wine should go with which food, a rosé can be offered since it is suitable for use in place of either a red or white wine. Many times, patrons who know very little about wines prefer a rosé with just a touch of sweetness. White wines usually have less body and less full flavor than reds. Reds are also slightly more astringent. Some whites have a flinty, harsh quality, as evidenced in a Graves from Bordeaux or in some German dry white wines. This in no way detracts from their quality, but some patrons, not appreciating these qualities, may prefer a softer, more delicate wine.

Exhibit 9.3 Matching Wine with Food

Menu Item	Wine Suggestion
Appetizer	Champagne, dry white wine, dry sherry
Salad	No wine (wine does not complement acidic dressings)
Fish or seafood	Dry or medium-dry white
Beef	Hearty red
Lamb	Hearty red
Veal	Light red or full-bodied white
Ham or pork	Dry or medium-dry white or rosé
Turkey, duck, chicken	Full-bodied white or light red
Game (venison, pheasant, wild duck)	Hearty red
Lasagna, spaghetti, pizza	Hearty red
Cheeses, full-flavored	Hearty red, sweet white (with roquefort)
Cheeses, mild	Sherry, port, Madeira, mild table wines of any type
Desserts, pastries, fruits mousses	Semisweet sparkling wine, sweet white table wine

Sweet wines, such as Muscatel, Tokay, or an imported Barsac or Trockenbeeren Auslese, complement desserts. Port and some other quite sweet, fortified wines are proper after dinner, but most Americans select brandy or a sweet liqueur.

If the management knows its wines, it can feature a wine that is not well known but is of fine quality. Egri Bakiver, a Hungarian dry red wine of considerable richness, bouquet, and body (Egri Bakiver means "blood of the ox"), can replace a Bordeaux or Burgundy wine. Aszu Tokay from Hungary is a fine offering as a sweet dessert wine. A Barbera from the Piedmont district in Italy is an excellent alternative to some of the higher-priced French red dinner varieties. (It may have to be *decanted* before serving because of its tendency to have considerable sediment.)

Merchandising Distinction and Variety

Wines are distinctive in numerous ways: they are produced from different varieties of grapes, from different vineyards, and in particular vintage years; they come from various districts, parishes, chateaux, or schlosses (castles), and are shipped by many different vintners. These factors offer many merchandising opportunities to foodservice operators.

Most wines have a story behind them, and good merchandising should make use of interesting wine lore. A good example of one of the romantic stories of wine that can be used is the famous remark of Dom Pérignon when he first tasted champagne, which he had invented accidentally. "I am tasting stars!" he exclaimed. The fact that the Aszu Tokay wine from Hungary has been called the "king of wines and the wine of kings" also makes good copy. Est! Est! Est!, a famous wine from Italy, derives its name from the exclamation made by the servant of a bishop who was sent ahead to sample the wine before his master came. The servant, who had heard of the wine's fame, said when he tasted it: "It is! It is! It is!" The fact that one of Napoleon's colonels thought so highly of the wines of the famous Clos de Vougeot vineyards that he ordered his soldiers to salute when they marched past the vineyard, also makes for interesting menu reading. A mention that Zinfandel, a red dinner wine somewhat resembling a Chianti, or Emerald Dry, a luscious, dry white wine resembling a Moselle with a bit of "spritz" (a term meaning small bubbles or effervescence), come only from grapes grown in California, can be used to increase these wines' prestige.

Use of proper terminology is crucial. To call a Moselle wine, which comes in tall green bottles, a Rheingau or Rheinhesse wine, which come in darker-colored bottles, is quickly noted by knowledgeable patrons. Similarly, labeling a German Sekt or an Italian Asti Spumante as "champagne" is deceptive. Wine descriptions can help sell, but they must truly represent the qualities and other factors found in the wine.

Merchandising the Formal or Catering Wine List

Operations such as clubs, hotels, restaurants, and others serving fine foods may wish to present the particular name of the wine served with a printed menu. This can be done in various ways. The U.S. State Department sets up the White House menus; often, when one wine is served, it will be listed at the bottom of the menu after the foods, as shown in **Exhibit 9.4**. At other times, the particular wine served with several courses will be listed to the left of the courses with which it is served, as in **Exhibit 9.5**.

The menu shown in Exhibit 9.5 is typical of those used for formal meals today. An appetizer course or a light soup might be used to start the meal and an Amontillado sherry (dry) would be proper with it, with the sherry noted on the left of the menu. Perhaps the most elaborate kind of a menu would be the seven- or eight-course meal served at very formal banquets. **Exhibit 9.6** shows a third way of listing the wines for a formal meal. (If an

Exhibit 9.4   Formal Wine Listing

Coquille of Seafood Neptune
Cheese Straws
Piccata of Veal Luganese
Saffron Rice
Asparagus Tips

Champagne Mousse

Bernkasteler Doktor 1969

Exhibit 9.5 Three Wines with a Several-course Meal

Johannisberger Klaus 1970	Timbale of Seafood Puff Paste Wafer
Louis Martini Cabernet Sauvignon 1968	Chateaubriand Béarnaise Soufflé Potatoes Artichoke Andalouse
Dom Pérignon 1964	Fresh Peach, Glacé Monticello Raspberry Sauce

Palace Hotel, San Francisco

Exhibit 9.6 Formal Seven-course Dinner Menu

Lobster Canapé
Small Cheese Puffs
Dubonnet

Double Consommé, Celestine
Cheese Straws
Amontillado, Dom Pedro

Celery   Olives   Salted Almonds
Poached Fillet of Turbot, Caper Sauce
Pouilly Fuisse 1955

Spooned Leg of Lamb
Mixed Spring Vegetables
Potatoes Anna
Egri Bikaver 1964

Fresh Asparagus, Vinaigrette
Camembert Cheese
Wafers
Chateau Margaux 1952

Schaum Torte
Schloss Johannisberger, Trockenbeeren Auslese, 1953

Coffee
Courvoisier, V.S.O.P.

Nuts   Mints   Bon Bons

Exhibit 9.7   Luncheon Menu with Wines

	Cream of Mushroom Potage
	Cheese Straws
Beaufort Pinot	Filet of Sole Marguery
Chardonnay 1969	String Beans, Amandine
Beaulieu Vineyards	Rice Croquette
	Citrus Fruit and Mango Salad
	Honey French Dressing
Chateau Yquem	Black Bottom Pie
1979	

eight-course meal were served, there would be a poultry course following the fish course; the Pouilly Fuisse, 1955, would be proper to serve with it. A dry, light, crisp wine, such as a Graves, might be then used with the fish course.)

Another method of presenting the wines served at a formal meal is to list the wines separately from the food. This would be done with a folded menu, which, when opened, has the wines listed on the left half and the food courses on the right half. **Exhibit 9.7** indicates the wines served for a luncheon.

The Spirit List

In simplistic terms, *spirits* are alcoholic beverages that are not wines, liqueurs, or beers. Spirits include distilled beverages, such as rum, scotch whiskey, gin, and vodka. Spirits generally have a higher alcoholic content than wines, beers, and liqueurs.

The list of menu spirits is rather traditional, and less variation is found on it than on a wine list. Only a few drinks may be on the menu, it being understood that the bar can furnish others if desired. Thus, a menu might list only those drinks that management wishes to push, as shown in **Exhibit 9.8**.

Exhibit 9.8   Spirit List

Special Decanter of Martini on the Rocks
or Manhattan on the Rocks
$3.35

Old-Fashioned   Gimlet   Whiskey Sour   Side Car
$3.25

The items on a spirit list should be balanced to provide what management feels will satisfy guests' needs. Normally, individuals ordering highballs, cocktails, or similar drinks know what they want, and a list is not required. In this case, the purpose of a menu is more to inform the patron about the prices rather than to spell out what is available. Most operations will find that they need a good list of "call" liquors, or brand names, Smirnoff's vodka, Chivas Regal scotch, or Beefeater gin are examples. The number of these should be limited as much as possible. Checks should be kept on how frequently requests are made for call items. Those that move slowly should be eliminated. If a couple of good call scotches, bourbons, ryes, brandies, gins, and, possibly, one rum are stocked, most requests can be filled. Often, if a patron who orders one high-quality spirit that is not in stock is offered another of equal popularity, he or she will accept it. If bartenders and service personnel keep track of how many call items are *not* requested and what they are, a better list can be built. Local tastes and value perceptions must be considered.

Proof

Alcoholic content of spirits is measured in *proof*, expressed as a percentage of volume of water to alcohol.

The term was originated by the British, who found that if gunpowder was mixed with alcohol and water, it would burn, but only if a specific amount of alcohol was mixed with the water *and no less*. If even the slightest amount of water above the limit was added, the gunpowder would not burn. The British used this test as a means of checking the alcoholic content of spirits. If the spirit burned, they said it was "proof" that the spirit contained an adequate quantity of alcohol. **Exhibit 9.9** indicates the equivalent proofs of British, European, and American standards.

Exhibit 9.9 Comparison of Proofs

	British	**American**	**European (Gay-Lussac)**
100% alcohol			
	175 proof	190 proof	100 proof
	100	114	57
	88	100	50
	85	98	49
	80	90	45
	75	86*	43
	70†	80†	40
	65	74	37
Water	0	0	0

*Many blends and lower-priced whiskies are 80 or 86 proof.

†The British and American governments do not allow spirits such as gin, rum, brandy, or whiskey to be less than this in proof.

In the United States, proof of a spirit is two times the percent of alcohol by volume or weight. Thus, if a spirit contains 50 percent alcohol, the proof is 100 (2 × 50). It is important to know whether alcohol content is based on alcohol by volume or alcohol by weight. A spirit that is 50 percent alcohol by weight contains more alcohol than a spirit that is 50 percent alcohol by volume. This is because alcohol is lighter than water, so it takes more alcohol to equal water weight.

Wines have less alcohol (7 to 14 percent) than spirits, and beers generally have the lowest alcoholic content (from 2.5 to 8 percent). Spirits range widely, from 50 to 190 proof, depending on the type of spirit and the brand.

Beers and Ales

On the liquor menu, the list of beers, ales, and similar drinks should be limited. A sufficient list would feature three or four domestic beers and ales and three or four imports. Of course, if the operation is a beer garden or a German or Bavarian restaurant, more beers from those countries should be offered. If several good draft beers are served as house beverages, the need for a bigger list, even in one of these restaurants, may not be necessary. On some beverage menus, one or two draft beers *must* be offered. "Light" beers are also popular, and a small selection of these should be available.

Local favorites may need to be included on the menu. Chicago beer drinkers, for example, have made Old Style a local favorite. Coors is practically a mandatory menu item in some western states. It's a simple matter of knowing the clientele.

Liqueurs and Cordials

The list of after-dinner drinks on a beverage menu should also be limited to what the trade requires and no more. Several domestic and imported brandies can be featured. Créme de Menthe, Créme de Cacao, a few fruit brandies, Curacao, Cointreau, Benedictine, Chartreuse, and a few others are likely to be sufficient. Often the menu can feature some mixed after-dinner drinks that the establishment feels can be sold at a good profit, and that will please patrons. These can be listed as clip-ons or boxed entries on the beverage menu to call special attention to them, in a way similar to that described for food menu items the management wants to feature. Table tents also work well.

WINE SERVICE

Servers must know all of the establishment's wines and which wines might be suitable with certain foods in order to make suggestions. With training, servers can home in on patron needs or tastes and follow through with proper service.

In large dining rooms, a wine steward or *sommelier* will be on staff. It is this individual's job to discuss wines with patrons, make suggestions, and take the order. Both sommeliers and servers should be able to present a good reason for a wine suggestion. For instance, if lamb and beef make up the entree orders, a red Bordeaux or Burgundy will have flavor qualities that go well with them. If the selection is seafood, a Chablis, Chenin Blanc, or German Reisling would bring out the best flavor qualities of the seafood. Lobster is a slightly sweet meat, and a wine that is crisp and delicate with just a touch of sweetness will be highly desirable. However, individual tastes vary and servers should be prepared to make secondary suggestions.

It is also necessary to enhance the proper wine with the proper service. Some wines should be served at specific temperatures. Some guests may desire wine at a different temperature, and service personnel may ask, when the wine is ordered, if a specific temperature is desired. If the guest prefers that a red dinner wine be chilled, the server should show no evidence that this is not the usual service but go ahead and serve it that way. (Chilling a red wine is thought to harm some of the flavor and bouquet.) It is proper for the individual ordering a red wine to ask the waiter to pull the cork ahead of service so that the wine can breathe. This allows the wine to oxidize slightly, giving it a fuller flavor and a better bouquet. Older, high-priced red wines should not be allowed to oxidize as much as newer reds.

Proper presentation and pouring are key elements of good service. It is customary for patrons ordering wine to be shown the label on a bottle before the cork is pulled to allow them to see that it is the right wine. The foil around the cork should be removed and the cork pulled following procedures. After the cork is pulled, white wine may be put back into the wine holder to continue chilling. Red wine may be placed directly on the table, the label toward the host, or it may be put into a basket. It is correct for the server to smell the cork to see that the wine in the bottle is good. The server may set the cork down at the host's right so that he or she, too, can smell it.

If there is any doubt about the quality, the server or *sommelier* may taste the wine in a silver *tastevin*. This should be only a tiny sip. The wine is then poured in a small quantity into the host's glass to judge whether it is a suitable wine to serve with the food. The host should nod or indicate approval. When this occurs, all of the other guests are served before the host.

The proper glass should be used. (See **Exhibit 9.10**.) Using small glasses that are completely or nearly full is a mistake. Only a part of the wine glass should be filled, "to leave room for the nose." A Burgundy wine requires a large, tulip-shaped glass, a claret needs a narrower one, a Rhine or Moselle should have a glass with a tall stem. The all-purpose wine glass is also proper. Champagne is best served in a tall, narrow tulip glass rather than a flat, open champagne glass. (Brandy should be served in a proper snifter and *not* in a small liqueur glass.)

The reason a wine glass is turned in slightly at the top is to concentrate the wine odor so that it is fuller as the wine is consumed. Before tasting, wine may be swirled in the glass, especially a red wine, to give it some oxidation and assist in building flavor and bouquet. It is proper to hold the wine up to the light to check its clarity and color, or to look at it through the glass against the white tablecloth to note these visual qualities. About two ounces

Exhibit 9.10 Wine Glasses Used for French Wines

Champagne Flute   Champagne Saucer   All Purpose

of wine should be poured into the taster's glass so that plenty of space is left for sensing the bouquet. Servers should leave the bottle on the table for the host to pour more wine for the guests if the server is not there to do it.

BEVERAGE SERVICE

Even if a menu has been masterfully planned to please patrons and meet profit needs, it can be completely negated by poor selling and service. It is essential that servers provide the follow-through that will obtain the proper sales mix and check average, and satisfy customers.

Beverage service should be built around the emphasis of relaxation and pleasure. Many people drink at social events, with friends, or to relax and spend a few idle, peaceful moments. Others want entertainment as well as drinks. Servers should be friendly, helpful, courteous, and know how to handle people and be able to sense their moods. Some will want drink recommendations and some conversation. Others will want only the service required and then to be left alone. Servers should know the liquor menu very well, how drinks are made, in which type of glass they are served, how they are garnished, and beverage prices.

The service of beverages in a bar or lounge will be slightly different than that in a dining area. In the bar or lounge people are there to drink and not especially to eat, although some operations may serve food in the bar or lounge. In the dining area, the patrons' main purpose is to have food and, possibly, to have a drink or two. Servers should be trained to quickly determine what guests want and then obtain it for them. Service should be sure, deft, and courteous. It is very important that servers watch their assigned tables for signals for repeat orders.

Drinks should be served in attractive, clean, sparkling glassware, be made from standardized formulas, and be attractively garnished. It is important in beverage merchandising to have drinks prepared to attract attention. An old-fashioned can be a conversation piece at the table if served with a beautiful garnish of fresh fruit. A martini served in a glass so cold it "smokes" will draw notice. Sometimes unusual glassware can be a differentiating factor. Serving drinks in a special glass that can be kept by the patron or in a hollowed-out pineapple or coconut is enjoyable. Beer steins may be used for German beers. Cocktail napkins should be presented before the drinks are served. If a snack or hors d'oeuvres are served, the proper serving utensils and dishes should be on hand.

When guests enter a dining area, a server should come to the table as soon as they are seated and ask, "What kind of cocktail may I bring you?" This question is more direct than, "Can I bring you anything?" Any special promotions should be described. If guests seem as though they would like a drink but do not know what to order, the server should promptly make a suggestion.

LIQUOR PRICING

Liquor is priced differently from food. Markups are usually higher, and there is a tendency to *average out* prices more by groups of similar drinks than by individual costs. Thus, a large group of mixed cocktails may be priced at $4.00 each, even though the cost of producing the different drinks may differ somewhat. With food items, individual pricing would likely be used. Many operations attempt to have an average ingredient cost for liquor items of around 20 to 25 percent, while at the same time they may want a food cost of 30 to 40 percent.

As in all menu pricing, a knowledge of cost is still desirable before establishing prices.

Pricing Wines

Wine prices should reflect the menu price range for food. Patrons like to see a bottle of wine priced somewhere around the price of entrees.

Some operations price wines at 200 percent of their bottle cost—the equivalent of marking them up 100 percent. However, this may increase the price of some rather expensive wines above what the market will bear, or it may bring in less total profit if only one bottle is sold when two could have been. Patrons often compare wine prices seen in stores and resent the higher markup in foodservice operations. Because of this, beverage pricing is more often done on the basis of competition or what the market will bear than food is. Servers working on a wine-selling commission also are happier if more wine is sold because it not only increases their commission, it also increases the amount of tips from the customer because of the larger bill.[1] Furthermore, it is desirable to have wines appear on tables because there is a greater tendency for patrons at adjacent tables to purchase wine if they see others having it. Therefore, some operations may price higher-costing wines at a lower markup to move them. Usually, the lowest limit used for the markup for wines is 50 percent over bottle cost. The reason for this is that costs on wine are usually calculated on the following cost percentages.

Interest on inventory[2]	11%
Storage and other space costs	5
Cooling and handling	3
Labor	15
Glassware	5
Breakage	2
Total	41%

The margin of 9 percent on a 50 percent markup (50% − 41% = 9%) must go for profit and variable and fixed costs. Because 9 percent may be insufficient to cover these, the markup may have to be higher.

Pricing Spirits

The costs of drinks made from spirits, such as highballs and cocktails, depend on the quantity and cost of the spirits used and the cost of other ingredients in the drink, such as a carbonated beverage, ice, fruit, or vermouth. To control costs, an operation should establish *exact* quantities to be used for all drinks and see that these limits are followed.

Usually the main ingredient cost of a drink is calculated, and then other costs are added to this. For instance, if two ounces of bourbon costs $0.62 and vermouth $0.08, the total cost to make a Manhattan is $0.70. If the beverage markup is to be based on a 25 percent product cost, the selling price will be about $2.80.

Some operations estimate the added ingredient cost over the main ingredient cost. Often this is considered to be around 20 percent of the main beverage ingredient cost.

In pouring liquor, there can be some miscalculation in determining how much is available for sale. There can be losses from evaporation, overpouring, or spillage. Often an allowance of about 5 percent is allowed for loss in spirit dispensing, and 7 to 10 percent in dispensing tap beer or other tap products. When the loss factor is figured in beverage yields, the calculation, based on a liter (33.8 oz), used for pouring $1\frac{1}{2}$-ounce drinks would be $33.8 \times 0.05 =$ a 1.7-ounce loss $(33.8 − 1.7) = 32.1 \div 1.5$ oz $= 21.4$. So about 21 drinks could be poured from a liter after the pouring loss is subtracted. Similarly, calculations should be used to find approximate portions obtained when pouring from irregular-sized bottles. In many operations this calculation will be unnecessary, thanks to computerized or electronic dispensing of drinks that count drinks poured from controlled stocks.

As stated earlier, there is a tendency to group prices in beverage menus around certain kinds of drinks. To get a group price, an operation may keep a record of the number of different kinds of drinks sold during a period and then make a study to see what the costs are. This will help determine an average selling price for each item in the group, along with the resulting profit

Exhibit 9.11 Record of Drinks Sold

	Ounce Per Drink	Cost Per Ounce	Cost Per Drink	Total Cost for Sale
DRINKS, PLAIN				
102 Scotch	1.5	$0.85	$1.25	$130.05
84 Bourbon	1.5	0.30	0.45	37.80
23 Gin	1.5	0.30	0.45	10.35
28 Vodka	1.5	0.30	0.45	12.60
6 Rye	1.5	0.65	0.99	5.85
4 Rum	1.5	0.30	0.45	1.80
Total plain drinks cost				$198.45
COCKTAILS, MIXED				
88 Gin or Vodka	2.0	$0.30	$0.60	$ 57.00
25 Manhattans	1.5	0.30	0.45	11.25
66 Other Bourbon	1.5	0.30	0.45	29.70
Total mixed cocktails cost				91.95
424 Total				290.40
Add 20% Other Material Costs				58.08
Total Cost of Pouring Drinks				$308.79

percentage. For instance, **Exhibit 9.11** shows that the total cost of pouring a certain group of drinks is $308.79. If the cost markup is 25 percent, then $1,235.16 should be taken in ($308.79 ÷ 0.25 = $1,235.16).

If management feels scotch at $5.00 per 1.5-ounce drink is too high (the markup at a 25 percent food cost) and wants to see what happens if it is sold for $3.00, and all other drinks and cocktails are sold for $2.00, the calculation would be: 102 × $3.00 = $306.00 and for the others 322 × $2.00 = $644.00, for a total of $950.00. At a cost of $308.79, this is a percentage cost of 32.5 percent. If management feels that it wants a percentage markup based on a 25 percent food cost, this is not satisfactory. A tight bar control must be practiced so basic ingredients are used in the amounts estimated.

Some operations have a high markup and charge one price, regardless of what the drink is. The price set is sufficient to cover all costs of drinks it produces. If any adjustment must be made, the amount of the main ingredient poured can be varied. This can be done by pouring two ounces of gin or vodka instead of 1½ ounces for a martini, or pouring 1¼ ounces of a call brand of scotch instead of 1½ ounces, thus covering the costs of an expensive item.

Pricing Tap Products

Draft products are usually priced on the basis of the unit cost. For instance, a 12-ounce pilsner beer glass holds about 10.4 ounces of beer. The amount held in a glass varies with the size of the head of foam—from ½ to 1 inch.

Operations should find out their own average serving amount. There is usually a 7 percent pouring loss when beer is poured from the tap. If a half-barrel of beer (1,984 ounces) costing $50.00 is used, the unit cost is calculated as follows.

1,984 oz × (100% − 7%) = 1,845 ounces
1,845 ÷ 10.4 oz = 177 glasses
$50.00 ÷ 177 glasses = $0.2825 cost per glass

If the operator wants a 25 percent product cost, the selling price is $1.13 ($0.2825 ÷ 0.25 = $1.13). If the operator wants a 20 percent product cost, the price is $1.41 ($0.2825 ÷ 0.20 = $1.4125).

Bottled beer is usually sold on a straight markup basis. For instance, if a 12-ounce bottle costs $0.50 and the desired cost percentage is 25 percent, the price is $2.40; if it is 20 percent, the price is $2.50.

Other pricing methods as mentioned in Chapter 6 on pricing could also be used for tap products. Charging only what the market will bear might be a good method for pricing tap products.

BEVERAGE CONTROL

Control of alcoholic beverages is essential to profitability of the liquor operation. Liquor that is "lost" cannot be sold. If controls are inadequate, potential profit can be lost. Through overpouring, spillage, improper mixing, improper ringing up of sales, customers who refuse drinks or avoid paying, and employee pilferage, liquor profits can be lost. Seeing that liquor items are served as planned and that costs are controlled comes with a program that includes good purchasing methods, standardized recipes, proper production, adequate record keeping, and financial controls. It is the purpose here to briefly summarize some of the factors that can lead to serving the right product at the right cost.

Purchasing Controls

The menu largely dictates what is to be held in stock for beverage service, and the stock requirements will, in turn, dictate what is to be purchased. The purchasing of alcoholic beverages is somewhat simplified in that items are usually purchased by brand name. Customers will often ask for a particular brand of scotch—a *call brand*. (Such an item is usually sold at a higher price than regular stock.) Thus, a certain number of standard brand items will be required to maintain a stock for patron calls. Wines, beers, and ales may be requested by brand, also.

Every establishment generally has in stock several *house* or *well* items. These are good-quality brands of spirits that are used for mixed drinks and for other drinks when no call brand is specified. Often these are selected on the basis of local tastes and price. Requests for wines, beers, and ales can also be filled from house stocks. For instance, if a customer orders a draft beer, the house stock is served. Similarly, a customer ordering a glass of dry, white wine will likely get a house brand.

Selection of alcoholic beverages must be based on several factors, including price, patron preferences, quality, and proof. Even though a particular item may be of high quality, it should not be stocked if only a few customers order it.

Value in spirits is often based on the quantity one receives plus the proof of the item for the price. A buyer should check the proof of items when purchasing, although if purchasing by brand, this may not be important since patrons who want a brand either know the proof or are not concerned. The buyer needs to be aware of proof, however, in order to price products. A spirit of 100 proof should sell for more than one of 80 proof, all other factors being equal. Buyers should also check the quantity of liquor in the bottle. A 750-ml bottle holds close to the same quantity as a fifth-sized bottle—the fifth holds 756.5 ml. However, in a case (12 bottles) of fifths one gets nearly three ounces more liquor than one does in a case of 750-ml bottles. A quart holds 945.6 ml, while a liter holds 1,000 ml, so when one purchases a case of bottles in liters, one is getting nearly 653 ml or about 22 ounces more. Many operations still use ounce measures in pouring. In pricing, it is necessary to convert bottled drink cost into item cost, so whichever form of measure is quickest for the operation should be used. (See **Exhibit 9.12**.)

The quantity purchased should be held to the lowest possible figure, with safeguards against running out. Usually an operation calculates its average use of items and establishes both a minimum and maximum level of stock for maintaining stocks between deliveries. The minimum level is set so that the stock will be available during normal usage, plus an additional safety factor. The maximum level is set so ordering is not too frequent. Occasionally, stocks may be raised above a maximum level if use is expected to be high. Seldom should it be allowed to go below the minimum level. Very slow-moving items are usually reordered when the last bottle is issued or the bar runs out.

Exhibit 9.12 Volume Measures for Standard Bottles*

Bottle	Ounces	Milliliters
750 ml	25.4	750.00
Fifth (1/5 gl)	25.6	756.50
Quart (U.S.)	32.0	945.60
Imperial Quart	38.4	1,133.54
Liter	33.9	1,000.00
1.75	59.3	1,750.00
3.00	101.6	3,000.00
Gallon	128.1	3,780.00
Imperial Gallon	153.7	4,534.15

*In these calculations the metric equivalent of 1 oz was taken to be 29.5 ml. If this had been weight and not volume, an ounce would be equal to 28.4 gm, approximately.

Buyers should not be misled by discounts into purchasing more than the maximum level, unless the discount is substantial. If the discount is less than the interest of money invested in a large stock, the deal will not be a favorable one for the buyer. Storage, risk of loss, and other factors also must be considered as costs.

Liquor purchase requisitions are usually the basis for purchase orders. Only those authorized to buy beverages should have access to purchase requisitions or purchase orders. They should be signed by management or the highest purchasing authority. A record should be maintained of all purchase orders for liquor. From the purchase record a *daily receiving report* should be set up, indicating what beverage orders are expected for delivery on what days, how much was ordered, and the price. The specification for each item can be consulted to obtain additional information for the receiving report.

Receiving

When goods arrive, they should be checked to see whether they are the right item and size ordered and the proper quantity. If the delivery matches both the purchase order and the invoice, the latter can be signed and a copy retained and sent to accounting with the receiving report. If the delivery is not correct, the discrepancy should be noted on the receiving report and on the retained invoice. If the discrepancy is major, delivery should be refused. After receiving, alcoholic beverages should be moved quickly to storage, since security is a factor during transport and until properly stored.

Goods should be stored on shelving in the same order as they appear on the inventory sheet. In this way, the items are easily found and checking is easier during inventory.

Issuing

The issue of bar goods requires special treatment. *Nothing* should be issued to the bar without a properly signed requisition. (See **Exhibit 9.13**.) The requisition with a duplicate is brought to the issue room and presented to the storeroom clerk who fills the order. Accompanying the requisition should be one empty bottle for every bottle to be issued. The storeroom clerk should check each empty bottle to note the code before disposing of it. Sometimes bars and lounges might lose track of a bottle. This can happen with full bottle spirit sales or wine sales, when a guest takes the bottle. In this case a sales slip for the item, signed by the bar manager, is presented to the clerk instead of the empty bottle. Issues for room service and catering operations may have to be handled a bit differently, but good control and security must be part of the procedure.

When the person to whom the items are to be issued receives them, the storeroom clerk and the receiver should each sign both copies of the requisition. The storeroom clerk keeps one copy and the receiver gets the other. Bars and lounges and other liquor-dispensing units should order on the basis of *par stock*, or an allowable inventory based on what management thinks is needed for the bar to operate over a specific period, usually a single shift or a

Exhibit 9.13   Beverage Requisition Form

BEVERAGE REQUISITION			

Dept: _____   Date: _____

Quantity	Item	Quantity	Item
	Liquor		Beer
			Soft Drinks
	Wine		Fruit, etc.

SIGNATURE: _____

full day. In that case, issues from the storeroom to the various units should take place at the beginning or end of a shift.

A bar stock inventory is done in tenths of a bottle or fourths of a bottle. Each time an inventory is taken, a check is made to see that all bottles bear the coding stamped on them by the storeroom clerk when the cases are opened. After cases are emptied, they should be broken down and folded. Unbroken cases can easily hide pilferage.

Bin cards for checking off items removed from storage can act as a perpetual inventory, but this is preferable kept on a computer. A regularly scheduled physical inventory should also take place. Two people should take inventory. One should identify items and count while the other checks the bin card and writes in the correct count on the inventory sheet. It is usually better for verification if one of the inventory takers is not a member of the beverage department.

Production Control

Bartenders may like to have the freedom to mix drinks according to their own formulas, but many operations find that consistent drink production ensures proper quantities and quality, keeps costs down, and contributes to responsible service. Standard recipes for drinks should be as well tested and costed out as food recipes. The cost of the garnish is added to the cost of the main ingredients. The standardized recipe should give the drink name, code number, list ingredients in amount in order used, preparation method, portion size, type of glassware, garnish, and any other information to produce the drink. (See **Exhibit 9.14.**)

Many bars that want to have control over the production of drinks publish manuals and brochures of recipes that standardize pouring. It is important for managers to see that these recipes are followed. When the standardized recipe is used, the cost and the resulting drink can help ensure patron acceptance and management control.

Some operations allow bartenders to *free pour* without measuring ingredients. With experienced personnel, an almost exact measure may be poured each time. Studies have shown, however, that better consistency in drink quality and better cost control occurs when measures are used.

Jiggers and *shot glasses* are often used as measures. A jigger is often a measure with two different size cups, one on either end. The most commonly used has a ³/₄-ounce and a 1¹/₂-ounce cup. Some jiggers are scaled in ¹/₄-inch markings and hold from 1 to 1¹/₂ ounces. The standard jigger size is considered 1¹/₂ ounces. A shot glass measures from ⁷/₈ ounce to several ounces. The standard is often set at 1 ounce. The jigger is usually used for mixed drinks, while shot glasses are used for making nonmixed or straight-shot drinks.

The lines on glass measures can be deceiving. Glasses are slightly concave or curved, so the patron seeing the glass sees the spirit above the line

Exhibit 9.14 Standardized Recipe for a Manhattan

Ingredient	Ingredient Unit	Drink Measure	Purchase Unit Cost	Measure Cost
Bourbon, whiskey	32 oz	2 oz	$11.75	$0.73
Vermouth, sweet	32 oz	1 oz	3.00	0.09
Bitters	16 oz	dash (¹/₂ oz)	3.25	0.10
Cherry (100 count)	1 gal	1 cherry	12.00	0.12
				$1.04

Method: On the rocks: Fill an old-fashioned glass (7 oz) with small ice cubes; measure with jigger; add bitters. Stir. Garnish with cherry on bar pick. Add swizzle stick.

Straight or up: Measure with jigger into shaker; add ice and stir. Drain into cocktail glass (4¹/₂ oz). Garnish with cherry on bar pick.

when it is actually just on the line. Some glasses are purposely lined just under the proper amount so that when a drink is overpoured, the exact amount is still given.

Caps that measure the exact amount poured can be put on bottles. When the established amount is poured through the cap, pouring automatically stops. Some caps also count the number of pours. Once used, a cap will not release liquor until the bottle is first set upright, then tilted for another drink.

Push-button pouring systems can be used to control drink amounts, and some attached to electronic cash registers or computers are quite sophisticated. Not only is the right drink poured in the right amount, but information on the drink, its price, and place of service is also recorded in the machine. Thus, at the end of the day a complete sales readout can be obtained.

Some patrons do not like to see drinks poured from caps or from push-button units, preferring the free-pour system. For this reason, when patrons can see service, such units might not be used, but they can be used as controls at service bars.

Service Control

Controlling the service of liquor is the final check in good beverage management. Bar checks for servers and bartenders should be numbered, and when issued, the check numbers should be recorded and the receiver should sign for the checks. When checks are returned unused, they are checked in. If a check turns up missing, the server who was issued the check is responsible.

The transfer of checks from the bar to the dining service should be worked out well. Usually the check and a transfer log are sent to the dining area by someone at the bar. The host, hostess, or maitre d' receives the check and signs a transfer log, which frees the bar of responsibility to obtain payment. Service personnel should use one check for each table served. (See **Exhibit 9.15**.) The bartender at the service bar should do the same. Sometimes bartenders do not use checks but cash registers instead. When the customer is ready to pay, the total bar bill is rung up and the paid check is then put into a locked box so it cannot be used again. This is done because if the server retains the check and gets a similar order, the check could be reused. The dishonest server could then pocket the extra cash since the recorded check has already been paid and rung up. Such checks held out this way by servers are called *floaters*. Using a locked check box helps prevent this from happening, but only if the check is placed there immediately after payment.

Some systems call for servers to obtain payment upon service for each check. If there is a reorder, the check is recalled, the additional items ordered sent out, and the additional amount totaled. Other systems call for cash to be presented by the server at the end of a shift. Then the receipts are totaled and the server presents the amount of cash matching the total, keeping the extra as tips. It seems that most establishments prefer the former method, where payment is received immediately.

Exhibit 9.15 Bar Check

TABLE	GUESTS	SERVER	DATE	CHECK NO.
				981201
1				
2				
3				
4				
5				
6				
7				
8				
9				
10				
11				
12				
13				
14				
15				
16				
17				
18				
19				
20				
BAR TOTAL ⟶				

SIGNATURE	ROOM NO.

CHECK NO.	DATE	GUESTS	CASHIER'S INITIALS	BAR TOTAL
981201				

Reconciling Sales

Beverage managers often try to establish methods that will allow a check on income received to determine whether income is what it should be. This is called *reconciling sales*. There are a number of methods for doing this. Reconciling sales can start with a daily cost sheet that includes the daily receipts, material use, food cost percentage, accumulated figures for these, and, perhaps, some historical data for comparison purposes. However, this sheet presents what *is* happening but not what *should* happen. Similarly, a profit-and-loss statement tells what *has* happened—not what should happen.

Some operations record inventory issues at retail prices, that is, what the item is to make in income. Theoretically, the cash or income received should then equal the issue price. There are problems in this, however. If only one type of drink is given at one price from the amount in each bottle, the system can work, but this is usually not the case in most beverage operations. Most often, different amounts are poured from one bottle for different-priced drinks. For instance, what should the retail value of a bottle of gin be if a gin fizz of 1½ ounces sells for $2.50, a martini with 2 ounces of gin sells for $2.75, and a Tom Collins using 1½ ounces of gin sells for $2.65? The answer will depend on how many of each are sold from the bottle, and the one-drink, one-price method will not work.

Another way to keep track of sales from bottles is to have a different bottle for each kind of drink sold in a different amount at a different price. This system may also break down, because of the number of bottles that have to be stocked at the bar and because during busy times the wrong bottle may be used.

Sales Tally

A more certain way to reconcile sales is to make a *sales tally* from guest checks and check the income against the amount of liquor used per drink for that day or that period. First, the exact amount of liquor used in each kind of drink must be known. Recipes will provide that information. Then multiply the total for the drink sold by the amount of liquor used per drink to get the total amount of liquor used for the day. This total is then multiplied by the selling price to get the actual income. This can be done for each drink made from each kind of spirit to see that sales come fairly close to matching the amount of liquor used. Thus, income can be determined for each type of drink sold, as shown in **Exhibit 9.16**.

The tally method can be cumbersome and time-consuming, but with electronic cash registers or computers, it is considerably simplified.

Averaging Drinks

Some operations make a tally, such as that shown in **Exhibit 9.17**, of every kind of drink sold over a period. Then, an average number of drinks sold from a bottle is obtained, and this, instead of a tally, is used to estimate how much income should be obtained for the amount of liquor used.

Exhibit 9.16 Income from Four One-liter Gin Bottles

Drink	Amount of Gin Dispensed per Drink, in ounces	Number Sold	Selling Price	Total Amount Used, in ounces	Total Income
Martini	2.00	34	$2.75	68.0	$ 93.50
Gin and Tonic	1.50	12	2.50	18.0	30.00
Tom Collins	1.75	8	2.65	14.0	21.20
Gimlet	1.50	6	2.75	9.0	16.50
Straight Gin	1.50	13	2.50	19.5	32.50
Totals		73		128.5 oz	$193.70

Exhibit 9.17 Drink Averaging

Drink	Average Number of Drinks Sold	Selling Price	Total Oz Dispensed	Income $
Martini	11.0	$2.75	22.0	$30.25
Gin and Tonic	2.0	2.50	3.00	5.00
Tom Collins	2.0	2.65	3.50	5.30
Gimlet	1.5	2.75	2.25	4.125
Straight Gin	1.0	2.50	1.50	2.50
Totals	17.5		32.25	$47.175

Averaging Percentage

Other operations use an *average percentage* of total sales instead of averaging the number of drinks. From the breakdown in Exhibit 9.17 of drinks sold from a liter, the following percentages are obtained: martini, 62.9 percent; gin and tonic, 11.4 percent; Tom Collins, 11.4 percent; gimlet, 8.6 percent; and straight gin, 5.7 percent. The next calculation required is to find out the number of drinks obtained from the bottle for each kind of drink served, allowing for about a 5 percent loss estimate. The results are shown in **Exhibit 9.18**.

Note that the income per liter of gin is about the same when using either the average percentage method or the drink averaging-method.

The advantage in using percentages is that they can be applied to any size bottle of beverage. Thus, it would be possible to calculate the potential value of a fifth of gin in the same manner as that of a liter of gin. First, estimate the percentage of drinks that will be obtained per bottle and then use the following formula.

Percentage of drinks sold × Number of drinks per bottle × Selling price of each drink

Then, total the income from each drink to get the expected income.

Exhibit 9.18 Average Percentage Method

Martini	1,000 ml ÷ 60 ml per drink = 16
Gin and Tonic	1,000 ml ÷ 45 ml per drink = 21
Tom Collins	1,000 ml ÷ 52 ml per drink = 18
Gimlet	1,000 ml ÷ 45 ml per drink = 21
Straight Gin	1,000 ml ÷ 45 ml per drink = 21

Next, the percentage of drinks served is multiplied by the number of drinks given per container times the selling price, which equals the contribution of each drinker to the total income per bottle.

Martini	62.9% × 16 × $2.75 = $27.676
Gin and Tonic	11.4% × 21 × 2.50 = 5.985
Tom Collins	11.4% × 18 × 2.65 = 5.4378
Gimlet	8.6% × 21 × 2.75 = 4.9665
Straight Gin	5.7% × 21 × 2.50 = 2.9925
Income per Bottle	$47.03

The percentage method can also be used to estimate the total income from different-sized bottles if the total amount dispensed is obtained. This figure is divided by the amount in one container for which the expected income is known. Suppose for a given period 12 1.75-liter bottles, 4 1-liter bottles, 6 quarts, and 8 750-ml bottles of gin were sold. The total sold would be as follows.

12 × 1,750 ml	= 21,000 ml
4 × 1,000 ml	= 4,000 ml
6 × (32 oz × 29.5 ml) =	5,664 ml
8 × 750 ml	= 6,000 ml
	36,664 ml
÷	1,000 ml
=	36.66 ml

If each liter is expected to bring in approximately $47.06, then $47.06 × 36.66 = $1,725.22, the expected total income from the sale of this gin.

Standard Deviation Method

Another method used to calculate income expected from a total amount of sales per bottle is called the *standard deviation* method. A calculation is made to ascertain what income would be obtained if one kind of standard size drink were sold at one price from a bottle. The amount of scotch, gin, rum, and bourbon sold in a period is then obtained, and the expected income ($31,600) is calculated, as shown in **Exhibit 9.19**. However, if sales from this amount of liquor during one period are $28,939 or only 91.68 percent of expected, a

Exhibit 9.19 Standard Deviation Method

Item	Number Sold	Drinks Sold	Price	Income
Scotch	150 qt (32 oz)	3,000	$3.00	$ 9,000
Gin	100 qt (32 oz)	1,600	2.50	4,000
Rum	50 qt (32 oz)	1,500	2.50	3,750
Bourbon	180 qt (32 oz)	5,400	2.75	4,850
Total				$31,600

check of the results from other periods may be needed. A study of several other periods may indicate that the difference between the expected income and actual gain may average out at 91.6 percent. Managers can typically expect a normal variance, and actual sales will usually be a percentage of potential or expected sales. A very low or high variation should be examined.

Potential or expected sales will only be realized if the planned sales mix holds. If the sales from a liter of gin, as shown in Exhibit 9.16, are not what is expected, there will be a definite variance in income from that expected. A sudden drop in sales of normally popular drinks should be investigated. There could be any number of reasons for a loss of sales. How large a variation should be permitted before an investigation is made? This depends upon the particular operation. A 1 to 3 percent variation probably does not warrant investigation, but beyond that point it is wise to find out whether something is wrong.

Drink Differential Procedure

The *drink differential* procedure is sometimes used to allow for the use of one type of liquor in a number of different drinks sold at different prices. Suppose management decides that each ounce of scotch should be sold at $1.50, each ounce of bourbon at $1.00, and each ounce of gin at $0.95. Next, an expected sales value is established for each bottle. If a liter is used, allowing for 5 percent spillage, each liter would give about 37.9 ounces, and the expected sales value per bottle would be as follows.

Scotch	$57.90
Bourbon	37.90
Gin	36.00

However, not all these items are sold straight. For example, 2 ounces of bourbon can be used in Manhattans selling at $1.75, 1.75 ounces in old-fashioneds priced at $1.50 each, and 1.5 ounces in whiskey sours priced at $2.50 each. The selling price should be Manhattan, $2.00 (2 oz × $1.00); old-fashioned, $1.75 (1.75 oz × $1.00); and whiskey sour, $1.50 (1.5 oz × $1.00). Thus, there is a $0.75 average over the selling price of Manhattans ($2.75 − $3.00), a $0.765 income over what management wanted ($2.50 − $1.75), and a $0.50 excess on whiskey sours.

The adjustment to be made in the drink differential method is to make a tally at the end of a typical day's sales of each of the different kinds of drinks sold, and then add the plus or minus differential to the expected cost. **Exhibits 9.20** and **9.21** show how this would be done. A calculation is made based on these drinks that shows how much of each kind was sold. Exhibit 9.21 shows the adjusted expected income.

Sometimes operations will use a different kind of differential based on the use of *secondary* ingredients. Thus, a bottle of vermouth holding 25.6 ounces is expected to provide 48½-ounce portions for preparing martinis; a quart bottle of tonic is expected to make 6 gin and tonics; and so forth. The theory is that by adding up the various quantities of secondary ingredients sold, one can arrive at the expected number of drinks sold and this multiplied by the selling price can give the expected income. This system works only when standardized recipes are used, but it is usually not workable because patrons want differing amounts of ingredients in their drinks.

There are other methods of trying to check on the ratio of income to inventory used, but these are the ones most commonly used. As the industry rapidly converts to electronic cash registers and computers, the prevailing

Exhibit 9.20 Determining Drink Differential

Drink	Ounce per Drink	Number Sold	Expected Price per Ounce	Selling Price	Drink Differential	Total $ Differential
Scotch, straight	2.00	84	$1.25	$3.00	+ $0.50	$ 42.00
Bourbon, straight	2.00	6	1.00	2.50	+ 0.50	3.00
Manhattan	2.00	18	1.00	2.75	+ 0.75	13.50
Old-fashioned	1.75	12	1.00	2.60	+ 1.49	17.88
Whiskey Sour	1.50	4	1.00	2.50	+ 1.50	6.00
Gin, straight	2.00	4	1.00	2.50	+ 0.50	2.00
Martini	2.00	26	1.00	2.75	+ 0.25	18.20
Tom Collins	1.50	8	1.00	2.60	+ 1.10	8.80
Gin and Tonic	1.50	12	1.00	2.50	+ 1.00	12.00
Total						$123.38

Exhibit 9.21 Adjusted Value per Bottle

Liquor	Ounces Sold	Expected Value
Scotch	168	$168.00
Bourbon	75	60.00
Gin	90	67.50
Total expected value drink differential		$295.50
		14.20
Adjusted expected value		$309.70

method is one in which a readout is obtained that will give the different kinds of drinks sold, the total income derived from each, the amount used, and a comparison with the expected sales income. The totals of actual sales and expected sales should be very close. Any system used should not cost more than the information it supplies is worth.

SUMMARY

Liquor menus differ in merchandising, pricing, and in other ways from menus offering only food, and they require special planning. Liquor menus can be separate from food menus or combined with them. Sometimes a few alcoholic beverages are offered with the food menu, and a much more extensive liquor menu is available as well. Sometimes a separate menu is provided for spirits and another for wines. Beer and ale menus may also be needed. It is sometimes desirable in fine-dining operations to have a separate liqueur and cordial menu to offer guests at the conclusion of a meal. Liquor menus should be simple and direct. Most patrons know what they want and just want to check prices.

It is not enough just to write a good beverage menu. Follow-through is important if the liquor menu is to be profitable. This involves seeing that the right service is given, the quantity and quality of each drink is controlled, and costs are controlled so the menu benefits the operation.

Liquor service should be fast, and proper for the beverage. Some drinks require special service. Servers should be salespeople, especially when it comes to liquor. The procedures used in serving should be those that will help develop sales.

Management should see that wine is served at the proper temperature in the right glass and in the proper manner. All of these require skill on the part of servers.

The pricing of liquors is often on the basis of material costs, being about 20 to 25 percent of the price. Spirit pricing is based more on competition and what the market will bear than food pricing is. There is also a tendency to group liquor prices within categories with a single price for all drinks in the same category.

Wine pricing is different from spirit pricing. Often the cost of the wine is doubled to arrive at a selling price. Many patrons like to see a bottle of wine priced at around the price of entrees.

Control of liquor costs and the control of liquor itself starts with purchasing and follows through receiving, storing, issue, preparation, and service. Purchasing is simplified because buys can be made on the basis of brands both for *call* liquors and for *house* or *well* liquors. The volume of alcohol obtained and the *proof* are other factors to weigh in purchasing. The quantity purchased should be based on usage during a certain time period between orders. The amount on hand should not only provide for the usage during the period but also allow for unexpected use.

Receiving is a critical step in liquor control, because it is here that a check is made to see that the right item is received in good condition. Immediately after receiving, deliveries should be sent to storerooms. As goods come into the storeroom they should be unpacked, marked with an operation code, and stacked properly on shelves or bins. Good security is needed in the storeroom, and only authorized employees should be allowed on the premises. Issuing only on the basis of properly signed requisitions, exchanging new bottles for empty ones, smashing or promptly removing the empty ones after verification of codes, and having all requisitions signed by the receiver and storeroom clerk are all procedures that help ensure beverage control.

All drinks should be made according to established, standardized recipes. Recipes and bar manuals may be used to standardize quantities and glassware and assure that proper garnishes are served. Recipes should be costed out, and pricing should be based on these recipes. Whether preparation personnel are allowed to free-pour or required to use jiggers, shot glasses, caps, or automatic pushbutton devices will depend on the operation.

Bar checks should be carefully controlled, and servers should sign for the ones they are given and account for each check received. Service personnel are usually held responsible for walkouts and lost checks.

Sales reconciliation methods are used to check expected income against actual income to see whether the bar is being operated and controlled correctly. These methods can include counting the drinks that can be sold per bottle, pouring drinks in different amounts at different selling prices, taking a sales tally of the drinks sold, averaging out expected bottle income by the number of drinks sold or percentages of drinks in a bottle, and the standard deviation method. The best record-keeping method is to use an electronic cash register or computer that can quickly give a full printout of sales, costs, and number of drinks sold.

QUESTIONS

1. The cost of gin is $0.30 an ounce, the cost of dry vermouth is $0.12 an ounce, and the cost of olives and ice is calculated as being 20 percent of the gin and vermouth costs. Calculate the cost of a martini made by the following recipe.

Gin	2 oz
Dry vermouth	$1/2$ oz

   Measure gin and vermouth into a shaker, add some small ice cubes, and stir gently. Strain into a 7-ounce cold barrel glass for on the rocks or into a $4^1/2$-ounce cold stem cocktail glass for regular. Add a green olive on a bar pick. If a lemon twist is ordered, twist the lemon over the completed drink and drop in the twist.

2. What are the selling prices of the martini in question 1 when the price is set at a 20 percent cost ratio? A 25 percent cost ratio? A 30 percent cost ratio?

3. A 2-ounce shot is given in a straight drink. What is the cost of the drink if a 1-liter bottle costs $9.46?

4. A 1½-ounce shot glass is used for a straight drink. The price is $12.00 for a 750-ml bottle. What is the cost of the straight drink? If the selling price is to be based on a 20 percent cost, what is the selling price?

5. The following information is obtained on bourbon sales during one shift. What is the potential or expected income per liter?

Drink	Number Sold	Ounces Served	Selling Price
Straight	27	1½	$2.00
Manhattan	32	2	2.50
Old-fashioned	40	1¾	2.00
Whiskey Sour	12	1⅕	2.00

🌿 10 🌿

Menu Planning and Health

Objectives

After reading this chapter, you should be able to:

1. Discuss why menu planners must be concerned with nutrition.

2. Describe the various nutrients and what each contributes to health.

3. Describe various special diets and ways that both institutional and commercial menu planners can provide such diets.

4. Indicate what can happen to foods' nutrients in storage, preparation, and production, and how to achieve maximum nutrient retention during these steps.

INTRODUCTION

Today, more than ever, we know that to live a long, healthy life, one must eat healthful foods. In the last several decades, Americans have become more and more concerned with the healthful qualities of foods served in the food-service industry. The result has been a change in eating patterns that has forced menu planners not only to change the types of items offered but the manners in which they are prepared and served. Fresh vegetables have become more and more popular. We often demand foods with less fat, cholesterol, sugar, and salt. One Gallup poll found that 70 percent of those interviewed said they were concerned about what they ate and how it affected their health; 40 percent said they had definitely changed their eating patterns to include more healthful foods. A wider variety of soups, salads and salad bars, and foods prepared in special ways now appear prominently on menus.

There is also a trend toward menus offering more raw fruits and vegetables, fewer red meats, and more poultry and lean meats. Many menus now have an area in which they feature healthful foods. The Hilton offers "Fitness First" items, which emphasize low-calorie, low-salt (sodium), low-fat, and low cholesterol items. Stouffer's "Light 'n' Lean" menu and Marriott's "Good for You" menu items have had similar success. Some operations, like the famous Four Seasons in New York, have found it profitable to have a complete healthful foods menu.

Quick-service operations have also responded to the desire of patrons for healthier foods. Almost all of them offer patrons who ask a small booklet indicating the nutritional value of the food they serve, and many offer salad bars, prepared salads, soups, and a variety of baked potato entrees.

NEW LABELING LAWS

New labeling requirements for packaged foods are designed to give more complete information about the ingredients and healthful qualities of foods. While these requirements do not apply to foodservice operations and their menus, foodservice operators, as consumers, have access to much more information on the foods purchased in packages than ever before.

While foodservice operators are not required to list ingredients on their menus, any nutritional or health claims made by the operation must meet labeling criteria established by the FDA. This includes using terms such as "low-fat" and "heart-healthy" on menus as well as on merchandising materials such as posters.

OVERVIEW OF FOODSERVICE INDUSTRY HEALTH ISSUES

While the trend toward emphasizing healthful foods on menus did not develop suddenly—it has been popular in health clubs, health spas, and specialty food services for a long time—it became popular in the early 1970s and then increased until it has become a significant factor in the entire industry.

One of the most successful early operations to offer health foods on menus was Chez Panisse in Berkeley, California, started by Chef Alice Waters. The restaurant emphasized natural, fresh foods, simply prepared and low in salt, fat, cholesterol, and calories. It was here that Chef Jeremiah Towers began his career. The operation soon had many imitators, and Chef Tower himself acted as a consultant in establishing many operations. Soon we had what some call the "American Nouvelle Cuisine" or just the "New Food Movement."

The movement has had several areas of emphasis. First, some menus have combined healthful foods with ethnic ones on the assumption that the traditional American diet too heavily emphasizes meat, fat, and sugar. Second, other menus have not especially emphasized health but, rather, natural foods or the organic type produced without pesticides or herbicides, or from animals fed only natural foods without any chemicals or growth stimulants. Another menu variation has been to obtain some legitimizer to approve foods on the menu, such as the American Heart Association, the American Dietetic Association, or the American Diabetes Association, which approves the menu and the preparation of some foods on the menu. The operator then indicates this on the menu. Finally, some operations make little or no change in menu offerings but offer patrons information aimed at helping them make informed dining choices.

Ethnic Foods

Ethnic foods have increased in popularity, partly because they often contain a greater proportion of vegetables and carbohydrates to meat than traditional American items do, something recommended today in healthful eating. The rapid growth of Chinese, Japanese, and other Asian cuisines and the enduring popularity of Italian cuisine prove this trend. Traditional Chinese food especially illustrates the way some ethnic foods meet healthful food standards. Only fresh foods, little meat—meat, fish, and poultry are used more as flavoring items—and the method of stir-frying with little fat contributes to its healthfulness. Madame Wu's restaurant in Santa Monica, featuring a "Long Life" menu, and the Hu Nan restaurants in Philadelphia have a healthful foods menu which the owners claim meets rigorous dietetic standards. However, it should be noted that a recent study of Chinese-food eating patterns in the United States indicates that the foods most commonly ordered by Americans are those highest in fat. It can be assumed that a perception of healthful eating is more important to many foodservice patrons than actual benefits of eating healthful foods.

Mexican restaurants may offer low-fat enchiladas, tacos with vegetable fillings, and Mexican salads. Japanese units serve many low-calorie broths, noodle dishes, and tofu dishes. Even Italian restaurants with their emphasis on pastas and cheese are offering lighter dishes. Since these dishes are often lower in cost than their heavier counterparts, the change can be a profitable one for food services.

Natural Foods

A second movement in the trend toward healthier foods has been to put more emphasis on serving menu items that are made from natural, fresh foods that are free of chemicals and naturally grown.

The USDA has set the criteria for advertising foods as "natural" or "organic." Animals must come from farms where no drugs, chemicals, hormones, or other compounds are used; they must be raised "without stress" and be "butchered at the peak of virility to ensure highest nutritive value." Eggs have to come from hens that eat a diet free of antibiotics and other drugs and that are allowed to run free. No chemicals, additives, or preservatives, such as stabilizers or emulsifiers, should be in such foods. Refined foods, such as white sugar, white flour, or white rice, are not approved. Vegetables must not be grown in soil fertilized with artificial fertilizers, nor treated with pesticides or herbicides.

Foodservice operators have learned, however, that many of these foods tend to be more perishable than their counterparts and must be used quickly. Menu planners must be cautious in their eagerness to jump on the natural foods bandwagon and recognize that foods must still be safe and sanitary when served. For example, raw, unpasteurized, certified milk is considered "healthy" by some people, but its sale to the public is banned in many states for sanitary reasons. Foodservice operators have also found that many of these foods often cost more and, therefore, the menu items must often command a higher price.

Vegetarian Foods

Along with the trend toward natural and ethnic foods has come a rise in vegetarianism. A number of foodservice operations offer vegetarian foods, which may include soy products or tofu (bean curd) as a meat substitute. Some vegetarian diets allow eggs (ovo-diet) or milk and dairy products (lacto-diet). Having one or two such menu offerings may serve this need and offer other patrons more menu variety. College and university operations, in particular, have had to change cafeteria offerings to enable students to "build" their own vegetarian meals.

Menu Approval

Some operations heavily emphasize healthy foods and have sought legitimization by such organizations as the American Heart Association, the American Diabetes Association, the American Dietetic Association, or even sponsors of popular programs, such as Weight Watchers. Their menu offerings may come from recipes and methods approved by the legitimizer. A very successful program like this started in Los Angeles. The Los Angeles Heart Association approved recipes, preparation procedures, and menu offerings of certain food services. The programs were called "Creative Cuisine," "Hearty Heart," or "Prudent Diet." Menus were augmented by dietary information in leaflets, posters, table tents, and pamphlets, along with advertising. In two years, 165 Los Angeles restaurants had joined the program along with 400 out-of-state units.

In any operation, menu items approved under the different food categories and cooked without adding much fat or salt may be depicted on a menu with a small heart in front of the menu item. General guidelines for making healthy menu choices when eating out are listed in **Exhibit 10.1**. A similar program has been started in Chicago, where it is also successful.

Exhibit 10.1   Guidelines for Healthier Dining

Dining Out Strategies
- Choose a restaurant that you know offers low-fat foods.
- Take time to survey the menu. Try ordering a few appetizers for your meal instead of a whole dinner.
- Don't be talked into selecting something you really don't want. If you do want something high in fat, share that food.
- Beware of buffets, salad bars or "all you can eat" situations. This is not an invitation to stuff yourself in order to get your money's worth. When satisfied, stop.

Ordering Basics
- Get your server involved in the ordering process. Ask questions about how a dish is prepared or for a low-fat recommendation.
- Request salad dressings, gravies, and sauces on the side. Remember to go easy on the salad dressing.
- Check if fresh, steamed vegetables or fresh fruit are available.
- Ask for unbuttered toast or vegetables.
- Praise a restaurant's low-fat option or willingness to accommodate your requests.

Menu Basics
- Request that margarine instead of butter be served with the meal.
- Ask for skim instead of whole milk.
- Order broiled, baked, steamed, grilled or stir-fried dishes instead of pan-fried or deep-fat fried items. Watch for words like buttery, crispy and cheesy.
- Limit foods with breading or stuffing. They usually are fatty and salty.
- Choose lean meats and trim the excess fat. Remove the skin from poultry before eating.
- Limit portion sizes of cooked meat to no more than 4 to 6 oz., or the size of a deck of cards.
- Pass on mayonnaise-based salads like tuna, egg, chicken, shrimp, potato, macaroni or coleslaw. Have salads made of fresh fruits or vegetables instead.
- Order a baked potato and top it with salsa. Order a green salad instead of coleslaw, french fries or fried vegetables because they have more fat.
- Skip the extra cheese on sandwiches.
- To flavor foods use sodium-free herbs and spices or lemon juice.
- For dessert, choose fresh fruit, fruit in a light syrup, fruit ice, sherbet, gelatin, or angel food cake.

Remember:
It is your right to request that foods be prepared the way you want.

Adapted by permission of the American Heart Association of Metropolitan Chicago.

Offering Nutritional Information

The fourth offshoot of the nutritional, healthy trend has been one in which the menu offerings are not really changed but nutritional information is offered, often to support the fact that what is on the regular menu is of good nutritional value. This information should follow the guidelines set for nutritional labeling on packaged foods. At most quick-service chains, information is dispensed through menus, table tents, posters, packaging materials, pamphlets, and leaflets. Burger King not only advertises that it broils instead of fries its hamburgers and offers low-salt fries—it is searching for a good salt alternative—but it also publishes a nutrition guide for patrons. Arby's went further and indicated what the nutritional values are for the foods it serves and how well they meet the needs for a balanced diet. McDonald's compares the nutritional value of its foods with the U.S. Required Daily Allowances. This information has been put on tray liners, bag-stuffer materials, and posters. McDonald's also publishes a pamphlet containing nutritional information titled "Good Food, Good Nutrition and McDonald's." A calorie counter and a diet and exercise card are given to patrons. Denny's indicates on its menu where to find the most healthful offerings.

These various areas of emphasis in the foodservice industry have resulted in a still-growing trend toward better nutrition and lighter, healthier foods by planning menus according to one, or all of the following criteria.

1. Stress fresh, natural foods. Avoid foods thought to contain chemical additives, and try to feature locally grown natural or organic foods.

2. Use methods of cooking that avoid greasy, overcooked foods in favor of preserving nutrients.

3. Stress foods low in fat, cholesterol, salt, and sugar while emphasizing foods higher in nutrients and fiber. Avoid refined and processed foods.

4. Present foods in innovative ways and use unusual foods or preparation methods, such as making French dressing from hazelnut oil, using goat's milk instead of cow's, or broiling foods over mesquite wood or charcoal.

5. Couple the healthy menu program with a thorough training program for cooks, chefs, servers, and others so the principles of the program can be implemented and the message can be well communicated to patrons.

The movement has probably had such a significant impact on the foodservice industry not only because it attracts patrons, but because it can be a very profitable venture for some operators with the right combination of proper purchasing, merchandising, and service. Lower-cost foods, such as fruits and vegetables, cheese, dairy products, fish, and poultry can be used. The production methods are often simpler, and the recipes call for less expensive ingredients. Healthful menus have helped increase patronage for many operations. The fact that dining operations such as Chez Panisse and Marriott's are happy with resulting profits also attests to the desirability of merchandising healthy foods.

Criticism of the Foodservice Industry

Some of the concern for better nutrition has found expression in criticism of what foodservice menus offer and how foods are prepared. Some nutritionists have claimed foodservice menus offer foods that are too high in calories, fat, cholesterol, and sugar. They say that many of the preparation procedures are also faulty, and many of the foods served have lost too much of their nutritive value, flavor, and texture. Tired salads that float in a sea of oily dressing are far too common, and too many snack and fast-food items are served which lack nutritive values. Some have gone so far as to say the foodservice industry is contributing to a nutritional breakdown in our eating patterns.

In the 1970s, the criticism focused in a movement in the U.S. Senate to push for passage of a law that would require menus to carry the nutritional values of all items. This move was strongly backed by consumers and consumer groups but was eventually defeated.

The criticism may have had some foundation, but it may have been extreme in some cases. Studies have shown that fast foods are nutritious—to a point. Often, they do not give nutritional balance, but if one watches the foods eaten during other meals of the day, nutritional needs can be met.

The problem is that while most Americans think they know what nutrition is, they are often lacking in actual knowledge of what a balanced diet is. There is a tremendous amount of erroneous general information which many people believe. Fad diets come and go. The grapefruit, macrobiotic, and all-rice diets are examples of diets that are considered not only fallacious but possibly harmful. The all-rice diet is said to have been responsible for deaths caused by malnutrition.[1]

The foodservice industry has sought to meet criticism in the area of nutrition and health, and to alert food services to the need to give attention to growing consumer interest in food and health. This reflects an industry awareness that about 25 percent of all meals Americans eat are consumed away from home, and this figure is expected to increase. This is significant and will affect menu planning in many foodservice segments. A great amount of publicity has been given to the need to provide healthful foods to patrons.

Although Americans on the whole are well fed, there are still many people who are hungry and undernourished. Also, many other people in other countries eat more nutriously, not because they can afford to, but because their diets, while basic, are naturally more nutritious. While repeated surveys show that many low-income Americans eat poorly, a nearly equal percentage of moderate- and high-income people also do. Twenty to thirty percent of Americans are either overweight or obese. (Persons are considered *overweight* if their weight is up to 10 percent above their normal weight; they are considered *obese* when they exceed 10 percent over normal weight.) Some health organizations have called our primary dietary problem *over-nutrition* rather than malnutrition.

Exhibit 10.2 USDA Food Guide Pyramid

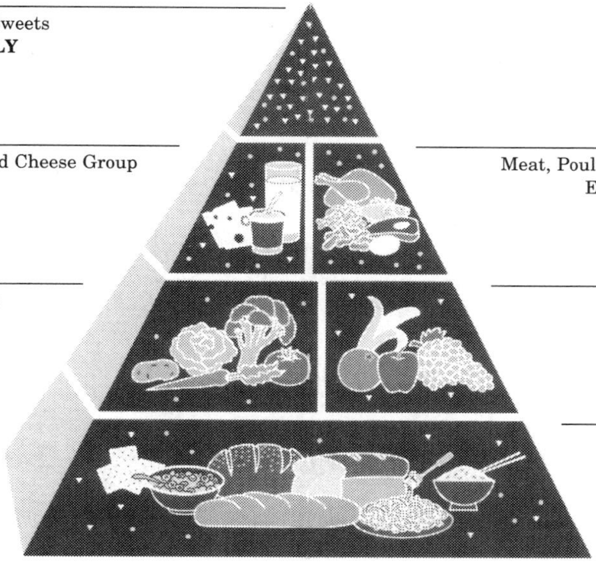

Fats, Oils, and Sweets
USE SPARINGLY

Milk, Yogurt, and Cheese Group
2–3 SERVINGS

Meat, Poultry, Fish, Dry Beans,
Eggs, and Nuts Group
2–3 SERVINGS

Vegetable Group
3–5 SERVINGS

Fruit Group
2–4 SERVINGS

Bread, Cereal, Rice,
and Pasta Group
6–11 SERVINGS

Overweight and obese people generally have more health problems and lower life expectancies than people with normal or near-normal weight. Recognizing this, the U.S. Department of Agriculture (USDA) in conjunction with the U.S. Department of Health and Human Services (HHS) has developed a brochure entitled "Dietary Guidelines for Americans," which basically urges Americans to eat less fat and less sugar and to increase their fiber intake. In addition, the USDA's new Food Guide Pyramid serves as a basis for healthy eating. (See **Exhibit 10.2**.)

The foodservice industry is at fault to some extent. Many who operate food services or write menus lack adequate knowledge of nutrition to do the job required. There is a need for further knowledge by these individuals in the area of nutrition or they should seek the help of others. However, foodservice operators often have to discuss nutritional problems with patrons or have to face patrons' criticism and then outside help is of no good. The operator must then be competent to discuss the problems or defend himself or herself against the criticism.

WHOSE RESPONSIBILITY?

It is estimated that the people in this country eat about 25 percent of their total food consumed away from home. This is largely served by the foodservice industry and, therefore, it can be said that the foodservice industry shares a 25 percent responsibility for meeting people's nutritional needs. But what exactly is that responsibility?

One of the problems with foodservice operations is that the responsibility to provide healthful foods has not been defined. Many believe there is little or no responsibility, while others feel there is a very strong one. Just what is the responsibility of foodservice operations? Undoubtedly there are degrees of responsibility among different operations—restaurants, schools, hospitals, nursing homes, etc.

When an operation, such as a restaurant or hotel draws patrons off the street, and when these patrons have free choice of what they select from the menu, the operator's responsibility for serving healthful food is probably not great. Commercial operations can really only offer patrons a chance to make a proper selection. They cannot force foods on patrons. The adult patron is responsible for knowing what his or her needs for healthful foods are and should select foods from the menu to meet them. If a patron orders a special meal for health reasons and then orders cream for coffee or tea, butter for bread, a scoop of ice cream, or other items that break this person's rules for diet, then this is the responsibility of the patron and not the food service. The food service can only have foods of various nutritional content available on the menu.

In this light, it seems that commercial operations' responsibility is to see that: 1) the nutrients that should be normally in a food item are there; and 2) foods that meet good health standards should be on the menu for selection by those who want them. If only partial meals are served, then what is served should be healthful but does not have to make a completely nutritious meal.

It should be noted that menu items in fine-dining operations can be made more nutritionally balanced while maintaining high profits. Drawing from Exhibit 10.2, one might develop a menu on which breads, vegetables, and fruits are emphasized and served generously throughout the meal, while the entree might consist of relatively small portions of meat served with a touch of a highly flavored sauce.

Noncommercial food services serving most or all the food patrons eat, such as prisons, universities, or in-plant operations, have a different responsibility. These operations must see that the menu is nutritionally balanced and healthful. If there is no freedom of choice, then the patron should be served a meal that is adequately balanced. The selection of a healthful diet can be promoted, but where patrons have free choice, they must be allowed to make the final decision. The institution might even have a dietitian on staff.

The greatest responsibility for providing nutrition belongs to those operations that fall in the category of health facilities, such as rest homes, mental health institutions, convalescent centers, retirement homes with limited nursing care, and hospitals. In most of these operations, the foodservice department is responsible not only for providing an adequate diet, but also for meeting all special dietary needs. It is also assumed that patrons will be urged to eat an adequate diet and that foods that should not be consumed will not be served. Even so, the difficulty in getting people to eat what is served may be a problem. They can hardly be forced to eat, and often, patrons have had poor dietary patterns for so long that they cannot give them up.

THE ABCs OF NUTRITION

Nutrition is a complex biological process, but to write menus containing healthful foods and to prepare these foods for service does not take extensive scientific knowledge. By following the USDA's Food Pyramid and other sources, one can plan an adequate diet. However, it is helpful to know what each nutrient does and how much of each is required.

Our bodies need calorie foods to produce heat and power, and regulators to run smoothly and function properly. The primary nutrients we get from calorie foods are carbohydrates, proteins, and fats. Regulators are largely vitamins and minerals, while we use minerals and protein to build body tissue. Some nutrients do more than one thing. Thus, calcium and phosphorus are important in building bones and teeth, but they also have very important jobs as regulators. Vitamins and minerals often have more than one job.

In addition to these basic nutrients, the body also requires water and fiber.

While alcohol is an energy producer, it is not needed in the body for this. Carbohydrates can take over the main job for this, with proteins and fats helping out some.

Carbohydrates

About 55 to 65 percent of our calories should come from carbohydrates. These are found in plentiful supply in starchy or sweet foods such as potatoes, syrup, honey, bread, macaroni products, corn, rice, dried legumes, cakes, and sweet potatoes.

The body breaks down carbohydrates into a simple sugar called *glucose* or blood sugar. In turn, the body converts this glucose to carbon dioxide and water, which releases energy during the chemical change we use for heat or power. Our reserves of glucose are small. We can store glucose as a starch called *glycogen* for quick energy release. If we use up our glucose and glycogen, the body then must turn to fat and protein to supply its energy needs. Authorities recommend that people eat more starchy foods than sweet ones to get their energy, since the energy from starchy foods is released much more slowly and as a result we get a longer period of steady energy production.

The measure used to quantify the amount of energy produced is the *calorie*, which is the amount of heat needed to raise one gram of water one degree Celsius.

Protein

Meat, milk, cheese, eggs, fish, shellfish, and poultry are foods that yield high amounts of protein. Protein is needed to promote growth and to regulate the body. Adults still need protein to replace worn-out body tissues and help make essential body components, such as blood. Most foods that come from animal sources are good sources of protein. A good amount of protein can also be obtained from cereals, nuts, legumes (such as dried peas, dried beans, or chickpeas), seeds, and from combinations of these foods. Vegetables and fruits also contain some protein.

Proteins are composed of chemical substances called *amino acids*. There is a fairly large number of these, but there are only eight needed by adults and nine or ten needed by children. These *essential amino acids* are found in meat, poultry, milk, cheese, eggs, fish, and in a few nonaminal products. (Thus, a certain amount—about 25 percent—of the protein we eat should be animal protein, or come from those few nonanimal products, such as soy, cottonseed, and rape seed, that also provide essential amino acids.) Some amino acids can be made from protein by the body, but not the essential ones. A protein containing all the essential amino acids is called *complete*. One or two servings of high-quality protein a day, from milk, as well as additional protein obtained from cereals and other foods, provides adequate protein.

It is possible to combine legumes such as beans, peas, nuts, and seeds with cereals and get a complete protein mixture with all the essential amino acids in adequate supply. What the legumes or seeds do not have, cereals provide; what cereals lack, the legumes have. Thus, a meal of Boston brown bread and baked beans gives a complete supply of the essential amino acids. This ability to combine cereal and legumes to make complete proteins is the reason some civilizations, such as the ancient Egyptians, could do so well without meat; millions in India and Pakistan do well today on the legume, *dahl*, and the wheat bread called *chapati*; the Chinese live largely on rice and soybeans.

Today we are able to process soy and other proteins from plants and make them into *analog* products that are very similar to meat. These are used to make imitation bacon bits, hamburger, sausage, ham, chicken, turkey, and beef. Many of these are made from soy. Since analogs are considered complete proteins, the USDA now allows the National School Lunch Program to use a certain amount of analogs with meats. People who must carefully watch their intake of animal fats find that meat substitutes can be eaten in normal amounts, and will not contribute the undesirable fat that meats would.

The federal government says that if a menu item contains an analog, it cannot be called by the same name as if the analog were not present. Thus, if one takes ground beef and adds a soy analog to it to extend it, shapes it into patties, fries it, and puts it between buns, it cannot be called a hamburger, but must carry another name such as beef and soy patty on a bun.

Fats

Fats are used by the body to promote essential body functions, to provide heat and energy, and to put a protective padding around body organs and the body itself. Fats stay in the stomach longer than carbohydrates and proteins, and so some fat in the diet helps to put off hunger. Not more than 30 percent of our calories should come from fats. Americans generally average more than this.

We differentiate between the kinds of fats in the diet. *Saturated* fats consist of carbon bonds filled with all the hydrogen they are capable of holding. Because the carbon bonds are all filled, they are called saturated; they cannot hold more. An *unsaturated* fat or oil is capable of picking up one other substance, such as an atom of carbon, nitrogen, hydrogen, or sulfur. If a fat or oil has two or more unsaturated double bonds, it is *polyunsaturated*. Some animal fats, such as beef suet, mutton tallow, and venison fat, as well as some vegetable fats, such as coconut oil and chocolate, are highly saturated. Pork lard and poultry fat are less saturated, and a number of vegetable oils are even less saturated. Fish oils and oil from corn, soybeans, and sunflower and safflower seeds are polyunsaturated.

Oils can undergo a process called *hydrogenation*, which changes them to a solid form by adding hydrogen, making an unsaturated fat saturated.

Cholesterol is a substance related to the fat family. When high amounts of calories or fats are consumed, many people tend to raise the level of cholesterol in their blood. Following a low-calorie or low-fat diet often helps lower the amount of blood cholesterol. A large percentage of individuals have cholesterol blood levels over what is considered desirable and, because of this, are at higher risk of developing high blood pressure, heart disease, strokes, and other health problems.

Cholesterol helps form a waxy, solid substance called *plaque* that deposits in the lining of the arterial system, sometimes to the point of stopping the flow of blood and causing either a stroke or heart attack. The large number of men and women that undergo heart bypass surgery each year indicates how common—and dangerous—high cholesterol levels are.

To try to reduce the amount of cholesterol in the blood, we eat fewer calories, fats, and foods that contain large amounts of cholesterol, such as liver and eggs. Those planning menus should know that any plant food is cholesterol-free, unless it is added in the preparation. Cholesterol is naturally found only in animal foods.

Some individuals may follow a very strict diet in cholesterol limitation and still run high blood cholesterol levels. Such individuals are born with cholesterol-making systems in their bodies. On the average, reducing cholesterol in the diet will reduce cholesterol in the blood about 5 to 10 percent.

While studies on cholesterol are still being conducted, most health authorities are certain that restricting butter and other dairy products, eggs, and fatty meats can lower cholesterol levels.

Vitamins

The word "vita" means life and the word "amine" means protein; the term *vitamin* originally meant "a life-giving protein." Now we know that not all vitamins are proteins, so the word is used to indicate a substance that is needed to control certain vital body functions.

The body uses most vitamins in extremely small amounts, but they have a great effect on essential body processes. For instance, the vitamin, *thiamin* must be present if the body is to use glucose. For this reason, an individual's carbohydrate and thiamin intakes should be somewhat correlated.

Vitamins usually do not work alone but together. Thus, even though the body may be plentifully supplied with some, if one or more are lacking, some vital body functions may not be able to take place.

When vitamins were first discovered, they were named after letters of the alphabet. Thus we have vitamins A, B, C, and D. About the time D was discovered, it was also discovered that what had been thought to be one vitamin, B, was actually a group of vitamins, now known as B_1 (thiamin), B_2 (riboflavin), up to B_{12}. Today the new vitamins are called by their chemical names, such as choline, folic acid, and pantothenic acid. It is becoming common to call the B vitamins by their chemical names, and to refer to vitamin C as ascorbic acid.

Vitamins are measured in very small quantities because that is the way they are found in foods and used by the body. Thus we may say that an individual needs only 60 milligrams of ascorbic acid a day. This is a very small quantity since a milligram is only one one-thousandth of a gram. Some vitamins are measured in *micrograms*, or one-millionth of a gram. Other vitamins are measured in International Units (IUs). The word *international* was used because investigators wanted to indicate that this was the international standard that had been established.

Vitamin A

A lack of vitamin A may cause night blindness, faulty vision, or even total blindness. It also helps to use proteins, build tissues and maintain other functions and growth. Vitamin A also helps keep the skin and alimentary and other tissue linings healthy. It is found in leafy green vegetables, yellow or orange fruits and vegetables, seafood and fish oils, cream, butter, cheese and organ meats.

One should have a substantial serving of a vitamin A-rich fruit or vegetable at least once a day. It can be stored in the body, so too much can be harmful. It is fat-, but not water-soluble, so it is fairly stable (it does not break down easily). Some foods have vitamin A added to them.

Vitamin D

Vitamin D is fat-soluble but not water-soluble so it is also fairly stable. The sun can change some fatty substances under our skin into vitamin D. Light-skinned people develop more of it this way than dark-skinned ones. We also can get it from fish liver oils, cream, butter, and eggs. Some food products, such as whole milk, have vitamin D added to them. It is required for growth. It works in the body to make teeth and bones. Children lacking it get *rickets*, a bone malformation.

Vitamin E

Our need for vitamin E is limited. It helps the muscles function, acts as an antioxidant in the body and may help in circulatory problems and in the body's use of proteins. It is fat-soluble and fairly stable. We usually get adquate amounts of vitamin E from whole-grain cereals, vegetable oils, and other foods in which it is fairly widely distributed.

Vitamin K

Another fat-soluble and fairly stable vitamin is vitamin K, found usually in good supply in fresh fruits and vegetables, especially green, leafy vegetables. We probably also produce enough to meet our needs in our intestines. Vitamin K helps the blood coagulate and may have other functions. Sulfa drugs and aspirin destroy it.

Vitamin B Complex

All the B vitamins are water-soluble and most are not very stable. Thiamin and some others are destroyed by too much heat and by alkaline substances. Because of the latter reason, putting soda into cooking water to keep vegetables green or to soften legumes in cooking is not recommended. The loss of many of the B vitamins can be high in some food preparation procedures, especially if the item is soaked in water.

Thiamin (B_1) is needed to promote the appetite, burn carbohydrates, and develop a stable nervous system. A lack of it can cause a disease called *beriberi*, evidenced by severe constipation and a soreness of the leg muscles, causing lameness or even inability to walk. It is plentiful in whole-grain cereals, fortified flours, yeast, meats (especially pork and liver), legumes, and milk. Menu planners should see that whole-grain products are offered on the menu.

Riboflavin (B_2) is important in developing body energy. A lack of it may show up as tiny sores on the skin, especially at the corner of the mouth. The eyelids also can become inflamed and sore. Riboflavin is plentiful in milk, cheese, eggs, meats, and whole-grain or enriched cereals. It is easily destroyed by sunlight; which is why milk used to be delivered in colored glass bottles.

Niacin (B_3) is rather stable in heat, but is very soluble in water. It works with thiamin and riboflavin to develop energy in the body. Niacin is plentiful in nuts (especially peanuts), seeds, brewer's yeast, meats, and enriched or whole-grain cereals. A lack of niacin can cause *pellagra*, a disease causing skin sores in the same place on both the left and right sides of the body. Pellagra is often called the "four Ds disease" because it causes dermatitis, diarrhea, dementia, and, eventually, death.

Pyridoxine (B_6) is important in metabolizing protein and fat and in changing the amino acid tryptophane into niacin.

Vitamin B_{12} is found in many foods but is most plentiful in fish, poultry, meat, cereals, dairy products, soy beans, yeast, nuts, and organ meats. It is important in preventing anemia and in generating a good supply of blood in the body.

Folic acid (folacin) is found in liberal supply in leafy vegetables as well as in liver, legumes, yeast, asparagus, and broccoli. It is important for the proper functioning of the body cells and in forming blood. A lack of it affects the oxygen-carrying power of the blood. It fights some forms of anemia.

Pantothenic acid is found in plentiful supply in foods high in pyrodoxine. It is important in promoting metabolic processes. It also supports the nervous system and is involved in the function of the adrenal glands and body oxidations.

The vitamins *choline* and *biotin* are involved in promoting growth and in regulating and promoting body functions. They are usually found in good supply in foods supplying adequate quantities of other B vitamins.

Vitamin C

Vitamin C (ascorbic acid) is important for the formation and maintenance of body tissue, bones, blood, and teeth. Individuals lacking vitamin C heal slowly. Vitamins A and C work closely together, and a lack of one may cause the other not to function well.

Scurvy is caused by a lack of vitamin C. It may first be evidenced by bleeding gums, lesions on the skin, and, later, by severe bruising. This disease was common among sailors who lacked fresh fruits and vegetables for long periods of time. (The explorer Magellan died of scurvy, and his men, many ill of the same disease, finally brought his ship back home after circling the globe.) Thus, British sailors were often called "limeys" because of the large stores of limes they learned to carry on board.

We should have at least one good source of vitamin C every day. It is plentiful in citrus fruits, tomatoes, cabbage, many fresh berries, bean sprouts, broccoli, cauliflower, rutabagas, kohlrabi, okra, onions, parsnips, fresh peas, peppers, persimmons, pimientos, fresh pineapple, potatoes, rhubarb, and spinach.

Vitamin C is easily oxidized and is quite perishable. Mincing vegetables and letting them stand will encourage oxidation loss. Cooking or soaking in water encourages a leaching loss. Heat destroys ascorbic acid, and when foods containing it are cooked in an alkaline medium, the loss is even more rapid. Acid protects it; thus, the ascorbic acid in tomatoes can withstand more heat than the ascorbic acid in blueberries in a muffin leavened by soda, an alkali.

Minerals

Minerals help to regulate our bodies and are important substances in body tissues, body fluids, and other body components. They also regulate the acid-base balance of the body, regulate fluid pressure (*osmotic pressure*), help the blood to clot, and promote nerve impulse transfer. We know the body needs specific amounts of some minerals. There are trace showings of some minerals (called *trace minerals*) in the body, but we are not sure whether these are there by accident or because the body requires them.

Calcium and Phosphorus

Calcium and phosphorus frequently work together in the body. They are important in the formation of bones and teeth and also in many vital functions. Together they can help to maintain a good acid-base ratio.

Independently, calcium maintains good muscle tone and helps the blood to clot, the heart to beat rhythmically, and the nerves to function. Phosphorus independently maintains normal muscle functions, is vital to the metabolism of carbohydrates, fats, and proteins, and is a part of some important enzyme activity. It is also an important substance in some vitamins and the brain and nerve cells.

Most children should have a quart of milk, or its equivalent, every day to furnish them with the calcium and phosphorus they need. Adults need a pint (two glasses) a day. The milk fat in milk usually carries vitamins A and D but can be omitted from milk that is consumed largely for its phosphorus and calcium content. Calcium can also be obtained from cereals, leafy vegetables, and other foods, but usually not as well as from milk.

Phosphorus is found in good supply in meat and other protein-rich foods, and in cereals and legumes.

Iron and Copper

Iron and copper work together in generating blood. A lack of either can cause anemia. If there is a loss of blood, the demand for these minerals increases. Thus women who menstruate, or any individual who has lost considerable amounts of blood, should have an increased supply of iron and copper.

Green leafy vegetables, meat, egg yolks, molasses, prunes and other dark dried fruits, whole-grain or enriched cereals and flours, legumes, organ meats, plums, and grapes are good dietary sources of iron. An adult needs about 10 milligrams of iron per day, which could be obtained from an egg, four servings of whole grain or enriched cereal, a pint of milk, or a serving of meat. Other foods in the diet would make up the balance. Copper is seldom lacking in diets since it is contained in many foods in good supply.

Sodium

Table salt is one of our main sources of sodium. Table salt is more than 50 percent sodium. This mineral helps maintain a proper acid-alkaline base in the body, promotes good muscle tone and contraction, and is associated with important tissue and fluid functions. A sodium deficiency may cause severe fatigue and even illness. Where there is a heavy loss of moisture, such as occurs in sweating, a doctor might recommend taking salt tablets.

Individuals with edema (swelling), high blood pressure, or kidney diseases may have to restrict their sodium intake, and, therefore, their salt consumption. Many food services can provide a restricted-sodium diet by request.

Potassium

There is seldom a lack of potassium in most diets, but some individuals who take medications for high blood pressure that eliminate salts from the body might lose a considerable amount of potassium. This must be replaced by potassium-rich foods, such as dried apricots, orange juice, and bananas.

Other Minerals

Numerous other minerals are found in the body tissues, but we do not know their function completely or what quantity we might need. Some found in minute amounts are called *trace minerals*.

We know that *magnesium* is important in regulating some functions, in forming bone, and in the use of protein. *Sulfur* is a significant substance in many tissues, but whether or not it plays a part in regulating body functions is unknown. *Zinc* is important in maintaining metabolic functions and is found in substantial amounts in the pancreas, which might indicate a role in the formation of *insulin*, a hormone that helps the body process glucose. *Fluorine* is important for teeth formation and, perhaps, for their maintenance. If children have small amounts of fluoride in the drinking water—often added by the municipal agency supplying the drinking water—their teeth are stronger and more durable. Some other minerals are known to be important in the functioning of the enzyme structure of the body. Most of the minerals mentioned in this section can be considered to be liberally supplied by a good, balanced diet.

Water

We should consume six to eight glasses of fluid per day—$1\frac{1}{2}$ to 2 quarts. This comes ideally from drinking water, but can also come in the form of milk, soups, juices, and other semiliquid foods. Fluids are vital for numerous body functions and to flush out undesirable or toxic substances. These substances usually are passed by the body. We lose water when we sweat and must continually replace it.

Fiber

Fiber is a nonfood item needed by the body. It is found mainly in the *cellulose* of plants. The two types of fiber, *soluble* and *insoluble*, cannot be digested by humans. However, insoluble fiber helps to separate foods in the digestive system and move them along. If it is lacking, poor absorption of nutrients occurs. Soluble fiber may help lower blood cholesterol levels.

NUTRIENT RETENTION IN QUANTITY FOOD PREPARATION

The preparation of foods in quantity can take a heavy toll on nutrients. Some of this loss can be avoided or at least minimized in the foodservice operation. For instance, a long soaking period for cubed potatoes will leave very little ascorbic acid in them. Cooking vegetables in water with added baking soda destroys the thiamin and ascorbic acid.

Storage and preparation procedures also can contribute to nutrient loss. Frozen foods, especially vegetables, will often retain nutrients better than canned foods, if the items are frozen quickly after harvest. Peeling some fresh vegetables and fruits removes nutrients.

It is important to see that foods are stored under proper conditions. Refrigeration can dry out foods, and nutrients can be lost when this happens. Fresh vegetables and fruits "breathe," so there must be space around them so they do not lose vitamin values. Cool temperatures help to delay reactions, and so the coldest temperature consistent with holding quality is recommended for most foods. There can be some vitamin loss in refrigerated or frozen foods. Minerals are fairly stable under frozen storage.

It is not easy to preserve the nutrients in foods in quantity cooking as it is in home cooking. Often there are necessary procedures that will destroy nutrients. For example, in mass cooking operations there must be a longer time period between the preparation of some foods and their service. At home, potatoes can be pared, cooked, and mashed in close sequence. In an institution, these procedures might take several hours or more.

Purchasing high-quality fresh foods and using them as soon as possible help to preserve nutrients. A food service should try to reduce the holding time of foods. Steaming, broiling, baking, and poaching reduce some of the nutrient losses that occur when foods are cooked in water.

Vegetables should not be held for more than 20 or 30 minutes in a steam table. After that, they should be replaced with a new batch. For this reason, it is recommended that food services cook their vegetables by *batch cooking*. This means that they should be cooked in batches only large enough to last for about 20 minutes of service. Cooks should watch to see how fast a batch is eaten and have another ready when the first is gone. The use of a small high-pressure steamer—17 pounds per square inch of steam—will process most small batches of vegetables in seconds. Vegetables cooked in smaller batches and sent to the service area as needed are much better in quality and more nutritious.

Some foods do not lose many nutrients when they are cooked. Vitamin A is fairly stable. The protein in meat, the carbohydrates in cereals, and the fat in pie crust are harmed little by cooking. Cooking too far in advance increases many nutrient losses.

In many cases, the loss of nutrients in quantity cooking cannot be avoided. Most foods do retain most of their nutrients, even in quantity cooking. So if an individual watches to see that a balanced diet is consumed, plus a few foods that are high in nutrients that one might be missing, an adequate diet will usually result.

When foods are prepared, they should be moved from storage to service as fast as possible. Oxidations and other chemical reactions after cooking can destroy vitamins and minerals. Peeling and soaking are also enemies of many vitamins and minerals. To reduce the need for soaking, citric acid or ascorbic acid products can be used to retard oxidations that harm greens, vegetables, and fruits.

Carbohydrates, proteins, and fats are fairly stable. Fat can oxidize. Fat can also break down in cooking and might give off-flavors in foods.

Vitamins are quite perishable, except for vitamin A. The B complex vitamins are highly water-soluble and are easily leached in water. Meat that thaws can lose a lot of the B vitamins in the drippings, and also in the juices that come out of the meat during cooking. Heat can destroy such vitamins as thiamin and pyridoxine, especially if the foods are cooked in an alkaline medium. Vitamin C is very unstable, as it is easily oxidized, can be destroyed by heat, and is also water-soluble. Vitamin D is fairly stable, as is vitamin E. Vitamin K is generally stable, except it can be destroyed in the body by aspirin and antibiotics.

The loss of minerals occurs largely through solubility, but some can be lost due to chemical changes that occur during storage, preparation, and cooking. Sometimes anti-vitamin factors in a food inhibit the availability of a mineral. This can happen to the iron in spinach or in a cereal when bran is present. Spinach and bran both contain factors that interfere with the absorption of iron during digestion.

The rules for the best preparation of foods from the standpoint of nutrition (not to mention quality) are the following.

1. Prepare foods for cooking as close to serving time as possible.
2. Reduce chances for nutrient losses: keep foods in large pieces, avoid soaking, and keep cutting to a minimum.
3. Cook foods as quickly as possible by the cooking method least harmful to the nutrients.
4. Cook vegetables only in small batches.
5. Avoid using substances, such as baking soda and baking powder, that can destroy nutrients.

MAJOR HEALTH CONCERNS ABOUT FOOD

Many patrons who eat in commercial operations are concerned about avoiding health problems, so they tend to want to eat foods low in fat to avoid calories or to avoid heart problems or other arteriosclerosis problems, or foods low in salt to avoid high blood pressure; or low-calorie foods to avoid adding weight or to lose it. People today want to consume foods containing less cholesterol because this is a substance associated with clogged arteries which results in heart, stroke or other problems. They, therefore, avoid organ meats, butter, eggs, and saturated fats which contain or help build up cholesterol in the body. They also try to eat meat items lower in cholesterol.

Low-calorie Foods

Almost all food contains calories, but some foods contain more than others because they contain different food components. Those components containing calories are carbohydrates (mainly members of the starch and sugar families) which contain 4 calories per gram and about 100 calories per ounce; protein (largely from meats, cheese, eggs, fish, and poultry, which have 4 calories per gram and 100 calories per ounce; fats and oils, with 9 calories per gram and 250 calories per ounce; and alcohol, giving 7 calories per gram of *pure* alcohol or about 200 calories per ounce. (This is the equivalent of 2 ounces of a 100-proof spirit.) Thus, a food containing a lot of fat or oil is high in calories, such as chocolate, over 50 percent fat, while one of the same weight containing mostly starch or protein, such as a potato, will be lower. However, add butter or sour cream to a baked potato and the calories jump because of the fat in the butter or cream. An 80 proof spirit contains only 40 percent alcohol; (always divide proof in half to get actual alcoholic content) and this 40 percent is only about 80% of 1 gram per cubic centimeter. To arrive at a close approximation, one can take the proof in a dry spirit and use the proof as the number of calories per ounce. In this case it would be 2 oz × 80 proof = 160 calories.

There are some components in food which the body does not turn into calories. An example is the cellulose or fiber found in fruits and vegetables. These foods are, therefore, low in calories.

Some foods are also high in water and so are quite low in calories. Thus, a number of vegetables such as cucumbers or lettuce fill one up, but contribute few calories. Of course, a part of this low calorie content is also because these vegetables also contain very little of any kind of calorie-containing nutrients.

Some foods are called "empty-calorie" foods. This does not mean they are low in calories; on the contrary, these foods are usually high in calories and low in nutritive value. They are usually associated with snack or "junk" foods and alcohol. Ironically, eating too many empty-calorie foods can make one fat yet undernourished. **Exhibit 10.3** shows a menu for a low-calorie breakfast, lunch, and dinner. Most adults need at least 1,200 calories a day to remain nourished. However, such a low-calorie intake allows little energy (calories) for much activity. Normally, active adults need at least double this amount.

Low-fat and Low-cholesterol Foods

Eating fats and oils can contribute unwanted calories and other problems, such as high cholesterol, high blood pressure, heart disease, and stroke. Some people with gall bladder or digestive problems may have to restrict all types of fats in their foods. We can separate fat or oil restrictions in foods into three broad categories: 1) general restriction of all kinds of fats; 2) restriction of saturated fats; and 3) restriction of fats and foods that contribute cholesterol.

Most health authorities agree that the number of calories one gets from fats and oils should not exceed 30 percent of the total calorie intake. This means that someone eating using 3,000 calories a day can get 1,000 of these from fats or oils, which means 111 grams or about 4 ounces. However, while this may seem like a lot, it is not hard to consume. Most Americans get about 40 percent of their calories from fats. We also eat too many saturated fats. We should try to divide our fat calories into three equal parts, a third only saturated, another third monounsaturated (a good portion of olive oil and

Exhibit 10.3 Low-calorie Meal Plan

Breakfast	**Approximate Calories**
Orange juice	60
½ cup cornflakes or cooked oatmeal	70
½ cup low-fat milk	50
Poached egg on dry toast OR	120
Scrambled egg with a slice of dry toast	120
Coffee or tea	0
Total calories	300

Luncheon	**Approximate Calories**
1 cup chicken broth	30
2 Melba toasts	30
Poached sole (4 oz)	125
Sliced tomatoes	25
Toasted raisin bread	60
Sherbet	120
1 cup low-fat milk	70
Total calories	460

Dinner	**Approximate Calories**
Broiled grapefruit	35
5 oz broiled chicken leg OR	250
4 oz broiled lean ground round	250
½ cup mashed Hubbard squash	35
Hard or soft roll	50
Mixed green salad with low-fat French dressing	35
¹⁄₁₆ angel food cake	100
Tea or coffee	0
Total calories	505

Daily Total Calories: 1,265

For a low-cholesterol diet the egg should be prepared from the low-cholesterol type of egg substitute and the poached egg or scrambled egg omitted. The chicken leg should also be used on such a diet and not the ground round. No butter should be served unless the calories allowed are higher. Fat restriction is usual in a low-cholesterol diet.

some other vegetable oils), and a third polyunsaturated, such as safflower and fish oils. A simple low-fat and low-cholesterol menu is shown in **Exhibit 10.4**.

Low-sodium Foods

Table salt is our main source of sodium which, for about 20 percent of Americans, has raised blood pressure to a point that causes hypertension. Nutritionists say many Americans consume too much salt and they have developed a

Exhibit 10.4 Low-fat and Low-cholesterol Meal Plan

Breakfast
Any fruit or vegetable juice
Whole grain cereal
Low-fat milk
Low-cholesterol egg substitute
Graham toast
Coffee or tea

Lunch
Fat-free soup with crackers
Low-fat cottage cheese in
    tomato cup
Hard roll
Fresh fruit or sherbet
Milk, coffee, or tea

Dinner
Fruit cup with crackers
Broiled cod
Baked potato
Green beans
Lettuce with low-fat
    French dressing
Pumpernickel bread
Apple snow
Milk, coffee, or tea

desire for a high amount of salt in their foods. Some individuals, they say, are "saltoholics" who grab for the salt shaker automatically before tasting their food. There is not much a foodservice operator can do about these people—except possibly offering a no-salt alternative or other flavoring along with salt.

If foods are cooked without salt and foods high in salt, such as potato chips, catsup, pickles, and sauerkraut are eliminated, about 2,500 milligrams of sodium might still be consumed per day. Normally, we get about one-third of our sodium from that naturally present in foods, one-third we add to food, and one-third is added to foods in processing them. One must be aware of many prepared, canned, and processed foods for their salt content. A menu for people on a 1,500-milligram, low-sodium diet must avoid these foods, as well as root vegetables such as beets and carrots, which contain a fair amount of sodium. When sodium is further restricted, even a sodium-free milk might have to be in the diet. In some areas, the water might be so high in sodium that it cannot be used for drinking or cooking. Distilled water or water coming from a low-sodium source must be used instead.

There are salt substitutes. These may use potassium chloride as a base flavoring. Also herbs may be used in place of salt for flavoring foods.

Baking soda, baking powder, and carbonated beverages contain sodium. Reading the labels on foods is important, and some manufacturers now put sodium content of the food on the label. If MSG or monosodium glutamate appears on a label, it is safe to assume that the product is high in sodium.

SUMMARY

Within recent years there has been a definite trend toward providing menus that give healthful food selections. The foodservice industry has responded to this trend by focusing on one or more of the following: 1) shifting menu emphasis to new and ethnic foods; 2) offering natural or organic foods; 3) having menus or menu items approved as "healthy" by various groups; and 4) dispensing information to indicate how the foods offered meet nutritional needs.

The responsibility for providing healthful foods varies according to the type of operation. Restaurants in which patrons are free to select what will be eaten usually have less responsibility than a hospital or rest home which must provide adequate nutrition in everything served, although marketing and promoting healthful menus has become quite profitable for commercial operations.

The role that nutrients play in a healthy diet is discussed. The major nutrients are carbohydrates, protein, fats, vitamins, and minerals. Water and fiber must also be provided. Menus can be planned to provide foods that meet patrons' health needs. Nutrients can be lost during storage, prepreparation, cooking, and holding, so care must be taken to retain nutritive value as much as possible.

QUESTIONS

1. Describe some of the characteristics of a healthful menu.

2. What responsibility might a full-service commercial restaurant have for the nutritional needs of its patrons? What are the responsibilities of a hospital or nursing home?

3. What are some of the ways to preserve nutrients during storage, preparation, and holding?

4. Name the five major groups of nutrients. Which three groups contribute calories in the diet?

5. What are the considerations involved in planning a low-fat menu? A low-sodium menu? A low-cholesterol menu?

11

Purchasing, Production, and the Menu

Outline

Objectives

After reading this chapter, you should be able to:

1. Indicate how purchasing and production help complete the task of menu planning.

2. Identify purchasing and production procedures needed to produce a menu.

INTRODUCTION

The menu cannot stand alone. By itself, it is simply a document that has *potential* for management of a food service. To be effective, the menu must be integrated with thorough purchasing and production procedures. No matter how well a menu is planned, if these two major steps are not done properly, the menu will fail.

While the menu is the central document that dictates what is to be done in almost every operating department of a food service, it is completely dependent on these departments for its fulfillment. It controls and directs, but it cannot act. In this respect the menu is somewhat like the staff member in an organization who originates directives but has no authority to take action. Instead, the person must make recommendations to a line member who then translates these into action. Similarly, the menu depends upon the purchasing and production departments to implement its recommendations.

Purchasing must correctly interpret what the menu calls for and procure the necessary materials *in time* for the items to be produced. Production must prepare the food in a timely manner with due regard to food quality, safety, and quantity. Both departments are a vital part of a complete foodservice system that revolves around the menu.

OVERVIEW OF THE PURCHASING FUNCTION

Purchasing is a complex function. It comprises the following steps.

1. Determine the need for an item, along with the quality, quantity, and other factors required to satisfy that need.
2. Search for the item on the market.
3. Negotiate between the buyer and the seller, ending in a transfer of ownership.
4. Receive and inspect, ending with acceptance or rejection of the item.
5. Storage and issuing items.
6. Evaluate the purchasing tasks, as judged by the performance of the product, and the economy and efficiency with which results were achieved.

In almost every purchasing task, these six steps must occur; only in rare instances can any be circumvented or omitted. The sixth step is extremely important, yet is often overlooked. Unless it takes place, the purchasing task may never be improved.

The Role of the Purchaser

The job of the purchaser is to interpret properly what is needed to produce the items listed on the menu, and to procure them at prices within constraints established by the operation. This is not easy, and some buyers fail because they do not understand the menu requirements or do not know how to satisfy them. Some buyers may lack sufficient background to search out the required products on the market. Many buyers act merely as order givers and not buyers. Some purchasers may know the market, food production, and service very well, but fail to do a good job because they are market-oriented; that is, they fail to follow through and see that their operation correctly receives and uses products. Some buyers may also be misled by bargain prices, and obtain materials that do not fulfill the menu's promise. Two factors essential to value in any menu are *quality* and *merchandising appeal*. If these are lacking, the price paid by the operation in lost profits may be high. On the other hand, a knowledgeable buyer who gets the right item at the right time and at the right price helps boost menu potential.

Expert purchasing requires knowledge of the production, processing, and marketing of products, their use in the foodservice establishment, and menu pricing. The buyer needs to know a lot about how the market operates, about markups, seasonal factors, and where to find specific items of the best quality for the best price. A good buyer is constantly in search of products that will simplify preparation and handling, improve quality, and facilitate service. A purchaser should also be active in analyzing cost and performance factors and in sorting out procedures that will improve the purchasing function.

Markets can change quickly and a buyer must be prepared to move with the changes. A rich background of information and knowledge about the market is needed if a buyer is to function adequately in it. A buyer must be sure to safeguard the interests of the enterprise for which he or she buys. The buyer must not waste resources and must not involve the enterprise in legal or ethical problems because of poor practices. Buying requires high ethical principles. The policies of the enterprise must be followed. Purchasing is a management function and, if delegated, must be given only to those who will protect the interests of the operation.

Orders often originate in the menu; items must be purchased to meet menu needs. Production notes the menu item and orders either from the storerooms or writes up a purchase/requisition requesting the buyer to obtain it. The buyer receives the purchase requisition and places and receives the order either sending it directly to the kitchen or to stores. Requisition from production moves items from stores, then go into use and service.

Determining Need

A production department lets the buyer know what products are needed by listing them on a requisition form. (See **Exhibit 11.1**.) Sometimes the amount of an item to order is based on a minimum amount that must be kept in stock (*par stock*), a safety factor, and an average usage amount from the time of ordering to delivery. For instance, if the par stock for tomatoes is four cases, the safety factor is two cases, and two more are needed for usage between order and delivery, the *reorder point* (ROP) for the item is eight ($4 + 2 + 2 = 8$). **Exhibit 11.2** shows an order list that holds orders to established par stocks.

Exhibit 11.1 Requisition Form

PANTRY REQUISITION

DATE: _____ ORDERED BY: _____

Quantity	Size		Quantity	Size	
		MILK			**PICKLES-OLIVES-SEAFOOD**
	1/2 pt	White		gal	Dill Pickles
	1/2 pt	Chocolate		gal	Sliced Pickles
	1/2 pt	Skim		gal	Olives
	1/2 pt	Buttermilk		qt	Olives, Ripe
	gal	Whole milk		gal	Sweet Relish
	each	Yogurt		case	Anchovies
		CREAM			Caviar
	qt	Whipping Cream		can	Tunafish
	gal	Sour Cream		lb	Crabmeat
	case	**EGGS**			**CONDIMENTS**
				#10	Catsup
		CHEESE		#10	Chili Sauce
	case	Bleu		14 oz	Catsup-bottles
	case	Cream		gal	Horseradish
	box	Bar		pt	Lemon Juice-bottle
		Cottage		gal	Vinegar, Cider
	box	Camembert		gal	Vinegar, White
	box	Liederkranz		gal	Vinegar, Red Wine
				gal	Wesson Oil
		VEGETABLES		drum	Mayonnaise
	case	Cabbage			Apple Sauce
	case	Cherry Tomatoes		can	Mint Jelly
	case	Tomatoes		can	Currant Jelly
	each	Cucumbers		qt	Low Calorie Dressing
	each	Green Peppers		pt	Peanut Butter
	case	Lettuce—Boston			
	bskt	Radishes			
	each	Red Cabbage			
	bag	Chives			
	bunch	Leaves Galax			**SEASONINGS**
	bunch	Celery hearts		box	Paprika
	bunch	Green Onions		can	Garlic Powder
				box	White Pepper
		FRUITS		box	Salt
	pts	Blueberries		box	Lawry Seasoning Salt
	pts	Strawberries		box	Dry Mustard
	each	Peaches		box	Celery Seed
	lb	Grapes			
	each	Apples			**JUICES**
	each	Oranges		case	Tomato
	each	Grapefruit		can	Grapefruit
	each	Watermelon		can	Pineapple
	doz	Lemons			
	#10	Fruit Cocktail			**MISCELLANEOUS**
	#10	Pears		lb	Sugar
	#10	Peaches		box	Ice Cream Cones
	qt	Cherries w/stems		can	Raspberry Jello
	can	Cherries, Bing		#10	Chocolate Sauce
	#2 1/2 tin	Pineapple, sliced		#10	Butterscotch Sauce
	each	Melons		box	Potato Chips
					PAPER SUPPLIES
				box	Wax Paper
				each	Doggie Bags
				box	Frill Tooth Picks
				box	Doilies for Pastry Tray
				box	Soufflé Cups
				roll	Saran Wrap
				box	Whippet Bombs

Exhibit 11.2 Order Sheet

PAGE 1			ORDERING SHEET						
DAY: _____			DATE: _____		DELIVERY: _____				
ON HAND	ORDER	PAR STOCK	SPECIFICATION AND DESCRIPTION	PURVEYOR	UNIT PRICE		EXTENSION TOTAL		
			—Meat Order—						
		12 pcs	Canadian Bacon 12–8 lb Stick						
		100 lb	Corned Beef, Ch. Deckle-Off 7–8 lb						
		25 pcs	Choice Top Butts 12–14 lb						
		8 pcs	Choice Strips 17–18 lb						
		300 lb	Commercial Chuck						
		20 lb	Beef Liver						
		15 pcs	Knuckles, Choice 8–9 lb						
		8 pcs	Choice Insides 16–20 lb						
		4 pcs	Hams, Round VC 10–12 lb						
		3 pcs	Hams, Pullman Canned 6–7						
		40 lb	Lamb Breast						
		12 pcs	Pork Loins 10–12 lb						
		12 pcs	Choice Beef Ribs 28–32 lb						
		30 lb	Spareribs						
		70 lb	Pork Sausage 5 lb						
		10 lb	Salt Pork						
		24 lb	Fresh Brisket, Ch. Deckle-Off						
		10 lb	Pork Tenderloins						
		30 lb	Veal Stew						
		100 lb	Beef Bones						
		12 lb	Wieners 8/lb						
			Total Meat						
			—Poultry Order—						
		8 cs	Turkeys 24–26 lb Toms						
		4 cs	Chicken $2^1/_4$ lb p.c. 65 lb/cs						
		40 lb	Chicken Livers, Fresh						
			Fowl Livers, Frozen						
		12 cs	Eggs, Grade A Extra Large 30 doz/cs						
			Total Poultry						
			—Fish Order—						
		100 lb	Halibut 40 lb						
		75 lb	Shrimp, Green 15–20 ct 10-5 lb						
		140 lb	Whitefish 3–3$^1/_2$ lb						
		4 pcs	Herring, 10 lb, Sour Cream						
		40 lb	Lobster Tails, African 10 lb 31–35 ct						
		150 lb	Filet of Sole 50 lb						
		60 lb	King Crab meat 6-5 lb						
		5 lb	Scallops 5 lb						
			Smelts 25 lb						
			Total Fish						
			—Produce—						
		20 cs	Head Lettuce 24's						
		12 cs	Tomatoes 20 lb flat 5x6						
		8	Potatoes, bakers,100 ct 50 lb bag						
		6	Onions, Spanish 50 lb						
		1	Onions, Red 25 lb						
		2	Cabbage, New Green 1 cs						
		1	Cabbage, Red						
		2	Celery Cabbage						
		2	Celery Pascal, Cal. 30/cs						
		2	Cucumbers 1 lb Med.						
		2	Carrots 50 loose						
		2	Romaine 24's						
			Total Produce						

Sometimes orders are automatic; an established amount is kept in stock and when replenishment occurs, the maximum level is reached. These are called *standing orders*. This can occur with many dairy, bread, coffee, or tea products where the supplier sees that a par stock level is maintained.

Searching the Market

A number of different methods for searching the market and ordering may be used. The most simple is to use a *call sheet* or *quotation sheet*. The list of needs is established and then copied on the sheet. Often the grade, quality, size, and other requirements for each product are noted, and then a number of purveyors are called and asked what their price is for each item on the sheet. This process can be quite complex when new menu items have unusual ingredients for which no specifications have been established. After this process is completed, the quoted prices are compared and the purveyor is chosen. The buyer then calls and places the order.

Bidding

Bidding is a *formal* method of buying. An operation indicates its needs to a number of purveyors, who quote prices for each item. The buyer then selects the most appropriate purveyor. The most formal bidding procedure is when specifications for items are written, indicating the quantity, quality, and packaging desired, and noting other factors such as billing, delivery periods, and general conditions of performance and responsibilities of the seller and buyer. Then purveyors offer items and prices in written bids based on these requirements. Sometimes samples are submitted by the supplier along with the offer to sell, and these samples are examined before a decision is made. Some samples may be retained to compare with the goods delivered.

In formal bidding, purveyors may have deadlines for submitting bids. Bids may be publicly opened and awarded. Bidders may be notified in writing of bid acceptance, and they will then have a specified time in which to perform. In many cases, a *bid bond* is required, which guarantees that if an award is made to a purveyor, performance is expected as agreed on the basis of the bid. If the purveyor does not perform as stated, the bonding company must either see that the purveyor does perform or pay the bond forfeit. Usually bidding of this form involves a rather large volume of business and is done by state, federal, or other governmental agencies, and by large enterprises, such as hospitals. Unless volume is large, the cost of administering a bid bond program is not worthwhile.

Informal (Negotiated) Buying—The most informal bidding method is called *negotiated buying,* which occurs when perhaps only one or several items are needed—and at least three purveyors are contacted over the phone—much as in call sheet buying. Then a decision is made as to who among the three will get the sale.

Cost Plus Buying—In *cost plus* buying, a purveyor buys items at cost with a specified markup added, part of which is the cost to the operator. For example, an operator agrees with a fresh produce purveyor to send him or her all produce orders in return for the purveyor's seeking out the best quality and price on the market. The buyer pays an agreed-on markup for this service. Such an arrangement may be limited to the purchase of specified products.

Blank Check Buying—Another method called *blank check buying* allows a purveyor to go out on the market and obtain necessary items no matter what the cost; the buyer agrees to pay whatever the market price is plus the purveyor's standard markup. In such cases, a purveyor may be instructed to purchase at the best possible price and bill the enterprise for it. Such an arrangement should be made only with reliable purveyors with whom the establishment has dealt for a long time.

Writing Specifications

The heart and soul of purchasing is the *specification*, which is the delineation of what the buyer wants in an item. It should cover all item characteristics and all other factors needed to get the right product at the right price. Some characteristics can be extremely simple and brief. They may only indicate what is wanted, how much or how many, the brand, and the packaging size. Involved specifications are needed when the item required is not common or well known and there are few quality or other purchase factors established for it. For instance, the purchase of vacuum-dried apricot nuggets may require a buyer to write up a detailed list of quality factors needed in the item. If an enterprise wishes something special that differs from the commonly marketed item, it may be necessary to prepare a detailed specification.

Buying should not take place until management determines exactly what is needed. Even a brief specification must include important item characteristics so that the right item is obtained.

Usually, a specification should include the following.

1. Name of the item
2. Quantity needed
3. Grade of the item, brand, or other quality information
4. Packaging method, size package, and special requirements
5. Basis for price—by the pound, case, piece, dozen, etc.
6. Miscellaneous factors required to get the right item, such as the number of days beef should be aged, the region in which the item is produced, or the requirement that all items be inspected for wholesomeness

When writing specifications, much detail can be eliminated if factors that apply to all items are detailed together in a "general specification" section. This section can carry instructions for delivery, methods of billing, and bid acceptance requirements. Buyers should learn the common procedures in marketing so that they use market terms correctly. Buyers and sellers use a language unique to purchasing. Terms such as "California lug," "No. 10," "18° Brix," and "5 × 5 tomato," have precise meanings that both understand. This code shortens and simplifies buying and communication between buyers and sellers. Some common terms are definitive enough to eliminate the need for further detail. All meat purveyors understand the meaning of the federal government's *Institutional Meat Purchase Specifications* (IMPS) commonly used on the market. The mention of any IMPS number for a meat item in specifications eliminates a great deal of detail that otherwise would have to be written out. If a specification requests a No. 109 rib roast, this number indicates the product's preparation, trim, and distance from the plate and from the ribeye of the meat. **Exhibit 11.3** indicates how a buyer might set up specifications for some market items.

Exhibit 11.3   Purchase Specifications

	Hamburger*	**Turkeys**
Name:	Hamburger, IMPS No. 136	Turkeys, Beltsville, Fresh-killed
Amt Needed:	150 lb (1,200 patties)	80 lb
Grade:	From U.S. Good (top)	U.S. Grade A, ready-to-cook, young toms
Packaging:	2 oz patties, frozen; packed in 25 lb lots, layer packed with wax paper separators	Wrapped in polyethylene and air exhausted, two to a carton, delivered at 40°F (4.4°C) or less but not frozen
Price:	Price per lb net	Price per lb net
Misc:	Conform to all IMPS requirements; only from chucks, rounds, flanks, or shanks; deliver at 0° F or lower internal temperature	Minnesota grain-fed birds each between 24 and 26 lb, no tolerance permitted over or under

	Fish	**Tomatoes**
Name:	Cod fillets, boneless, no skin	Tomatoes, canned
Amt Needed:	40 lb (about 60 to 70 fillets)	10 cases
Grade:	Strictly fresh caught cod processed in plants meeting federal sanitary standards	U.S. Grade B or Choice
Packaging:	Dry layer packed in 20 lb lots	6/10's
Price:	Per lb	Per dozen 6/10's
Misc:	Shall be treated with no preservatives or seasonings; from Boston docked cod, hake, pollock, cusk or haddock 1½ to 3 lb size (scrod)	Shall be tomatoes with no added juice or other liquid, California pack

Exhibit 11.3 Purchase Specifications *(continued)*

Pears

Name: Pears, halves, Bartlett

Amt Needed: 2 cases

Grade: U.S. Grade A or Fancy

Packaging: 24 2½'s

Misc: 7 to 9 count per can; minimum drained weight 17 oz; heavy syrup (18 to 22° Brix).

Shrimp

Shrimp, headless, frozen, in shell (raw green)

120 lb (24 5-lb packages)

Highest quality, pink shrimp

In 5-lb blocks with no added moisture in wax paper wraps and in cardboard boxes, 8 boxes to the carton

Shall be large size, 21 to 25 per lb

Eggs

Name: Eggs, fresh, in shell

Amt Needed: Two Cases (1 lot)

Grade: U.S. AA

Packaging: 30 doz paper cartons

Price: Per dozen

Misc: Size large, min. wt. net per case 45 lb; no dozen shall weigh more than 25 oz nor less than 23 oz

Butter

Butter, sweet cream

400 lb

U.S. Grade A (93 score)

5-lb packs, 72 pats per lb

Per pound

Pats shall be individually separated by waxed paper and layer packed; deliver over two-month period in lots not under 40 lb each

Apples

Name: Apples, fresh, Rome Beauty

Amt Needed: 20 Washington cases

Grade: U.S. Extra Fancy or Washington Extra Fancy

Packaging: 100 size, minimum net weight per box 45 lb

Misc: Paper cartons; apples shall have been stored in federally supervised environment controlled warehouses

Milk

Milk, fresh, homogenized, 3½%

60,300 half pints

U.S. Grade A, pasteurized

In sealed ½ pt paper containers; 64 containers per carton

Flash pasteurized; milk shall not be over two days old from milking time; shall conform in all respects to local and state ordinances

*Institutional Meat Purchase Specifications of the USDA.

When a considerable amount of market information exists on food products, the writing of a specification is not difficult. When items are not well known, writing specifications becomes more difficult. Buyers have been especially hampered in writing specifications for many convenience foods because there are few factors in the market that differentiate item characteristics, and the quality and other elements needed for their purchase. However, many federal and state agencies have begun to develop specifications for these items, which can be of considerable assistance to enterprises writing similar specifications. Others may take a recipe for a product, and from this prepare a specification indicating the ingredients that must be in it. Government agencies or other organizations may have good information on the quality factors for some items that are very much like the one to be purchased. For instance, there are some good standards and purchasing criteria for canned meats. If these are studied, perhaps the necessary standards for the frozen equivalent can be developed.

Two code numbers are often used in purchasing and foodservices may use these even as their code numbers for items. The two are the Institutional Meat Purchases Specifications (IMPS) and the Universal Product Code (UPC).

The IMPS are code numbers used to indicate specific kinds and cuts of meat. Numbers such as 109 and 190 indicate beef, the 200's indicate lamb and mutton, 300's veal and calf, 400's pork, etc. Portion cuts are identified by placing a 1 in front of the cut number. Thus, a 109 rib is a beef rib ready for the oven and 1109 is a rib steak ready to cook. Using the number makes it simple and easy for buyers to indicate exactly what they want without a lot of writing.

The *Universal Product Code* (UPC) is another method used to standardize purchasing. It consists of a series of numbers with lines of different width and boldness which indicate specific food items. We see these used at supermarket checkout counters, where the bar code is drawn across a light which reads the code and records the sale, indicating the product and price. UPC's also have specific numbers related to the lines and, if the light will not read the lines, the operator can punch in the number and the machine will record the information in the same way it would if it read the lines.

Quality Standards

Buying quality can be defined in different ways. Many buyers use a brand name to assure consistent quality. Thus a buyer may order Heinz catsup because it is a recognized item of a certain quality. Brands, however, are only as good as the manufacturer that makes them. Their quality is generally not based on any standard other than that observed or established by the manufacturer.

Quality definition can also be established by *grade*. Federal standards are usually the basis for these grades. Many food grades exist. Grading is the separation of a product into different quality levels. Thus, for canned fruits there may be three quality levels: Grade A (highest), Grade B, and Grade C. Buyers and sellers need to know what quality levels these grades represent.

Exhibit 11.4 Quality Grade Symbols

SOURCE: U.S. Department of Agriculture

Grades are usually established on known quality factors and do not change. **Exhibit 11.4** shows quality grade symbols for several items.

Trade grades may be used that have recognition only in specific markets. Thus, trade grades have been established for fresh fruits and vegetables, dried fruits, eggs, and poultry, but many of these are rapidly losing out in market use as federal grades take over.

For instance, very few markets now use the trade grades for eggs because federal grades are more universally known. At times the federal government may adopt a trade grade and copy it. This has happened with meat and canned items. A federal grade is established after consulting with industry and is issued as a *tentative grade*. It is tested for a time to see how it works, and buyers and sellers can suggest changes. After a period of testing, the grade may be revised and then be made official. Federal grades are usually established for different levels of the market—the *consumer*, the *wholesale*, and the *manufacturing* levels. A food buyer may use all three. However, consumer or retail grades dominate the foodservice market because these are how most foods are graded, and processors and producers tend to follow these standards more than any others. Thus, eggs today move almost totally on the basis of consumer grades and not wholesale ones.

The federal government's grading system for processed foods is based on the development of scores for certain items. Then, based on the total score of an item, a grade is assigned to it. Thus, an item scoring anywhere from 90 to 100 may be Grade A; another, scoring from 80 to 89, Grade B; and another, from 70 to 79, Grade C. Anything below a score of 70 is said to be "below standard." This does not mean that the food is inedible or not suitable for some uses, but that it is below the lowest standard.

Various methods of scoring have been developed for different groups of foods. The scoring for meat varies considerably from the scoring of fruits and vegetables. Buyers must learn the basis for scoring different food products, the value given different quality factors, and what the scores mean in item quality.

A very important standard for food buyers is called *standard of identity*. This is a statement by the federal government that defines exactly what an item is by its characteristics. Thus, no manufacturer of egg noodles can use the term "egg" to describe noodles unless the noodles contain 5½ percent dry egg solids. Unless a product comes from a specific species and variety recognized in the standard of identity, it may not be called by the name of the product that does come from that particular species and variety. Juice from anything other than *citris paradisi* cannot be called grapefruit juice. Standards of identity also indicate what is meant by terms such as "diced," "salt-free," "shoestring," and "cream." When a standard of identity is established by the government, it is a legal description of what the item is. The buyer and seller can negotiate more easily when such terms are defined in this manner. Many of these standards are also used to establish truth-in-menu requirements. (See **Appendix A**.)

Other standards that assist in promoting buying and selling in the food product market are those of *fill* or *weight*. Canned items must be filled to a specific level in the can, and cereals must settle only to specific levels in the packages. Standard sizes for barrels, hampers, bushels, crates, and other package units have been established, along with their fraction units.

There are also laws to control market interaction and establish procedures for manufacturing and handling. Some laws, such as the Pure Food, Drug and Cosmetic Act, provide standards for food sanitation. Others, such as the Federal Trade Commission Act, the Agricultural Marketing Act, and the Perishable Commodities Act, deal with how the market is to function and what constitutes legal actions in the market. These acts protect both buyers and sellers. They also give order, reliability, and stability to the marketplace.

Purchasing Controls

Good purchasing is not simply deciding what, when, and how much; it requires further efforts in accounting, controlling, and monitoring the flow of materials within the operation from receipt until they are used. All of these functions must be well coordinated, organized, and simplified as much as possible. Management should scrutinize the purchasing system to see if any procedure can be streamlined or eliminated. The system should provide procedures for an adequate flow of information between departments and for maintaining good records to provide accountability.

Much of the paperwork for purchasing procedures can be handled by a computer, which helps simplify, speed, and improve the purchasing process.

Purchasing needs arise from different areas in an operation. Various units within the food and beverage department may prepare requisitions. Store-room personnel or a check of the computer file may alert the buyer to the need to bring stores up to a par or maximum level. All this information is consolidated by the buyer and usually put on a purchase order or on a call sheet and the order placed. Note that each purchase order carries its own number, and this must usually appear on all related invoices, packages, and shipping papers so they can be readily identified with the order. (See **Exhibit 11.5**.) **Exhibit 11.6** shows a daily order and receiving record. These forms help ensure accurate order placement and the delivery date. All order lists and purchase orders should be properly signed and executed. Many purchase orders include a copy that is signed by the seller and returned to the buyer, indicating that an exchange of goods will occur.

Receiving

Receiving is an important step in the sequence of obtaining menu supplies. If done efficiently it allows management to see that the goods delivered meet the terms in every respect as described in the specifications, the purchase order, and other purchase documents, so menu items can be the proper cost and quality. Deliveries should be accompanied by proper invoices and package lists. After a thorough check is made of quantity, quality, temperature, and weight, any discrepancies are noted both on the receiving sheet and on the *invoice* acknowledging receipt that is returned to the deliveryman. The invoice copy is sent to accounting with the receiving report. If items are returned, a form such as the one shown in **Exhibit 11.7** might be used. Such a form might also be used to note any credit that might be given or any discrepancy in the delivery.

Storage and Inventory

It is the responsibility of receiving personnel to move the goods to storage as quickly as possible. To ensure the safety of perishable incoming food items, it is important that foods be placed in proper storage immediately after they are received and checked. Food safety and quality can be compromised if products are left out too long. Of course, it is important to try to prescribe delivery times so that delivery does not occur during peak times when employees are unable to give attention to proper receiving procedures.

The storage step should include *inventory control* procedures. Goods should be either removed from packing cases and stored on shelves or stored in their packing cases on shelving. The order of arrangement of items should follow some logical method of use, such as *first in, first out* (FIFO), in which items are stored and used in the same order as they are received. Minimum and maximum quantities should be established for each item. When supplies reach the minimum on the ROP (reorder point), a notice is given to the buyer taking the stock up to maximum or par.

Sometimes inventory must be taken daily, for example, of quantities of foods on hand in the kitchen or available bar supplies. This inventory form may also be used as a requisition to bring items up to par level. It is important that management establish good policies and procedures for taking inventories.

Exhibit 11.5 Purchase Order Form Indicating Account Number

		PURCHASE ORDER NO.	**45845**
		REQ. NO. _____	
		DATE _____ 19 ___	

S
H
I
P

T
O

FOR	DATE REQUIRED	HOW SHIP	F.O.B.

QUANTITY	PLEASE SUPPLY ITEMS LISTED BELOW	PRICE	UNIT
1			
2			
3			
4			
5			
6			
7			
8			
9			
10			

❑ CAPITAL EXPENDITURE   ❑ OTHER _____

❑ CONFIRMING ORDER—DO NOT DUPLICATE

IMPORTANT

OUR ORDER NUMBER MUST APPEAR ON ALL INVOICES, PACKAGES, ETC.

PLEASE NOTIFY US IMMEDIATELY IF YOU ARE UNABLE TO SHIP COMPLETE ORDER BY DATE SPECIFIED.

PLEASE SEND _____ COPIES OF YOUR INVOICE WITH ORIGINAL BILL OF LADING.

PURCHASE AGENT

Exhibit 11.6 Daily Order and Receiving Record

QUOTE FROM AND PRICE				ITEM DESCRIPTION	SUPPLIER ITEM CODE	DATE ORDERED	QUANTITY ON HAND	QUANTITY ORDERED	PERIOD REFERENCE NUMBER	RECEIVED		DATE INVOICE PROC.	REMARKS
FROM	UNIT PRICE	FROM	UNIT PRICE							DATE	QUAN.		

DAILY ORDER AND RECEIVING RECORD

FOR THE _____ PERIOD

(OPERATION STAMP)

Exhibit 11.7 Returned Merchandise Report Form

RETURNED MERCHANDISE OR SHORTAGE REPORT

Name of Supplier _____ Invoice # _____

Amount of Correction _____

Reason _____

_____

_____

_____

_____

Date _____ Deliveryman's Signature _____

By _____ Company _____

Exhibit 11.8 Perpetual Inventory Sheet

PERPETUAL INVENTORY SHEET																								
DATE	ORDER NO.	IN	OUT	BALANCE	DATE	ORDER NO.	IN	OUT	BALANCE	DATE	ORDER NO.	IN	OUT	BALANCE	DATE	ORDER NO.	IN	OUT	BALANCE					

Remarks			PRICE	
LOCATION	MINIMUM	MAXIMUM	ARTICLE	SIZE OR PART NO.

There are two main kinds of inventories: perpetual and physical. A *perpetual inventory* is derived solely from records, such as delivery reports indicating what items have been received and put into storage and from requisitions indicating what items have been withdrawn from storage. In many operations today, the perpetual inventory is maintained by computer. As food items are received, the kind, amount, and cost are fed into the computer. As the items are withdrawn, the computer updates the inventory. Thus, one can quickly find out from the computer how much of an item is on hand plus what the maximum/minimum level should be, the average usage, and other valuable information. A perpetual inventory sheet is shown in **Exhibit 11.8**.

In a physical inventory, each item is counted by hand and recorded on a sheet. (See **Exhibit 11.9**.) Often, two individuals are assigned to participate in a physical inventory, one of whom comes from the accounting or a department other than receiving. The inventory sheets must be signed by whomever does the counting. Counting devices, such as a laser gun, that record items by name, size, value, and other data needed for inventorying, are now used. Some of these feed the information into the computer.

Some experience and knowledge are required to take a good inventory. Those taking the inventory must, for example, know the various can sizes and package quantities to obtain accurate data.

It is usually considered normal to have a 1 to 2 percent difference between the perpetual inventory and the physical inventory, but if it varies much from that range, management should investigate. The food and beverage department or the accounting division may also maintain perpetual inventories of items on hand.

Some operations use a slightly different inventory system for meats. When a meat order is received, it is tagged with the proper receiving information, indicating the weight, the value, and the name of the item. A copy of this record is used to indicate on the perpetual inventory that this item is on hand. When the item is withdrawn from storage for use, the tag is taken off and sent through proper channels, and the item is deducted from the perpetual inventory.

Exhibit 11.9 Physical Inventory Sheet

DAILY MEAT INVENTORY

Date _____ Day _____

Item	Drawer	Cooler	Freezer	Total	Purchases
New York					
Filet 9 oz					
Filet 6 oz					
Scrod					
Lobster tail					
Chicken breast					
Lbs chopped sirloin					
Prime rib					

Issuing

Issuing is another critical step in the series of activities related to purchasing. Requisition forms are usually completed to indicate what items various departments want to withdraw from stores. These are signed by the person needing the items and approved by the manager or the person's supervisor. The requisition is then presented to the storeroom, and the goods are withdrawn. When tagged meats and other tagged items are issued, the tag is removed and sent with the requisition to the accounting department to indicate issue.

Issues from the storeroom plus *direct deliveries*, which go directly from the receiving dock to production, should be totaled to obtain the amount of food used for the day, week, or month.

Value Analysis

A *value analysis* is a review of the purchasing process to evaluate whether the best possible purchasing job has been done and determine whether it can be improved. After purchase, the items themselves are analyzed to see if they meet the needs for which they were purchased. If they prove inadequate, an alternative should be investigated. An operation purchasing No. 189 tenderloins may decide to eliminate all the trimming and labor necessary to bring them to a usable condition by purchasing No. 190 tenderloins, which come well trimmed. Also, prepared grapefruit sections may be purchased instead of fresh whole grapefruit, which require labor to section. Many operations obtain most of their beef packaged and deboned, with most fat removed, and divided into quantities based on the cooking methods required to cook each item. This removes the necessity of cutting the meat after it is received, which, if done improperly, can result in high waste. In addition, the shipment of bones and fat, which are usually waste products, is eliminated. Working out solutions, such as these helps operations simplify procedures and reduce costs.

Value analysis also includes observing items as they are processed to see whether preparation procedures can be improved and to ascertain the actual cost of preparation.

The supplier must also be appraised. A supplier should not be judged by the price of items alone but by the quality of service and performance. Some purveyors perform more or better services and, in turn, charge higher prices.

Some value analysts say that value is *quality divided by price* ($Q \div P = V$). If quality can be increased and price held stable, value is increased. If quality drops and price remains stable, value is lost. If price drops but quality remains the same, value increases. If price rises but quality remains the same, value is lost. Buyers should constantly attempt to increase value.

There are numerous variables in the quality or price of items purchased on the market, and buyers must seek constantly to equate one with the other. One of the prerequisites for doing this is to know the yield of items purchased. Schuler's restaurant in Michigan weighs every rib before roasting and keeps accurate track of the number of servings that are obtained from each rib.

Schuler's can look over a year's record of rib yields and obtain accurate portions costs. It can also evaluate the method it uses to purchase ribs and see whether it can be improved to get a better product at a lower cost.

There are many things that can be done by buyers, if value analysis is practiced, to bring down costs and improve procedures. It is usual for buyers and purveyors to work together to improve purchasing methods and reduce costs. It may be possible for a group of food services to consolidate their orders with one purveyor so that the supplier can make more deliveries in a given area, which reduces costs and results in a more favorable price for each operation. This is known as *cooperative*, or *co-op*, buying. Since some food services are slow in paying bills, those who pay promptly can help to defray the cost burden this places on the purveyor. By guaranteeing payment within a specified period, some enterprises may obtain lower charges from purveyors. It may be possible to work out arrangements, such as cost-plus buying or providing guarantees to a purveyor for a specific amount of business during a period, in return for the purveyor's seeking out the best possible products for the enterprise, adding only a specific amount above costs for this service. Orders may be placed farther in advance so that purveyors can do a better job of searching the market and making the most favorable buys.

Simplifying purchasing procedures and reducing paperwork can do much to assist in reducing costs, as can improving the purchasing task to reduce inventories kept on hand.

Good value analysis is a constant search for ways to improve purchasing performance and, if consistently practiced, can lead to worthwhile savings. It is the search for facts, their analysis, and then action on the basis of the information gained.

PRODUCTION

Menu writing and food production are mutually dependent. The success of the menu depends very much on how well the production system interprets what the menu offers. Conversely, successful production depends on how completely and accurately the menu itself is prepared, just as it depends on the purchasing system to provide the right materials at the right time and at the right cost. No menu writer should place items on a menu when workers lack the skills necessary to produce them or when equipment is lacking. If the menu properly reflects the limitations and assets of the production department in layout, equipment, and personnel, production can implement it correctly.

Good forecasts, recipe preparation, and portioning information must be provided so that the production department knows the quantities, methods, and times required to prepare items. Coordination of service, management, purchasing, and other departments of the operation is essential. It is necessary for management to study the production system used and develop the flow of information and the controls that are required. Patron forecasts must be coordinated with accurate purchase quantities, and the production depart-

Exhibit 11.10 Production Sheet

PRODUCTION SHEET

DAY _____   DATE _____

AMOUNT	• ITEM •	LOCATION	TEMP.	TIME	REMARKS
	• REHEATS •				
					EMPLOYEES' CAFETERIA
	• VEGETABLES •				
	CASES OF SPINACH				
	PANS OF BAKING POTATOES				

• OUT AT •

AMOUNT OF RIBS LEFT: _____

BAKED POTATOES LEFT: _____

AMOUNT OF GREENS LEFT: _____

AMOUNT OF SPINACH LEFT: _____

GREENS IN WALK-IN ICED: _____

FISH PROPERLY ICED: _____

STOCKPOTS CHECKED (SIMMER): _____

TOTAL NUMBER OF DINNERS: _____

GENERAL REMARKS: _____

_____

_____

_____

ment needs to know what quantities to expect and when foods are to come. The production department should also be advised of menu forecast requirements so that personnel can be properly scheduled. This information should be recorded on a production sheet. (See **Exhibit 11.10**.) The production department must also establish procedures to ensure that items are produced in the proper quantity and quality at the time when they are required.

Management should ensure that the production department knows exactly what each menu item is and what it consists of. A menu item and its recipe should be explained to production in precise detail as to ingredients required, their amounts, and the procedures used to produce the item. *Standardized recipes* should be used and controls established to produce exactly the same item each time it is offered to a patron. Costs should be accurately known. The most successful enterprises are those that establish good information flow so the production department knows what is to be done and how to do it. Failure of management to see that the production department is informed and is able to perform as expected can result in an unprofitable menu because the work may be haphazard and the product frequently disappointing. It is easy to put items on a menu. It is not so easy to put them on the menu *with adequate planning* for the expected result, the item cost, and customer acceptance.

It is sometimes said that a menu promises and the production department reneges. There should be a complete understanding by the menu planner, the patrons, and the food production department of what is promised in the menu. What is promised should be delivered. A toasted sandwich should be made with toast, not bread that is browned on a griddle on both sides—the latter is a "grilled" sandwich. A consomme is not a bouillon or rich broth but a special soup produced by specific methods from specific ingredients.

Each item on the menu should be thoroughly tested and standardized so the food production department can produce the correct quantity and quality. Recipes must be complete, precise, and carefully followed. **Exhibit 11.11** shows a form that can be used to record recipes. **Exhibit 11.12** shows a standardized recipe. A wide variance in quality, portion size, or appearance of menu items can result in dissatisfied customers. Service personnel should check foods they receive, and if they are not correct, let the food production department know.

Exhibit 11.11 Standard Recipe Card

STANDARD RECIPE CARD Number ____________

Recipe For ____________ Restaurant ____________ Date ____________

Portion Size ____________ Meal Period ____________ Number Portions ____________

INGREDIENT	WEIGHT	COST PRICE			INGREDIENT	WEIGHT	COST PRICE		
		Pur. Unit	Per Unit	Ingredient			Pur. Unit	Per Unit	Ingredient

Cost Per Portion ____________

Menu Price ____________

Food Cost ____________

Exhibit 11.12 Standardized Recipe

Barbecued Spareribs
Yield: 10 portions
Portion: ½ lb

Ingredients	American Weight	Metric Weight	Amount	Method
Hoisin sauce	2 oz	57 g	4 T	1. Combine all the ingredients except ribs and honey in a large bowl.
Bean sauce	2 oz	57 g	4 T	
Apple sauce	2 oz	57 g	4 T	
Catsup	5 oz	142 g	⅝ c	2. Score the ribs with a sharp knife.
Soy sauce	2 oz	57 g	4 T	
Rice wine	4 oz	114 g	½ c	3. Place the ribs in the marinade. Marinate them for at least 4 hours at a product temperature of 45°F (7.2°C) or lower in refrigerated storage.
Peanut oil	3 oz	85 g	⅜ c	
Red food coloring (optional)	½ oz	14 g	1 T	
Ginger, minced	1 oz	28 g	2 T	
Scallions, minced	8 oz	226 g	1 c	
Garlic cloves, minced	6 oz	170 g	½ c	4. Place the ribs in a smoker at 425°F (220°C) for 30 minutes.
Sugar	4 oz	114 g	½ c	5. Reduce the heat to 375°F (190°C) and continue smoking the ribs for 50 minutes. Brush the honey on the ribs during the last 5 minutes of smoking. Final internal product temperature must reach 150°F (65.5°C) or higher.
Salt	1 oz	28 g	2 T	
Pork spareribs, trimmed	5 lb	2.27 kg		
Honey	8 oz	226 g	1 c	6. Slice the ribs between the bones and serve.

Foods should be prepared at the proper time. Some can be prepared ahead and are often better if they are. Others should be prepared as close to service as possible. Foods that sit too long after preparation can lose culinary and nutritional quality and may become contaminated and unsafe. Production schedules will help indicate the amount of food required and the times it should be ready for service. Checks should be made to see how much is carried over after the service period. Runout times should be noted.

Good organization is required of supporting units. Thus, the butcher shop should have items on hand as they are needed. The vegetable preparation cooks should be informed as to the amounts of vegetable items required and have them ready at the proper times. Purchasing must take place sufficiently in advance to allow proper preparation. Guests dislike ordering an item from the menu and then being told the operation is out of it.

There is a certain amount of prepreparation work to be done in the production operation. Soup stocks need to be made in advance, as well as sauces and other preparations. Long before service begins, a check should be made to see that supplies and foods required are on hand. Good organization and coordination will make the mealtime rush go a lot smoother and promote high-quality production.

Spending some time with food production staff to show them what is intended by the menu as written can help them provide tasty, satisfying meals that will make patrons want to come back.

Production Personnel

The people working in food production must be trained to produce what the menu lists. In a quick-service, limited-menu operation, the skill, abilities, and knowledge of food production employees may be limited to preparing only a few simple items. If the menu is more extensive, more production skills, experience, and training, will be required.

Often the reason employees produce foods of poor quality is that they have little knowledge of what is expected. It is essential that food production people know enough about production principles to understand what is happening when they prepare foods. Workers may know from experience that a steak or hamburger changes color when subjected to heat and that it becomes slightly more firm and less moist. However, if they understand the reasons for these phenomena—how some of the more desirable changes can be encouraged and some of the less desirable ones limited in the food production task—higher quality items will be produced. Teaching employees why procedures are important is frequently required to ensure adequate performance. A manager who tries to discourage an employee from cooking hamburgers too far in advance of service may not be able to prevent this practice until the employee learns that heat and extended holding increase the toughness and shrinkage in meat. Employees must be shown what their finished products should look like. This type of thorough training usually results in higher productivity.

Personnel organization should be functional. In many operations, a chef may be in charge and may have assistants, called *chefs du parti* in formal, continental kitchen organizations. In other operations, a food production manager may be in charge of several head cooks. Whatever the organization, it should lead to efficient, smooth production of high-quality menu items. Those in charge should constantly seek to develop high standards of performance that employees must meet. The organization should ensure that workers are adequately supervised and are assisted by superiors when they need help.

Control Documents

Labor can be controlled through the use of documents, such as production schedules, time cards, payroll records, training records, and health records. Written and communicated *production schedules* are vital to a smooth pro-

Exhibit 11.13 Food Production Schedule

Day: Tuesday Date: 2/3 Meal: Dinner
Volume Forecast: 412

Menu Item	Forecast	Portion Size	Production Method	Portions on Hand (Prepped)	Needed Production	Left Over
Chicken Tetrazini	84	6 oz	Recipe #46	12	72	7
Sole Mornay	76	6 oz	Recipe #42	0	76	—
Crab Cakes	115	3 cakes	Recipe #57	16	99	13
Blackened Swordfish	84	8 oz	Recipe #39	0	84	—
Blackened Tuna Steak	53	8 oz	Recipe #41	0	53	—
TOTAL	412					

duction process. (See **Exhibit 11.13**.) Employees must be properly scheduled to see that work is done. Improper scheduling is often the cause of high labor costs, poor-quality food, and waste. Sales histories are a big help in predicting quantities to prepare and reducing excess production and cost. Comparing the amounts prepared with amounts sold can give valuable information and reduce waste. As much as possible, one form should do the work of many, to reduce the amount of copying and to eliminate errors. Some forms in use have been presented here. However, each operation should design a system to meet its needs. There is less uniformity here than in purchasing, and one will find that the number and kind of forms used will not be consistent. Using a computer to do much of this can reduce time and costs, and generate more accurate information in this area.

As with purchasing, management should study the production system to see that it is efficient. The entire program should be coordinated to bring the efforts of the production team together so that menu items will be produced as planned at the right time. This coordination is a complex, sometimes difficult task, but a very important part of implementing a menu.

SUMMARY

The purchasing and production systems of a food service are critical factors in ensuring a menu's—and an operation's—success. When purchasing and production are performed well, the menu can be expected to live up to its potential.

Purchasing entails supplying an operation with the right products at the right price at the right time. Thus price, while important, is not the only criterion. How a product *performs* is the essential measure of successful purchasing.

Purchasing includes a number of steps that need to be coordinated to ensure good results. The first step is to determine need. This may be done by checking inventory levels, the weekly menu, or discussing needs with production, or by the production staff, who may use a *purchase requisition* form to request items. Searching the market is the next step. This may include accepting bids from suppliers and choosing from among the offers. The third step is to negotiate services from the chosen purveyor. Fourth, deliveries are inspected and received, and the next step involves storage and issuing. The last step involves evaluating the entire process.

Controls must be established in all phases of purchasing to ensure the proper handling and security of products until issue.

Value analysis, an important, often neglected step in purchasing, is a method used to evaluate the purchasing process itself, the product, and the supplier.

Production can make or break a menu. If food products are not what they should be, the results will eventually show up on the bottom line. An operation must have the right staff and implement schedules to ensure that foods are prepared according to standardized recipes and as close to service times as possible.

There are a number of control documents that can assist in production and purchasing to ensure proper coordination and communication among departments, tight controls, and good recordkeeping. These include the production sheet, standardized recipe, production schedule, and carryover food report.

QUESTIONS

1. Set up a flow chart that shows the steps in procuring items, starting at the definition of need and ending at production. Indicate some of the forms used in the various steps.

2. How can using a standardized recipe control quality and quantity?

3. List the factors a good specification should include.

4. What should be included in a thorough value analysis? What are the benefits of implementing this process?

5. How do production sheets, standardized recipes, and production schedules work together to ensure efficient production?

12

Service and the Menu

Outline

Introduction

Serving Guests
 Mise en Place in Service
 Greeting Patrons
 Serving Food

Types of Service
 Counter Service
 Cafeteria Service
 Buffet Service
 Table Service
  American Service
  French Service
  Russian Service
  English Service
  Organization for Table Service
 Room Service

Handling the Guest Check
 Tipping

Summary

Questions

Objectives

After reading this chapter, you should be able to:

1. Indicate the importance of service in fulfilling the objectives of the menu.

2. Explain what service entails.

3. Identify the essential elements of good service.

4. Differentiate among types of table service.

5. Explain how checks should be handled.

INTRODUCTION

Service is the point at which all of the work previously done to create a menu comes to fruition. The menu's objectives are to communicate and sell the items the menu offers and to please patrons. Along with walking into the operation and being seated, the menu is the patron's introduction to the enterprise. How patrons are served can mean much in fulfilling a menu's goals.

The manner in which food is served is a critical step in the menu's success. Poor service can ruin otherwise fine food. Time is always important, even where the dining is leisurely; there should be little delay in serving menu items. Hot food should be hot; cold food should be cold. This is often stated, but violated almost as frequently. Water, butter, rolls, and other foods must be replenished as needed, condiments must appear at correct times, empty coffee cups should be refilled, and all other service details handled in an efficient manner. Serving should be suited to the dining pace of each party. Service that proceeds smoothly and efficiently—without patrons noticing that it is very hard work—should always be the goal.

SERVING GUESTS

When a menu does not measure up to expected profit potential, then, and purchasing and production procedures seem to be efficient, managers must next evaluate whether service is consistent with the goals of the operation and the menu.

In the hospitality industry, when we serve guests, we try to satisfy their personal needs. In this way, food service is considered a *service industry*. Today there are more people employed in the foodservice industry than in any other industry.

As an industry we render a special service, one in which we not only take care of the sustenance and nutritional needs of individuals, but also seek to please people in the manner in which we provide service. Patrons in a food service are guests, and while they are in an establishment, our managers and employees have the responsibility to see to it that they are courteously treated and are made happy and satisfied.

Being responsible for a guest's comfort and pleasure is an ancient tradition in many cultures. The principle of *sanctuary* arose from the tradition that people must be cared for and not injured while in an establishment. Under an ancient Irish custom, guests were offered wine and a pinch of salt as they came through the door. Today, when a headwaiter or hostess greets guests as they come into the dining area to be seated, the same spirit of hospitality should prevail. We should be proud to maintain these traditions and see that guests are properly greeted. There is a great satisfaction and reward in knowing we can please others with our food and service. When this pleasure is lost, employees lose something extra that should come with their jobs.

When the foodservice industry first came into being, the feeling was that customers were guests coming into the home of the proprietor, and in many areas of the world customers are still treated as if they were coming into a home rather than into a business establishment. The Arab merchant goes through a considerable ceremony to let you know how pleased he is that you are his guest. Guests should be made to feel that they are friends whom we wish to serve and make happy. Doing this is not an act of servility but the performance of a skill that the server possesses and is proud to possess. In many of today's food services courtesy is lacking. This loss in service can be like the loss of rain to a fertile plain. If rain fails to come, the plain dies and becomes a desert.

Good service is not always easy to give. It takes a lot of skill, effort, and knowledge. Employees who give good service work at it. They study their jobs to find out how they can make serving more efficient and better. They are constantly alert to find ways to please their guests. This pays off in personal satisfaction—and in tips—and in happier clientele and higher profits for the establishment.

Employees who serve guests directly should have pleasant personalities and enjoy interacting with guests and fellow workers. They should want to do the best possible job. Often guests may try a server's patience and be difficult to serve, but those people should still be given the best service—with a smile.

Servers must also have stamina. They often must work under pressure. They also should have an appropriate appearance: neat and clean. Hands and fingernails should be immaculate. The hair should be neat and clean. The uniform should be crisp and clean.

The type of service provided will depend on the type of operation, the food, and what patrons expect. Patrons of a quick-service operation will generally not expect—nor will they have time for—fine seated service. Some establishments will have different types of service within one operation. The major types of service are discussed here.

Mise en Place in Service

Good service does not begin with the arrival of patrons. It depends very much on the preparations made for patrons ahead of time. *Mise en place* means getting ready for the job to be performed. Service personnel should see that the necessary preliminaries are taken care of before guests arrive so that service can proceed smoothly and efficiently. Without this, the job may be poorly done, and both the server and the guest will be dissatisfied with the results.

Before service begins, butter packets must be arranged in bowls and iced. Ice, silverware, napkins, water, condiments, juices, salads, dressings, and other items needed for service should be assembled and put where they can be obtained quickly.

It is essential for service personnel to be briefed on how foods are prepared and how they are to be served. Sometimes this is the job of the dining room supervisor, and a short meeting just before service may be held to cover the menu and its items for the day.

Dining room employees also should see that all dining areas are clean and in good order. Chairs, tables, and other items in the area should be clean and in good condition. In a full-service operation, linen should be clean and neat, and tables should be properly set with sparkling glassware and bright silverware. Menus should be clean and in good condition.

Managers and employees should continually ask themselves, "Would I dine here?" Supervisory personnel should submit survey reports to management on the condition of the dining room. Management should see to it that repairs, maintenance, and other needs are taken care of. Outside areas should also be checked. Patrons are likely to think that a poorly maintained operation will offer poor food and service.

Greeting Patrons

A maitre d'hôtel, headwaiter, host, or hostess may greet patrons as they enter a foodservice establishment, take them to their places, seat them, and give them menus. If some individual is not immediately available to do this, the first employee encountered should greet patrons and make them feel welcome. Benjamin Franklin said, "The taste of the roast is often determined by the handshake of the host." Greetings should be warm but not so overly friendly that guests are embarrassed. Knowing exactly how to give a greeting takes training and practice. All patrons should be made to feel welcome.

It is not easy to greet 200 guests during a meal and escort them to their places, but this fact should not be conveyed to guests. Every greeting should be distinctive and special so that guests feel that they have been especially identified and welcomed. A mechanical greeting from someone who simply grabs menus and recites, "This way, please," will do little to make guests feel welcome.

Serving Food

A good serving system is needed so that orders will be properly taken, properly given to the production department, properly prepared, and, finally, properly served. It is wise to have a service manual that service personnel and other employees will read to see how service is performed in the operation. This should cover rules of conduct and procedures for doing the job, from greeting guests to resetting tables. Service personnel should be informed about where to place orders in the kitchen for different kinds of foods. They should also be told the times required for preparation.

Different foods require different kinds of service, and servers should know these requirements. There is also a proper sequence to be observed in giving good service. Water should be brought immediately. The server must time the service so that groups of foods, such as a main dish and accompaniments, come to the table together. Personnel should not serve food that is not up to expectations. A good motto is: "If you are not proud of it, don't serve it." Thus, food must not only taste good but be served at the right temperature, be appealing, and be of sufficient quantity to satisfy patrons. Servers should be aware of these factors when serving menu items.

Servers need to have good organizational abilities and be competent to follow the systems used. They should be trained in how to present the menu, how to pour water, how to take orders, how to communicate with guests, and how to write orders in detail so that production personnel can follow them. Servers should also follow a system designed to help them remember which guest has ordered which menu item. This usually requires a set procedure for writing down the orders and numbering the guests, starting always in one specific place and going around the table clockwise.

A good system for placing orders in the kitchen is also needed. Usually orders are given in written form. Some operations use a circular rack so that orders come in proper rotation as the rack is turned. Some use a computer, an electronic cash register, or other system to order, thus establishing a record that the order was placed. Whatever the method, it should be simple and workable. Service personnel should develop a system for informing production workers when to start orders so that they are ready on time but are not prepared so far in advance that they lose quality. A good communication system is needed to inform service personnel when their orders are ready.

A method needs to be worked out for keeping hot foods hot and cold foods cold after they are prepared and while they are awaiting pickup by service personnel. Infrared lights over a table on which hot foods are placed is sufficient for hot foods, though items should spend as little time under lamps as possible. A refrigerated shelf may be used for cold foods. The method should include storage areas where dishes can be properly warmed or chilled should be available.

Some method for checking foods as service personnel pick them up can be devised, so that the right foods are taken and foods for each course are presented in order. A food checker can serve these functions.

Tableware must be handled properly. Glassware should be handled so that the fingers do not touch the tops or insides. Silverware should be held by the handles. A dish should be held with four fingers under it and the thumb steadying it at the edge.

Serving should proceed from a selected spot at the table. It is traditional to serve women first, but wherever serving starts, service goes to the server's left in a clockwise fashion. As the server moves left from the next guest to be served, he or she turns to the right, using the right hand to put down the main dishes and items from the guest's right side. With the left hand, the server puts down items to be served at the guest's left, such as a salad. While this procedure is common, there is no reason why the service *has* to move in this fashion, as long as *good service occurs.*

It is proper, after guests have been served and sampled their food, to ask whether everything is satisfactory. Prompt attention should be given to complaints. Servers should never argue with patrons. If necessary, supervisory personnel should be called to the table to correct any problems or smooth over difficulties. It is also wise after service has ended to have some means for addressing problems that have arisen in the dining area during a shift. A problem can be reviewed and discussed, and perhaps a recurrence can be avoided. It is a grave error to allow the same mistakes to occur over and over again without making an attempt to correct them.

TYPES OF SERVICE

The type of service an operation uses depends on the type of establishment and its clientele. Putting good of service into effect is a matter of training people and having the right combination of equipment and atmosphere to make it work. At minimum, a standard for a particular type of service should be achieved so that patrons will be served properly and consistently.

Counter Service

Counter service is fast and usually has a high rate of customer turnover, since patrons can be seated, order, and eat in a short period of time.

Contrary to some thinking, counter service does not necessarily save space. The space needed behind the counter, the service area, counter and seats, plus aisle space for traffic, is rather large. In some cases, seated service requires less space.

A server may have from 8 to 20 seats to serve at the counter. Everything possible should be within easy reach so that the server has little need to go to other parts of the operation frequently. The counter should also be close to the production area to permit orders to be placed, picked up, and served quickly. Work simplification is desirable, and work center arrangements should be studied. The use of a communication system that gets orders into the kitchen without service personnel having to go there to place them speeds service and allows servers more time to help guests.

In some counter-service operations, places may be preset for guests: a placemat, knife, and spoon to the guest's right, and forks and a napkin to the left. Only water and a menu need to be handed to guests when they sit down. Menus and napkins may also be available on the counter for self-service. Water should be placed to the guest's right. If other silverware is needed, it is put in proper position after the guest has ordered.

Good counter service is not easy; it is fast-paced work. The individual doing it must have exceptional organization skills and work quickly. While their minds are constantly on orders and details of service, service persons must also manage to be pleasant and make guests feel welcome. Good teamwork is required with other counter servers and with production personnel. When not serving, it is usually necessary to keep busy cleaning up behind the counter, replenishing supplies, and otherwise organizing the station. Salt and pepper shakers, sugar bowls, and napkin dispensers always need filling;

failure to perform these tasks in slack moments can mean that service goes slowly at peak times. Getting behind can make counter work hard and frustrating. Learning how to keep ahead is essential.

After a guest has been given a check—with a "thank you"—and has paid and left, the soiled dishes should be removed quickly. Some sorting of items is usually desirable. Counters should be arranged so that boxes used for dishware are handy and workers do not have to walk long distances with used tableware. Buspersons should remove bus trays and tubs filled with dirty dishware and replace them with new ones.

Cafeteria Service

In cafeteria service, guests go to a counter and select foods that are dished up by service personnel and then take these foods to a table. There may be modified types, such as in some cafeteria operations where service personnel stand at the end of the line, pick up the tray, and take it to a table for the guest. Water, silverware, and beverages may also be served by service personnel. Good cafeteria service should put about six people per minute through the cafeteria line. A cafeteria line over 50 feet long is usually not as efficient as a shorter one.

A *scramble* cafeteria system is one in which guests go to specific locations to get certain types of foods. For instance, beverages may be obtainable at an island in the center, salads and entrees at one counter, and desserts at another counter. Hot entrees may be obtainable at a central location. None of these locations is connected to another; guests must pick up their trays and move to the next location without sliding trays along in a line. This prevents the formation of long lines and allows the individual who wants only a few items to get them quickly and leave the service area. Thus, patrons do not wait in line while someone else wanting more items takes time to make the selections. Patrons pay as they leave the service area before proceeding to a table. Some cafeteria lines have a checker who adds up the cost of the food on the tray and hands the guest a slip with the total on it. The guest then moves to the cashier and pays the check. In some cases, guests may pay at the door after finishing a meal. If this second method is used, some system needs to be worked out so that a guest cannot go through the line and get food and a check, eat this food, go through the line again for only one or two items, and then use only the smaller check for payment. If every patron picks up a check when entering, and all charges are entered only on one check, a fairly secure system exists.

Some cafeteria lines can move more quickly by having lines where only certain foods are obtainable. Thus, some cafeterias have cold-food or snack-food lines that relieve the hot-food line of patrons who want only a limited amount of food.

Self-bussing of trays may be used. If this is done, the station where guests carry their used dishes should be located on the way out. If this is not done, most guests will walk out and leave their dirty dishes on the table. Many cafeterias find it more efficient to have floor personnel who bus dishes; clean tables; replenish salt, pepper, sugar, and condiments; see that napkins and glasses are available; and do other general dining area work. It is important that they work diligently and establish good procedures for clearing tables.

Buffet Service

Buffet service has the advantage of reducing service personnel, but the disadvantage of being quite wasteful of food. In times of high food cost, the cost of the food may outweigh the advantage of a lower labor cost, with a result that final costs are higher. Normally, a buffet is served at a set price with guests taking whatever and as much as they want. Sometimes food portions may be controlled, as when service personnel serve guests or a service person carves the meat. However, second helpings are usually allowed.

Buffets make it possible to display and merchandise food attractively. They are being used more and more to give simple, fast service for continental or regular breakfasts, light lunches, or for meals where service must be fast and guests wish to come and go quickly. They are also good for handling large numbers of people who may wish to eat at different times. When seated service cannot handle the numbers to be served, a buffet may work best. For instance, the Hawaiian Regent Hotel of Honolulu found that with large tours in the hotel, the seated-service restaurants could not handle the demand. For a set price to tour groups, guests were invited to go to the banquet room of the hotel, in which a buffet was set up. This enabled the hotel to accommodate them adequately with good guest satisfaction. Likewise, special dinners, receptions, luncheons, and other special occasions lend themselves to buffet service.

A *smorgasbord* is a Swedish buffet that includes a large assortment of cold foods after which hot foods and then a dessert and beverage are offered. A true smorgasbord must include pickled herring, rye bread, and Swedish *mysost* or *gjetost* cheese. Similarly, a Russian buffet must include caviar in a beautiful glass bowl (or in a carved-ice bowl), rye bread, and sweet butter.

It is possible for a buffet to be combined with other kinds of service. For instance, guests may pick up only cold foods and order the remainder of the meal. Or they may eat the cold and hot foods and then be served a dessert and beverage, or just a beverage. Water is usually poured by service personnel.

When buffet service is used, dishware, silverware, and a napkin are usually preset on the table for each cover. Plates and other dishes needed for the buffet are set at the front of the line where guests can pick them up. If silverware, napkins, and water are to be picked up by guests, they are usually placed at the end of the line or in a separate area. Desserts may be set on another table. Using separate tables can speed service. It is also faster to have personnel behind the buffet to serve guests than to have guests serve themselves. It is best to have meat carved at a separate station.

Foods served at buffets should be colorful and attractively arranged. It is aesthetically desirable to have different shapes and sizes of dishes. *Réchauds*, *bains-marie,* and other holding units can be used to keep foods hot. The heights of foods and dishes should be varied to give an interesting pattern. Buffet tables can be arrayed with candles, flowers, or more elaborate decorative pieces to give an attractive display.

The buffet table should be neatly spread and have a cover on the front that completely hides the underside and table legs from view. Table linen or snap-drapes in various colors can be used to achieve an interesting effect. The table shape can vary, but consideration should be given to flow, since some shapes will not speed service and may even hinder it.

A good system for replenishing the buffet should be developed. Some buffets have service from both sides, and these are difficult to replenish. The table should be as close as possible to the food preparation point, but this convenience factor will be influenced by service considerations. Some operations may have a rule that when a dish is about two-thirds empty, it will be removed from the table and another, full one put in its place. The one removed is returned to the preparation area to be cleaned and refilled later. Vessels containing food should be about two to three inches from the table edge. Do not have one food in back of another—making guests reach over the food in front—unless the food in front is on tiers so that it is easy to reach.

Food served at a buffet should be of a kind that lends itself to self-service. Items that require a thin sauce or are not easy to handle should be avoided. It is usual to put both cold and less impressive foods first in line. However, the proper sequence may be dictated by the type of food and when it should be eaten during the meal.

Table Service

The foodservice operation that serves its guests at their tables in the familiar way is classified as seated-service establishment. This is the basic, traditional method of serving food and drink. The term is used to distinguish it from other service methods, such as drive-in or carry-out.

There are three distinct types of table service used in this country—American, Russian, and French—and English service is seen occasionally.

American Service

The simplest and least expensive type of seated service is American service. It is also fast and does not require a great amount of labor. The table setting for this service places the knife (blade side in) at the right, the soup spoon next, and the tea spoon next on the outside. Normally settings are made so that the first utensil on the outside, on either the left or right, is used first, then the next utensil to it, moving in as the courses progress. Placing the soup spoon inward from the teaspoon violates this rule, but it is a more common way of positioning the soup spoon. However, it is not improper to put the soup spoon on the outside, where it is used first with the first course, the teaspoon next, and the knife on the inside. The dinner fork and then the salad fork are placed on the left. In the center, a service or hors d'oeuvre plate is set. The water glass is set at the tip of the knife and about an inch away. The coffee cup and saucer are usually placed on the table next to the teaspoon

Exhibit 12.1 American Service Setting

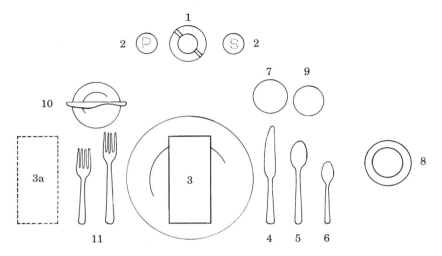

(1) Ashtray, (2) salt and pepper, (3) napkin on service or hors d'oeuvre plate. (3a) an alternate position for the napkin, (4) dinner knife, (5) soup spoon, (6) teaspoon, (7) water glass, (8) cup and saucer, (9) wine glass, (10) bread and butter plate with butter knife, (11) salad and dinner fork. (The salad usually will be served where the napkin is, at 3a, after the napkin is picked up by the guest.)

bowl to speed service. The ashtray and salt and pepper should be in the center. (See **Exhibit 12.1**.)

If a wine glass is used, it is placed to the right of the water glass. The bread and butter plate should be above the forks and perhaps a bit to the left of them. The butter knife should be at a right angle to the forks on the butter plate with the blade turned toward the forks. For a normal meal the table may be covered first with a *silence cloth* and then a table cloth. However, placemats alone may be used for an informal meal. Silverware and dishes should not be any closer than a half-inch from the edge of the table. Chairs should be out from the table, away from the tablecloth.

In American service, food is dished onto plates in the kitchen. The server takes plates to the dining area. Coffee is often served with the meal. The coffee cup and saucer may also be on the table to speed service.

American service, or a modified version of it, is used both in operations requiring fast turnover, such as coffee shops, and in fine-dining restaurants. When it is used in a fine-dining operation, the coffee cup and saucer are not on the table, since hot beverages generally are served later in the meal. Procedures vary with different operations.

It is common to serve foods from the left and beverages from the right, moving around the table from right to left. However, much variation occurs. All clearing may be done from the right using the right hand. The general rule in all service is that when serving at the guest's right, use the right hand; when serving at the guest's left, use the left hand. Whatever method is used, it should be based on what is easiest to do most efficiently and quickly for the guest. It is not proper to remove dishes or to start a new course in American service, or in any other type of service, until everyone at the table has finished eating the present course.

Soiled dishes are removed from the table as follows: items to the left, from the left-hand side using the left hand; central items and items to the right, from the right-hand side using the right hand.

American service is frequently used at banquets because a large number of guests can be handled quickly by a limited number of servers. The banquet head server is responsible for all dining room service. This person directs set-up of tables, arrangements for the head table, setting of silverware, decorations, and, in general, all service. If wine is served, the head server will plan its service. On the average, between 15 and 25 guests will be assigned per server. Buspersons may assist.

French Service

The most elegant service is French service, but it is also slower and more expensive. At one time it was even more elaborate than it is today. It consisted of three or four table settings, with each setting accommodating a number of courses. Guests would sit down and eat all the courses for a given setting. Then they would leave the table while it was being cleaned and reset. They would then sit down again and eat another series of courses. As many as 48 or more dishes might be served at one meal. The goal was for guests to taste many foods rather than eat large quantities. To a large extent, the purpose of all the food was to make for a lavish display. French service reached its peak in the court of Louis XIV. At that time it was called the grand cover (*le grand couvert*). A good part of the service was the ceremony that accompanied each setting and the serving of the courses. The French service of today is descended from this service but has been considerably simplified.

Modern French service is performed from a cart called a *guéridon,* which has a *réchaud* or heating unit on it. The réchaud is usually heated by an alcohol lamp, but some guéridons may be equipped with a small bottle of butane or propane, which fires a gas burner. Food is brought raw, or partially prepared, to the cart, where it is prepared next to the table. Meats, poultry, and fish may be cooked in the kitchen, but they will be carved or deboned on the cart. Some food preparation must occur in the kitchen, and only service is done at the cart. Salads, desserts, and other foods may be prepared completely at the guéridon from raw foods.

Employees who perform French service must be more numerous and more skilled than in any other service. A dining room using a French service has a *maitre d'hôtel* in charge. In Europe, this person excercises much more authority than in the United States. Here, maitres d'hôtel are in charge of making reservations and assigning tables as well as determining service procedures. They may greet guests, and some may even take guests to the table and give them menus. In some operations, the menu may be presented by a captain, waiter, or *chef du rang*. Captains usually supervise about four servers. The *chef du rang* has charge of a table and is assisted by an apprentice, called the *commis du rang*. The dress is usually formal, with servers wearing white gloves. Large napkins, called *serviettes*, are carried on the arm (not under it). Apprentices wear white server jackets with a white shirt, black bow tie, and dark pants.

The chef du rang usually takes the orders and gives them to the commis, who takes the orders to the kitchen. The commis gives the orders to the *aboyeur* (announcer) who, in a loud, clear voice, calls them out. (The aboyeur is said to have been introduced by Escoffier, who wanted to reduce loud talking in the kitchen between cooks and servers.) When the foods are ready, the commis takes them to the chef du rang, who takes them to the guéridon. The commis must also bring plates, dishes, and other items required for service.

As the chef du rang prepares the food on the réchaud or in other equipment and then dishes it onto the service dishes for guests, the commis serves the guests. Service is from the right, with the right hand, except for items to be placed on the left. (If the server is left-handed, the service may differ.) Removal of plates and dishes is usually from the right with the right hand, but this too can vary. Plates and items should not be removed until all individuals have finished eating. Second servings are not given in French service.

If guests want alcoholic beverages before the meal, the chef du rang will take the orders and serve them. However, today some dining rooms allow a cocktail waitress or waiter to do this. A wine steward, or *sommelier*, should bring the wine list, make recommendations, take the order, and then later serve the wine. Glasses should be on the table so that the first wine to be consumed is poured into the glass on the right. The progression is inward, as it is with the silverware. However, some variation in wine glass placement may occur. It is not proper to have wine glasses inverted on the table when guests come in, since this indicates that the room is not ready for them.

All the silverware needed may not be on the table, but will be put down as required. It is not considered proper to have more than three or four pieces of silver on either side at one time. A *service* or *show plate* is usually in the center when the guest is seated, and an hors d'oeuvre plate may be on top of this, if required. The napkin can be put on the hors d'oeuvre plate with the fold to the left, making it possible to pick it up with the right hand so that it opens as it is lifted. It is proper for the server to pick the napkin up, open it, and hand it to the guest. (See **Exhibit 12.2.**)

The dinner fork and other forks should be to the left of the service plate. The cocktail fork can be on the plate on which the item is served, or placed in a position on the service plate so that the diner's right hand can pick it up. The dinner knife is to the right of the service plate with the cutting edge toward the plate. The soup spoon is usually to the right of the knife. The dessert fork and spoon are placed lengthwise across the top of the service plate. If a bread and butter plate is used, it is above and to the left of the

Exhibit 12.2 French Service Setting

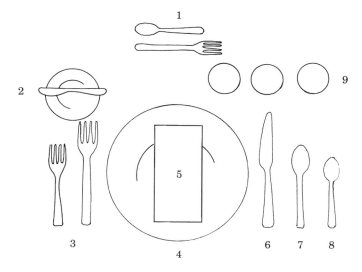

(1) Dessert spoon and fork, (2) bread and butter knife (omitted in formal French service), (3) forks, (4) service plate, (5) napkin, (6) dinner knife, (7) soup spoon, (8) teaspoon, (9) wine glasses.

dinner fork, with the butter knife at a right angle to the dinner fork and the blade facing the forks.

The number of courses in a French meal is limited today. A dinner can consist of a soup, main course, salad, and dessert, served in that order. The salad is served as a separate course after the main course. If there are more courses, an hors d'oeuvre may start the meal, a fish course may then follow, with a poultry course next. The main course should then be served. The salad may be followed by a cheese course. Coffee in a demitasse is proper after the meal.

The service plate is left on the table until the main course is served. It is replaced when the salad course is served and remains until the end of the meal. Soup is brought from the kitchen in a tureen or other container, placed on the réchaud, ladled from there into cups or bowls, and served to the guests.

Different foods require different eating utensils, dishes, and methods of service. The knowledge of what is correct and proper takes considerable study and training. The skill required of the chef du rang is considerable and must be coupled with showmanship.

Fingerbowls are proper after each course, at the end of the meal, and at any other time required. Fresh napkins also may be given at any time during the meal. In very formal French service, rolls and butter are not served, and salt and pepper are not on the table. Water is not served—only wine—

and, at the most, only three wine glasses are in place at a setting. More are placed on the table as needed. Ashtrays are not on the table, since guests are expected not to smoke until the meal is completed. However, if guests request them, they are brought to the table.

The chef du rang usually presents the check and collects the money. The commis clears. In some large dining rooms, the person who comes around with the cart of attractive pastries or other foods may be called the *chef du trancheur. Curry persons* are those who serve condiments and other food accompaniments.

French service usually requires more equipment and space than American or Russian service. French service is designed for the operation that specializes in emphasizing the finest dining, decor, service, food, conversation, and wine. It connotes leisurely dining. French service has many traditions, but modern practice may vary these. Purity for purity's sake is not necessarily the most desirable procedure to bring about good service; some license may be permitted, providing it leads to better service. However, tradition and some of the finer points of French service should be preserved because they help maintain those aspects that give much grace and elegance to dining.

Russian Service

Russian service has great elegance and showmanship. It is also efficient and relatively fast. It requires less labor and skill than French and is also suitable for elaborate banquets.

The table setting for Russian service follows what is common for French service, but a water glass may be on the table just above the tip of the knife, and an ashtray may be on the table. A bread and butter plate and butter knife are also used. Since Russian service is considered slightly less formal than French, the rules for setting the cover are not quite as strict.

In Russian service, the plates for the course to follow are put down in their proper places before the guests. If the food is to be served hot, the plates should be hot; cold foods should be served on chilled plates. Sometimes, salads are brought to the table already dished onto cold plates. To put the plates down for a course, a server uses the right hand to place the item on the right side of the guest. The movement is then to the next guest on the left, and proceeds clockwise. When all plates are in position, the serving dish is picked up by the waiter and held in the palm of the left hand, or by the left arm and palm for a tray or large platter. The right hand serves the food from the serving dish to the guest's plate at the right. Soup may be ladled into soup dishes from a tureen or it may be brought to the table in small, individual serving dishes on a tray. Servers take these, one by one, and pour the hot soup from them into the guest's soup bowl or cup.

Considerable dexterity is required to perform good Russsian service. The silver tray on which the portions of food have been dished can be heavy and very hot. Some servers wrap a towel lightly around their left arm before putting on the jacket to protect the arm from being burned by the hot dish. The serving dish must be held securely and balanced, while the right hand manipulates a large spoon and fork to grasp the portion and move it without spilling it. The right hand holds the serving spoon with its bowl facing up. Directly over this, with the tongs up, is the fork. The spoon is used to scoop up the item while the fork, with some pressure on the top, holds the item on the spoon as it is being transferred to the guest's plate. The spoon can be used to pick up a bit of sauce from the platter and pour it over the plate. The spoon is also used to serve some vegetables and sauces.

Coffee is served after the meal. Coffee cups, saucers, cream, and sugar are not on the guests' table; coffee may be poured from a buffet and served.

English Service

English service, sometimes called formal family service, is most often used in family-run inns and on special occasions in other food services. Foods are brought from the kitchen on platters and in serving dishes. The host, who remains at the table during the meal, carves the meat while the hostess serves the vegetables, salad, dessert, and beverage. The host places the meat portion on a hot plate and then passes it to the hostess, who puts on the other foods and then passes it to a guest. The host is served last, or next to last before the hostess. The meat should be in front of the host, with plates used for service immediately in front of him. It is desirable to work out a passing pattern that requires the least handling of plates. Sometimes servers may take plates and carry them to the guests instead of having them passed. It is proper to have the first course placed on the table when guests come into the dining room. Water can be poured and butter placed on the butter plates. Coffee cups and saucers will not be placed on the table but brought at the conclusion of the meal or when dessert is served. Small tables may be placed to the right and left of the host and hostess where service dishes can be placed when the service is ended. However, servers may remove these.

Place settings may be similar to those used in American service, but they can vary. Normally, knives and spoons are to the right and forks are to the left. The order of placement is from the outside in as the courses occur. Wine glasses are placed to the right of the water glass, which is placed just above the tip of the knife.

Organization for Table Service

The organization of the dining area may vary considerably with different operations. Some food services may have no head of services but will have the task handled by the assistant manager. Some may use a host or hostess who, in addition to supervising the dining room, greets and seats guests. Sometimes the individual in charge is a head server. In the most formal establishments, a maitre d'hôtel performs this task. Whatever form of organization is established should be effective and well managed. The number of hours usually clocked in a food service is substantial, and unless the operation is managed properly, costs can be unnecessarily high. Usually, the ratio of hours used for service, or front-of-the-house, to the hours used for food production, or back-of-the-house, is 10 to 7.

The individual in charge of service should see that service proceeds properly, servers are neat and clean, and they follow established policies. This person should handle any personnel problems and, perhaps, may be responsible for hiring and firing, although management may reserve this right. This person should schedule servers and assign work stations and days off. Work assignments should be made on an impartial and balanced basis. Schedules should be posted sufficiently in advance so that members of the service staff can make personal plans. A rotation system should be used in allocating days off and the stations at which servers will work. In this manner, the same day off will not always fall to the same person and, from time to time, the days off will fall on a weekend. Of course, this can be varied if personnel wish to have the same days off regularly. Any system devised should be fair to all. Some stations in the dining area are better than others because they are easier to work or provide more tips. Unless there is a policy that the service personnel longest on the payroll get these stations, the work stations should be rotated.

A policy should be established for taking breaks and eating meals. Some type of rotation system usually works well. A policy should exist on what can be eaten by the help for free or for minimal payment, and the head of the service or production department may have to check this. Some type of record should be maintained on employee meals so that costs can be calculated.

Room Service

Room service represents an important source of revenue for the food and beverage departments of hotels and motels, as well as a significant factor in the satisfaction of guests. Special organization may be required to give good room service. Some hotels even have special room service production kitchens.

Considerable space must be available so that small mobile tables can be stored and ready to be moved with the items ordered to guest's rooms. Mise en place is extremely important since distances are usually great, and hot foods can quickly cool down and cool foods can warm up. A special service elevator is desirable if the amount of room service is large.

Most hotels and motels with room service have a special telephone number for guests to call for room service. The order is taken and transferred to the proper personnel so beverages and foods can be prepared. Timing is important, since items must be ready at the same time. Service personnel must be trained to assemble all of the tableware required, as well as butter, rolls, and other items.

Many operations follow the practice of having the check time-stamped when the order is received, when it leaves for the guest's room, and when the signed check is brought back.

HANDLING THE GUEST CHECK

After guests have finished eating and drinking after-meal drinks, the check is brought. If the server knows who is to get the check, it can be placed upside down to that person's right. If not, it should be placed in the middle of the table. If there are to be separate checks, this should be known when first taking orders. The check should be totaled and placed on a tray. The server should always say "thank you." It is proper for guests to check the accuracy of the check. Prompt attention should be given to questions about charges.

Some system for maintaining a record of service checks should be established. Each service person, at the start of a shift, should be given and sign for a set of consecutively numbered checks. Later, a consecutive count of checks turned in by guests to cashiers should be made by the accounting department; if the count is made by the service department, problems can occur. Missing checks should be investigated. Some operations charge servers a certain sum for each missing check. Rarely will guests walk out without paying, but this can occur, and it may be necessary to make allowances for it. Some operations say that to anticipate walkouts numbering one-tenth of a percent of sales is not unrealistic.

In addition to its own serial number, a service check should have a space for identifying the server who used it and for showing the number of persons served, the date, and, perhaps, the table number. Only one item should be put on a line on the check. Some checks provide a ticket that the server can tear off and keep as a record. Many different kinds of checks are used. Each is designed to fit some special need of the operation. (See **Exhibits 12.3** and **12.4**.)

When point-of-sale (POS) electronic cash registers or computers are used, servers no longer have to go to bartenders or to the kitchen to place orders. These devices can transmit the order by sending a coded message through to a printer at the bar or kitchen. Even more sophisticated is the use by the server of a small hand-carried POS register. The server can code in the number of the item ordered, and this will send out a signal that will activate the electronic register or main computer so it prints out the order and sends it to the bar or kitchen.

Some operations use checkers, who usually station themselves at the kitchen entrance and review orders coming to the kitchen to ensure that only the foods ordered on the check are taken out. Portions are checked by this individual to see that they are adequate but not too large. The appearance and garnishing of the food can also be inspected at the same time. For instance, if tea is on the tray, the checker will see that a slice of lemon goes with it. Checkers frequently price out individual items and total the bill. The checker should initial it so that the cashier will know it has been checked. Checkers can also act as cashiers. There will be variations on what checkers do in different operations.

There are many occasions for mishandling of checks, especially when ser-

Exhibit 12.3 Full-Service Sales Check

Date 4-13	Server LPG	Table No. 11	No. Persons 4	No. 2370
1				
2				
3	1 mush			4.95
4	1 shr			6.95
5				
6	1 — SALM rice bl. ch			14.95
7	2 — SNAP B-BSc bl. ch			12.95
8	3 — PASTA veg v.o.			12.95
9	4 — LAS fr			10.95
10				
11				
12				
13			SUBTOTAL	63.70
14			TAX	4.46
15			TOTAL	68.16
				No. 2370
Date 4-13	GUEST RECEIPT	Persons 4	AMOUNT OF CHECK	68.16

vice personnel collect the money. If a check goes out at 6:00 PM and is still out at 10:00 PM, one might suspect that the check is being held by the service person as a "floater"—being reused for orders and presented to different guests. To avoid this and other abuses, an operation should establish control procedures.

Missing check reconciliation is done each day by the accounting office, *not* by service personnel. A locked box is provided into which checks can be inserted immediately after they have been rung up on the cash register, thus eliminating floaters. The accounting department or some authorized person should have the key to the box. Often the food and beverage director has a key. The box is emptied whenever cash register readings are taken. A time stamp is also provided to stamp each check with the time the first item is served and the time the check is paid. This indicates how long the check was in use. Some operations allow service personnel to time-stamp the checks; others require that the bartender, host, or hostess do it.

Computers and electronic cash registers automatically time-stamp checks and price items as the order is placed. They make it difficult to use a check again, as a floater, since the machine reads the number, and will reject a check the second time around since the number has already been placed in

Exhibit 12.4 Quick-Service Sales Check

Frank-n-Burger							
Go	Stay						
No. of Items	1	2	3	4	5	W	WO
Hamburger	.70	1.40	2.10	2.80	3.50		
1/4 lb. Burger	.80	1.60	2.40	3.20	4.00		
Cheeseburger	.80	1.60	2.40	3.20	4.00		
Dbl. Chsburger	1.40	2.80	4.20	5.60	7.00		
Combo Meal	2.10	4.20	6.30	8.40	9.50		
Salad	.90	1.80	2.70	3.60	4.50		
Fries	.60	1.20	1.80	2.40	3.00		
Lg. Order Fries	.80	1.60	2.40	3.20	4.00		
Cola-Lg.	.80	1.60	2.40	3.20	4.00		
Cola-Reg.	.70	1.40	2.10	2.80	3.50		
Cola-Sm.	.60	1.20	1.80	2.40	3.00		
Orange-Lg.	.80	1.60	2.40	3.20	4.00		
Orange-Reg.	.70	1.40	2.10	2.80	3.50		
Orange-Sm.	.60	1.20	1.80	2.40	3.00		
Van. Shake	.80	1.60	2.40	3.20	4.00		
Choc. Shake	.80	1.60	2.40	3.20	4.00		
Straw. Shake	.80	1.60	2.40	3.20	4.00		
Coffee	.40	.80	1.20	1.60	2.00		
Milk	.40	.80	1.20	1.60	2.00		
Hot Choc.	.40	.80	1.20	1.60	2.00		

Subtotal _____
Tax _____
Total _____

the machine. (Collusion between the bar person and the server, however, can still make it possible to misdirect funds. For example, the bar person fills the order without putting the check through the machine, the server collects for it and doesn't bring in payment, and the two share it later.)

In some cases, such as hotel room service, checks require special handling. Checks are usually issued to room service personnel, and when an order is placed, they are filled out and placed with the order. A record must be maintained of which room service checks are out and who has them. **Exhibit 12.5** shows one form used to keep track of room service checks. (Chapter 9 describes other methods to control checks and to maintain records.)

When guests have charges put on their bills, as in a hotel or club, it is important that these charges be forwarded promptly to the accounting department. Some hotels give a guest a code number that identifies his or her account. When a charge is given to a cashier by a guest, the total of the charge, the department where the charge is being made, and the guest's code number are put into the cash register. Electronic registers or computers are connected with the accounting department, so charges are automatically put on the guest's bill as they are made. This prevents hotel guests from checking out before all charges are on their bills.

Exhibit 12.5 Room Service Control Sheet

ROOM SERVICE CONTROL SHEET
Coffee Shop

PERSON RECEIVING ORDER	ROOM NUMBER	NO. OF GUESTS	WAITER'S NAME	TIME ORDER PLACED	TIME ORDER LEAVES	TIME TRAY PICKED UP	CHECK NUMBER

DAY OF WEEK_____ DATE_____ HOTEL_____

Tipping

Some guests indicate on a sales check that a tip is to be given to an employee. The amount of the tip is noted by the accounting department and added to the employee's wage check. However, some operations pay the employee the amount of these tips each day. For this it is necessary to maintain a *charge summary sheet*. The information required on this sheet is compiled before checks are sent to the accounting department for posting. Usually this information includes the check number, tip, and total charge. The total column is also a cross-reference to balance guest charges. (Tax and miscellaneous information are not necessarily recorded.) The employee getting the tip should sign for it in the "tip received" column to substantiate the paid-out tips reading on the register or to reconcile the cash. This is also proof that the service person received the tip. The sheet is turned in to the food and beverage department daily.

Tipping varies from 10 to 20 percent of the total bill, depending on the style of service; 15 percent is common. The term originated as an abbreviation of "to insure promptness." It was—and is—given as a token of appreciation for service above the ordinary. There is no reason for patrons to tip if the service is mediocre or poor. In fact, no guest should be expected to encourage continued poor service. It is common for servers to give about 15 percent of their tips received to buspersons or others who have assisted in service.

SUMMARY

Good service is crucial for a menu to fulfill its purpose. Good service requires many things; proper preparation, courteous and helpful order taking, and rapid and efficient service. Servers should follow established procedures for the kind of service being given. Major kinds of service are counter, cafeteria, buffet, and seated service. Seated service includes American, French, Russian, and English service. Each requires different table settings and number and tasks of service personnel. Dining rooms can be organized differently according to kind of service and need. Service should be concluded with a courteous presentation of the bill. Controls can be established to ensure that checks will be handled carefully.

QUESTIONS

1. What are the most important considerations involved in getting ready for service (*mise en place*)? In greeting guests?
2. What are the major differences between French and American service?
3. What are the advantages and disadvantages of buffet service?
4. What are the primary responsibilities of the person supervising the dining room?
5. Describe some common methods used for controlling guest checks.

13

Management by Computer

Objectives

After reading this material, you should be able to:

1. Explain uses for the computer in front-of-the-house activities, including guest sales transactions, server productivity reports, sales analysis, and sales forecasting.
2. Describe uses for the computer in back-of-the-house activities, including purchasing functions, and vendor transaction.
3. Describe various financial reports generated by computers.
4. Explain the role of computer-generated reports in management decision making.

INTRODUCTION

It is hard to imagine that only 20 years ago, the only computers were monstrous mainframe machines that could take up an entire city block. Today there are over 100 million personal computers in use world-wide, and the number is growing by millions per month. Restaurants, except huge chains, couldn't afford mainframe computers, but today, even the tiniest operation can have the power of a computer for use in business analysis. We truly are entering a new age in business. We have left the Industrial Age and have entered the Information Age.

Exhibit 13.1 shows the way computers can be used in foodservice facilities. The foundation of any system is made up of both front-of-the-house and back-of-the-house applications. When combined, these two applications supply the data required for management decision making. The various applications are listed in rough order from the most fundamental applications at the bottom of each box to the most complex applications toward the top. The ordering of these applications revolves around two factors: the amount of input or raw data entered into each application, and the usefulness to management of the resulting output.

Exhibit 13.1 Computer Applications in the Foodservice Industry

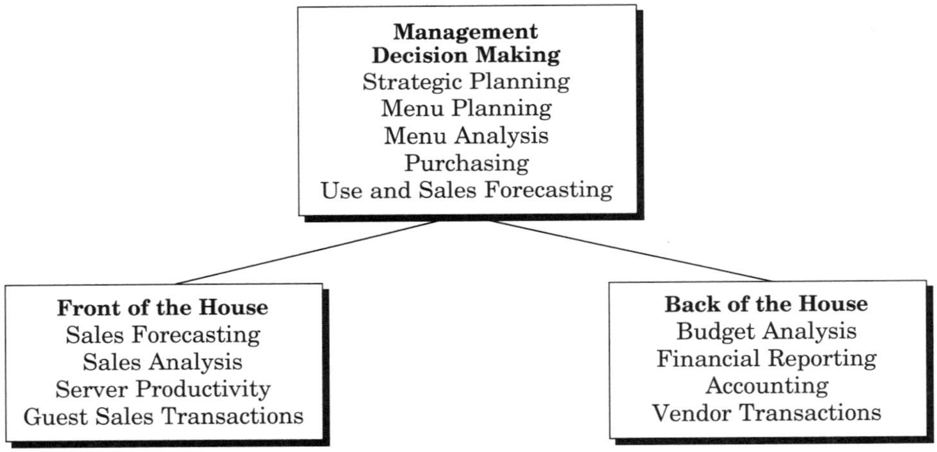

> **Management
> Decision Making**
> Strategic Planning
> Menu Planning
> Menu Analysis
> Purchasing
> Use and Sales Forecasting

> **Front of the House**
> Sales Forecasting
> Sales Analysis
> Server Productivity
> Guest Sales Transactions

> **Back of the House**
> Budget Analysis
> Financial Reporting
> Accounting
> Vendor Transactions

Once the foodservice manager knows *what* computers can do, the question is *how* to get the computer to do these tasks. There is a wide range of software available to do the tasks required. We will look at generic software packages, general application software, and then industry-specific software. While discussing these program categories and how they can perform the tasks required, we will also discuss *who* in the foodservice organization must work with computers.

FRONT-OF-THE-HOUSE COMPUTER APPLICATIONS

In those operations where computers are used, by far the most computer equipment is found in the front of the house. It is easier to computerize the front-of-the-house since the old-fashioned cash register has already mechanized the many activities found there. Also, since this is where cash is handled, operators are especially concerned about maintaining tight controls.

Guest Sales Transactions

In Exhibit 13.1, guest sales transactions are shown as the first building block of computerization. Guest sales transactions are those associated with the cash register: recording sales, totaling the bill, and recording how the bill was paid. In an operation that does not require guests to pay directly for what was consumed (such as a hospital or military foodservice facility), there is still the necessity to record the quantities of food dispensed. The recording of what was consumed is vital for further analysis. Production figures (quantities produced of a recipe item) alone do not tell the whole story. The amount consumed versus the amount left over tells the manager how to adjust future production of the item to reduce waste or even to remove a particularly disliked item from the menu cycle.

Computers that record guest sales transactions are called *point-of-sale (POS) equipment*. Many POS vendors enhance their product with report-generating capabilities that encompass most front-of-the-house activities as well as some back-of-the-house reporting. As with most things in life, you get what you pay for: the more sophisticated POS machines cost much more than simple computerized cash registers.

The typical POS system has a preset keyboard. (See **Exhibit 13.2**.) The keyboard is divided into sections and menu items are shown in each section. The user presses buttons in the appropriate section for the specific menu item and that item is recorded by the POS as a sale. The usual system includes a guest check printer (shown in the figure) or a receipt printer, the preset keyboard, some form of display in order to show the user what he or she has done, and a cash drawer (optional, as cash drawers may be used by individual servers and located away from the machine itself). Options include remote terminals for use throughout the dining room, remote terminals in the kitchen or bar area to show the cooks or bartenders what orders to produce, disk drives for recording transactional data, a printer for printing management reports, and an electronic link to an operation's other computers.

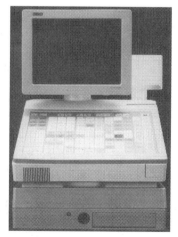

Exhibit 13.2 Computerized Cash Register with Preset Keyboard

Courtesy of NCR Corporation, Dayton, Ohio.

Exhibit 13.3 Computerized Guest Check

Courtesy of NCR Corporation, Dayton, Ohio

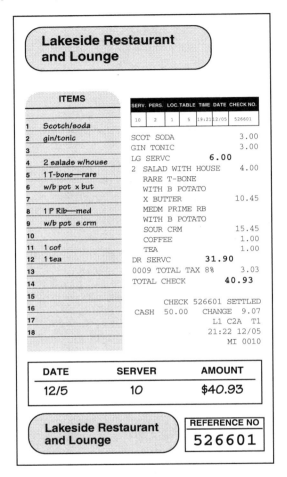

DATE	SERVER	AMOUNT
12/5	10	$40.93

Some POS systems use a light pen or other reading device that the server can use to point to an item on a screen or to read a bar code (as seen in supermarket checkout lines). **Exhibit 13.3** shows a bar code on the guest check, which the POS reads when the check is inserted into the machine. This allows the computer to bring forward a *pick-up balance* (those subtotals shown in Exhibit 13.3 in bold large type and called "TOTAL CHECK"). Other systems have a computer keyboard on which the user types short command codes. Voice recognition systems are becoming practical, although few if any have been installed in the foodservice industry.

The usual procedure for transacting a guest sale is to take the order from the guest and write the items ordered on the guest check. The server then proceeds to the POS terminal to begin a new transaction by inserting the guest check into the printer and then entering the server number, table occupied, number of guests, and items ordered. The POS then prints the various items on the guest check and then prints a total for the items ordered. In sophisticated POS applications, the various items ordered are routed to remote terminals in the kitchen depending on which kitchen worker is responsible for producing the item. Hence, an order for a salad item would go to the terminal in the salad station, while an order for a grilled item would be transmitted to the fry cook's station. Such systems are very complicated, requiring a great deal of time to set up and "debug." Their complexity may also lead to a resistance to change the menu due to the cost and time involved in reprogramming the system.

This whole process can be shortened by having servers carry a device in which the order information is punched and then sent to the computer, which is then activated to send the orders to the various stations.

As guests order items throughout the meal, the server writes the items on the guest check and takes the check to the POS terminal. There the server inserts the check, types in the check number (if there is no bar code on the check), and the POS system adds the new items to the previous balance and computes a new sales total. After the meal, the server presents the bill to the guests, collects the payment from the guest, goes back to the POS terminal, and settles the check. A settled (closed out) check copy is presented to the guest as a receipt.

A variety of reports can be retrieved from a POS system. An *open check report* shows which guest checks have not yet been closed out and for which the company has not received payment. These checks could represent *skips* (people leaving without paying), input errors by servers, or a failure by the server to deposit the payment into the system.

Another report is the *charge tip report*. Charge tips must be reconciled with the amount charged by the POS for sales and tax, thus providing the Internal Revenue Service with a record of tip transactions. Servers should be warned that these tip amounts are easily audited, and that it is their duty to report all tips received but, most importantly, those recorded through the POS system.

Study of guest satisfaction can be performed by management by taking the total charge sales where a charge tip is shown and calculating the tip percentages left to the various servers. Those servers with high tip percentages presumably have found a way to increase guest satisfaction. These results could be useful in training those providing lower guest satisfaction in addition to providing management with a guide to who might bear watching for ideas on how to increase guest satisfaction.

Server Productivity Reports

One of the most rudimentary reports a POS system can provide is a report showing the sales each server makes during a shift. While on any one night server sales averages may be affected by a multitude of events beyond the server's control (such as having a less desirable station in the dining room,

Exhibit 13.4 Server Productivity Report

Server	Today's Shift	Today's Sales	Customer Count	Average Sale	30-day Sales	30-day Sales Average
Betty	Lunch	$218	49	$ 4.45	$ 4,702	$ 4.05
Pam	Dinner	455	43	10.58	9,885	10.68
John	Lunch	193	42	4.59	5,012	4.22
Sue	Dinner	410	41	10.00	10,010	10.85
Lunch Average		$205	45	$ 4.52	$ 4,857	$ 4.14
Dinner Average		433	42	10.29	9,948	10.77

or serving poor tippers) trends emerge over time that indicate the server's overall productivity (assuming negative events are evenly distributed among servers). One such report is shown in **Exhibit 13.4.**

Notice in this report that Betty served more customers today than John. But John sold slightly more to each customer than Betty did. (This advantage of John's ability to sell shows up more clearly in the 30-day Sales Average column). While the difference is small (about a 5 percent difference between the two servers), a more detailed analysis may show that John is consistently selling more desserts than Betty is. Such user-defined custom analysis is possible using many software packages and is generally called "what if" analysis.

Other server productivity analyses may include: *sales per hour* (showing how productive the employee is regardless of how long they work), *item sales analysis* (showing the ability to "sell up" or convince customers to buy more expensive items), *group sales analysis* (showing how well an employee sells extras like soup, salad, appetizers, and desserts), and *specials analysis* (an analysis of who sells those items selected for special promotions).

One report often touted by POS machine salespeople is the *payroll report*. The servers must log on to the POS system at the start of their shift and log off at the end. A report can be produced showing the hours worked for each employee. Care must be taken not to violate the Fair Labor Standards Act, especially those provisions that relate to start and finish times. The start time for an employee is the time he or she arrives at the job site, so all time spent changing into a uniform or in setting-up the dining room is time for which the employee must be paid. There is no substitute for a time clock located at the employee's entrance to the establishment for recording times on and off the job. Computerized time clocks can be used that do much more of the payroll work than simply recording times in and out.

Most POS equipment has limited capability to store more than one shift or one day's transactions, so the ability to transfer the daily data into another computer for cumulative analysis is important.

Sales Analysis

Most of the same analysis done on a per-server basis can be performed on a per-shift or per-day basis. A POS system can print out a report showing the sales and numbers sold for each menu item. It may also show an analysis of sales by time of day. One example of such a comprehensive report is shown in **Exhibit 13.5**. In this case a computer has received the information directly from the POS on each of the past 30-days and produces a report showing not only the daily sales results but the 30-day moving average results as well.

The unit sales report in Exhibit 13.5 shows only the entrees from the menu, but it could show all the menu items and subtotals for each group. Another report often run from the POS system is one showing the food cost per item and the gross profit margin (the sales received minus the food cost). Since food cost fluctuates due to market conditions, waste reports coming out of a POS system generally serve as a rough guide only. The manager is much better served by relying on reports generated through a back-of-the-house system run after the food cost has been recalculated to take current market prices into effect.

Sales Forecasting

To forecast sales, managers can assume that past sales are a good indicator of future sales. Sales forecasting usually consists of forecasting for the very near future, often less than two weeks away. Based on history, reservations made so far, forecasts of weather, and special events which may impact sales, the manager can usually come up with a fairly accurate prediction of sales for tomorrow and the rest of the week. Such sales forecasts are used in sched-

Exhibit 13.5   Unit Sales Report

Menu Item	Today's Quantity Sold	Today's Popularity Index	Total Sales Today	Today's Sales Percent	30-day Quantity Sold	30-day Popularity Index	30-day Total Sales	30-day Sales Percent
NY Steak	18	14.4%	$135.00	18.7%	555	14.3%	$ 4,163	18.6%
Filet Mignon	7	65.6	57.75	8.0	208	5.4	1,716	7.7
Hamburger	15	12.0	63.75	8.8	466	12.0	1,981	8.9
Cheeseburger	22	17.6	106.70	14.8	598	15.4	2,900	13.0
Pork Chops	8	6.4	54.00	7.5	285	7.4	1,924	8.6
Lamb	3	2.4	21.00	2.9	99	2.6	693	3.1
Chicken Wings	10	8.0	39.90	5.5	385	9.9	1,536	6.9
Chicken, Grilled	16	12.8	84.00	11.6	415	10.7	2,179	9.7
Fish Sandwich	9	7.2	44.55	6.2	333	8.6	1,648	7.4
Fish, Broiled	5	4.0	28.75	4.0	154	4.0	886	4.0
Shrimp	12	9.6	87.00	12.0	377	9.7	2,733	12.2
TOTAL	125	100.0%	$722.40	100.0%	3,875	100.0%	$22,358	100.0%

uling labor, purchasing supplies, and even in deciding on hours of operation. While this activity is well beyond anything done by a typical POS system, computers can easily be programmed to analyze computerized guest reservation information, historical sales and item popularity data, and apply a *heuristic* (a set of rules programmed into the machine) to compute a sales forecast. One foodservice operation, for example, knows that the day of the week impacts sales, and that a nearby opera house brings in added late night business. This operation programs the forecasting system to look at the previous night's sales (an indication of current business activity) and increase or decrease those figures based on what day of the week it was (hence, if the day was a Tuesday the program adds 15 percent to the sales figures as Wednesday sales are usually 15 percent better than Tuesday's sales) and to add an extra 100 sales because the opera house is going to be open that night. These forecasts can be highly accurate, often achieving an error rate of less than 5 percent. Since each operation's heuristic is different (i.e., each operation has a different set of rules to be put into the program) it is hard to purchase these programs "off the shelf." But savvy operators can use a programmable spreadsheet to forecast sales and achieve similar results.

BACK-OF-THE-HOUSE COMPUTER APPLICATIONS

Back-of-the-house computer systems generally consist of a variety of programs designed to computerize the basic accounting functions. The most generic packages are known as *4GL* software, which refers to the four basic functions of accounting: accounts receivable, accounts payable, payroll, and general bookkeeping. Generic accounting software has only limited use in the foodservice industry since often there are few, if any, receivables (amounts owed the organization by people who have purchased meals). Credit card sales are the biggest receivable item, and there are only a few credit card companies, so their accounts can usually be maintained by hand. The accounts payable function in a foodservice operation can be minimal. Many small operations are on a COD basis with vendors and, hence, owe little. Another dimension to the accounts payable function—vendor transaction recording and analysis—is vital to the foodservice organization. The standard functions of purchasing, receiving, storage, and issuing, and use constitute a chain of events that presents numerous opportunities for costly mistakes to occur. Computers can help the manager stay on top of food costs and significantly boost profits.

The Purchasing Function

Hospitality operations, to operate successfully, must have a large number of supplies. Deciding what is needed, what to purchase, the quantity needed, where to get it, and how much to pay for it is just a part of the work required to have these supplies on hand. In addition, after the need and quantity are established, orders must be placed, received, stored, and issued to users.

The computer was first used in purchasing to keep perpetual inventory records, so the amount on hand could always be available. Today the computer is used to do many more tasks related to the purchasing function.

Computer programs are used to maintain a record of all of an operation's specifications. These can be used each time a particular item is needed. Computers also can inform the purchasing agent of when supplies are low, according to the perpetual inventory records, and must be reordered. This is done by setting the reorder point (ROP) for each item in the computer.

Ordering of inventory items is still often by telephone or in person, but some operations now connect their computers to a *modem* which uses telephone lines. Modems make it possible not only to place orders quickly, but to gather information and prices to help managers make quick buying decisions.

Computers can print out copies of orders placed and send them directly to accounting and other departments that need to be informed that an order has been placed. The computer also can compile a list of orders pending.

While the use of computers in purchasing began slowly, their use in this area undoubtedly will continue. Links between buyers' and sellers' computers will be further perfected, and it is entirely possible that computers will be able to "make" certain buying decisions and even place orders. It is already possible to have a computer transfer an authorization for payment of a delivery upon signing of the delivery order. The operation's bank will automatically be notified of the debit and transfer the funds out of the buyer's account into the supplier's fund.

Computers will no doubt improve operators' forecasting capabilities and accuracy. Computers will be further used to increase accountability for supplies among employees. In fact, one can imagine nearly every technological development expected in the future and see applications somewhere in purchasing.

Vendor Transaction Systems

Exhibit 13.6 shows the flow of information through a typical computerized vendor transaction system. Notice that a sales forecast is used in conjunction with the standardized recipes and a record of the food items on hand (which appears on an inventory report) to determine what items need to be ordered and in what quantity.

An example of an order report is shown in **Exhibit 13.7**. The items may be printed out in a variety of sequences. The most common is a printout of items by type or group (such as all dairy items or all frozen items). Flexible programs allow the operator to choose the way the program sorts out the list, so an operator may print out a list by preferred vendor or alphabetically. No matter how the report is sorted, the reports are used to solicit prices or formal bids from vendors. If prices seem out of line, something that often happens with commodities like vegetables, the manager may wish to revise standardized recipes, make substitutions, or eliminate an ingredient. These revisions to the standardized recipes in turn change the order report.

Exhibit 13.6 Flowchart of a Computerized Vendor Transaction System

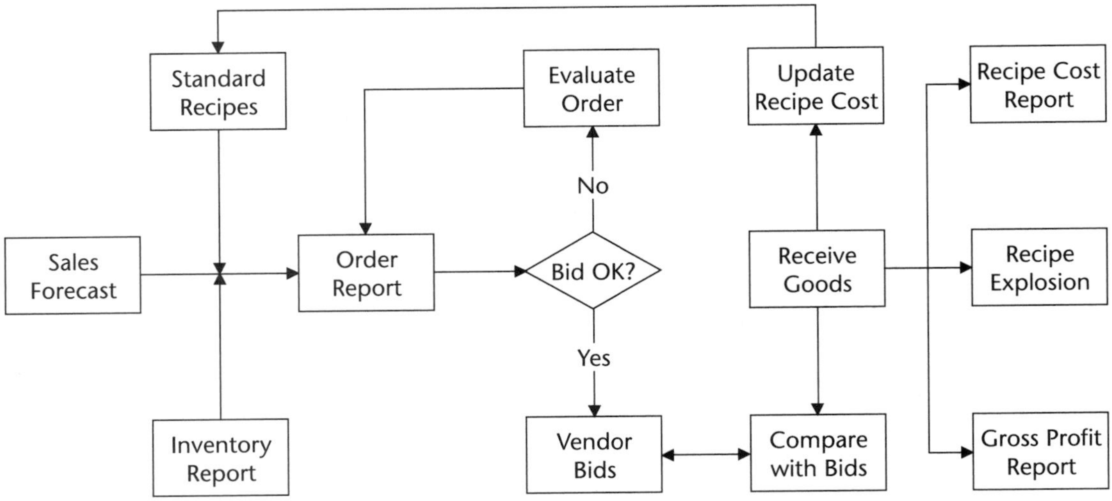

(These changes should be communicated as much as possible to customers to prevent allergic and other dietary reactions.)

Note that the ordering report in Exhibit 13.7 calculates ordering quantities from the greater of either the par inventory amount or the amount actually used. Here again, the computer has to be told how to calculate the reorder amount, and company policy, not the whims of a programmer, should be the source of such calculations. This company obviously believes in having greater inventory and not risk running out. Other operations may follow a different philosophy.

Looking back at Exhibit 13.6, we see that when merchandise is received, a comparison is made of the shipping invoice and the bid amount. Vendors often forget what price they bid, or the bid price is not updated by the vendor in the billing system. Such comparison is easy to do in a computer system:

Exhibit 13.7 Order Report

Item Code	Brand	Description	Last Cost	Par Inventory	Average Usage	On Hand	Order Amount	Bid 1	Bid 2	Bid 3
3.10	K Bros.	109 Prime	4.88	100 lb	98 lb	21.5 lb	78.5 lb			
3.11	SRK	NY Strip	3.91	125 lb	133 lb	75.2 lb	57.8 lb			
3.15	Certify	Tri tip	1.89	55 lb	51 lb	18.8 lb	36.2 lb			
4.01	Select	Veal Leg	1.99	65 lb	48 lb	31.0 lb	34.0 lb			
4.02	K Bros.	Veal Chops	2.89	30 lb	38 lb	28.2 lb	9.8 lb			
4.11	Select	Veal Roast	2.50	25 lb	21 lb	7.7 lb	17.3 lb			
4.88	Select	Sweetbreads	2.25	6 lb	5 lb	2.6 lb	3.4 lb			

the invoice data must be entered in order to update the inventory files. Note that it is at the time of receipt that the standard recipe files are updated with current price information. This is in adherence with good accounting principles and allows for an accurate inventory valuation. The information is also used to produce three reports; the recipe cost report, the recipe explosion, and the gross profit report. Each of these will be discussed later.

Accounting Systems

As mentioned previously, a computerized accounting system usually consists of four components: the accounts receivable system, accounts payable, payroll, and general bookkeeping. Often foodservice operators use the general bookkeeping system to handle the small number of accounts receivable found in most foodservice operations. We have also seen how the accounts payable system can be quite unique and comprehensive, as a part of a cost accounting system. The payroll system is another area that can benefit from computerization.

Computerized time-keeping systems are now available that provide payroll reports breaking down employee hours by shift and by department within each shift. Some time clocks even *interface* (connect) directly to the back-of-the-house computer so that payroll information is available immediately for analysis. Problems often encountered with payroll include the production of paychecks, various governmental payroll reports, and payment of numerous payroll taxes. The payroll laws change constantly, often unexpectedly, and usually at the worst possible time (like just before a payday). In an effort to keep up, many operations rely on outside computer service bureaus to process the payroll and produce the paychecks, tax forms, and deposit notices. These services often are quite inexpensive and may even guarantee their work. Using their services also can verify thorough practices in case of an IRS audit. Managers who do their own payroll should be aware that they will have to upgrade their payroll software periodically, probably at least once a year, in order to stay in line with new laws. Given the costs of these software updates in both time and money, a service bureau may be the most economical choice.

The program most often used by those wishing to computerize their accounting is the *general ledger program*. The general ledger is a record of a company's assets, liabilities, owners' equity, revenues, and expenses. A good software program can tie all the various transactions together and can produce a set of financial statements on a timely basis. The most important advantage of this is that timely financial statements allow management to make decisions before a crisis has occurred; to act "proactively."

Financial Reporting

There are others beside the foodservice manager who want to know how a business is doing. These include owners, lenders, the government, and a host of other people who may have a stake in the company. Accordingly, and under strict rules of accounting, the organization must produce a periodic series of financial reports. A computerized accounting system helps managers produce these reports, which include the balance sheet, income statement (or profit-and-loss statement, or statement of revenue and expenditures), and statement of cash flow.

Budget Analysis

Budget analysis reports compare actual financial results of operation with budgeted figures. In many operations, these are the true "report card" for how management is doing. The budget process consists of forecasting sales and costs for a period. However a budget is arrived at, the budgeted amounts are entered into a computer and the accounting software packages use those figures to produce reports showing the actual results, budgeted amounts, and comparisons of these figures. (See **Exhibit 13.8**.)

COMPUTERS AS A TOOL IN MANAGEMENT DECISION MAKING

Use and Sales Forecasting

When the front-of-the-house system and the back-of-the-house system are coordinated, managers have the information necessary to make key decisions. The most common type of decisions involve those dealing with forecasting sales and use. *Use forecasts* predict how much labor and materials will be used during a period—a day, week, or longer. At this level of decision making, forecasts rarely exceed one fiscal year in length.

Once a consistent popularity index has been obtained, the computer can perform *sales forecasting* menu item with a minimum of assumptions from management. Predicting sales is done two ways. A manager might predict, for instance, that gross sales will increase by 5 percent next month. Using this figure, the computer runs a sales forecast in which the forecasted gross sales figure is broken down into sales per menu item. **Exhibit 13.9** shows one simplified printout using this technique.

Exhibit 13.8 Budget Comparison Report

Account	Actual	Budgeted	Variance $	Variance %
Food Sales	$35,000	$30,000	+ $ 5,000	+ 0.16%
Bar Sales	15,000	10,000	+ 5,000	+ 0.50
TOTAL	$50,000	$40,000	+ $10,000	+ 0.25%
Food Costs	12,250	9,900	+ 2,350	+ 0.24
Bar Costs	3,000	2,000	+ 1,000	+ 0.50
TOTAL	$15,250	$11,900	+ $ 3,350	+ 0.28%
Gross	$34,750	$28,100	+ $ 6,650	+ 0.24%

Exhibit 13.9   Sales Forecast Using Increase in Gross Sales

	Menu Price	Actual Popularity Index	Forecasted Sales	Units Sold
Beef	$4.50	41%	$ 5,513	1,225
Lamb	4.75	17	2,363	497
Chicken	3.75	42	4,725	1,260
TOTAL		100%	$12,601	2,982

Note that the forecasted sales column reflects the 5 percent increase in sales forecasted by management. The units sold column is used in production estimation and is simply the item forecasted sales divided by the menu price for that item.

A second way to forecast sales is to use a *bottoms-up* approach of forecasting increases in menu item units sold, multiplying the forecasted unit sales by the sale price of the item, and then totaling the item sales figures. This procedure is best when management is considering using promotions aimed at increasing sales of specific menu items, such as featuring a special item or using coupons. The effect of these marketing techniques on item sales can be significant. Spreadsheet programs are ideal for analyzing sales since many different marketing strategies can be compared in a very short time.

Use or production forecasts and sales forecasts are produced together. They depend on each other, since sales forecasts are needed in order to calculate production forecasts, and production forecasts often lead to buying decisions that affect sales forecasting. For example, if sales become large enough that an operation can place a very large order with a vendor for some item, such as shrimp, then the volume purchase may become the basis for a marketing promotion built around shrimp. This decision would, in turn, affect the sales forecast. These circular decisions are frequently encountered when making management decisions, so the ability to quickly analyze a wide variety of options is critical.

Recipe Files and Reports

Computer files of standardized recipes provide managers with information concerning the cost of producing menu items, and a tool for forecasting future use. The invoice data entered into the computer can be used to generate several reports. One is a revised *recipe cost report*. The computer also can access a standardized recipe file and update it with a use forecast to make a recipe cost report in which the recipe has been resized to the number of servings anticipated by the forecast. A recipe cost report is shown in **Exhibit 13.10**. Amounts are shown in terms of total recipe amounts (the costs involved in producing one recipe of the item as required by the forecast) and in terms of individual serving cost.

Exhibit 13.10   Recipe Cost Report

Item:	Teriyaki Steak w/ Mango		Yield: 24	Sale Price: $4.75		Cost: $1.57 Cost Percent: 33.1		

Item #	Item	Description	Quantity	Yield %	$ Cost	P/S Size	$ P/S Cost
3.310	Flank Steak	Trimmed	6.0 lb	100.0	17.28	4.0 oz	0.72
80.117	Soy Sauce	Brushed on	3 tsp	100.0	0.30	0.125 tsp	0.01
18.139	Mango, Haden	Peeled, sliced	6 ea	44.6	5.94	0.25 ea	0.25
80.125	Teriyaki Glaze	Brushed on	18 oz	100.0	2.98	1 oz	0.12
18.311	Fruit Salad	Menu Item	96 oz	100.0	5.68	4 oz	0.24
79.31	Sesame Seeds	Toasted	0.5 cu	100.0	2.25	0.0416 cu	0.09
18.208	Mint Leaves	Sprig	3 ea	80.0	1.08	0.0416 ea	0.05
81.101	Fruit Dressing	Ladle	36 oz	100.0	3.28	1.5 oz	0.14

The printout of all standardized recipes for a menu is useful for managers who may wish to re-evaluate certain recipes due to current price conditions or when recipe sizes no longer make certain items cost effective (such as when too small a demand means that large packages of expensive foods are being wasted). But a recipe cost report is not as useful for that purpose as a *buying list*, which totals ingredients for all recipes and tells the manager what total quantities of all food items are required to produce the menu for that day.

Once the recipes have been established and the manager is ready for production, then the manager can have the computer produce a recipe *explosion*. The computer explodes a recipe using the desired portion amounts based on the day's forecast. A recipe explosion is shown in **Exhibit 13.11**.

The last use report the computer can generate for recipes is the *labor report*. This report takes into account all recipes to be produced, how long they will take to produce, and who produces each one. These reports are normally possible only when the operation has designed customized software. The problem is further complicated by individual skills and abilities. Often certain workers are better able to produce certain recipes than are others. The operator must then assign production to those best able to produce a quality product in a reasonable time.

Purchasing Decisions

At the management decision-making level, purchasing involves decisions that may affect operations for years. The decisions to buy preportioned foods, precooked foods, or large quantities of frozen foods at optimum price levels to store for long periods of time greatly affect the operation. Purchasing in large quantities to take advantage of volume discounts may mean that management must create innovative merchandising campaigns in order to sell in such volume. Or world conditions may change the way the public accepts a product, such as the impact on African lobster tails of the embargo on South

Exhibit 13.11 Exploded Recipe

RECIPE NO. 2520

ITALIAN SPAGHETTI & MEAT SAUCE	99 EL. SERVINGS	99 SEC. SERVINGS

PREPARATION CONTAINER: STOCK POT OR KETTLE   PAN SIZE: 12 x 20 x 1½

SERVINGS PER PAN	TEMPERATURE	ELEM. PORTION	SEC. PORTION	PANS REQUIRED ELEM.	SEC.
33	155–165°F	6.2 OZ (AC)	6.2 OZ (AC)	3.00	3.00

GROUND BEEF, USDA   9 LBS

ONION, FRESH, CHOPPED   1 LB 2 OZ

    WHEN PREPARED AS STATED, THE YIELD SHOULD BE
    1 LB

GARLIC, FRESH, GROUND   1¼ OZ

    PARTIALLY BROWN MEAT. ADD ONION AND GARLIC.
    FINISH BROWNING. DRAIN EXCESS FAT.

TOMATO PUREE   4 LBS 8 OZ *OR* ¾ NO. 10

TOMATO PASTE, MKT.   3 LBS *OR* ½ NO. 10

WATER   3 QT

SUGAR, GRANULATED   1/2 OZ *OR* 1 TBSP ¼ TSP

SALT   2 OZ

WORCESTERSHIRE SAUCE   2¼ TSP

OREGANO FLAKES   ¼ OZ *OR* 2½ TSP

BASIL FLAKES   ¼ OZ *OR* 1 TBSP ¾ TSP

    ADD TO BROWNED MEAT. SIMMER ONE HOUR. STIR
    TO PREVENT BURNING. REMOVE FROM HEAT.

CHEESE, PROC., USDA, GRATED   3 LBS 1 OZ

    ADD GRATED CHEESE. BLEND UNTIL MELTED.

COOKED SPAGHETTI (REC. 160)   12 LBS (SEE SEPARATE RECIPE.)

    PREPARE COOKED SPAGHETTI (RECIPE 160). SCALE
    4 LBS OF COOKED SPAGHETTI INTO EACH 12 x 20 x 2
    PAN. POUR 8 LBS 3 OZ (APPROXIMATELY 3 QT +
    3¼ CUP) OF SAUCE OVER COOKED SPAGHETTI IN
    EACH PAN. MIX WELL.

MOZZARELLA CHEESE, USDA   3 LBS

    GARNISH EACH PAN OF SPAGHETTI & SAUCE WITH
    1 LB OF GRATED CHEESE. BAKE AT 350°F (MODERATE
    OVEN) FOR 15 TO 20 MINUTES, UNTIL CHEESE MELTS.

    SERVE 6.2 OZ (APPROXIMATELY ¾ CUP OR 2 NO.
    12 SCOOPS) TO EACH STUDENT.

RECIPE YIELD   38.43 LBS

African products in the 1980s. A whole host of "what if" strategies can be run through computer programs and their financial consequences measured and evaluated. Spreadsheets incorporating macroeconomic models can run to thousands of lines in length. The possibilities concerning management decision making are virtually boundless.

Menu Analysis

Perhaps the greatest benefit of computerization is most apparent in the area of menu analysis. Computerized menu analysis can be performed on a routine basis, even daily if desired. Any of the methods mentioned in chapter 8 can be computerized; only two examples are given here. Hurst's menu score is one example. (See **Exhibit 13.12.**) The effect of daily specials on sales and profitability will change the menu score every day. Maintaining a record of menu scores over a period of several months will help in judging the interplay of daily specials with the regular menu, and even writing new menus.

Another analysis involves scoring various sections of the menu rather than individual menu items, such as beef, lamb, and other red meats; poultry; seafood; and miscellaneous or other. This type of scoring helps menu planners decide which broad categories guests prefer, and which types of items might be added.

Ongoing Menu Planning

The menu analysis stage inevitably leads to further menu planning. Computers provide a much easier and faster way to calculate the possible popularity and profitability of several alternative menus. They can help the operator zero in on the need for major overhaul or simply minor changes. Unfortunately, operations often tinker with menus, adding a few items now and again. The result is usually a horrible mess of conflicting flavors, styles, and tastes that confuses patrons' impression of the establishment and why they chose it in the first place. The generic "road house" menu popular now is an excellent example of this, offering items ranging from Chinese foods to Mexican food to steaks, seafood, barbecue, and everything in between. Patrons can come to believe that all these restaurants are alike, and that there is no compelling reason to go to one versus the other. When this happens, only price can attract more patronage, and few operations can compete for very long on price without suffering a loss in profitability.

One way to avoid this problem is either to follow Harvard strategy specialist Michael Porter's advice to "stick to one's knitting," or to develop at periodic intervals whole new dining concepts. McDonald's is a classic example of the first strategy, while General Foods and its constant development of new dining concepts is an example of the latter. If frequent change is the chosen strategy, then computer analysis of menus and computerized menu planning is crucial.

Menus can be planned using software that reviews a master list of recipes and creates menus based on rotating the items in some pattern of prefer-

Exhibit 13.12 Computerized Menu Scoring Worksheet

```
A1                                                                    READY

          A            B            C          D          E          F
  1                            MENU SCORING WORKSHEET
  2
  3  -------------------------------------------------------------------------
  4          1            2            3          4          5          6
  5      MENU ITEM   NUMBER SOLD  ITEM SALES  FOOD COST  TOTAL SALES  TOTAL FOOD
  6                                PRICE    PERCENTAGES  (2 × 3)     COST (4 × 5)
  7
  8  Shrimp          100         $3.00       33.3%      $   300     $   100
  9  Prime Ribs      500         $4.00       41.0%      $ 2,000     $   820
 10  Turkey          400         $3.00       40.0%      $ 1,200     $   480
 11                                                     $     0     $     0
 12                                                     $     0     $     0
 13  -------------------------------------------------------------------------
 14                  1,000                              $ 3,500     $ 1,400
 15  -------------------------------------------------------------------------
 16
 17          7                          8                       9
 18  MEAL CHECK AVERAGE            GROSS PROFIT            GROSS PROFIT %
 19      (5 ÷ 2)                     (5 − 6)                  (8 ÷ 5)
 20
```

MENU SCORING WORKSHEET

1	2	3	4	5	6
MENU ITEM	NUMBER SOLD	ITEM SALES PRICE	FOOD COST PERCENTAGES	TOTAL SALES (2 × 3)	TOTAL FOOD COST (4 × 5)
Shrimp	100	$3.00	33.3%	$ 300	$ 100
Prime Ribs	500	$4.00	41.0%	$ 2,000	$ 820
Turkey	400	$3.00	40.0%	$ 1,200	$ 480
				$ 0	$ 0
				$ 0	$ 0
	1,000			$ 3,500	$ 1,400

7	8	9
MEAL CHECK AVERAGE (5 ÷ 2)	GROSS PROFIT (5 − 6)	GROSS PROFIT % (8 ÷ 5)
$3.50	$2,100	60%

10	11	12
GROSS PROFIT AVERAGE PER MEAL (7 × 9)	TOTAL MEALS SERVED	PERCENTAGE OF CUSTOMERS EATING MEALS COUNTED (2 ÷ 11)
$2.10	1,500	66.7%

13	REMARKS:
MENU SCORE (10 × 12)	
$1.40	

Exhibit 13.13 Menu Planned by Computer

SERVING PERIOD: F29

				91F Monday/15	92F Tuesday/16	93F Wednesday/17	94F Thursday/18	95F Friday/19
E N T R E E S	SECONDARY (STUDENT CHOOSES 1 OF 5)	ELEMENTARY (STUDENT CHOOSES 1 OF 4)	1	Oven Grilled Cheeseburger on a Bun	French Bread Pizza Boats	Marathon Spaghetti	Oven Fried Chicken	TEACHER PLANNING DAY
			2	Corn Dog	Rib Sandwich on a Bun	Tri-decker Peanut Butter and Jelly Sandwich	Oven Grilled Frankfurter on a Bun	
			3	Hard Cooked Egg	Hard Cooked Egg	Hard Cooked Egg	Hard Cooked Egg	
			4	Cottage Cheese	Cottage Cheese	Cottage Cheese	Cottage Cheese	
			5	Oven Grilled Sausage Sandwich	Egg Salad Sandwich	Meatball Sandwich	Cold Cut and Cheese Sandwich	
F R U I T S A N D	V E G E T A B L E S	STUDENT WILL CHOOSE 2 OF 4	6	Chilled Fruit Cocktail	Chilled Applesauce w/Cherry Garnish	Blue Ribbon Fruit Choices	Chilled Peaches w/Cherry Garnish	
			7	Elementary—OJ Bars Secondary—Juice	Lime Gelatin w/Pears	Juice	Juice	
			8	Whole Kernel Corn w/Butter Sauce	Mixed Vegetables w/Butter Sauce	Southern Style Green Beans	Broccoli w/Butter Sauce	
			9			DO NOT USE THIS LINE		
			10	Wedge Cut Potatoes	Tater Tots		Individual Baked Potatoes	
			11			Maestro Tossed Salad		
	BREAD		12			Honor Rolls	Flaky Biscuit	
	DESSERT Elementary only		13			Oatmeal Cookie of Champions		
	Suggested a la carte Secondary Dessert		14	Butter Cookie	Chocolate Honey Cake w/Frosting	Oatmeal Cookie of Champions	Chocolate Chip Cookie	
	MILK		15	Milk	Milk	Milk	Milk	Milk

ences. Management can choose to specify constraints on the program, ordering it to feature a chicken dish on Sunday or a seafood item on Friday, for example. Other constraining factors may be put in the program such as nutritional constraints, overall cost constraints, or variety constraints. The computer then generates several complete menus for the period and managers choose the best. One menu planned by such a program is shown in **Exhibit 13.13**.

Strategic Planning

Computers are one important tool in making strategic decisions. They provide the information needed by management to make correct decisions and to accurately weigh alternatives. No computer is infallible; the old computer expression of "garbage-in, garbage-out" is still true today, and what comes out of the computer is only as good as the data that goes in. If menu items are not actually produced according to standardized recipes, or if food prices are not updated, or if sales information is incomplete or incorrect, the best computer in the world will not give managers useful information on which to base a decision. Too often failures occur in our industry when managers are not aware of what is really going on at the unit level. A good computer system with tight controls can provide a channel of information through the organization and ensure that top managers get reliable information they need.

Also keep in mind that no computer is smart enough to replace the people responsible for running the company: managers. Computers should never tell managers what to do. Rather, they should provide managers with the calculations needed to make intelligent, informed decisions. While computer experts talk about artificial intelligence and creating computers that can think, this is a long way in the future. How can any computer reflect the lifetime of experiences found in a typical foodservice manager? Computers are a tool, like a knife or an oven, they are a means to an end, not an end in themselves.

SUMMARY

Computers have applications in nearly every area of foodservice operation and management. In the front of the house, they are commonly used to provide managers with automatically totaled guest checks, server productivity reports, sales analyses, and sales forecasts.

In the back of the house, computerized purchasing records—specifications, purchase orders, perpetual inventories, and automatic reorder points—make the purchasing function much quicker. General bookkeeping, accounting, financial reporting, and budget analyses are also made faster and easier by computer programs made especially for hospitality operators.

While computers cannot and should not replace the human element necessary for sound management decision making, they can provide managers with useful information in the form of use and sales forecasts, standardized recipe files and reports, detailed menu analysis, and ongoing menu planning reports. All strategic planning can be made easier and faster using computer applications, provided the information put into the computers is accurate and relevant, and the information is used wisely.

QUESTIONS

1. What are the most common applications for a computer in the front of the house? In the back of the house?

2. What financial reports are possible through a computerized financial reporting system? What is the function of each report?

3. A restaurant manager must plan its staffing strategy for next year. What computerized reports will help this manager make these management decisions? How should these reports be used?

14

The Menu and the Financial Plan

Objectives

After reading this chapter, you should be able to:

1. Explain the need for a menu to cover capital costs and (for commercial operations) contribute to profit.
2. Identify some of the basic costs of going into the foodservice business and indicate how to calculate them.
3. Review some of the methods used to calculate whether a menu is providing an adequate return on investment.

INTRODUCTION

This book has dealt with the menu as a basic document to be used in planning, operating, and controlling a foodservice operation. In the process of our discussion, we moved from a simple definition of the menu as a mere listing of what is offered to a more complex definition. We established the menu as a merchandising tool, and elaborated on that definition to say that the menu is *the* management tool of *primary importance* for initiating and controlling all work systems in a foodservice operation.

This chapter discusses financial aspects of establishing a foodservice operation and how the menu can be evaluated in terms of satisfying the required return on capital investment. When a commercial menu does not produce enough revenue, or when the institutional menu does not stay within reasonable budgetary limits, financial failure is certain to result.

Operators can analyze the operating results generated by a menu and determine whether the menu has met the financial tests placed on it. The menu itself creates financial needs, and it must meet financial burdens to be effective. Several financial tests are used to determine whether the menu meets these tests, and certain strategies help managers adjust menus to meet financial needs.

THE MENU AND FINANCIAL PLANNING

Any menu requires an initial capital investment. The menu will dictate the facilities, equipment, decor, inventory, and space needs. The menu reflects the essence of the operation that is planned and will have a strong influence on atmosphere, staffing, and a host of other factors.

Capital Investment

A well-planned menu can help eliminate or alleviate many capital costs. Many institutions, for instance, can operate quite well with only ovens and steam-jacketed kettles for heavy cooking equipment. It takes a very well-planned menu in order to scale down capital needs to this level. Other operations might need specialty equipment, such as large woks or tortilla-making equipment. These may be quite necessary in certain ethnic situations, but many operations do not have the money or floor space to satisfy only a small portion of their market.

Some equipment is used so infrequently that it is possible to do certain operations by hand. The capital needed to start an operation, be it a not-for-profit hospital kitchen or a for-profit large restaurant, can easily reach hundreds of thousands or even millions of dollars. Regardless of the intended nature of the operation, there will be some pay back of capital required, either in the form of moneys owed to lenders and investors, or in terms of community benefit. The savvy menu planner tries to keep initial capital investments at a minimum so as to maximize the payback ratio.

Food Service: A High-Risk Business

Banks frequently label the industry as "easy to enter without business skill, high-risk, and low-profit." The number of business failures in the foodservice industry is very high—among the highest of any industry. Therefore, controlling business costs is one of the primary management tasks in any foodservice operation. Since cost control is so complex, and the cost of supplies and the amount customers are willing to pay change so frequently, a business can quickly get into financial trouble. Bankers have seen many losses when making loans to the foodservice industry making them quite wary of making new loans.

It usually takes several investors going in together to spread out the capital requirements and risk of starting a new foodservice business. Sometimes limited partnerships are formed with investors who act as silent partners, or small corporations are formed with numerous shareholders investing relatively small amounts of capital. Often these investors are passive, meaning they contribute only capital, while in other situations several people with good professional knowledge of the foodservice business may get together and contribute their expertise, as well as money. Regardless of the type of business formation—corporation, partnership, *limited partnership,* or individual owner—the investor(s) seldom supply all of the capital needed for start-up. Some form of borrowing must take place.

Most foodservice operations require from $500,000 to well over $1 million in capital investment. Lenders frequently require the investors to put up between 20 percent and 50 percent of the total capital cost for an operation. This can mean that the investors must invest between $100,000 and $500,000 of their own money. Franchises may be purchased for as little as $10,000, but the more financially worthwhile ones require the franchisee to invest considerably more. Given these large dollar amounts, one can easily see why lenders and investors are so careful when making a commitment, and why the wise use of the capital investment is so critical.

Running a foodservice operation is a complex task, requiring not only good merchandising skills, but a knowledge of food purchasing, production, and service, as well as high competency in finances. A large business organization can afford to hire managers who specialize in one of these areas, but most foodservice operations are small, and the investor or a very limited group of partner-managers usually try to perform these tasks themselves. The requirement that one person be experienced and successful at such diverse activities means that only a few, unusually talented people are successful running a foodservice operation. This situation may explain why there is such a high failure rate of foodservice businesses. In addition, the foodservice industry is highly competitive. Even hospital, airline, and other institutional foodservice operations are in a competitive environment. Competition means that only the best survive.

The Feasibility Study

Any planning for the opening of a new foodservice operation should include a *feasibility study* designed to answer the basic question: "Will the business pay?" This question, if applied to a commercial operation, should include the phrase, ". . . and turn a profit?" If it is an institution, a better question would be, "Can it be operated within budgetary cost constraints?"

The feasibility study is the detailed report produced to show exactly what the capital investment is to be used for and precisely how the operators plan on generating the revenues to pay back that investment. It must be realistic and constructed from the best available facts and projections. The study must take the broad estimates from the initial phase of considering the project and show a detailed accounting of what really will be designed, built, and purchased. While preliminary estimates, such as using the standard rule-of-thumb of $50 per square foot for equipping a kitchen, were fine for determining the general cost of a facility, such estimates are not good enough for a formal feasibility study. Investors and lenders want to know exactly what their money will be used for, and how their investment will pay off.

Independent contractors will work with an operator to write a feasibility study. These companies usually have expertise in writing such studies, and some lenders give more credence to studies written by well-known firms. They can be expensive (another possible pre-opening capital cost), but if they can convince a banker to lend an operator money, they will be worth the cost.

A typical feasibility study looks like the one shown in **Exhibit 14.1**. The study essentially shows the prospective lenders or investors exactly what the foodservice operation is all about—its concept, the potential market, how it will satisfy the market, what it will cost to accomplish these objectives, and what kind of payback one may expect.

A complete feasibility study can easily be hundreds of pages in length. Accounting firms generally offer services concerning the creation of proforma financial statements. Vendors often can help in writing what equipment will be needed. Marketing consultants can help analyze the market and propose advertising budgets. But with all these parties participating, the operator must not become a passive observer. The manager should understand fully and approve all aspects of the study.

The Short-Form Feasibility Study

A *short-form feasibility study* is no substitute for an in-depth one, but it can help managers and investors see whether a project is worth the time and investment a detailed feasibility study will entail. Suppose a steak house is planned in a downtown area that will be about average in profitability. A short-form feasibility study for this operation is shown in **Exhibit 14.2**.

The example shown states that the project is feasible, although by only $63.83 per day. This represents an *error factor* (financial cushion) of about 2.4 percent ($63.83 ÷ $2,693.67 in sales needed = 0.0236%). This is not a very large margin for error, but at least the investor knows that a more detailed feasibility study is probably warranted. The turnover data can be ob-

Exhibit 14.1   Feasibility Study

		FEASIBILITY STUDY
SECTION	**SUBSECTION**	**DESCRIPTION**
Introduction		Brief summary of the proposed foodservice operation
	Mission	Brief statement of the type of operation planned
	Location	Description of the facility's site
	Capital	Summary of how much it will cost and where the money will come from
Target Market		Purpose of the operation
	Demographics	Who the operation is meant to serve
	Competition	Which other operations directly compete for the same market
	Economy	Overall economy of the market and economic trends
Site Selection		Describes location in more detail
	Community	Description of the community, its history, future, etc.
	Site Location	Specific description of the site
	Traffic Flows	How people will gain access to the site, how many potential customers come by the site, how they will know the operation is there
	Rent vs. Buy Analysis	Analysis of the cost of purchasing the site and building a facility versus renting the site
	License Costs	Cost of all permits, licenses, and fees
	Utility Costs	How accessible utilities are, cost to provide on site
Operation's Concept		What the operation plans on providing the market, how it plans on satisfying that market
	Theme/Style	Description of the theme, ambiance of operation
	Menu	What food and beverages will be offered and when
	Marketing	Promotions and advertising will be used to bring in customers and keep them coming back
Capital Budget		Statements concerning what money is required for opening the operation and what that money will be used for
	Design	The design of all facilities
	Equipment	Equipment needed to operate the facility
	Supplies	Inventories and operating supplies required
	Pre-opening	Detailed list of all money used prior to opening
	Working Capital	List of funds necessary to operate on a continuous basis
Financial Statements		Pro forma statements of projected income and expenses and projected cash flows for a five-year period
	Income and Expense Statements	In a not-for-profit operation, this may be called a *statement of revenue* and expenditures or an *operating budget*
	Balance Sheet	Shows projected assets, liabilities, and owner equity
	Cash Flow	Shows how cash will come into the operation, how it will go out, and how much will be left for debt and as a return on the investment
Staffing Plan		Description of how the operation will be staffed
	Personnel Policies	Policies and procedures concerning hiring, training, compensation, benefits, discipline, and advancement
	Service Standards	Descriptions of what each job requires of an employee; also describes education, experience, and other requirements
	Organization Chart	Shows lines of authority and relationships among employees
Advertising Plan		Description of planned advertising, promotions, and other marketing to be done in the first year of operation

Exhibit 14.2 Short-Form Feasibility Study

SHORT-FORM FEASIBILITY STUDY

Operating Data

Lunch: turnover 2.5 times   Occupancy average: 75%   Check average: $5.00

Dinner: turnover 2 times   Occupancy average: 80%   Check average: $9.50

Bar and special catering income per day (average): $300

Number of seats in restaurant: 100

Closed Mondays, Christmas, and New Year's Day; average days of operation per year: 312

Return on investment desired: 12%

Net profit before taxes projected: 5%

Feasibility Data

Amount invested $350,000

Return on investment ....($350,000 × 12%) = $42,000

Sales needed @ 5% profit to yield ROI..................................($42,000 ÷ 5%) = $840,000

Average check required to yield sales*.......................................$7.07

Number of checks needed to produce sales ....($840,000 ÷ $7.07) = 118,812 checks needed

Checks per day needed ....(118,812 ÷ 312 days) = 381 checks per day

Income per day needed ....($7.07 check average × 381 checks) = $2,693.67

Estimated Income per Day

Lunch: 100 seats × 75% occupancy × 2.5 turnovers × $5.00 check average...............................$937.50

Dinner: 100 seats × 80% occupancy × 2 turnovers × $9.50 check average...............................$1,520.00

Bar and catering business per day $300.00

Estimated income per day $2,757.50

Income needed per day $2,693.67

Income surplus per day...$63.83

Detail of how to calculate average check:

		CALCULATION	LUNCH	DINNER
1	Seats	from part 1	100	100
2	Occupancy percent	from part 1	0.75	0.80
3	Turns expected	from part 1	2.5	2
4	Checks required	Line 1 × 2 × 3	187.5	160
5	Check	from part 1	$5.00	$9.50
6	Total	Line 4 × 5	$937.50	$1,520.00
7	Overall average check	Total in line 6 ÷ total in line 4		$7.07

---

tained from observing potential competing restaurants in the target area, or from averages obtainable from the National Restaurant Association. (The check average can be calculated from the proposed menu the various items' popularity indexes times the sale price per item). The estimated bar business can be arrived at by observing potential competitors.

Location and the Market

One of the most important factors affecting the success of a food service is *location*. Location alone may be decisive in determining whether the operation even has a market. Some have put it more emphatically. The Pioneering hotelier, E.M. Statler, once remarked, when asked what three things a hotel had to have for success, that it was "Location, location, location."

Some operations get 95 percent of their patrons from within a relatively small area, while others may have to try to lure them from a considerable distance away. It is important to know how many potential customers go by the door, either on foot or in a car. It is also important to know whether or not they *might* come in. For instance, an operation might be successful on one side of the street and unsuccessful on the other side. For example, on the Ohio State Turnpike, patronage at a rest stop restaurant was good from westbound traffic but poor from eastbound traffic. It was found that people traveling west had set a goal—to reach the state border—and eastbound travelers had not.

The speed of traffic also may be important. Signs must be strategically set to coincide with speed so that people can see them ahead and make plans to stop, but not so far ahead that they forget they wanted to stop. The orange roof of Howard Johnson's and the golden arches of McDonnell's were designed purposely to show up some distance away so that motorists could identify the unit before they come to it.

An operation also must be suited to its traffic. A quick-service or carryout operation may do well near a public transit center, but a sit-down unit may not. People are in a hurry to catch their trains and want something quick.

Parking can be important for some locations, though not for others. A food service in an area to which people come in cars should have parking spaces for a fourth of the house seats. An establishment on a highway should have one parking space for every two seats.

The location should be investigated for environmental factors. The location may be undesirable because it is in a deteriorating neighborhood, or it may be desirable because it is in a growing or trendy area.

Competition should also be checked. The effect of it can vary. It may be harmful if the new operation will be in direct competition with existing services. However, it may not be harmful if it is a complementary type of operation. Many food services may be in close proximity to each other but each, by emphasizing a different product, do well. Thus, within a block one may find a McDonald's, a Kentucky Fried Chicken, an International House of Pancakes, and an Arby's—all doing well. However, if two operations in the same area offer identical or similar products, one or the other seems to fade away.

A market may already exist for a certain location, or there may be a market potential that must be developed. Even with an existing market, it should be well researched because it may not be durable. A very popular owner may sell, and the buyer may think the operation itself has inherited the clientele, only to find that the market has followed the former owner who has set up in a new location. Unless a market is well established, well defined, and can be held, it is best to interpret market projections conservatively. Studies show there is a tendency to overestimate, rather than underestimate, markets.

It is important to get an estimate of the number of potential customers. A close examination of the market is also necessary. Income levels, social habits, eating patterns, ethnic background, age level, sex, and many other factors about potential customers must be investigated as thoroughly as possible when designing an operation and a product for the market.

Good market studies ask questions such as the following.

- Who are the customers or potential customers? Can they be well defined?
- What do they want? Can it be produced for them at a price they want to pay?
- Why will they come to this establishment?
- What are their incomes? When do they get paid?
- What is their age level?
- What is their background?
- How many potential customers are there in the area?
- What percentage of these will come in on a single day?
- Where does the market eat now? What do they eat?
- What is the competition for this market?
- Is the market steady and reliable?

Own, Rent, or Lease?

To determine initial capital costs, it is important to look at how the operation is to be established. There are a number of ways in which a foodservice can be established. How an operation is established will identify the costs that must be paid by the foodservice owner/operator. A new building can be erected on a site with land, equipment, and furnishings belonging to the owner. Or the land can be leased, with the landowner putting up the building and equipping and furnishing it. Or the site and building can be built by someone else and leased; the owner of the building then furnishes and equips it. Sometimes furnishings and equipment are leased.

There are various ways to make arrangements to rent or lease a building and its furnishings. A straight rental of so much per year, per month, or for a certain period, such as five years, may be arranged. This rent may be 2 to 20 percent of gross sales, depending on what is included. The highest rent would be for a *turnkey operation*, called a grade 4 lease, with everything ready to go. Even some utilities may be paid by the landlord. A *net, net, net* lease is one in which the business owner pays rent, taxes, and insurance. In a *net, net* lease, the operator pays only the rent and taxes. A *net* lease means that only rent is paid, and the owner of the building pays rent and taxes and insurance on the property. The owner of the business, and not the landlord, usually must carry insurance on equipment and furnishings he or she owns. When the landlord owns them, the procedure will vary.

The length of the lease is also variable. If the operator has a good track record in business, the lease may be written for ten years. Because of the instability of many food services, leases often run for five years or less. The lessee must usually guarantee the lease. This guarantee may require that two to four months rent be applied on the final months of the lease. Options to renew the lease may be included. Transfer of the lease may be allowed only with the property owner's approval. The seller of the lease may be able to get the lease guarantee back from the new buyer.

A grade 3 lease is one covering an improved building shell with food preparation equipment in it. New furnishings and some decor and other changes may be required. Rent is lower than for a grade 4 (*turn-key*) operation.

A grade 2 lease is for a slightly improved shell. It should include partitions, finished floor (carpet, tile, and hardwood), finished coiling, heating, ventilation, electrical wiring and outlets, air-conditioning runouts for wiring, finished plumbing with fixtures, and drains. The rental cost for this may run 6 to 8 percent of gross sales.

The lowest-level rental arrangement is a grade 1 lease, which is an unimproved shell. It has completed exterior and interior walls and has basic floors. Almost any business could go into it. The rent per square foot per year for this type of lease will vary, depending on the area.

A rental agreement can also be set up so that a variable rent is paid, usually based on a percentage of gross sales. Another method is to pay a minimum rent plus a percentage of gross sales. Rent can also be set at a sliding percentage of gross sales with the percent figure declining as sales increase. Usually, there is not much difference in the final amount. A return of 8 percent on the capital investment by the operator is normal, and the profit for the individual leasing the property is around 2 to 5 percent of sales.

It is important in negotiating a lease to establish exactly when it is to start. If rent is paid during remodeling or building for a period before the business opens, the property may have to be operated for some time to erase the rental deficit and begin to show a profit.

Other Capital Costs

Pre-opening expenses are funds spent prior to opening for non-assets. These include salaries paid to management or key workers before opening, pre-opening marketing expenses, licenses and other prepaid expenses, utility deposits, and other costs incurred before the first patron walks in the door. *Working capital* is the money necessary to keep the operation afloat once it is in business. This includes sufficient cash reserves to meet emergencies, funds needed to buy supplies, money needed to buy inventories at quantity discounts, and money tied up in cashier's banks.

Pre-opening expenses often overwhelm a new operator. It can seem like everybody in town has his or her hand out. A lawyer must set-up the business entity. An accountant must set-up the books. Both these professionals are expensive and costs often amount to several thousand dollars prior to opening. Next are the various permits, licenses, and fees collected by federal, state, and local government. Liquor licenses in some states are very costly, often as high as $100,000. Regardless of the cost, liquor licenses usually take several months to obtain and hearings and bonds are usually required at a minimum. Insurance for the business is expensive, liability insurance being the principal expense. Insurance companies want payment in advance, and many localities will not issue permits to do business without proof of adequate insurance. The utility companies usually want deposits before hooking up their services. Newspapers and other advertising services usually want payment up front. The menu printer wants payment before he will deliver the menus. All of these expenses, while often individually quite small in amount, add up. It would be a shame if you ended up not opening because you were a few thousand dollars short!

Stocking the business with inventories can be quite expensive. Suppliers often require payment of purchases either C.O.D. or weekly. With exceptionally good credit, an operator may secure 30-day accounts, but the new operator should not plan on this. The average food inventory turns over about once every two weeks. This means that if opening inventory is $5,000 (a very small inventory), about $130,000 will be spent per year on food ($5,000 times 26 turns = $130,000). One way of looking at this is that the food inventory is like a checking account, where funds move in and out rather quickly. However, some operators look at food inventory as a savings account, where funds sit and gain interest. The "interest" is gained through volume purchasing. When commodities are at their lowest, savings of 20% or more can be obtained. With freezing and other long-term storage techniques, products can last six months or longer. Not everything can be stored, but some operations can save money this way.

Liquor inventories are said to turn about eight times a year. Many operators keep two inventories, one for wines and one for beers and spirits. Beers and spirits should turn over about every two weeks. Liquor can usually be bought at a large discount when buying cases at a time. Here, again, operators who stockpile goods will see the cost per unit drop, but the total investment cost rise. If you borrowed your capital at 10 percent interest, you must factor in the cost of borrowing against any savings in purchase price. You break even if the liquor price drops by 10 percent while you have to pay the bank 10 percent for the cash to buy the goods.

One final pre-opening expense is the hiring of staff. Skilled employees should already be trained and on the payroll when the business opens.

Once the doors of a new business are opened, working capital, in the form of cash for cash registers and money to buy more food, liquor, and incidentals, is needed. There should be a positive cash balance in the operation's checking account. As a rule of thumb, many operators maintain a checking account balance equal to one-half their normal monthly expenses. Thus, an operation with a projected $100,000 a month in expenses would keep a balance of $50,000. In addition, the operation must keep a *contingency fund* for emergencies. This is usually kept in the form of a savings account or certificate of deposit. This contingency amount could be one additional month's expenses. This contingency amount may be replaced by a short-term borrowing agreement with your banker. For a fee, most banks will negotiate a short-term loan agreement that allows you to borrow on an as-needed basis.

FINANCIAL ANALYSIS AND THE MENU

A foodservice operation's financial success is measured by profitability and return on investment. Both will be discussed here in detail.

Measuring Profitability

The most common measure of how well a business is performing is to calculate the ratio of net profit to total assets. This ratio is called a *return on assets*, and it shows how well the assets entrusted to the management have been used. A return on assets of from 3 to 6 percent is considered a fair return. For example, if assets are $500,000 and $25,000 is the profit, the ratio of profit to assets is 5 percent ($25,000 ÷ $500,000 = 0.05).

Another way is to measure net profit. Net profit in this instance is the profit left over after operations, interest, other non-operating expenses, and business taxes have been paid. It is the amount of money which is left to the owners and investors after everyone else has been paid.

Return on Investment

Another way of measuring the financial health of an enterprise is to calculate the *return on investment* (ROI). The ROI is the amount of money obtained as a profit in relation to the actual amount invested by the owners of the firm. ROI is compared across investments; that is, investors calculate the ROI of the foodservice enterprise and compare the results to what would have happened had they invested their capital in an interest-bearing bank account, or government bonds, or the stock market. Given the higher risk in investing in food service, investors usually demand that the ROI be higher than that on relatively safer investments like government bonds. Thus, if the owner of a business has invested $200,000 in it, and it makes a profit of $20,000, then the ROI is 10 percent ($20,000 ÷ $200,000 = 0.10). Some calculate ROI the following way.

1. Calculate the sales turnover using gross sales divided by the investment.

   1. $\dfrac{\text{Sales}}{\text{Investment}} = \dfrac{\$400,000}{\$200,000} = 2$

2. Calculate how much profits is in every sales dollar.

   2. $\dfrac{\text{Profit}}{\text{Sales}} = \dfrac{\$15,000}{\$400,000} = 3.75\%$

3. From these two equations, calculate the percent return on investment by multiplying the sales return times the profit in every sales dollar.

   3. (Sales Turnover) × (Profit) = ROI
   2 × 0.0375 = 0.075
   (0.0375 = 3.75%) (0.075 = 7.5%)

Given this example, the investors would receive a 7.5 percent return on their investment. One advantage of investing in a food service is that often it may be highly leveraged. *Leverage* is the amount invested versus the asset value. If investors can get very high amounts of financing, they can often buy an operation that generates high profits on relatively little investment. An operation where 90 percent of the assets were bought using loans and 10 percent of the assets were purchased using investor dollars could easily yield an ROI of 15 percent or more. Naturally, finding lenders willing to take the risk of loaning a high percentage of the asset value of the business is difficult.

Cash Flow

Simply stated, *cash flow* is the dollars generated in the operation during an operating period—dollars that can be used to pay off obligations plus other costs. In other words, cash flow is the excess of dollars available after cash paid out for operating costs and represents money coming from all sources in the operation. The sources of cash include sales revenue, but may also include additional cash put into the operation by investors, or the net proceeds from additional loans secured during the period. Cash flow is calculated by deducting payments made during the period to banks to repay principal on loans and other cash uses not ordinarily recorded on profit-and-loss statements. Cash flow represents the actual money left over at the end of the period without the artificial contrivances of general accounting practice. As such, it is a good management tool usable primarily to determine what strategies to use to continue operations.

A food service needs cash to operate. Due to accounting conventions such as the expensing of depreciation on assets, and accruing certain expenses not yet payable, the usual financial statements do not completely show what cash is really available to the operators. Operations may do well and be profitable from an accounting viewpoint, but poor managerial decisions, such as allowing inventory levels to rise or spending too much money redecorating, may leave little money left to pay creditors when their bills are due. Dollars, not book profits, are what is needed to actually pay the bills. Cash flow calculations can indicate the number of dollars available to do this.

Management should know the cash flow, and the impact on future cash flows, before making capital investment decisions such as remodeling or expansion. Of course, such decisions can be funded from cash reserves, but management must be assured through a *cash flow analysis* that such investments will pay off. No investment is sound if the cash flows generated after the investment are insufficient to repay the loans. As a minimum, an investment must generate the cash flow to pay off the amortized loan payments, but ideally an investment should return additional cash to the owners as well.

LIQUIDITY FACTORS IN FOOD SERVICE

Most businesses must function in the black, and most standards of evaluation are often based on dollar revenue in relation to debt and can be obtained either from the balance sheet or the profit-and-loss statement. *Liquidity* means that *current assets*, such as accounts receivable, inventory, cash, and other convertible assets, exceed *liabilities*, or debts, such as capital payments due within a current operating period and accounts payable.

To determine whether a business is liquid or not, a factor called the *current ratio* may be used. This is a comparison of current assets to current liabilities. Assets should be greater than liabilities. A ratio of 1:1 is barely satisfactory; a 2:1 or 3:1 ratio is better. Food services can often function well on a low ratio because they have little or no accounts receivable and thus can have a good cash flow. If a business has no historical records, then it is necessary to make the best possible estimate of potential liabilities. This is always assumed to be the case when new operations are set up and some projections for the future have to be made.

Another standard method of evaluating liquidity is to calculate the ratio between dollar sales and working capital. Working capital is current assets less current liabilities. The ratio between dollar sales and working capital can indicate good or poor financial management. A high ratio of sales to working capital, such as $40:$1 or $50:$1 is desirable. Thus, if an operation has $1,320,000 in gross sales per year, the working capital should be between $33,000 and $26,400 ($1,320,000 ÷ $40 and $1,320,000 ÷ $50). This shows a low ratio of required working capital. However, food services can operate fairly well at lower ratios.

Another ratio called the *solvency ratio* may be used to indicate worth with respect to debt. This is a ratio of the dollars an owner has in the business owner's equity to the dollars owed to creditors. Thus, if one has $250,000 in a business but owes $500,000, the solvency ratio is 1:2 ($250,000 ÷ $500,000). A 1:1 ratio is considered adequate, but the more dollars an owner has in the business, as compared to money owed, the stronger the business will be. A ratio of 1:4 indicates the food service is operating more on the money of creditors than on that of ownership, a condition that might initially seem desirable but could be quite dangerous if creditors press for payment. Creditors generally prefer to see the solvency ratio at around 2:1.

NONCOMMERCIAL OPERATIONS

Measuring the operating efficiency of a noncommercial operation is often simpler than for a commercial operation. The most common check is to compare operating costs and sales to budgeted figures. Many institutional food services are operated for reasons other than dollars and it may be important to compare other factors as well. However, a satisfactory performance must be achieved in income, or an operation cannot last very long or achieve other goals.

MENU STRATEGIES AND FINANCIAL SUCCESS

How might a change on menu affect the feasibility of an operation? The menu prices may be changed to increase the check average (usually this requires a change in the menu items to increase the perceived value). Prices could be lowered and anticipated volume could be increased. A restaurant in a downtown area with a large business luncheon market can perhaps increase volume with a less elaborate menu and longer serving times. Clearly, the feasibility study should not be thought of as a static or fixed document. It is highly dynamic and changes in operating assumptions can have a significant effect on the feasibility of a project.

However, while a food service must operate at a satisfactory financial level, the success of an operation is not measured in dollars alone. The experience of eating out, whether that experience is of necessity or for pleasure, is important to patrons. But a creative and profitable menu can help fulfill the expectations of the owner and customer alike.

SUMMARY

The foodservice business is a risky one, and many enterprises fail. One factor in making the foodservice business a high-risk one is the high capital required to open and run an operation. Factors within the operation also make for risk. The products are mainly perishable and must be produced to order; the industry is very labor intensive, and labor costs are high in comparison with material costs. Management must be strong in many areas, including financial management and accounting.

Anyone wanting to start a food service should use extreme caution in going into the venture. Many costs must be analyzed in the initial planning to assure sufficient cash balance to carry through the early stages of operation. Hidden costs, such as licenses, bonds, advertising, and insurance, should be considered.

A detailed *feasibility study* should be made before opening. The potential market, competition, and finances should be carefully assessed.

A number of tests should be made to see whether there will be sufficient *return of investment* (ROI). These tests include comparing current assets to current liabilities, calculating the ratio of dollar sales to working capital, using the *solvency ratio*, and calculating the ratio of net profit to total assets. Nonprofit operations usually make a test based on budgetary considerations. If all tests turn out satisfactorily, management can then turn with greater confidence to bringing the menu to life. If everything has been properly done, the result should be a menu that performs successfully for the operation.

QUESTIONS

Use the following summaries of a foodservice balance sheet and a profit-and-loss statement to answer questions 1 and 2.

Balance Sheet
Assets

Cash	$ 86,000	
Payroll account	51,000	
Accounts receivable	6,500	
Inventory	12,400	
Total current assets		$155,900
Equipment and furnishings	$ 62,000	
Building and grounds	112,000	
Total assets		$329,900

Liabilities

Accounts payable	$ 37,400	
Note payable in 30 days	8,500	
Vacation payable	1,800	
Taxes payable	3,200	
Total current liabilities		$ 50,900
Mortgage payable	$108,000	
Ownership	171,000	
Total liabilities and ownership		$329,900

Profit-and-Loss Statement

Gross sales	$878,000	
Cost of goods sold	270,000	
Gross profit		$608,000

Operating Expenses

Labor	$265,000	
Other operating expenses	181,000	
Capital and Occupation Costs	86,000	
Total operating expenses		$532,000
Profit before taxes		
Reserve for taxes		$ 23,000
Net profit		

1. Calculate the following.

   a. Profit before taxes

   b. Net profit

   c. Percent of costs of goods sold, gross profit, labor cost percentage, total labor and operating costs, and capital and occupational costs

    d. Net profit percentage

    e. Current ratio (assets to liabilities)

    f. Ratio of dollar sales to working capital

    g. Solvency ratio

    h. Return on initial investment

    i. Percent of net profit to total assets

2. Would you say this business is in good financial shape and is being well operated? Explain your answer.

3. Set up a feasibility study as was done in the text, based on the following facts.

    A downtown cafeteria serves three meals a day. Breakfast occupancy is 62 percent, 83 percent for dinner and lunch combined. There are 240 seats. Turnover rates are: breakfast, $1\frac{1}{2}$ times; lunch, 3 times; and dinner, 2 times. The average check for breakfast is $2.80, lunch $3.10, and dinner $6.80. Additional income per day of nonrush-hour income is $186.00. The cafeteria is closed on Sundays and holidays, so use 312 days as the number of operating days of the year. The business wants an 8 percent profit on sales and 12 percent ROI. It has $405,000 in capital invested.

    Project the expected income per day and the income per day needed to make the operation a successful one.

✿ A ✿

Accuracy in Menus

REPRESENTATION OF QUANTITY

If standard recipes and portion control are strictly adhered to, no quantities of menu items should ever by misrepresented. For instance, it is perfectly acceptable to list the precooked weight of a steak on a menu; double martinis must be twice the size of a regular drink; jumbo eggs must be labeled as such; petite and supercolossal are among the official size descriptions for olives.

While there is no question about the meaning of a "three-egg omelet" or "all you can eat," terms such as "extra large salad" or "extra tall drink" may invite problems if they are not qualified. Also remember the implied meaning of words: a bowl of soup should contain more than a cup of soup.

REPRESENTATION OF QUALITY

Federal and state quality grades exist for many foods including meat, poultry, eggs, dairy products, fruits, and vegetables. Terminology used to describe grades include Prime, Grade A, Good, No. 1, Choice, Fancy, Grade AA and Extra Standard.

Care must be exercised in preparing menu descriptions when these terms are used. In some uses, they imply a definite quality. An item appearing as "choice sirloin beef" should be USDA Choice Grade Sirloin Beef. One recognized exception is the term "prime rib." Prime rib is a long-established, well-understood, and accepted description for a cut of beef (the "primal" ribs, the 6th to 12th) and does not represent the grade quality, unless USDA is used also.

Ground beef must contain no extra fat (no more than 30 percent), water, extenders, or binders. Seasonings may be added as long as they are identified. Federally approved meat must be ground and packaged in government-inspected plants.

REPRESENTATION OF PRICE

If your pricing structure includes a cover charge, service charge, or gratuity, these must be brought to your customers' attention. If extra charges are made for special requests, guests should be told when they order.

Any restriction when using a coupon or premium promotion must be clearly defined. If a price promotion involves a multi-unit company, clearly indicate which units are or are not participating.

REPRESENTATION OF BRAND NAMES

Any product brand that is advertised must be the one served. A registered or copywritten trademark or brand name must not be used generically to refer to a product.

A house brand may be so labeled even when prepared by an outside source, if its manufacturing was to your specifications. Contents of brand-name containers must be the labeled product.

REPRESENTATION OF PRODUCT IDENTIFICATION

Because of the similarity of many food products, substitutions are often made. These substitutions may be due to stockouts, the substitutions' sudden availability, merchandising considerations, or price. When substitutions are made, be certain these changes are reflected on your menu. Substitutions that *must* be spelled out as such include the following.

Maple-flavored syrup for maple syrup
Nondairy creamer for cream
Boiled ham for baked ham
Ground beef or chopped beef for ground sirloin
Capon for chicken
Veal pattie for veal cutlet
Ice milk for ice cream
Cod for haddock (or vice versa)
Powdered eggs for fresh eggs
Picnic-style pork for pork shoulder or ham
Light-meat tuna for white-meat tuna
Skim milk for milk
Pollack for haddock
Pectin jam for pure jam

Sole for flounder
Whipped topping for whipped cream
Processed cheese or cheese food for cheese
Chicken for turkey (or vice versa)
Nondairy cream sauce for cream sauce
Hereford beef for Black Angus beef
Peanut oil for corn oil (or vice versa)
Bonita for tuna fish
Blue cheese for Roquefort cheese
Beef liver for calf's liver (or vice versa)
Diced beef for tenderloin tips
Half & half for cream
Salad dressing for mayonnaise
Margarine for butter

REPRESENTATION OF POINTS OF ORIGIN

A potential area of error is in describing the point of origin of a menu offering. Claims may be substantiated by the product, by packaging labels, invoices or other documentation provided by your supplier. Mistakes are possible as sources of supply change and availability of product shifts. The following are common assertions of points of origin.

Lake Superior whitefish
Bay scallops
Gulf shrimp
Idaho potatoes
Florida orange juice
Maine lobster
Imported Swiss cheese
Smithfield ham
Wisconsin cheese
Puget Sound sockeye salmon

Danish blue cheese
Louisiana frog legs
Alaskan king crab
Colorado brook trout
Imported ham
Colorado beef
Florida stone crabs
Long Island duckling
Chesapeake Bay oysters

There is a wide spread use of geographic names used in a generic sense to describe a method of preparation of service. Such terminology is readily understood and accepted by the customer and their use should in no way be restricted. Examples of acceptable terms follow.

Russian dressing
French toast
New England clam chowder
Country fried steak
Denver sandwich
Irish stew
French dip
Country ham
Swiss steak

French fries
German potato salad
Danish pastries
Russian service
French service
English muffins
Manhattan clam chowder
Swiss cheese

REPRESENTATION OF MERCHANDISING TERMS

A difficult area to clearly define as right or wrong is the use of merchandising terms. "We serve the best gumbo in town" is understood by the dining-out public for what it is—boasting for advertising sake. However, to use the term "we use only the finest beef" implies that USDA Prime Beef is used, as a standard exists for this product.

Advertising exaggerations are tolerated if they do not mislead. When ordering a "mile high pie" a customer would expect a pie heaped tall with meringue or similar fluffy topping, but to advertise a "foot long hot dog" and to serve something less would be in error.

Mistakes are possible in properly identifying steak cuts. Use industry standards such as provided in the National Association of Meat Purveyors *Meat Buyer's Guide.*

"Homestyle" or "our own" are suggested terminology rather than "home-made" in describing menu offerings prepared according to a home recipe. Most foodservice sanitation ordinances prohibit the preparation of foods in home facilities.

The following terms should be used carefully.

Fresh daily	Aged steaks
Corn fed	Milk fed
Fresh roasted	Low-calorie
Flown in daily	Low-fat
Kosher	Low-sodium
Black Angus beef	Low-cholesterol
Center cut ham	

REPRESENTATION OF MEANS OF PRESERVATION

The accepted means of preserving foods are numerous, including canned, chilled, bottled, frozen and dehydrated. If you choose to describe your menu selections with these terms, they must be accurate. Frozen orange juice is not fresh, canned peas are not frozen and bottled apple sauce is not canned.

REPRESENTATION OF FOOD PREPARATION

The means of food preparation is often the determining factor in the customer's selection of a menu entree. Absolute accuracy is a must. Readily understood terms include the following.

Charcoal broiled	Broiled
Deep fried	Prepared from scratch
Sauteed	Roasted
Barbecued	Fried
Baked	Poached
Smoked	

REPRESENTATION OF VERBAL AND VISUAL PRESENTATION

When your menu, wall placards or other advertising contains a pictorial representation of a meal or platter, it should portray the actual contents with accuracy. Following are several examples of *visual misrepresentation.*

- Using mushroom pieces in a sauce when the picture shows mushroom caps
- Using sliced strawberries on a shortcake when the picture shows whole strawberries

- Using numerous thin sliced meat pieces when the picture shows a single thick slice
- Using four or five shrimp when the picture shows six
- Omitting vegetables or other entree extras when the picture shows them
- Using a plain bun when the picture shows a sesame topped bun

Examples of *verbal misrepresentation* include the following.

- A server asking whether a guest would like sour cream or butter with a potato, but serving an imitation sour cream and margarine
- A server telling guests that menu items are prepared on the premises when in fact they are purchased preprepared

REPRESENTATION OF DIETARY OR NUTRITIONAL CLAIMS

Potential public health concerns are real if misrepresentation is made of the dietary or nutritional content of food. For example "salt-free" or "sugar-free" foods must be exactly that to assure the protection of your customers who may be under particular dietary restraints. "Low-calorie" or nutritional claims, if made, must be supportable by specific data.

Sections adapted from *Accuracy in Menus*, Copyright © 1984 by the National Restaurant Association, Washington, DC.

B

Number of Portions Available from Standard Containers

HOT AND COLD FOOD VESSELS

Portion size	2½ oz	3 oz	3½ oz	4 oz	5 oz	6 oz	7 oz	8 oz	10 oz	12 oz
					NUMBER OF PORTIONS					
No. 2 can	7	6	5	5	4	3	2	2	2	1
No. 2½ can	10	9	8	6	5	4	4	3	3	2
1 quart	13	11	9	8	6	5	5	4	3	3
5 lb tin (80 ounces)	32	27	23	20	16	13	11	10	8	7
7 lb tin (No. 10 can)	45	37	32	28	22	19	16	14	11	9
1 gallon	51	43	37	32	26	21	18	16	13	11
10 lb can	64	53	46	40	32	27	23	20	16	13

SOUFFLE CUPS, CREAMERS, ETC.

Portion size			¾ oz	1 oz	1½ oz	2 oz	3 oz	3¾ oz	5 oz	5½ oz
					NUMBER OF PORTIONS					
No. 2 can			24	18	12	9	6	5	4	3
No. 2½ can			34	26	17	13	9	7	5	5
1 quart			43	32	21	16	11	9	6	5
5 lb tin (80 ounces)			106	80	53	40	27	21	16	15
7 lb tin (No. 10 can)			148	112	75	56	37	30	22	20
1 gallon			171	128	85	64	43	34	26	22
10 lb can			212	160	107	80	53	32	29	

PORTION CUPS

Cup number		050	075	100	125	200	250	325	400	550
Cup size		½ oz	¾ oz	1 oz	1¼ oz	2 oz	2½ oz	3¼ oz	4 oz	5½ oz
					NUMBER OF PORTIONS					
No. 2 can		36	24	18	14	9	7	5	5	3
No. 2½ can		52	34	26	20	13	10	8	6	5
1 quart		64	43	32	26	16	13	10	8	6
5 lb tin (80 ounces)		160	106	80	64	40	32	24	20	15
7 lb tin (No. 10 can)		224	148	112	90	56	45	34	28	20
1 gallon		256	171	128	102	64	51	39	32	22
10 lb can		320	212	160	128	80	64	50	40	29

C

Menu Evaluation

MENU PROFITABILITY

	4 Excellent	3 Good	2 Fair	1 Poor	Comments
1. Does the menu have an adequate number of high gross profit items?					
2. Has there been a good selection of popular items?					
3. Is there a good balance between high- and low-priced items and no concentration of either?					
4. Does pricing meet competition?					
5. Are menu prices changed frequently enough to reflect costs?					
6. Are portion costs based on reliable cost information?					
7. Is portion size adequate?					
8. Are menu items selected with a view toward reducing waste and other risks?					
9. Are menu items selected to reflect labor requirements?					
10. Are menu items selected to reflect energy needs?					
11. Does the menu encourage a higher check average?					
12. Can items be controlled in cost?					

	4 Excellent	**3** Good	**2** Fair	**1** Poor	Comments

PRESENTATION OF WORDING

1. Are menu items described accurately and truthfully?
2. Does the menu avoid indicating weight, size, using pictures and other factors that can cause problems in patron interpretation?
3. Are effective descriptive words used to indicate menu item qualities?
4. Is the choice of words adequate to describe the item? Is overkill avoided? Is the wording simple and easy to understand?
5. Are truth-in-menu requirements met?
6. If pictures are used, are they exact replicas of what is delivered?
7. Does the wording do a good job of merchandising?
8. Do menu items appear at consistent quality, size, etc.

MENU COMPREHENSION

1. Do menu items stand out?
2. Is print legible and easy to read quickly?
3. Are words and reading matter not crowded?
4. Is the menu free from clutter?
5. Are menu items presented in a logical order, usually the order of eating?
6. Are prices presented clearly?
7. Are items easy to find?
8. Will patrons know what to expect from items from the menu listing?

	4 Excellent	3 Good	2 Fair	1 Poor	Comments

9. Are any unexplained foreign words used?

10. Is there adequate space between menu items so there is no confusion?

11. Does the print stand out from the background?

12. Are headings prominent and of sufficient size?

PHYSICAL SUPPORT

1. Is the menu appropriate for kitchen equipment production capability?

2. Is the menu appropriate for servers to do a proper job?

3. Is the layout of the operation adequate to meet menu needs?

4. Is there adequate storage to support the menu?

5. Are menu items matched to the ability of kitchen employees to produce them?

6. Is the distance between the kitchen and dining area reasonable?

7. Is lighting adequate to read the menu?

8. Is a comfortable environment provided for guest comfort?

9. Do patrons have adequate space?

MENU MECHANICS

1. Is the cover durable, easily cleaned, and attractive?

2. Is the menu on strong, sturdy paper?

3. Is the menu easily read and understood?

4. Can one find things easily?

	4 Excellent	3 Good	2 Fair	1 Poor	Comments
5. Does the menu appear neat and clean?					
6. Is the menu free of cross-outs and handwritten changes?					
7. Are color combinations effective?					
8. Is the shape appropriate?					
9. Is it of proper size to be easily handled?					
10. Are decorative features appropriate?					
11. Are the style of the menu and wording in keeping with the decor, atmosphere, and logo of the operation?					
12. Does the menu have good symmetry and form?					
13. Does the menu look professional?					
14. Is information given on operation time, address and telephone number, special catering, etc.?					
15. Is the logo prominent on the menu?					

ITEM SELECTION

	4 Excellent	3 Good	2 Fair	1 Poor	Comments
1. Is the selection of items balanced and varied?					
2. Do items offer variety of form, color, taste, and temperature?					
3. Are seasonal foods offered?					
4. Is preparation of items varied among broiling, frying, steaming, boiling, etc.?					
5. Are items suited to the preparation skill of employees and servers?					
6. Has simplicity been preserved and not too much lavish ornateness attempted?					

	4 Excellent	3 Good	2 Fair	1 Poor	Comments
7. Is there a wide enough selection to appeal to most patrons?					
8. Is the sales mix effective?					
9. Are specials prominent but not over-emphasized?					
10. Are items balanced in their popularity?					

MENU AND ITEM PRESENTATION

	4 Excellent	3 Good	2 Fair	1 Poor
1. Are items served in the proper dish or the right packaging?				
2. Are they well garnished?				
3. Are items attractive?				
4. Are items offered in the order of eating or in an otherwise logical manner?				
5. Are items not offered by order of price?				
6. Are long columns broken up in some way?				
7. Are items that management most wants to sell put in the most prominent places?				
8. Are children's menus offered and do they suit children's need?				
9. Is the use of clip-ons or inserts well done (not repeating menu items, covering other material, etc.)?				
10. Do menu items reflect a manageable inventory?				
11. Are high-risk items limited?				
12. Do most items have a high volume potential?				
13. Is there good presentation of high gross profit items?				
14. Is attention given to nutritional concerns?				
15. Is there a proper balance between a la carte and table d'hôte items?				

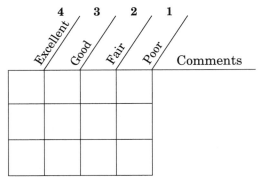

16. Are ingredients available on the market without great price fluctuations?

17. If it is a cycle menu, is the cycle repeated at a reasonable length of time?

18. Is there good and adequate presentation of alcoholic beverages?

To score: Analyze the menu, evaluating each factor in the menu evaluation form and scoring 4 for excellent, 3 for good, 2 for fair, and 1 for poor. Do not score factors that are not applicable, but keep track of those omitted.

When scoring is completed, total the numbers. Next, count the factors not considered applicable and deduct the number from 85 (the total factors in this menu evaluation form). Multiply the result by 4, which will be the total of a perfect score. Divide the actual score given the menu by the perfect score. This will give a menu evaluation percentage.

Anything from 90 percent to 100 percent is excellent, anything from 60 percent to 69 percent is poor. Most likely, any menu scoring below 80 percent should be redone.

The comment column should be used to indicate how a factor might be improved if it is not satisfactory.

D

Menu Factor Analysis

The following information is known:

Salad Item	Number Sold	Selling Price	Total Sales	Food Cost	Total Food Cost	Item Gross Profit	Total Gross Profit
Crab Louis	25	$6.00	$_____	$2.10	$_____	$_____	$_____
Chef's	40	5.00	_____	1.25	_____	_____	_____
Fruit	30	5.50	_____	2.10	_____	_____	_____
Vegetable	45	4.25	_____	1.10	_____	_____	_____
Total	140		$_____		$_____	$_____	$_____

Calculate the popularity index, sales index, food cost index, and gross profit index in column 1 below and then convert to the proper factors in column 2. The expected index for all four in popularity, sales, food cost, and gross profit is 0.25.

Crab Louis salad   (1)   (2)
    Popularity _____ _____
    Sales _____ _____
    Food cost _____ _____
    Gross profit _____ _____

Chef's salad
    Popularity _____ _____
    Sales _____ _____
    Food cost _____ _____
    Gross profit _____ _____

Fruit salad   (1)   (2)
    Popularity _____ _____
    Sales _____ _____
    Food cost _____ _____
    Gross profit _____ _____

Vegetable salad
    Popularity _____ _____
    Sales _____ _____
    Food cost _____ _____
    Gross profit _____ _____

Study the factors. What do they tell management about popularity, sales dollars, food costs, and contribution to gross profit?

Salad Item	Total Sales	Total Food Costs	Item Gross Profit	Total Gross Profit
Crab Louis	$150.00	$ 52.50	$ 3.90	$ 97.50
Chef's	200.00	50.00	3.75	150.00
Fruit	165.00	63.00	3.40	102.00
Vegetable	191.25	49.50	3.15	141.75
Total	$706.00	$215.00	$14.20	$491.25

	Indexes	**Factors**		**Indexes**	**Factors**
Crab Louis salad			*Fruit salad*		
Popularity	0.179	0.716	Popularity	0.214	0.856
Sales	0.212	0.848	Sales	0.234	0.936
Food cost	0.244	0.976	Food cost	0.293	1.172
Gross profit	0.198	0.792	Gross profit	0.208	0.832
Chef's salad			*Vegetable salad*		
Popularity	0.286	1.144	Popularity	0.321	1.284
Sales	0.283	1.132	Sales	0.271	1.084
Food cost	0.233	0.932	Food cost	0.230	0.920
Gross profit	0.305	1.220	Gross profit	0.289	1.156

Comments:

Crab Louis salad has poor popularity, sales, and gross profit, its food cost is about right but does not help generate profit. It needs to be given more sales emphasis. Perhaps it also needs better presentation on the menu.

Chef's salad does well. It has a good food cost and also good popularity, sales, and gross profit.

Fruit salad is another problem. It does not have good popularity and is slightly below expected sales. It has a high food cost and this contributes to its low gross profit margin. The salad should be changed some to lower its food cost. Perhaps the price could be raised slightly to solve the problem

Vegetable salad holds it own in every category. In fact, it is the best of the four. Do not change.

❧ E ❧

A Brief History of Food Service

Year	Region	General History	Foodservice Events
Before 4500 B.C.	Denmark and Orkney Isles	Stone Age	First volume-feeding seen by 10,000 B.C.
	Switzerland	New Stone Age	Swiss Lake Dwellers eating in groups by 5000 B.C.
3000–500 B.C.	Egypt	Age of the Pharaohs	Art depicts food prepared for and served to large groups.
2500–1000 B.C.	Mohenjo-Daro Pakistan		First evidence of restaurant-type facilities, including ovens and stoves.
2200–1000 B.C.	China		Roadside inns appear for travelers, restaurants appear in larger cities.
900–500 B.C.	Middle East	Assyrian Empire	Evidence of production of both beer and wine. King Soloman holds great feasts.
500–300 B.C.	Europe	Classic Greek civilization	Inns, restaurants, copyrights for recipes, and first known school for chefs all appear.
300 B.C.–320 A.D.	Europe	Roman Empire	Romans hold lavish banquets. "Tabernas" (taverns) appear.
200 B.C.			Apicius writes first cookbook, which is resurrected after the Dark Ages.
1300s	England	Middle Ages	Chaucer and others write about inns for travelers and pilgrims. Monasteries develop various liqueurs still known to us today. Rise of guilds, whose members produce specialty foods.
1300s	France	Middle Ages	First reintroduction of a complex meal with separate courses.
1491–1547	England	Reign of Henry VIII	Henry VIII, known for his rotund figure and voracious appetite, encourages elaborate dining.

Year	Region	General History	Foodservice Events
1400s	Italy	European Renaissance	Great merchants like Marco Polo expand trade and bring new foods and spices to Europe. Rise of gourmet recipes and elaborate banquets.
1500s	France	Age of Discovery	Catherine de Medici of Italy marries Henry II, king of France and brings Italian cooks and recipes to the French court. Starts French tradition of fine dining.
	England		Mary, Queen of England, brings Spanish dining traditions to England.
1589–1610	France	Colonial Expansion	Henry IV, king of France, encourages nobility to become gourmets. Beginnings of sauce-making as an art. Good chefs are prized by nobility. First coffee houses appear and quickly spread throughout Europe.
1600s	France	Age of Reason	Bourbon kings bring French cuisine to its grandest heights. Louis XIV (the Sun King) builds his palace at Versailles. Foods are named after members of the nobility.
1700s	France	Age of Enlightenment	Louis XV marries Polish princess who, like de Medici, supervises kitchens and sets new standards of excellence. Very elaborate meals, with 100 or more dishes served, become common.
	Russia		Catherine the Great of Russia introduces French language and customs to the court. Introduces concepts of appetizers, dishes like caviar, etc., to European tables.
1760	France		Boulanger opens *"restaurants"* serving "restorative" soups. Legal fight with guilds results in legalization of the restaurant concept. Chef Carême simplifies and codifies the royal cuisine, and trains many famous chefs.

Year	Region	General History	Foodservice Events
1792	France	French Revolution	First books appear detailing the ideal life of a gourmet. First gourmet magazine appears.
1800–1815	France	Napoleonic Period	While not much of a gourmet himself, Napoleon's wife and counselors are. They inspire a rebirth of imperial style of food presentation and service. About 500 restaurants are now operating in Paris. Appert invents the canning process, used by Napoleon to feed his army.
1760–1800s	England and Europe	Industrial Revolution	The Industrial Revolution changes the way people live, work, and eat. With mass production, items once reserved only for the rich become available to a large new economic class, the "middle class." With the Industrial Revolution comes a faster-paced lifestyle. Eating out becomes both affordable and necessary.
1700s– early 1800s	United States	Colonial Period	President Thomas Jefferson, remembering the foods he ate in France while he was an Ambassador, appoints a French chef to the White House kitchens.
1818	New York City		There are eight hotels in New York City. There will be more than 100 hotels by 1846.
1800–1850	England		Great chefs trained by Carême serve the English elite. They introduce French eating styles to England and create first English-language cookbooks of French recipes. Private clubs, like the Reform Club, become popular with English gentlemen. Alexis Soyer, chef at the Reform Club, invents the mobile army field kitchen, feeding over 10,000 Irish citizens a day during the potato famine.

Year	Region	General History	Foodservice Events
1850–1938	Europe	Age of Grand Hotels	César Ritz and Auguste Escoffier serve the wealthiest Europeans in their grand hotels and restaurants. Escoffier revolutionizes the kitchen by applying principles used in industry and introducing personnel changes. He codifies and further simplifies *haute cuisine*. His idea is copied for restaurants. More than 1,000 chefs trained by Escoffier revolutionize the entire foodservice industry.
1850	Chicago		There are more than 150 hotels in Chicago.
1849–1892	United States	California Gold Rush	Gold is discovered in California in 1849. By the end of the Civil War in 1865, extremely luxurious hotels become more common.
1890s–1915	United States and Europe	Victorian Era	Delmonico's and Rector's are famous New York City restaurants. Fine dining reaches levels not seen again until after World War II. Restaurant chains, such as Harvey House and Schrafft's, bring consistent, good food to the masses.
1920s	United States		With Prohibition, the "speakeasies," usually bar or nightclubs, become popular. Some famous speakeasies, like The 21 Club, later become famous fine-dining establishments.
1946	United States	Post-World War II	The National School Lunch Act introduces the start of large-scale public feeding programs.
1950s	United States		Quick-service chains, such as McDonald's and Kentucky Fried Chicken, appear.

Year	Region	General History	Foodservice Events
1960s	France		French chefs develop *nouvelle cuisine*. Chef Bocuse, Gaston Lenetre, and the Trosgros brothers define the new cuisine with healthier foods that are lower in fats, starches, and sugars.
1970s	United States		American chefs discover regional specialties. New awareness of locally grown produce creates an explosion of innovation in the fine-dining field.

 Notes

Chapter 1

1. The earliest record of ice cream is that it was made for the Persian kings by freezing cream, honey, and other flavorings in snow in the high mountains. This was then packed in snow and taken by runner down the mountain to the king's court. The Carthaginians learned how to make ice cream from the Persians and carried the knowledge to the Sicilians who, in turn, brought it to Florence. Benjamin Franklin, when he was ambassador to France, liked it so much that he brought the recipe to the United States, where both Martha Washington and Dolly Madison made history by serving it at the White House.

2. Alexander died of eating a dish of poisonous mushrooms several years after Carême left him to go to the Rothschild household.

3. This did not occur until the 1920s and 1930s. As late as the 1940s, foodservice operations used electricity only for lights.

Chapter 2

1. Much of the material in recreational feedings was originally supplied by Professor Mickey Warner from his 1982 Masters degree thesis, "Recreational Foodservice Management," School of Hospitality Management, Florida International University.

2. Locally operated programs existed before this. In 1884, in Boston, Mrs. Ellen H. Richards, a home economist, started what was probably the first program. It was not until after World War II, however, that a broader need for such programs was shown when figures for malnutrition and physical defects, and some data obtained on the nutritional status of school children, were analyzed.

Chapter 4

1. John Rosson, "Menus Still Have a Long Way to Go." *National Restaurant Association News*, Volume 3, Number 5, May 1983, pp. 15–17.

Chapter 5

1. The frozen, preblanched strips usually contain around 11 percent fat when purchased. Thus, the finished potatoes will contain around 17 percent fat when sold.

2. *Standards, Principles, and Techniques in Quantity Food Production, Third Edition*, by Lendal H. Kotschevar, published by Van Nostrand Reinhold Company, New York, has a large number of tables indicating portions and yields.

3. John F. Johnson, "A Statistical Analysis of the Relationship between the Number of Meals Served and Number of Employees in 171 Cafeterias." Masters degree thesis, University of Chicago, School of Business, 1950.

4. C. Broton, "Controlling Restaurant Costs." Masters degree thesis, College of Hotel Administration, Cornell University, 1953.

Chapter 8

1. Michael Hurst owns the very successful 15th Street Fisheries in Florida, teaches at Florida International University, and is a past President of the National Restaurant Association.

2. David K. Hayes and Lynn Huffman, "Menu Analysis: A Better Way." Cornell Quarterly, Vol. 25, No. 4, February 1985, pp. 64–70.

Chapter 9

1. Commissions range from around 10 to 20 percent, or a cork price may be given, such as $0.59 for each bottle of wine (cork) sold.

2. Wine inventories usually do not turn over more than four times per year.

Chapter 10

1. Even some authorities in the nutrition field have been accused of peddling poor, and sometimes harmful, nutritional information. Adele Davis, who had some nutritional training, was taken to task for claims about vitamin E and other nutrients. In 1984 her estate settled out of court a number of suits that claimed harm from her dietary recommendations. One of the problems is that anyone can call themselves a dietitian or a nutritionist. Knowing the claimant's actual credentials is important.

Glossary

Accuracy-in-menu guidelines Guidelines that specify general terminology for menus to ensure that what is listed on a menu is what is actually served

Acid-base ratio Balance in the body between alkali and acid; an individual must maintain an almost neutral acid-base ratio to stay alive; the body does this automatically, except in the course of some diseases

Actual (cost) pricing Pricing method based on actual costs, including purchasing, labor, and operating costs

A la carte Literally "to the card"; term used to indicate that a menu item is ordered with few or no accompaniments and has its own price

Apéritif Alcoholic beverage drunk before a meal

Aquaculture Raising fish or other marine life in an artificial environment as close to the natural environment as possible

Aquavit Clear Scandinavian liquor that is very high in proof, often flavored with caraway seeds; it can be seasoned with other items, such as orange peel or cardamom

Assets Property, capital, and other resources available to meet cost or debts as needed

As purchased (AP) cost As the product is purchased, in the raw state before production

Baby boomer Person born in the period from after World War II through the early 1960s

Back of the house Area where food production occurs, as distinct from the service area, which is called the front of the house

Bain marie Small steam table

Base pricing Pricing based on what a certain market will pay and what is needed to cover costs

Batch cooking Cooking foods in small batches so foods will be at their peak freshness when served

Bid Price quote made by a supplier, using a written form

Bin card   Card attached to a storage area that indicates what items are stored and their quantities

Blank check buying   Asking a purveyor to supply an item without knowledge of the price

Bouillon   From the French verb meaning "to boil"; a soup usually made from a rich beef stock

Break even   Point at which an operation neither makes a profit nor loses money

Buffet   Type of service in which guests are served foods from a long table

Café   Literally "coffee"; a place where beverages and light meals are obtained at a moderate cost

Cafeteria   Type of food service where patrons select their own food from a counter

California menu   Menu that offers breakfast, lunch, dinner, and snack at any hour

Call brand   Popular brand of liquor often requested by name by patrons

Call sheet   Market list on which suppliers are named; used for calling for prices and market information (also called quotation sheet)

Calorie   One unit of heat energy

Canapé   Small, open-faced sandwich served as an appetizer or hors d'oeuvre

Capital costs   Funds spent to supply land, building equipment, and other investments

Captive market   Market that must, because of circumstances, eat at a particular food service

Carafe   Container used for serving small amounts of wine

Carbohydrate   Family of organic compounds that the body needs to produce energy

Cast type   Type that is set by pouring molten lead into molds that form letters

Catering   Dispensing food away from the production facilities for parties or special occasions

Central commissary   Large kitchen that prepares food for satellite service areas

Chain   Group of foodservice units related to each other through some corporate or other business group; often they have similar themes or menus

Check average   Total dollar sales divided by the number of patrons served

Checker Back-of-the-house employee who checks food orders as they leave the kitchen

Chef du parti Chef in charge of a particular production section, such as the broiler section, roasting section, or sauce section

Cholesterol Substance necessary for some vital functions in the body; some forms can cause arterial problems that lead to strokes, heart attacks, and other health problems

Clip-on Temporary attachment to a menu to announce special items

Club Organization that often has a private or special membership and that serves food and drinks

Commercial feeding operation Operation serving food and beverages for profit

Consommé Soup made of rich, concentrated stocks or broths, seasoned with herbs and spices, and often garnished with vegetables, dumplings, or other items

Contract feeding operation Organization that has a contract to produce and serve food for an organization involved in some other business activity

Convection oven Oven with a fan that circulates heated air, allowing for efficiency and heat distribution

Convenience foods Foods prepared to such a state that very little further preparation is needed for service

Cordial Sweet, aromatic liquor

Cost allowance Cost of food groups allocated to feed individuals based on a budgeted figure

Cost-plus buying Making an arrangement with a supplier to purchase items at cost plus a set markup

Cost-plus-profit pricing Adding the desired profit to the total cost of an item to arrive at a selling price

Counter service Service style in which guests are served at a counter rather than at a table

Cover charge Basic charge added to a guest's bill, usually for entertainment or some special feature that the enterprise offers in addition to food

Current ratio Current assets less current liabilities

Cycle menu Menu for a certain number of days, weeks, or meals, that is repeated after a set amount of time

Daily receiving report Summary of items received each day by the receiving department

Dietetics   Application of the science of nutrition through diet

Dietitian   Individual trained to apply the science of nutrition through diet

Differentiation   Act of making an enterprise and/or menu unique in the marketplace so patrons are drawn there, rather than to the competition

Direct labor cost   That part of the labor budget that is spent directly preparing or serving a menu item

Directs   Deliveries that go directly into use and not into inventory and are charged on the day received

Draft (draught) beer   Beer drawn from a keg and propelled by a carbonating unit

Drive-in   Food service that serves food to people in vehicles in an area provided for their parking or at a drive-up window

Du jour   French term meaning "of the day"; often used on menus with daily specials; a du jour menu is a daily menu

Edible portion (EP)   Portion of food that is edible and that must be separated from any inedible portion, such as fat or bone

Entree   Main dish on a menu, as opposed to accompaniments

Executive chef   Head of the chefs in a kitchen

Feasibility study   Compilation of data made before opening a new operation to see how successful a foodservice business is expected to be

Fixed costs   Costs that do not fluctuate with changes in business volume

Floater   Check held by a server and used more than once, usually as a means of stealing money

Food cost   Cost of the portion of food used in a menu item

Food cost pricing   Basing a selling price on the cost of the food by using a percentage markup

Forecasting   Estimating future sales, costs, and other factors

Front of the house   Service and sales area of a foodservice operation

Grade   Standards of quality established for some foods

Gross profit   Sales revenue less cost of materials sold

Gross profit pricing   Pricing method based on the cost of profit

Haute cuisine   Literally "high cooking"; refers to fine and elegant food and service

Healthcare feeding   Food services typical of hospitals, rest homes, and convalescent centers where diet and health considerations are stressed

Hospitality industry   Overall industry that provides lodging, food, and entertainment through hotels, restaurants, airlines, resorts, etc.

House wine   Bulk-stocked wine usually taken from a jug, cask, or other large container; it can also be a specially bottled wine that the house serves as its own

Hydrogenation   Adding hydrogen to make an unsaturated fat into a saturated one; hydrogenation will change a liquid oil into a solid fat

Institutional feeding   Food service in institutions such as schools, prisons, and industries

Invoice   Form given by a delivery person to the purchaser that indicates what is delivered and other information about the delivery

Issuing   Function of giving food, materials, and supplies to employees from inventory

Jigger   Small measure used for alcoholic beverages

Lamination   Cover, such as a stiff plastic, to give paper a sturdy feel and texture

Light beer   Beer that contains fewer calories and less alcohol than normal

Limited menu   Menu offering only a few items

Liqueur   Liquor often made from a brandy or grain alcohol base that is usually sweetened and flavored

Liquidity   Financial solvency of a business

Logo   Distinctive mark or emblem that differentiates an operation from others and identifies it to patrons

Low-sodium diet   Diet in which the salt and sodium are restricted

Maitre d'hôtel   Literally "master of the hostel or place"; person in charge of the service in a dining room

Malnutrition   Poor nutrition; a diet that lacks adequate nutrients

Marginal analysis pricing   Pricing method based on maximum net profit

Markup   Amount added to a basic cost to arrive at a selling price

Meal pattern   1) Kind of foods served along with their progression through a meal, 2) Federal guidelines for elementary and secondary school food services that establish what should be included in school lunches

Meal plan   Sequence of different foods in a meal without mention of specific food items, only of their kind, such as "meat," "fruit," etc.

Menu   List of food offerings and major operational document

Menu factor analysis   Method of analysis in which items are tested for their popularity, sales revenue, food cost, and gross profit

Mineral   Group of elements used by the body to produce bones, teeth, and other substances

Mise en place   Literally "to put in place"; getting everything ready for a job or task to be done

Negotiated buying   Purchasing after negotiation with a number of suppliers

Noncommercial operation   Food service that functions without the objective of making a profit; often the unit is part of some other type of enterprise

Non-cost pricing   Pricing method based on factors other than cost, such as on what the market will bear

Occasion meals   Meals that have special significance, such as the celebration of a wedding or a holiday

Par stock   Established minimum stock level that must be on hand at all times

Perpetual inventory   Inventory that is maintained solely through records

Physical inventory   Inventory that is conducted by hand

Polyunsaturated fat   Fat that has two or more unsaturated double bonds of carbon

Precosting   Calculating costs ahead of actual operation by forecasting sales or the cost of menu items for those sales

Prime cost   Food cost plus direct labor cost

Printout   Hard copy of information that has been fed into a computer

Productivity   Amount of work or output produced by human resources

Promotion   Selling efforts aimed at getting new business or moving special items

Proof   Alcoholic content of liquor; American proof is based on two times the percentage of alcohol

Proprietorship   Ownership of a business by an individual

Protein   Nutrient that provides amino acids for building body tissues

Purchase order   Formal presentation from the buyer of a purchase requirement in written form

Quotation sheet   Market list on which suppliers are named; used for calling for prices and market information (also called call sheet)

Ration allowance   Rationing of specific amounts of certain foods based on nutritional requirements and budgetary constraints

Receiving   Function of receiving and checking deliveries from suppliers

Réchaud   Small heating unit used to keep foods warm in French service

Recipe costing   Calculating total and portion costs of a recipe

Recipe forecasting   Estimating portions from a standardized recipe

Recreational food service   Food service established to serve individuals at a recreational park, sports stadium, athletic club, theme park, theater, etc.

Restaurant   Food service that operates commercially to sell food and beverages to patrons

Retail host   Foodservice operation in a retail establishment

Return on investment (ROI)   Profit made on what owners have invested in the business

Rosé   Pink or reddish wine, often slightly sweet, with a very delicate flavor

Roughage   Fiber or bulk in food that provides for efficient digestion and elimination of wastes

Sales mix   Selection pattern of patrons in choosing menu items

Satellite feeding   Food services that heat up and serve foods that are to be prepared elsewhere, often at a central commissary

Saturated fat   Fat that has all its carbon bonds filled with hydrogen

Seated service   Food service that serves patrons who are seated at tables

Service bar   Bar that dispenses alcoholic beverages to servers who serve guests

Shot glass   Measure for dispensing liquor

Silk-screening   Method of printing that uses a stencil to transfer print onto an object

Smorgasbord   Scandinavian buffet

Snack bar   Counter selling snack items, to be eaten there or taken away

Snifter   Large, bowl-shaped glass into which only a small amount of brandy or other aromatic liqueur is poured

Social caterer   One who caters meals to social affairs such as receptions, private parties, and other special occasions

Solvency ratio   Ratio calculated from assets and liabilities to indicate how liquid (able to meet financial obligations) an operation is

Sommelier   Wine steward

Sous chef   Assistant to the executive chef

Specification   Written statement of all characteristics needed in an item to be purchased

Spirit   Distilled alcoholic beverage

Standard(ized) recipe   Recipe that gives a known quality and quantity at a known cost

Supply and demand   Two factors in economics that are influential in establishing the price of commodities; a large supply usually lowers price while a large demand raises it

Table d'hôte menu   Meal or a group of foods sold together at one price

Tastevin   Small silver cup used for tasting wine

Tavern   Operation that sells mainly alcoholic beverages

Truth-in-menu guidelines   Group of laws and guidelines that require that what a menu offers must be truthful in describing and delivering what it offers for sale

Turnover (customer)   Number of times a seat in a foodservice operation is filled during a meal period, day, etc.

Unsaturated fat   Fat that has double carbon bonds that can pick up other substances, such as nitrogen or sulfur

Value analysis   Study used to assess how well the purchasing function (or another function) was performed

Value perception   Perceived value of an item in comparison to its cost

Variable costs   Costs that change with changes in business volume

Variable cost pricing   Pricing method based on the variable costs of the menu item, usually based on a set food cost markup

Vending   Service of foods from vending machines

Vitamins   Nutrients that in small amounts can help regulate the body and promote essential body functions

Walk-out   Individual or group of customers that has walked out of the operation without paying the bill

Wine steward   Individual who discusses and recommends wine to patrons (*sommelier*)

Working capital   Assets minus liabilities

Index